Home Front Battles

Home Front Battles

World War II Mobilization and Race in the Deep South

CHARLES C. BOLTON

OXFORD
UNIVERSITY PRESS

Oxford University Press is a department of the University of Oxford. It furthers
the University's objective of excellence in research, scholarship, and education
by publishing worldwide. Oxford is a registered trade mark of Oxford University
Press in the UK and certain other countries.

Published in the United States of America by Oxford University Press
198 Madison Avenue, New York, NY 10016, United States of America.

© Oxford University Press 2024

All rights reserved. No part of this publication may be reproduced, stored in
a retrieval system, or transmitted, in any form or by any means, without the
prior permission in writing of Oxford University Press, or as expressly permitted
by law, by license, or under terms agreed with the appropriate reproduction
rights organization. Inquiries concerning reproduction outside the scope of the
above should be sent to the Rights Department, Oxford University Press, at the
address above.

You must not circulate this work in any other form
and you must impose this same condition on any acquirer.

Library of Congress Cataloging-in-Publication Data
Names: Bolton, Charles C., author.
Title: Home front battles : World War II mobilization and race in
the deep South / Charles C. Bolton.
Other titles: World War II mobilization and race in the deep South
Description: New York : Oxford University Press, [2024] |
Includes bibliographical references and index.
Identifiers: LCCN 2024004665 (print) | LCCN 2024004666 (ebook) |
ISBN 9780197655610 (hardback) | ISBN 9780197655634 (epub)
Subjects: LCSH: World War, 1939–1945—Southern States. |
World War, 1939–1945—Social aspects—Southern States. |
World War, 1939–1945—Economic aspects—Southern States. |
African Americans—Southern States—History—20th century. |
Rural-urban migration—United States—History—20th century. |
Southern States—Politics and government—1865–1950. |
Southern States—Race relations—History—20th century. |
World War, 1939–1945—Manpower—Southern States.
Classification: LCC F215.B65 2024 (print) | LCC F215 (ebook) |
DDC 975/.042—dc23/eng/20240130
LC record available at https://lccn.loc.gov/2024004665
LC ebook record available at https://lccn.loc.gov/2024004666

DOI: 10.1093/oso/9780197655610.001.0001

Printed by Sheridan Books, Inc., United States of America

For my teachers

Contents

Introduction ... 1

PART I: ECONOMIC MOBILIZATION

1. World War II and Agriculture in the Deep South ... 15
2. Ingalls Shipyard: Pascagoula, Mississippi ... 37
3. The FEPC and Black Workers ... 65
4. "A Typical Crowded War Community": Pascagoula, Mississippi ... 93

PART II: MILITARY MOBILIZATION

5. Military Mobilization and Black Troops ... 125
6. The 364th Infantry Regiment, Camp Van Dorn, and the Crisis of 1943 ... 149
7. A Conservative Revolution ... 173

PART III: SOUTHERN POLITICS

8. Ellis Arnall: Southern Liberal ... 201
9. Theodore Bilbo: Southern Reactionary ... 222
10. Political Crossroads, 1946: Black Voters and White Resistance ... 244

Epilogue ... 273
Acknowledgments ... 279
Notes ... 281
Bibliography ... 345
Index ... 363

Introduction

In the early 1940s, the Delta and Pine Land Company was the largest cotton plantation in the United States. Owned by British investors and managed by the company president, Oscar Johnston, who also had title to part of the property, the plantation occupied parts of two Mississippi Delta counties and measured roughly 40,000 acres, approximately 10,000 planted in cotton. As many as 1,000 Black families worked the land of the company, more than 80 percent of them as sharecroppers, toiling for half of the cotton and corn crops they raised (minus the "furnish"—expenses for supplies and food advanced by the company during the growing season). The company hired the remainder of the families as wage laborers, who often worked by the day and were paid weekly, sometimes in food or livestock. For most of the workers at Delta Pine, life was better than for the typical landless farmer of the Deep South. Johnston was a paternalist, and he brought the ideas of welfare capitalism used by northern factory owners to the massive Mississippi plantation. It had a hospital, a school, a recreation center, and better housing than the typical tenant shack.[1]

Although World War II offered the company the potential of new cotton profits, thanks to an anticipated spike in demand from both the military and civilians, that possibility was tempered by concerns about how to maintain enough workers to staff the labor-intensive plantation. Soon after Pearl Harbor, Johnston recognized an already significant loss of labor to the military draft, which had begun in the fall of 1940. He worried that other farm workers would soon move to take industrial war jobs. By the spring of 1942, the federal government had initiated programs to ensure that new war industries around the country had sufficient labor to meet the nation's ambitious production goals. The War Manpower Commission (WMC), created in April 1942 and charged with mobilizing and managing the US labor force for maximum production, distributed an occupational questionnaire to all men between the ages of eighteen and sixty-five who had registered with the Selective Service System. In June 1942, workers at Delta Pine received the questionnaires, and based on their answers, some received notices to appear for an interview at the Greenville, Mississippi, office of the US Employment Service (USES)—another federal agency established by President Franklin D. Roosevelt in December 1941 through a consolidation of all state employment agencies. There, employment officers determined whether the men were "capable of performing service in an essential occupation," and if so, USES employees had instructions to encourage the men to move to war production jobs. Johnston thought that work at Delta Pine qualified as an essential activity, but farm work did not make the government list. Johnston's workers increasingly moved to other jobs because of the federal efforts. In mid-July, he noted that the plantation had lost six workers to war jobs in three days. He believed the company would face a serious labor shortage by the time of the fall harvest.[2]

Labor problems plagued the owners of Delta Pine throughout the war, but despite Johnston's concerns, federal wartime agencies and mandates generally operated in ways that preserved their prerogatives. In December 1944, David Reed, who worked at Delta Pine, decided to leave the plantation. He felt he earned little and decided to go to Chicago, where defense jobs were plentiful. He applied for work in the city through Chicago's USES office, but the Greenville USES staff of local white administrators would not clear Reed. Even though he was in his forties and unlikely to be drafted, the Greenville USES officials claimed Reed did not have a release from his draft board, run by local planters. When Reed appealed the decision, the local panel in Greenville concluded that he offered no "justifiable reasons for leaving the farm" (low pay did not count).[3]

The case of Delta Pine and David Reed offers a window into life in the Deep South during the World War II years.[4] On the eve of the war, much about the region's economic and social relations seemed stuck in time, reminiscent of a world deeply connected to its antebellum past. The unprecedented national economic and military mobilization that accompanied the global conflict of World War II, however, brought change to the Deep South. A series of home front battles erupted—between Black and white people, between poor white people and wealthier ones, between workers and employers, between the federal government and local communities, among others. At the same time, as the account of David Reed suggests, the upheaval of World War II left much about life in the Deep South unchanged. For the elites who had always wielded economic and political power in the region, winning the war was not their only priority; preserving as much of the status quo as possible represented an important home front battle.

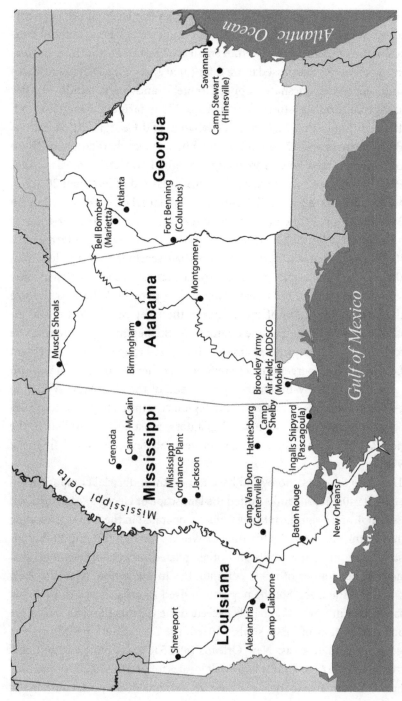

The Deep South during World War II, Created by Jeffrey Patton

The Delta Pine plantation sat at the apex of the Deep South's agricultural economy, which dominated the rural districts where roughly two-thirds of the region's people lived. A small group of Deep South farms (less than 1 percent) encompassed more than 1,000 acres. Like Delta Pine, these plantations relied on sharecroppers, renters, and hired hands—mostly Black agriculturalists—to work their land. Many farmers owned no land. In 1940, in Louisiana, Mississippi, Alabama, and Georgia, 51 percent of all Black farmers and 17 percent of all white farmers sharecropped. Those who possessed land tended to occupy marginal concerns; in Mississippi in 1940, more than one-third of all farms consisted of less than 20 acres. Landless farmers and small farmers relied largely on family labor to make their crops. While other parts of the country had large agricultural populations, the South had an atypically large number of poor farmers. In 1940, 67 percent of southern cultivators had yearly incomes of less than $1,000; in the Midwest the percentage of farmers with such a small income was 17 percent and in the Great Plains only 7 percent. Whatever the size of the farm or the status of the farmer in the Deep South, cotton was almost always produced in some quantity. At the beginning of the war, the percentage of cotton growers among all farmers ranged from 76 percent in Louisiana to 89 percent in Mississippi.[5] In other words, cotton was still king in 1940, seventy-five years after the end of the Civil War. While the one-crop system of agriculture in the region continued to generate wealth for a small minority of Deep South planters, most agriculturalists in the region achieved bare subsistence but secured few additional financial rewards.

The Deep South economy did have important industrial components in the early 1940s. Textile mills dotted the landscape of Georgia, Alabama, and Mississippi, and a significant steel industry operated in the area surrounding Birmingham, Alabama. By the time of World War II, a thriving timber industry, including paper mills and other related processing facilities, sustained the economies of many communities in the region. Approximately one-third of the Deep South's population lived in urban areas in 1940, but most resided in towns that barely exceeded the Census Bureau's minimum urban designation of 2,500 souls. Indeed, the Deep South had only three large metropolitan areas: New Orleans (494,538), Atlanta (302,288), and Birmingham (267,583). Only two other locales topped the 90,000 population plateau—Savannah, Georgia, at almost 96,000, and Shreveport, Louisiana, at just over 98,000.[6]

Over the years, Deep South leaders had constructed an economy that impoverished many white people and kept almost all Black men and women in a position of poverty and subservience. In the countryside, Black people worked largely as sharecroppers or tenants in a status of neo-slavery, tied to the land, penniless, and with few opportunities for advancement. Those in the towns and cities fared no better, with most confined to labor as domestic servants or unskilled laborers. Black freedom and opportunity were limited in other ways. By the early twentieth century, most Black men had lost their right to vote—seemingly won during Reconstruction—through various state-sponsored disfranchisement mechanisms. As a result, the region had a political system dedicated to limited participation and one-party Democratic rule. To maintain white supremacy, white people also enforced a system of racial segregation, in both town and country, and constructed a legal system run by and for white people and with extralegal violence directed at Black citizens for any violations, or even perceived breaches, of the color line. Between 1888 and 1938, Mississippi had 476 recorded lynchings, although additional racial killings went unreported. Most of these murders occurred prior to the mid-1920s, but racial violence and its threat continued to prop up the region's racial caste system well into the mid-twentieth century.[7]

In the decade prior to World War II, FDR's New Deal began to alter life in the Deep South. Most important, the Agricultural Adjustment Act (AAA), designed to boost low farm prices, paid landowners to take acreage out of production. The South had suffered from a scarcity of capital ever since Black emancipation wiped out the massive investment white Southerners had made in the ownership of other human beings. The AAA brought federal money into the South and began to ease the region's capital problem. This infusion of cash into the Deep South's rural environs led to the beginning of the end of the region's plantation system and its reliance on abundant cheap labor. Increasingly, landowners could hire temporary labor to plant and harvest their crops, rather than furnish landless families to do this work. Landowners could also invest in new machinery, such as tractors, to complete farming tasks formerly performed by hand. Only the largest plantations, such as Delta Pine, seemed immune to the changes wrought by the AAA.[8]

Other New Deal programs, such as the Works Progress Administration, the Civilian Conservation Corps, the Tennessee Valley Authority, and Social Security, brought additional federal funds into the South, providing jobs and relief for the many people battered by the Great Depression. To receive federal money, state governments in the Deep South had to invest a portion of their own resources in public welfare operations—relatively small contributions but greater than ones they had previously made. White leaders tried to make sure that the federal spending did not come with strings that required any substantial changes, especially to the edifice that assured white supremacy. FDR himself did not make such demands, but white elites still worried about the long-term implications of federal involvement in their affairs. While New Deal agencies preserved the racial inequities that defined life in the region, some New Dealers, including First Lady Eleanor Roosevelt, advocated for civil rights reforms for Black Americans. Even though little changed for most Black men and women in the Deep South during the 1930s, the seeds of racial change were planted during the Great Depression.[9] While the New Deal began a transformation of the Deep South's economy and social structure, mobilization for World War II pushed those changes forward even more, as federal spending and federal policies expanded their reach into southern society.

In popular memory, World War II is often remembered as the "Good War," even if such an understanding never existed among Americans during the years of fighting. In retrospect, World War II seemed "good" because the conflict pitted the democratic nations of the United States and Great Britain against the forces of totalitarianism. The United States had to fight to prevent Germany and Japan from subjugating other nations and dominating the world. And the US involvement in World War II certainly seemed more justified than later military adventures. On the World War II home front, American citizens came together and sacrificed in ways largely unimaginable today: launching scrap-metal drives, rallying to buy war bonds, submitting to government rationing and price controls on essential goods, and volunteering in large numbers for military service. Yet wartime mobilization also generated tensions on the American home front.[10] These battles brought change to the area's economic, social, and political systems during the war years and set the stage for even greater shifts in the decades that followed.

Wartime mobilization transformed the Deep South's economy. The agricultural revolution begun during the 1930s advanced further during the war years. Wartime imperatives pitted the interests of larger growers against those of smaller ones, including many Black landless farmers. The Deep South's largest farmers, however, especially cotton planters, wielded extensive power and succeeded in shaping wartime agricultural policy and production primarily in ways to maintain their economic advantages.[11] Mobilization also brought a new wave of industrialization to the Deep South, especially in shipbuilding, aircraft assembly, rubber manufacturing, and ordnance factories. The new industries, such as the Ingalls Shipbuilding Corporation in Pascagoula, on the Mississippi Gulf Coast, contributed significantly to the war effort, while also providing substantial financial benefits to the industrialists who built the concerns. War businesses gave rural migrants a chance to earn more money than they ever had, yet it introduced them to an unfamiliar world of work. Black and white Southerners sometimes toiled at the same companies, women played an essential role as wartime employees, and organized labor fought to secure a foothold in a region that had long been hostile to labor unions. Because of the South's largely rural profile at the beginning of the conflict, many of the new war industries were located in small towns and mid-size cities, such as Pascagoula. As rural migrants swarmed into these places, they faced a host of difficulties: housing and food shortages, health problems, overcrowded schools, and increased exposure to vice and crime. Although the federal government provided help to booming war towns in the Deep South, federal assistance often proved inadequate, especially given traditional southern antagonism toward the federal government and urban life, as well as entrenched patterns of racial discrimination.[12]

In the Deep South, mobilizing for total war occurred in a region with racial apartheid. As national leaders proclaimed the war a struggle to preserve freedom and democracy, mobilization heightened racial tensions and led to home front battles along the color line. The federal government decreed the need for nondiscrimination in employment in war industries and military training and service, but those mandates did not propose the abolishment of racial segregation. Basically, the federal wartime orders embraced the ideal of the 1896 *Plessy v. Ferguson* mandate of "separate but equal," a US Supreme Court directive routinely ignored in the South (and beyond) for decades. While some federal officials and some white Americans may have still honestly believed that racial segregation could exist on a nondiscriminatory basis, in the Deep South, racial segregation operated in an openly discriminatory manner. So, as World War II mobilization proceeded, federal nondiscrimination directives and southern racial practices clashed.[13]

President Roosevelt created the Fair Employment Practices Committee (FEPC) with Executive Order 8802 in 1941 after Black leaders—including A. Philip Randolph, head of the Brotherhood of Sleeping Car Porters, and Walter White, executive secretary of the National Association for the Advancement of Colored People (NAACP)—threatened a massive march on Washington, DC, to protest racial discrimination in the defense industry and the military. The directive that established the FEPC boldly proclaimed that "there shall be no discrimination in the employment of workers in defense industries or government because of race, creed, color, or national origin."[14] Ideally, this edict would have united all Americans in the drive to attain maximum war production. This aspiration, reflected in the federal government slogan, "United We Win," proved particularly difficult for federal administrators to realize. With no real enforcement powers, the FEPC depended on the goodwill of white employers to treat potential Black employees fairly. The FEPC proved unable to uproot the private white economic privilege inherent in the South's system of racial segregation. So Black workers in the Deep South (and elsewhere) faced severe difficulties gaining equal opportunities in war industries, and the nation's manpower needs sometimes suffered as a result.

The service of Black men in the World War II military also generated racial conflict in the Deep South, a region that provided training sites for most Black GIs. Black soldiers had fought in all of America's wars dating back to the American Revolution and had long viewed military service as one way to stake their claim to equal treatment. In 1881, Frederick Douglass had noted that "if the negro knows enough to fight for his country, he knows enough to vote." When W. E. B. Du Bois urged Black Americans to support American entry into World War I, he hoped that the sacrifices made by Black soldiers would "show the world again what the loyalty and bravery of black men means." Many white Americans, however, both within the military establishment and in the larger society, always claimed, unfairly and inaccurately, that Black warriors were cowardly and inefficient. Throughout American history, these stereotypes helped justify confining most Black troops to labor details and limiting the opportunities for Black men to serve in the officer corps, which blunted their claims to first-class citizenship and full manhood. During World War II, however, various groups challenged traditional white beliefs about Black soldiers: Black civilians, especially in the North; Black soldiers from both the North and the South; and eventually even some white military officials, who tried to enforce the nondiscrimination principles proclaimed by the Roosevelt administration in the Selective Service and Training Act (1940).[15]

During the early years of the war, the US Army's efforts to implement the nondiscrimination mandate at its own facilities meant that it sometimes did not enforce racial segregation or maintained racial separation less rigorously than white Southerners desired. Off-base, however, the army made little effort to enforce the principle of nondiscrimination. As a result, communities in the areas near army camps became the site of racial conflict nationwide. In the spring and summer of 1943, these troubles led to violent clashes, including at a number of Deep South military sites. Following the racial unrest of 1943, the US military cautiously moved to bolster its nondiscrimination efforts. Beginning in the summer of 1943 and continuing into 1944, the army improved conditions for Black officers, utilized more Black soldiers as combat troops, and desegregated base recreation and transportation facilities. Despite these changes, which represented the most visible and sustained challenge during the war to established racial arrangements in the Deep South, the military refused to condemn the system of southern racial segregation more directly. That decision catered to white public opinion—North and South—but it did not end the racial unrest in and around Deep South military facilities. It also potentially imperiled the US manpower needs for a total war against the Axis Powers.

As wartime mobilization upended daily life, some African Americans in the Deep South pressed for changes to the system of race relations. Black people throughout the region clearly understood the contradictions that the war created. Even if they did not use the specific language of the Double V slogan popularized by the *Pittsburgh Courier* in 1942, Black citizens regularly pointed out the inconsistencies between fighting a war to preserve democracy against a racist enemy and their own struggles at home for equal treatment and the basic rights of citizenship. Black activists in the Deep South created NAACP chapters, teachers mounted salary equalization challenges, and individuals tested racial segregation on buses and elsewhere. Even small acts of defiance undermined southern racial practices; one Black man in Alabama in 1942 told a store clerk writing out his bill to put "Mr." in front of his name, a demand for a small form of respect typically denied Black people in the Deep South. Historians have rightly suggested that the Black activism of the World War II years was not as militant as during the previous decade. The dislocations and everyday struggles created by wartime undoubtedly increased the difficulties of sustained activism during those years. But the war did help to refocus the tactics of the struggle. Indeed, the World War II years represented an important stage in the "Long Civil Rights Movement."[16]

The most sustained fight for Black rights in the South during the war years revolved around securing the vote for Black citizens. In 1940, Lonnie Smith, a dentist in Houston, Texas, challenged that state's Democratic white primary.

By barring Black voters from participation in the Democratic Party primary, white leaders excluded Black citizens from the only election that mattered in a region dominated politically by the Democrats. Aided by the NAACP, Smith's case eventually reached the US Supreme Court, which declared, on April 3, 1944, in *Smith v. Allwright*, that the white primary in Texas was unconstitutional. The ruling spurred Black activists across the Deep South, often led by war veterans. The campaign for the right to vote peaked in the Deep South in the elections of 1946—when Black citizens attempted to vote on a scale unprecedented in the twentieth century. Black Southerners, however, faced overwhelming obstacles in their effort to exercise this basic right of citizenship. White Southerners beat back the effort with tactics ranging from verbal intimidation to violence, and the federal government refused to intervene. Black voter suppression in the 1946 elections in Mississippi and Georgia undermined the notion that Americans—including Black Americans—had fought (and died) for four years to preserve democracy.[17]

If most Black people in the Deep South saw wartime mobilization as presenting opportunities for change (for the most part, unrealized), white political leaders in the region disagreed about the impact of the war on their economic and social systems. Some, such as Ellis Arnall, governor of Georgia from 1943 to 1947, embraced the federal model promoted during the war: supporting a "fairer" type of white supremacy, one in which segregation might remain while addressing some Black demands. This strategy, which tended to ignore racial issues while focusing on regional economic problems, reflected the gradualist style that had long defined southern liberalism. Only a small group of white leaders in the Deep South embraced this approach, but it dovetailed nicely with national liberal thinking on race.[18] Most southern white leaders, such as Theodore Bilbo of Mississippi, who served in the US Senate from 1935 to 1947, reacted to the changes of the war years by calling for renewed vigilance and action to prevent any alterations to racial segregation and Black disfranchisement. The elections of 1946 in Georgia and Mississippi highlighted these competing southern political visions, including the limitations of both, and foreshadowed the contours of the region's postwar politics. Much like their Black neighbors, white Southerners used the language of wartime to justify their actions; however, instead of viewing the war as a struggle to expand democracy, most claimed they fought to defend white democracy.[19]

The two-act crisis response of the FDR years—the federal programs of the New Deal and the economic and military mobilization of World War II—

challenged a status quo in the Deep South that had largely defined the region since the Civil War. Despite FDR's reluctance to confront white southern leaders directly, especially on matters of race, his twelve years in office established programs and policies that initiated generations of transformation in the region. At the end of the war, plenty of continuity accompanied undeniable change: racial segregation and Black disfranchisement were challenged and slightly dented but still stood; industry had further increased in importance, but agriculture (though restructured) remained the essential lifeblood of the economy; and the Solid Democratic (white) South endured, increasingly worried about its racial future, but unbroken. Greater transformations would follow in the postwar decades, though the deeply ingrained traditions of the Old South never completely disappeared.

PART I
ECONOMIC MOBILIZATION

1
World War II and Agriculture in the Deep South

On Saturday, October 3, 1942, 10,000 people gathered in the small town of Tylertown (population 1,400) in southwest Mississippi for the Food for Freedom Thanksgiving Harvest festival. In addition to a parade and a picnic, Claude Wickard, secretary of the US Department of Agriculture (USDA), addressed both the crowd and a national radio audience on the "National Farm and Home Hour." Wickard announced a projected increase in the 1942 harvest, which would meet the USDA's Food for Freedom goal of 1942 and boost agricultural production by 12 percent over that of 1941, a one-year growth record for American farm products. But Secretary Wickard worried about the future. People were leaving the land for the military and to work in war jobs. Farm machinery parts, fertilizers, and other necessary agricultural materials were in short supply. Wickard predicted that "the road ahead for farmers is long and difficult." As the secretary later explained, the USDA's Food for Freedom program required that "farm resources must be used toward but one end—Victory . . . production which does not contribute to winning the war must be discarded. We must turn all of our energy to production of agricultural products essential in this war."[1]

Despite Secretary Wickard's concerns, World War II did not necessarily produce hard times in the Deep South countryside. The war years, however, did bring both change and conflict in the region's farm districts. Migration from rural areas created labor shortages and raised agricultural wages. However, wealthy landowners used their power to compel the federal government to act on their behalf to keep farm wages low and farm workers on the land, especially Black tenants and wage hands who provided much of the essential labor for key parts of the regional farm economy. All farmers, from the largest cotton planter to the smallest dirt farmer, could lay claim to helping with the war effort, although the region's wealthiest farmers focused much of their efforts on maintaining high prices for their favored agricultural products, especially cotton. Large growers also undermined the work of other farmers in the region by attacking the Farm Security Administration (FSA), the federal agency most committed to helping hundreds of thousands of small producers in the Deep South, agriculturalists who had proved the most willing to reshape their farming for victory.

The vision that wealthier landowners increasingly had for southern agriculture—for a more modern, industrial type of farming—was promoted during the war by the work of private interest groups, such as the American Farm Bureau Federation (AFBF), led by Alabamian Edward O'Neil. That vision also became the dominant policy of the USDA in the years after Henry Wallace, secretary of agriculture since 1933, became FDR's vice president in 1940. Wallace had promoted progressive thinking while secretary, but his successor, Wickard, had a hands-off management style that allowed those parts of the USDA that favored big agriculture, such as the Agricultural Adjustment Administration (AAA) and the Extension Service, to gain greater influence within the agency over the course of the war. At the same time, the more progressive parts of the USDA, such as the FSA and the Bureau of Agricultural Economics (BAE)—entities interested in advancing the concerns and fortunes of smaller producers, including landless farmers—lost a key ally with the change in agency leadership and saw their influence over agricultural policy evaporate by the end of World War II.[2]

During World War II, Black and white migrants left the rural South in droves. About 3.2 million out of a population of 14.6 million in southern farm districts relocated during the war years, and by the end of the conflict, the South's rural population had declined by 20 percent; the Black rural population dropped by 30 percent. Economic opportunity, in the form of war production jobs, lured most migrants from the land. At the beginning of the war, federal economic planners worried little about the migration of farm labor to defense work since they correctly recognized that rural America—especially in the South—had a surplus of underused labor. Two-thirds of the southern rural migrants headed north or west, but perhaps a million people moved to urban areas in the South. During World War II, manufacturing employment rose 75 percent in the South, from 1.6 million to 2.8 million. Despite the overall loss of population in the South, urban areas in the region expanded by 30 percent, with the most dramatic growth occurring in coastal cities. Two of these in the Deep South, Pascagoula, Mississippi, and Brunswick, Georgia, had population increases between 1940 and 1943 that ranked them in the top ten nationally among the fastest-growing locales.[3]

As with other migrations, the movement of the southern rural population to war jobs followed well-worn paths—roads local populations perceived as leading to economic opportunity.[4] The migration also unfolded differently in the small farming areas and the plantation districts of the Deep South, as a closer look at two areas in Mississippi reveals. In northeast Mississippi, where small farm operators and their families comprised most of the population, there were two main groups of war workers. Most who sought war jobs did so in a way that kept them connected to their local communities. In the counties adjoining the Alabama line, residents commuted to Muscle Shoals, Alabama, often to work in the nitrate plants that supplied the munitions industry. In other parts of northeast Mississippi, those looking for war jobs headed to the area around Grenada, Mississippi, where they worked on constructing Camp McCain, and later, took civilian jobs at the military outpost. A second, but smaller, group of migrants from northeast Mississippi, typically those who were younger and not well established financially, left the area for more distant war jobs. They moved away for months, for years, or in many cases, permanently. Among this group, those heading to southern locales often went to the shipyards of the Gulf Coast or to help construct air bases in Pensacola, while those going north typically landed in Detroit—a major national site for war industry—or Akron, Ohio, where by 1942, the Goodyear Aircraft Corporation already employed 35,000 workers.[5]

Migration for war work in the Mississippi Delta looked different. First, a more significant number of residents, both white and Black, left the area. An FSA official noted in 1944 that "both whites & Negroes have left in considerable no." from Clarksdale in Coahoma County. A white widow in the county who lived with her sharecropper son similarly observed that people who had been working in the towns at sawmills, garages, and the light company left the town for war jobs. Black people from the countryside also left the area, especially "young fellows from [the] cropper group." Others working on plantations in Coahoma County moved to places like Clarksdale to take the jobs vacated by town residents. Unlike northeast Mississippi, most of the Delta residents who sought war jobs did not commute to nearby opportunities, in part because of fewer opportunities for local war work but also because those looking for new economic prospects could not afford a daily commute for employment. Residents of Coahoma County observed that some who left the area for war jobs went to the shipyards in New Orleans or Mobile or to aircraft plants in Texas, although most of the Black migrants who left the area went to the North, to what one called "big cities a long way off."[6]

As federal officials originally believed, the migration from the southern countryside had some positive effects. Those in small farming areas often improved their economic position because of the new job opportunities. The farm owners who commuted to war jobs in Muscle Shoals or Grenada generally prospered. As one dairy farmer in the area observed, those working in Muscle Shoals were "doing fairly well—behaving themselves and a lot saving some money." But the buzzing war economy nearby even meant economic improvement for some landless farmers or laborers in northeast Mississippi. The FSA supervisor in Lafayette County reported that several FSA clients who combined war jobs with farm work had managed to pay their loans and become landowners. At least a dozen other landless farmers receiving FSA assistance had earned enough at war work to buy farm equipment or household appliances. A Black laborer in the area reported in 1944 that he "worked just about full-time" and had jobs all winter for the first time in over a decade. Working at a variety of positions across north Mississippi—as a cotton picker, as a janitor at the University of Mississippi, at a pulp yard in Batesville, and as a pipe layer near Holly Springs—he made enough money to take on a home mortgage. A white farmer in Tishomingo County observed that because so many white residents who worked in Iuka left to take war jobs, local businesses that "used to employ none but whites" started to hire Black labor.[7]

In plantation areas, such as the Mississippi Delta, the thinning of the Black labor ranks also led to a variety of positive changes for those who remained. When F. D. Patterson, president of Tuskegee Institute, and Claude Barnett, founder of the Associated Negro Press, toured the South on behalf of the USDA in 1942, they found that landowners "who formerly refused space for gardens and discouraged taking time for their care, . . . are now encouraging and occasionally requiring their tenants to grow a variety of foodstuffs." These new arrangements for landless farmers reduced their typical reliance on overpriced foodstuffs at a plantation commissary or local grocery. In Coahoma County, some sharecroppers who stayed on the land got extra acreage to work during the war—the fields abandoned by their migrating neighbors. In addition, some plantation owners in the county reportedly quit cheating their tenants and sharecroppers on credit terms. Fewer Black workers also meant better housing arrangements for some Black landless farmers in plantation areas. Several plantation owners also demonstrated more interest in providing education for their Black workers. During the war, the Delta Council, an association of Mississippi Delta planters, backed the creation of a Black teacher training school in the region.[8]

Despite the positive developments that wartime migration brought to rural residents in the Deep South, the movement of large numbers of people from these areas also created problems. Small towns in rural districts clearly felt the effects of the migration. A southern official of the US Commerce Department concluded in early 1943 that in the Deep South "thousands of small and rural communities . . . have suffered from loss of population, trade, and essential services." A small town with one doctor or pharmacist lost that essential service if the sole practitioner left for the army or migrated to an area experiencing the growth associated with economic mobilization. Small-town merchants had fewer customers as local populations declined.[9]

In the countryside, the biggest problem created by wartime migration was the disruption of rural labor markets. Residents noticed a decline in local labor supplies soon after America's economic mobilization began, a situation that persisted throughout the war years. In September 1941, the county agent in Calhoun County, Alabama, estimated that 50 percent of the adult male labor working on area farms in 1939 was no longer available for agricultural work. A farmer in east-central Mississippi complained in February 1942 that "we farmers have no labor and cannot get any . . . there is no hope of getting farm labor in this part of Miss. and we have done all we could." By the summer of 1944, planters in the Mississippi Delta had only about half of the laboring force they typically relied on to harvest their vast cotton crop.[10]

In addition to the rural migration to war jobs, other factors altered the labor equation in the rural South during the war. W. R. Brumfield, a white farmer with substantial holdings in southwest Mississippi, blamed a host of factors for the scarcity of agricultural workers: "Selective Service, High Wages Being Paid at Government Projects and Industrial Plant, Surplus Commodities, Works Project [sic] Administration and Civilian Conservation Corps." Joe Watson, a farmer sixty miles north in Hazlehurst, disliked the relief provided by the Federal Surplus Commodities Corporation (FSCC), a New Deal program that provided excess farm products to poor families. He complained that he could not secure any reliable farm workers and believed that "Negroes and a lot of white men will not work as long as the Government feed them. They leave their field in the middle of the week to go for the commodity." Farmers who needed extra labor were also upset that the Work Projects Administration (WPA), another New Deal relief agency, still provided government jobs until the summer of 1943. Theodore Bilbo, US senator from Mississippi, claimed in 1942 that "the WPA has just about ruined me as a farmer and what the WPA lacked completing the job, the high prices paid by the Government projects finished me."[11]

The military also took away farm labor. A prosperous farmer in Crystal Springs, Mississippi, south of Jackson, reported in the spring of 1943 that he had four vacant tenant houses because of the draft, which significantly reduced his farm's production. In addition, soldiers often sent a portion of their military pay back home, which provided an economic boost for wage laborers. Planters in the Mississippi Delta were convinced that a major portion of their Black labor force moved to town and worked less because they were getting "some of that soldier pay." In 1943, Mississippi governor Paul B. Johnson suggested that employers use the state's existing vagrancy law to compel such individuals to return to the fields. Even some white observers, however, disagreed that military payments reduced the number of black laborers. A white government official in Coahoma County believed that while "there are some very obvious cases among Negroes," most of those receiving military checks from relatives were white women. The official noted that planters never complained about this group, since "you can't force white women to work!"[12]

When farmers complained about a shortage of labor, what they really bemoaned was the absence of extra workers available to help during the busy planting and harvesting periods. In northeast Mississippi, one county agent in 1944 noted a shortage of labor at certain times of the year but also observed that despite all those who had left for the army and for war work, there was "still on hand in [the] country more people than needed to tend the present acreage of crops." The county agent believed that many in his area were underemployed. A Black tenant farmer agreed with this assessment when he told an interviewer in 1944 that he did not "know what to do here as [there are] more people than jobs & farms even now." In the Mississippi Delta, the surplus labor of Black men and women powered the plantation economy of the region, and World War II migration threatened this system by creating an unfamiliar labor shortage. As a young white woman who worked for the FSA in Coahoma County understood, "It seems like we got just too many people except in wartime."[13]

To deal with the rural labor shortage, especially at key points in the agricultural cycle, farmers in the Deep South turned to a variety of strategies. As in other parts of the country, small farmers often increased their own labor or that of family members. For example, during the 1941 harvest in Calhoun County, in north Alabama, some farmers reportedly worked as much as ninety hours a week to bring in their crops. Other farmers looked for extra help during critical times of the year wherever they could find it. In the fall of 1942, as thousands of migrants—at least a third of those from rural districts—moved to Atlanta for war-related jobs, the mayors of several towns in the farming areas south of the city declared holidays so that town folk, including bankers and city officials, could help pick cotton for the typical, prewar wage rate of $1 per 100 pounds picked. In Georgia during the 1943 harvest season, farmers received help from both soldiers detailed to the fields (Washington County) and from town residents and children let out of school early (Thomas County). Some farmers in the Deep South also utilized imported Mexican labor through the bracero program, which the USES and the FSA managed during the early years of the war.[14]

Farmers facing labor shortages in the Deep South and elsewhere also relied on two other sources of workers not typically used in peacetime: women and Axis prisoners of war. Women had long contributed valuable labor to farming enterprises, though only women from the poorest families typically worked at the most demanding jobs of planting and harvesting crops. Those numbers grew as men left the countryside for the army or to work in war plants, and nationwide, by July 1943, 19 percent of all agricultural workers were women (up from 9 percent in July 1940). In April 1943, Congress passed the Emergency Farm Labor Program, which revived the Women's Land Army (WLA), an organization that had existed during World War I. The WLA helped recruit female labor to fill some of the labor shortages in the Deep South, although it had less success there than in other parts of the country. Obstacles included the failure to enlist white, middle-class women in urban areas to help on the farm. Agricultural work—especially planting and harvesting—was widely perceived in the region as a "Black" job, one a "respectable" white woman would not undertake. At the same time, the WLA tended to shun Black women when recruiting in the South, largely to dampen white associations of farm labor with Blackness. As elsewhere, the lack of adequate childcare also limited how many women the WLA could muster to work on southern farms.[15]

By 1943, war prisoners represented another option for filling rural labor shortages. Planters in the Mississippi Delta urged their congressional delegation to secure the location of prisoner of war camps in their area, preferably German or Italian POWs (rather than Japanese). And by the time of the 1943 cotton harvest, five POW camps operated in the area: at Clarksdale, Cleveland, Greenville, Indianola, and Belzoni. Although the POWs filled a yawning labor gap for the 1943 harvest, they also put downward pressure on the wages for Black cotton pickers still in the area. Eventually, more than 12,000 German and Italian POWs worked on cotton plantations in Mississippi, Arkansas, and northern Louisiana. Through the successful lobbying of Mississippi's junior US senator, James Eastland, Axis POWs remained in the Mississippi Delta through the 1946 cotton harvest, a full year after the war ended.[16]

These additional sources of labor could not, however, completely replace all the Black labor that typically worked the Deep South's largest farms. White citizens also utilized several methods that had long played a role in controlling Black labor in the South. In the years following the end of Reconstruction, most southern states had passed emigrant-agent laws, which instituted difficult registration requirements and exorbitant fees for labor recruiters, all designed to limit the movement of labor—especially Black workers—from the region. Most southern states still had such laws in the early 1940s and sometimes used them during the war to prosecute out-of-state labor recruiters. In 1942, Georgia officials arrested a New Jersey man trying to attract Black workers to move to his company in Newark. In 1944, the Delta Council recommended that law enforcement pay attention to Mississippi's emigrant-agent law to prevent "unethical labor recruiting practices." Although only selectively enforced during the war, these emigrant-agent laws undermined the efforts of the USES, which tried to manage manpower issues with a nationwide focus on labor shortages and surpluses.[17]

Landowners in the South, especially in plantation districts, also relied on maintaining unequal credit arrangements to keep Black laborers on the land. Although the US Congress officially abolished debt peonage—forcing people to work to clear unpaid debts—in 1867, southern states had continued to maintain laws and customs that preserved exploitative systems of debt and credit that limited Black movement. The sharecropping system, with its advancement of food and supplies against the future value of a growing crop, which often proved to be less than any furnish, was one such practice. Poor Black farmers trapped in endless cycles of unfair credit and debt arrangements with wealthy white landowners still had freedom of movement, but in some cases, they believed that indebted people had to remain at work or on a particular piece of property until they settled their accounts. When interviewers asked Coahoma County residents in 1944 why they had not joined the wartime migration, some respondents, Black and white, thought the county had strict debt laws, especially for Black people, who "can't leave the county if in debt." At the same time, some white Southerners did impose debt peonage on Black workers. Black men and women who faced court fines and fees frequently had those charges paid by white landowners, who then required labor—of an often-indeterminate length—to work off the debt. Although debt peonage had begun to decline because of the Black migration from the South that began around World War I and because of New Deal programs that undermined traditional sharecropper/tenant patterns in the region, in 1942, the federal government investigated more than thirty cases of peonage, almost all of them in the southern states.[18]

Unlike white people, Black individuals trying to take advantage of wartime economic opportunities in the Deep South sometimes had to navigate a landscape of unscrupulous white landowners willing to use debt to exploit Black labor. Consider the wartime saga of Lonnie Kimbrough. He was born in 1913 in Meridian, Mississippi, in the eastern part of the state, but his family moved to the Mississippi Delta, where his father worked as a sharecropper. Lonnie did not particularly like the farming life, and when wartime economic mobilization began, he secured a job working for the US Army Corps of Engineers as a bulldozer operator, earning $270 a month. He helped construct the new army airfields in Greenville and Indianola. When construction shut down in winter, he found work at the Phoenix Hotel in the little Delta town of Moorhead, where he lived with his wife and two children. One December night in 1942, Kimbrough went to a Moorhead roadhouse and got into an altercation with some other Black patrons, tenants on a Sunflower County plantation. Kimbrough flaunted his prosperity by flashing cash, and the tenants took umbrage. One complained, "Here is a town Negro working for the government and making big money while we poor devils are just farm hands." A fight broke out, and the police soon arrived and arrested the men. The employer of the tenants backed their story that Kimbrough had caused the affray, and the police released them. Kimbrough, however, who realized "that a city negro could not exert much influence in Moorhead," turned to the best white "protector" he knew, W. P. Scruggs, who owned the Sunflower County plantation where his father worked.[19]

Scruggs solved Kimbrough's problem with law enforcement, but only at a steep price. According to Kimbrough, the planter told him that he could make the pending prosecution go away if he would "remain forever with his wife and children on Mr. Scruggs' plantation and make Mr. Scruggs a good hand." Kimbrough agreed, and Scruggs gave him nine acres to grow cotton, as well as 100 rows of corn and a small garden patch to tend. Kimbrough received one-half of the cotton crop, and Scruggs provided supplies and a $20 per month furnish, all of which had to be repaid after the crop sold. At the end of 1943, after deducting what Scruggs said was a $300 debt, Kimbrough received $42 for his year's labor. He wanted to quit the plantation, but he did not, because he had heard stories that Scruggs had beaten others who tried to run off. By the summer of 1944, however, with that year's crop well underway, Kimbrough finally decided to leave. He asked relatives in Chicago to send him the $7 train ticket and left for the city at the end of August. From Kimbrough's perspective, he thought he and Scruggs were square, as the tenant's share of the cotton crop then coming to fruition would cover the furnish. Kimbrough found a job at the Howard Foundry in Chicago, and his family joined him in the city. Kimbrough, however, had heard correctly: Scruggs did not just let his tenants leave. He tracked Kimbrough down in the Windy City and had him arrested on the assault charge from 1942. The Illinois governor, Dwight Green, approved the extradition request, but a federal judge, Walter LaBuy, blocked that move, remarking that "some of these plantation owners apparently don't know that slavery has been ended in the United States."[20]

Even as rural white Southerners continued to utilize traditional tools to limit Black movement, they turned to the federal government to help stabilize local labor markets and preserve their economic position. Although wealthy farmers like Oscar Johnston of Delta Pine and Land Company initially believed the economic mobilization plans for the United States devalued agriculture, the nation's powerful Farm Bloc (a bipartisan, national coalition of members of the US Congress) soon adjusted that calculus. Farmers rightly argued that agricultural production was as important to military victory as the manufacture of tanks and planes. By early 1942, agriculturalists throughout the country, including in the Deep South, called on the federal government to help with their labor problems. By the summer of 1942, state officials stepped up the complaints to federal officials about a shortage of agricultural workers. National political leaders soon heeded these pleas.[21]

Farm interests sought federal help to exclude agricultural labor from the draft. In November 1942, Congress passed the Tydings Amendment to the Selective Service Act of 1940, which allowed local draft boards to issue a military deferment to those found "to be necessary to and regularly engaged in an agricultural occupation or agricultural endeavor essential to the war effort." The amendment came with a set of regulations that rated farm labor in terms of "war units" required to produce various commodities and in terms of their essentiality to the war effort. A deferment required at least eight war units. A dairyman tending one cow received credit for one war unit, a chicken farmer needed to manage 600 broilers for the same unit, and a cotton farmer had to till two acres of cotton to receive credit for a single war unit. By February 1943, local draft boards had approved exemptions for more than 560,000 agricultural workers, a number that had grown to 2 million by September 1943. The latter number represented 47 percent of the agricultural labor force between eighteen and forty-four, compared to 7 percent of all nonagricultural workers in the same age range who received other military exemptions, typically because of employment in war-related industrial concerns.[22]

Local draft boards, typically staffed by the most substantial farmers, had wide discretion in implementing the Tydings Amendment. As a result, local concerns and existing social arrangements shaped how they applied the law. In small farming areas, such as northeast Mississippi, draft boards generally sympathized with what one Tishomingo County resident described as farmers "too old to do plowing, cultivating, etc." who asked for the deferment of a "son or hand." Draft boards in these areas also protected local farmers, who typically depended on family labor, from having all their male children taken by the military. Some employers secured military deferments for their employees, at times without their knowledge. A Black wage hand in northeast Mississippi worked primarily for a single landowner, who also provided a cabin where the laborer and his family lived. The farm laborer claimed his boss secured his exemption from military service without his knowledge. When a BAE interviewer asked him in 1944 whether his employer's action meant he had to stay on that landowner's farmer for the duration of the war, the wage hand replied, "I don't know, but I reckon maybe yes." While some Black laborers had white patrons who actively shielded them from the draft, many Black wage laborers had no such protection.[23]

In plantation districts in the Deep South, draft boards focused not only on ensuring an adequate supply of Black laborers but also on shaping the Black population that remained. In the Mississippi Delta, planters typically disliked the work of the FSA; an agency official from Coahoma County believed that the draft boards "were inclined to think FSA clients [were] to [be] taken if at all possible." An official with the AAA office in Coahoma County believed that local selective service officials generally selected the cream of the local Black population when filling draft quotas—Black residents with the "most schooling, best health, most ambition and dependability." That strategy may have been a way to remove young Black men from the area (among those who had not already left) who were the least likely to accept the oppressive conditions of life for Black landless farmers. At the same time, the AAA man noted that members of the draft boards applied a different logic when dealing with their own Black workers: "they naturally take care of keeping their own croppers they want but can't do that for all."[24]

The Farm Bloc from the South and elsewhere pushed for a more expansive military deferment program for agricultural workers than was provided in the Tydings Amendment. Bills considered in the US Congress during the first several months of 1943 proposed to eliminate both the "necessary to" standard and the requirement to produce a certain amount of farm product to qualify for an agricultural exemption from military service. Instead, farm interests wanted the military deferment applied to all who had "substantially full-time" farm jobs. Black leaders and the Black press denounced this measure, in the words of the *Baltimore Afro-American*, as an effort to impose "a system of virtual peonage wrapped in the clothes of patriotism" on rural Black Southerners. Another measure, the Austin-Wadsworth bill, proposed in February 1943, would have given local draft boards almost total power to determine how their local populations contributed to the war effort, whether that be military service or "noncombatant" service. As the *Atlanta World* pointed out, from the perspective of African Americans in the South, the Austin-Wadsworth law "would be just the needed power in the hands of local draft boards which their members have long desired"—the power to force Black labor to work wherever it most benefited white elites. None of these measures ever received congressional approval, although in March 1944, the Selective Service System agreed to end the unit system for farm deferments.[25]

By the fall of 1942, the federal government had identified agriculture as an "essential activity" necessary to the successful prosecution of the war, so rural workers had to secure a release from their employers and local draft boards to get clearance from local manpower offices to take other war-related jobs. Farmers and draft board members did not always approve releases, even if a farm or timber employee could only secure sporadic work in the community. Many rural Southerners, however, left the countryside without going through the red tape of the WMC and USES, and by the spring of 1943, the new War Food Administration (WFA). And not all employers fully complied with the employment procedures mandated by the wartime bureaucracy. In October 1943, the WMC began to allow agricultural workers to look for employment in other industries for up to six weeks during the slack times in the agricultural cycle without receiving the required releases. Landowners, however, complained about this new policy, as it was essentially a loophole for people to leave the countryside for other war jobs without getting permission from employers and draft boards.[26]

Southern landowners relied on the federal government to help keep their prices as high as possible during the war while also holding down labor costs. To check wartime inflation, Congress and the Roosevelt administration tried several programs to limit wage and price increases. The Farm Bloc managed as well as any economic entity to limit the impact of these efforts to regulate the prices of its products. The Emergency Price Control Act of January 1942 included an amendment by Alabama senator John Bankhead that placed the oversight of the prices of agricultural commodities not with the Office of Price Administration, which managed all other price control efforts, but with the USDA, an agency more sympathetic to farm owners. The president of the Alabama Farm Bureau Federation, Walter Randolph, told Senator Bankhead that his amendment had "saved agriculture from a Pearl Harbor catastrophe." The bill also created a generous ceiling on farm prices, set at 110 percent of 1910–1914 farm prices, the most prosperous years for agriculture in recent memory. Since most farm prices in 1942 remained well below the 110 percent threshold, controls on agricultural prices were essentially nonexistent. In October 1942, FDR created the Office of Economic Stabilization (OES), in part to stabilize rising farm prices. The agricultural parity formula became less generous to farmers, but at the same time, the government offered subsidies to farmers by purchasing commodities at prices above market value. As a result, agricultural prices continued to rise, even after the implementation of another federal anti-inflation effort, FDR's wage and price freeze order in April 1943.[27]

Southern politicians, in alliance with their colleagues from other farm states, continued to seek additional price-control exemptions for agricultural commodities throughout the war, and almost all landowning farmers in the South prospered during the war. The price that growers received for cotton, the primary cash crop in the Deep South, more than doubled. Selling for 10 cents a pound in 1940, cotton soared to 18 cents a pound in 1942 and rose to as high as 26 cents a pound by the end of the war. The prices for many other southern farm products doubled during the war, and farm income increased by 300 percent. A 1943 survey by the BAE showed that farm values in the southern states grew faster during World War II than in any other section of the country.[28]

Despite this period of prosperity for southern farmers, escalating costs threatened profit margins, especially for those with the most labor-intensive operations. As the 1945 crop season approached, Walter Sillers, a Mississippi Delta cotton planter and speaker of the Mississippi House of Representatives, calculated the impact that rising wages for farm labor had on Delta cotton operations. Cotton pickers had received $1 per 100 pounds picked in 1940, a rate that by 1944 had risen in some places to as much as $3 per 100 pounds picked. Sillers believed that Delta cotton in 1944 was "cultivated at costs entirely too high and far out of proportion to the value of the services rendered." He estimated labor costs that year for cotton cultivation at 35 to 75 percent of the total value of the crop. After factoring in other costs of production, Sillers believed that the 1944 cotton harvest resulted "in many cases in losses and in many more with little if any profit to the operation." Cotton farmers with medium-sized holdings also complained about relatively small returns despite higher prices for the staple. In Floyd County, Georgia, in the northwestern part of the state, a farmer who had previously raised ninety acres of cotton decided not to grow the crop in 1945. Even though the Georgia farmer knew that cotton brought more than 20 cents a pound, he could not secure enough cheap labor, and both the cost of fertilizer and ginning his crop had risen substantially.[29]

As wage costs continued to rise during the war, large growers in the South pressed the federal government for help. Committed to a relatively free supply-and-demand market for cotton, even in wartime, wealthy landowners viewed a similar market in wage labor as a threat to their economic existence and asked the USDA to intervene. In the Delta regions of Mississippi, Arkansas, and Missouri in 1945, both the Southern Tenant Farmers Union (STFU)—active in the Mississippi Delta since the late 1930s—and the Congress of Industrial Organizations (CIO) helped organize a campaign among cotton pickers for a minimum wage of $3.50 per 100 pounds of picked cotton. Flexing their political muscle in Washington DC, Delta planters convinced the USDA to halt the movement by having local USDA Wage Boards call for a referendum on the need for a wage ceiling for the 1945 harvest. According to agency guidelines, such a ceiling required that a majority of the producers of the crop in an area agree to such a regulation. In late August, a referendum was held in nineteen Mississippi counties. Cotton pickers, not classified as producers by the existing rules, could not vote. Though sharecroppers and tenants were considered producers, the STFU reported that on many plantations, Black sharecroppers were instructed to vote for the ceiling. The final tally in the referendum was 22,193 for a ceiling and only 313 against the action. Following the vote, the USDA established a 1945 wage ceiling in the nineteen counties of $2.10 per 100 pounds of cotton picked.[30]

Prosperous landowners in the Deep South were united in their reliance on the Roosevelt administration's wartime bureaucracy to help with their labor problems and to shield them from the worst effects of government price controls. Many of those same farmers, however, did not support federal help for poorer southern farmers. Specifically, big agricultural interests tried to eliminate the FSA, a federal agency that did more than any other to help improve the lives of smaller producers, including landless farmers, and that also played a significant role in promoting increased food production during the early years of the war.

The FSA, created in 1937 to address rural poverty, administered several programs. The farm ownership program provided landless farmers with low-interest, forty-year loans to buy their own land. By the end of World War II, Black growers represented about one-third of the participants in this program in the South. A rehabilitation program offered money and advice to both tenants and small owners to encourage good farm management. Short-term loans helped small growers buy seed, feed, and farm tools. The rehabilitation program also encouraged diversification among southern FSA clients, most notably by increasing livestock-tending. In addition, the agency provided credit and advice to create co-ops for everything from farm machinery to insurance to veterinary services to prepaid medical care plans. The FSA also ran several communal farming experiments, which resettled poor rural residents on leased or purchased plantations. FSA programs touched the lives of many small producers in the Deep South. In 1942, the FSA helped 25,000 Mississippi farmers. Twenty-six hundred participated in the farm purchase program, while more than 20,000 had rehabilitation loans.[31]

Rural southern leaders disliked the FSA. For one thing, the FSA's mission, to reduce landlessness in rural America and to assist poorer farmers in other ways, challenged the existing hierarchies of southern agriculture and challenged practices used by large farm owners in the South to cheat tenants and sharecroppers, such as unwritten leases and the control of credit. The National Cotton Council (NCC), formed in 1939 and led by Oscar Johnston, organized cotton growers, ginners, warehousemen, and merchants in nineteen cotton-producing states and regularly criticized the FSA. The NCC concluded in January 1942 that the agency "threatens the foundations of American agriculture." The NCC specifically denounced the FSA for its advocacy of a minimum wage for cotton pickers, because such a reform threatened "to disrupt a fair and satisfactory system that has successfully operated in the Cotton Belt for over 100 years," in other words, dating back to the days of slavery. The Delta Council, for its part, discounted the need for the credit arrangements provided by the FSA, since there was "sufficient credit in the Mississippi Delta for every legitimate farmer," though not necessarily credit relations administered as equitably as the FSA loan programs.[32]

Farmers, especially cotton planters who still largely depended on Black landless labor to make their crops, had little sympathy for a federal agency that helped their Black workers become landowners, even if those total numbers remained small. Planters like Oscar Johnston claimed that his operation, worked by hundreds of Black sharecroppers and wage hands, operated more productively and efficiently than a small family farm could. What that assertion discounted was the almost universal desire of landless farmers to achieve the independence and freedom promised by landownership, still perceived as one of the essential pillars of the American Dream. Overall, the FSA helped more white than Black landless farmers, which limited the attacks FSA critics in the South could make against the agency's farm ownership program. In 1944, the Delta Council prefaced its critique of the FSA with a statement supporting the effort to help "worthy families desiring to purchase family-type farms." The Council and other white residents of the Delta did not typically count Black tenants among the "worthy."[33]

Yet when a landless Black farmer secured land during the war, the FSA had typically helped. Overall, landless Black farmers had fewer opportunities to climb the agricultural ladder to the ranks of landownership than their white counterparts. Between 1940 and 1945, the number of white landowners in the southern states increased by 1.6 million, raising the overall percentage of white landowners in the region from 50 percent to 60 percent. During the same period, only 19,000 additional Black farmers became landowners in the region, which increased Black ownership from 21 percent to 24 percent. The ratio of white farmers who became landowners during the war to Black ones was eighty-four to one, even though the ratio of white farmers to Black farmers in the region overall was only four to one in 1940. At the same time, while the FSA helped 18,302 new landowners in the states of Alabama, Florida, Georgia, and South Carolina between 1940 and 1945, 3,932 of these were Black agrarians. In other words, African American farmers represented 20 percent of the FSA clients in these four states who became landowners during the war.[34]

Rural elites saw the FSA as too interested in reforming southern society in other ways. In early 1942, after the AFBF charged that the FSA paid poll taxes for its clients in the South, a probate judge in Hale County, Alabama, R. K. Greene, confirmed the reports. Judge Greene disclosed that local FSA officials had searched tax records to calculate the amount of delinquent poll taxes owed by FSA's white clients. The FSA then increased loans to these farmers by an amount that allowed them to settle their poll tax debts. Similar efforts were underway in other parts of Alabama, Georgia, and South Carolina. After the practice came to light, the regional administrator for the agency in Montgomery, E. S. Morgan, admitted to the practice but clarified that it was not extended to Black clients, since "the Farm Security Agency has not and never will do anything contrary to local custom and regulations." Despite this reassurance, which angered the NAACP, among others, Judge Greene castigated Morgan for the practice, especially since "our country is now engaged in a life struggle with the Axis Powers. . . . We will give our all for defense but we are in open rebellion against this iniquitous [sic] stab at our homes and institutions."[35]

FSA critics also denounced the cooperative farming activities promoted by the agency. The AFBF claimed the FSA carried on "experiments in collective farming under a plan which appears to resemble the practice of collective farming in Russia." The Delta Council also disliked the FSA's cooperative programs, which the Council described as a departure "from our American way of life." These criticisms even extended to such programs as the farm machinery co-ops. FSA administrator C. B. Baldwin denied such operations equaled "collectivism"; rather, he claimed they were "in the best American and in the best democratic tradition." Even if some FSA initiatives did go beyond long-standing cooperative agricultural practices, many of these proved beneficial to both the South's poorest agriculturalists and to a nation at war. In the late 1930s, the FSA settled 123 Black families on some abandoned lands in Randolph County, in southwest Georgia. The families worked cooperatively to raise livestock and vegetables, including potatoes, beans, and onions. When America entered World War II, the cooperative farm used part of the proceeds from the sale of its products to buy War Bonds and Stamps. White law enforcement in the county described the Black collective as "one of the most law-abiding groups in the county."[36]

Oscar Johnston proved one of the most persistent critics of the FSA. He bemoaned the fact that local FSA administrators had close ties with labor groups, such as the STFU, which Johnston labeled "a purely socialistic or communistic movement." After Johnston gained access to a planning document for a May 1941 regional FSA meeting, he went on a speaking tour of Mississippi, Arkansas, and Tennessee in the summer and fall of 1942 and used the agency's plans to argue that it had gone beyond its original purpose of helping landless farmers acquire property. The FSA document had some laudable and seemingly unassailable goals, such as reducing the number of tenant farmers and improving rural housing. Johnston, however, objected not only to the FSA's plans for more cooperative enterprises but also to those parts of the plan that directly threatened large growers: a minimum wage for farm laborers, a graduated land tax on large holdings, and a government land-purchase program. Johnston's speaking tour succeeded in helping to diminish the standing of the FSA among southern leaders. Mississippi congressman Will Whittington claimed that Johnston's speeches had convinced him that the FSA "is not executing the Farm Tenant Act as it was intended. Its purpose was not to socialize or Sovietize, but its purpose was to enable worthy tenants to become landowners."[37]

Despite the criticism, the FSA received positive publicity because of the contribution that its clients made to the war effort, specifically the Food for Freedom program promoted by the USDA early in the war. Small farmers in the Deep South, including those receiving assistance from the FSA, answered the national call for increased food production. In 1942, FSA clients represented 9 percent of all southern farmers, typically those with the lowest income. While 1942 saw a record increase in the production of almost all agricultural products, FSA farmers in the South provided 61 percent of the increase in milk production in the region, 22 percent of the additional output of chickens, and 14 percent of the growth in egg production. In Mississippi, the 25,000 FSA borrowers there boosted their output of a variety of food items in 1942: peanuts (121 percent), beef (104 percent), soybeans (93 percent), chickens (43 percent), and milk (35 percent).[38]

The initial endeavor to enlist the nation's small farmers in increasing production to aid the war effort, however, began to fade soon after the 1943 harvest. In early December 1942, FDR issued an executive order creating the Food Production Administration within the USDA. Secretary Wickard named Herbert W. Parisius, an enthusiastic supporter of the New Deal, to head the new organization. Parisius worked with the FSA to develop a proposal to continue promoting increased food production among small farmers by providing them with advice and credit, exactly the kind of work the FSA had done for years. Wickard initially approved the plan but then reversed course after opposition emerged from the Farm Bloc, which disliked the proposal and preferred to encourage production increases through higher prices for agricultural products. Parisius resigned in protest, five weeks after taking the job. With his new food oversight bureau in disarray, in March 1943 FDR created a replacement agency, the WFA. The new entity, also located in the USDA, had a new administrator, Chester Davis, a former member of the AAA and an ally of the AFBF, who reported directly to Roosevelt. The FSA continued to work with its clients, and in the South, FSA farmers, including more than 35,000 Black ones, again increased the production of key food products in 1943—milk, chickens, eggs, beans, potatoes, hogs, and soybeans.[39]

After the creation of the WFA, however, the FSA's influence over farm policy began to decline, especially as a years-long effort by congressional opponents to dismantle the agency made headway. Originally launched by Representative Malcolm C. Tarver of Georgia in the spring of 1940—just before the departure of Henry Wallace from the USDA—what became an annual assault on the FSA finally resulted in a significant cut in the agency's budget in the summer of 1942. Then, in the spring of 1943, the House Appropriations Committee, which a South Carolina representative characterized as "dominated by a certain group interested in the big farmers," voted to eliminate all funding for the FSA. The full House restored some minimal funding, but only enough, as Oscar Johnston put it, to provide for "a reasonably economic funeral." The US Senate restored much of the FSA's funding, with only two senators from the South voting against continuing to support the agency: Virginia's Harry Byrd, a passionate anti–New Dealer, and Mississippi's James Eastland, owner of a large plantation in the Mississippi Delta.[40]

Most southern senators, answerable to statewide constituencies that contained sizable populations of poor white farmers, acknowledged the value of the FSA to their state's citizens. Senator Bilbo, unlike his Mississippi colleague, defended the agency during the Senate's floor debate on FSA funding in 1943 by noting that the agency helped the poor farmers of his state. While Congress deliberated the FSA's fate, Bilbo heard regularly from state residents touting the value of the organization. W. A. Dallas, of Collins, who received an FSA loan in 1939 that allowed him to transform his small plot into a productive farm, called the agency the "poor man's friend." Another farmer in south Mississippi denounced the move to eliminate the FSA as an effort to dismantle a part of government that had helped "the poverty stricken small farmer of our nation ... lift his head above the surging waves of financial distress." He believed opponents of the FSA wanted small farmers to "beg the scrapings from the tables of Oscar Johnston and his associated ilk." As a self-described champion of the common man, Bilbo embraced the sentiments of these poor white farmers. When he heard from FSA opponents, Bilbo responded by acknowledging the legitimate criticisms of the agency while also noting that the FSA had "rendered a great service to the under-privileged farming class of this Nation, especially of the South."[41]

Like Bilbo, other southern senators did not like everything the FSA did, failings they in part blamed on the agency's leadership, specifically administrator C. B. Baldwin. Several southern senators (though not all) had long denounced the FSA chief as a communist. During the negotiations in 1943 between the House and the Senate over FSA funding, some congressmen promised support for the agency if the president removed Baldwin. Jonathan Daniels, adviser to FDR on southern issues, told Roosevelt about these conversations and encouraged him to continue to support Baldwin, a man who "undoubtedly has his faults" but who had "become almost a symbol of the New Deal so far as it relates to agriculture." Daniels argued that Baldwin's removal would not increase congressional support for the FSA. Eventually, the House and Senate negotiators reached an agreement, which Roosevelt accepted. The political compromise led to drastic reductions in FSA funding, and soon thereafter, Baldwin resigned. Both the large budget cut and the change in leadership seriously undermined the work of the FSA. The agency slashed staff and eliminated programs. Even so, the now-crippled organization continued to provide some limited assistance to poor southern farmers until the end of the war. In late November 1944, Georgia governor Ellis Arnall addressed eighty-seven white Georgia farmers who had moved from tenancy to landownership with help from the FSA. Held at the Henry Grady Hotel in Atlanta, the event was billed as the first annual "Paid Out Dinner." But it was actually more of a final act than a beginning. In August 1946, a new federal agency, the Farmers Home Administration, took over what remained of the FSA's functions.[42]

During World War II, large growers in the South, particularly cotton planters, helped to dismantle the FSA, and they also received special considerations from the federal government concerning prices for their crops and in maintaining a cap on farm wages. Despite these victories, the world of cotton production underwent significant changes during the war years. Production of the staple in the United States declined over the course of the war. In 1942, farmers planted 22.6 million acres in cotton, producing more than 12.8 million bales of cotton. In 1945, those numbers had declined to only 17.2 million acres and 9 million bales. Already by the 1944 harvest, the US cotton industry faced a looming crisis. High government-supported prices for domestic cotton and increasing competition from cheaper producers of the fiber in places like Brazil and India generated large domestic cotton surpluses.[43]

Before the war, southern farmers had begun to diversify their production, and the trend continued during the war years, although some of the largest cotton planters, like Oscar Johnston, resisted the changes. In November 1942, Secretary of Agriculture Claude Wickard set the 1943 cotton production goal at 22.5 million acres, 1.5 million acres lower than the previous year. He required cotton farmers to replace some of their acreage with either peanuts or soybeans. Johnston and other large cotton planters complied, but only to avoid a $15 per acre penalty against their AAA benefits. In fact, Johnston planted 400 acres in soybeans in 1943 but did not harvest them, because, he claimed, he did not have the necessary machines to bring in the soybean crop. During the war, however, southern farmers overall accelerated the trend toward greater diversification, in part to answer the call to increase the variety of farm products needed during the war emergency. They raised livestock in unprecedented numbers during the war years, and they also started growing more peanuts, potatoes, and especially, soybeans. The FSA played an important role in encouraging diversification among smaller growers, especially in 1942 and 1943, but by 1944, even the Delta Council recognized that farmers would produce less cotton and more soybeans, corn, and other crops.[44]

Increasing mechanization also promoted agricultural diversification in the Deep South. Farmers in the region had experimented with mechanization, especially the use of tractors, since at least the early 1930s, but the dire outlook for southern cotton by 1944 convinced growing numbers of cotton planters to further mechanize their segment of the agricultural economy. In December 1944, Secretary Wickard met with cotton growers, distributors, and processors in Washington, DC. He told the group that US cotton could not compete in world markets unless it cut costs and increased mechanization. Other production priorities during the war, however, limited the complete transformation to industrialized cotton farms. In the fall of 1944, International Harvester gave the first demonstration of a mechanical cotton picker on the Hopson plantation near Clarksdale in the Mississippi Delta, but these machines, which would eventually transform the annual cotton harvest and allow cotton planters in places like the Mississippi Delta to modernize and continue to play an important role in the production of the fiber, did not become widely available until 1948.[45]

As early as 1943, the signs that mechanization and diversification had transformed southern agriculture were everywhere, although no one knew what those changes, when fully realized, would mean for the people of the South. Would all those who left the land during the war return, and if they did, would they have jobs in the new agricultural landscape of the South? In 1943, a writer for *Fortune* magazine looked at the changes in southern agriculture underway and predicted the arrival of "an efficient diversified economy" by the end of the war, one where the use of more farm machinery would mean the need for fewer farm workers. The Deep South's largest cotton farmers, those who had most depended on a large Black labor pool to make a profit, disagreed on how quickly such changes would come and whether they even wanted the rural migrants, especially the Black ones, to return. R. N. Hopson, the business manager of the Hopson Plantation, told Senator James Eastland in 1944 that he wanted to see "the farmers of the Mississippi Delta changing as rapidly as possible from the old tenant or sharecropping system of farming to complete mechanized farming." First among the benefits of this change for Hopson: agriculture would require fewer Black people and would "equalize the white and Negro population which would automatically make our racial problem easier to handle."

Other white Deltans, however, believed that area planters would still need a large supply of labor after the war and worried that Black workers would not return. Some even hoped for "race riots" in the North at the end of the war—like the conflicts that occurred at the end of World War I—to drive Black labor back to their southern homes. Black Southerners who had stayed on plantations during the war doubted that many of those who had left would return. As one Coahoma County sharecropper told a white interviewer in 1944, "No Cap'n, when colored folks get out of Mississippi & has a job—he ain't coming back to picking cotton." He was right. Not only did the rural migrants of World War II not return to southern farms, but they continued to depart in the decades that followed. In 1940, 14 million Southerners had made their home on the region's farms; by 1970, that number had shrunk to just 3 million. While agriculture continued to be important in the Deep South's economy at war's end, the era when labor-intensive cotton plantations dominated the region had finally begun to end.[46]

2
Ingalls Shipyard: Pascagoula, Mississippi

During World War II, the USS *Pocomoke* spent most of the conflict ferrying supplies and troops between the United States and various points in the Pacific theater. Like thousands of other vessels, the *Pocomoke* was but one small cog in the larger US effort to defeat the Japanese. Despite its humble service during the war, the *Pocomoke* had a much-heralded beginning. On June 8, 1940, more than 10,000 spectators at a shipyard in Pascagoula, Mississippi, waited for the launching of the nation's first all-welded steel ship, the *Exchequer*, into the Pascagoula River. Mrs. Max O'Rell Truitt, wife of a member of the US Maritime Commission and daughter of US Senate Majority Leader Alben Barkley, did the honors of christening the C-3 cargo liner. Months later, the Maritime Commission sold the ship to the US Navy, which reconditioned it and renamed it the USS *Pocomoke*. Boatbuilding had been a significant part of the economy of the Mississippi Gulf Coast since at least the eighteenth century, but the launching of the *Exchequer* signaled a new era for the shipbuilding industry in the area.[1]

Economic mobilization for World War II reshaped life and labor throughout the Deep South. As the country began to mobilize its economy for war production in 1940 and 1941, much of the increased economic activity took place outside the South, in areas that already had significant industrial capacity easily converted to the production of airplanes, tanks, ships, and munitions. Although southern states received a relatively small share of the billions that the federal government expended on military and industrial contracts during the war, wartime mobilization still brought significant change to even the poorest parts of the region. By the end of 1942, more than 60 percent of all men and more than 10 percent of all women nationwide toiled in war-related industries. During the World War II era, Mississippi gained 750 new industrial plants, and the state's per capita income tripled between 1940 and 1946.[2]

In the Deep South, the coastal rim experienced the most profound economic change associated with wartime mobilization. Beginning several years before Pearl Harbor, federal spending bolstered the shipbuilding industry and reordered the economies of five locales in the Deep South: New Orleans (Louisiana); Pascagoula; Mobile (Alabama); and Brunswick and Savannah (Georgia). Many of these areas had shipyards that had operated during the World War I era but quickly retrenched after the short American involvement in that conflict. In 1937, however, the Roosevelt administration, worried about the potential for war in Europe and Asia, worked through the recently created US Maritime Commission to initiate a program to build fifty high-speed standard merchant ships a year for ten years. After France fell in July 1940, that target was raised to 200 merchant ships a year, and the US government made plans to mass-produce a simple-design, steel merchant craft, known as Liberty Ships. In 1941, US shipyards produced 1.1 million deadweight tons of merchant shipping. By 1943, the tonnage of such vessels had ballooned to 18 million tons. The US Maritime Commission and the US Navy contracted for other types of ships as well, including transports, tankers, and attack ships. Between 1941 and 1945, American shipyards produced $18 billion worth of sea vessels for the Navy and another $13 billion for the Maritime Commission. In the Deep South, approximately half of the government contracts received by the region through February 1943 went to shipyards.[3]

The men who owned these shipyards made millions during the war and sometimes laid the foundations for enterprises that continued to prosper in the postwar years. Rural Southerners, especially white men and women, found well-paying jobs in the shipyards but also a workplace unlike the ones in which they and their ancestors had toiled for generations. Even as critical labor needs brought women workers to the shipyards, racial discrimination limited the opportunities for Black workers to find work in the industry, despite the favorable labor market created by the global conflict. Labor unions, which the US government had belatedly recognized in the 1930s as legitimate organizations, saw economic mobilization for war as a chance to build their memberships. While unions did enroll new members in the war years—even in the anti-union South—they failed to build the kind of institutions that secured much lasting economic power for working people.

Southern businessmen took advantage of the opportunity presented by the federal support for shipbuilding that began in the late 1930s and created industrial enterprises on a scale not typically seen in the Deep South. One of those men was Robert Ingersoll Ingalls, a Birmingham, Alabama, steel magnate. Ingalls was born in 1882 in Huntsville, Ohio, north of Dayton. His father, Horace Ingalls, who had remarried and started a second family in his mid-fifties, operated a hotel. The elder Ingalls, however, had recently retired as an organizer and manager of "freak shows," a popular form of American entertainment in the post–Civil War decades. Styling himself Judge H. P. Ingalls—though he had no legal training—Ingalls worked with the flamboyant showman P. T. Barnum and managed two sets of Siamese twins, Chang and Eng Bunker and Millie and Christine (the so-called Two-Headed Nightingale), as well as Captain and Mrs. Bates, "The Tallest Couple Alive," whose combined height was almost sixteen feet. Robert Ingalls may not have known all the details about his father's early life, but he likely heard stories about his father's career as a risk-taking showman traveling around the United States and Europe, a man who had "won and lost a half-dozen fortunes," according to one account.[4]

Though Robert Ingalls shared his father's entrepreneurial spirit, his approach to making money was more no-nonsense and risk-averse. Ingalls moved to Dayton while still in his teens and worked as a bookkeeper for the National Cash Register Company. He studied accounting for a time at Ohio Normal University and then secured a job with the S. J. Patterson Coal Company of Dayton. He later became an investor in the company and eventually assumed the position of secretary/treasurer. At some point, his job took him to the coal country of Alabama, where he met Ellen Gregg, daughter of a Birmingham real estate lawyer and city attorney. The two married in 1909 and settled in Birmingham. Ingalls initially opened a small iron shop there. He later said he started out "with one Negro, one mule, [and] a busted crane." Within a short time, however, perhaps with help from his well-connected father-in-law, he built the Ingalls Iron Works Company into a major player in the city's iron and steel industry. By the early 1920s, the company was prospering, and Robert Ingalls had become an important corporate leader in Birmingham, serving as president of the city's Chamber of Commerce in 1923.[5]

When the US Maritime Commission announced its new shipbuilding program in 1937, Robert Ingalls resolved to get some of the government contracts. He already owned two small shipyards at inland locations in Alabama—at Chickasaw, north of Mobile, and at Decatur, on the Tennessee River. He sent two of his top executives, Monro B. Lanier and W. R. Guest, to scout out a bigger location. They initially liked Pensacola, Florida, until city leaders in Pascagoula, in Jackson County, Mississippi, about forty miles southwest of Mobile, came through with a financial incentive. The Magnolia State had recently created an initiative, the Balance Agriculture with Industry program, that provided public funds to attract industry. Jackson County voters overwhelmingly approved a $100,000 bond measure to deepen the channel of the Pascagoula River to the Gulf of Mexico and to acquire and prepare a proposed site of forty-six acres with 3,000 feet of waterfront.[6]

Ingalls secured a government contract for four ships, and he created a subsidiary company, the Ingalls Shipbuilding Corporation, in 1938. His shipyard at Pascagoula opened in 1939 with three shipways, and within a year, the yard completed work on the *Exchequer*. By that time, more than a thousand people worked at the facility. With help from the US Navy, Ingalls acquired nearby properties and eventually expanded the business to ten shipways. During the war years, Ingalls received contracts from both the Maritime Commission and the US Navy to build C-3 cargo ships, the largest of the C-type vessels. The C-3, bigger and faster than the Liberty Ship, was easily converted to other uses beyond transporting cargo, and C-3s built at Ingalls were eventually used as net layers, troop ships, and aircraft carriers. Between 1939 and 1947, the Pascagoula shipyard built more than 40 percent of the C-3s constructed, and between 1940 and 1945, Jackson County received $350 million in war contracts, almost all of which went to the Ingalls Shipbuilding Corporation.[7]

Robert Ingalls liked to say that "conservative people made the world," but he was an innovator when it came to production techniques. He helped pioneer the all-welded ship in the United States, at a time when ship construction still involved riveting steel plates together. His workers began using the procedure on smaller craft in the 1930s at his Alabama shipyards, and with this limited experience as a shipbuilder, Ingalls designed the Pascagoula shipyard as the first in the country to focus solely on building all-welded ships. Eighty percent of the steel used to construct vessels in Pascagoula was manufactured and pre-assembled in Birmingham at the Ingalls Iron Works Company. A "300-mile assembly line"—actually a rail line—delivered the processed steel to Pascagoula. Ingalls built long open shops at the Pascagoula yard so that workers could take the sub-assemblies from Birmingham and turn them into various large ship parts, some weighing as much as seventy-five tons. The yard also had wide erection platforms so that large cranes could easily move these massive pieces from the shops to the shipways for assembly. Unlike traditional ship construction, workers laid out the ship's deck first and supported it by gigantic timbers. Then the prefabricated steel pieces were hung, and workers known as tackers would use arc welding to join the pieces together to form the ship's keel and hull. One tacker could do the job that formerly required four riveters. The all-welded technique of Ingalls Shipbuilding saved the US government money in a variety of ways, according to Ingalls, and also reduced labor costs, since the all-welded process required fewer man-hours per ship constructed.[8]

In 1941, Ingalls made Lanier president and Guest vice president of the Ingalls Shipbuilding Corporation. However, Ingalls retained the position of chairman of the board of Ingalls Iron Works, and he maintained tight control over his entire company, including the operations at the south Mississippi shipyard. A hands-on manager, Ingalls believed in cutting costs, including wages. He could be a difficult taskmaster, both with his closest associates and with the government men who provided him with the bulk of his shipbuilding business. Lanier later recalled, "If Mr. Ingalls got a little rough with me, I knew I was doing all right." In his dealings with the federal government, Ingalls adopted the same blunt approach he took with everyone else. Frank Constangy of the Atlanta War Manpower Commission (WMC) office noted in 1943 that Ingalls was "a very difficult man to work with." Likewise, Mark O'Dea, head of public relations for the US Maritime Commission, termed Ingalls "always cantankerous."[9]

At the beginning of the war, the government wanted private shipbuilders to accept cost-plus contracts, which provided for a builder's actual costs plus a minimum fee, with certain bonus payments for efficient production. Ingalls protested this arrangement because he thought it led to excessive expenditures for materials and labor. He convinced the government to let him continue with the lump-sum contracts he had negotiated before America entered the war. Such contracts provided a set fee for each ship built. The government agreed to Ingalls's terms; he was the only southern shipbuilder to secure such an arrangement. The lump-sum contracts required that Ingalls and his managers carefully monitor costs, including labor expenditures, to earn maximum profits. Ingalls opposed premium overtime pay and wanted wages frozen at late 1940 levels. The federal government eventually adopted Ingalls's way of thinking about government contracts. By 1943, the US Maritime Commission had made an about-face and urged all private shipbuilders to accept lump-sum contracts.[10]

Ingalls's expansion of his shipbuilding enterprise in the World War II era proved a profitable undertaking. Shipbuilding work was important to winning the war, but the federal government never intended for capitalists who built wartime businesses to forgo a profit. Since business records for the Ingalls Shipbuilding Corporation during the war years are unavailable, the exact profits received by the company during the war are unknown, but evidence of the profits produced by other, nearby shipbuilders offer some sense of the company's earnings. In 1942, New Orleans shipbuilder Andrew Jackson Higgins made $8 million in pre-tax profits on $47 million in sales, a profit margin of 17 percent. However, since the effective corporate tax rate at the time was 40 percent, Higgins's actual profit that year was $4.8 million, a margin of just over 10 percent. Ingalls likely had a profit margin in line with Higgins's earnings, especially since Ingalls worked on a flat-fee basis and cut costs whenever possible. With the approximately $325 million in war contracts that the Pascagoula Shipbuilding Corporation received between 1940 and 1945, it is reasonable to think that Robert Ingalls's pre-tax profit margin could have averaged at least 5 percent, which would have earned his company more than $16 million in gross profit, or perhaps more than $9.6 million in after-tax earnings (more than $148 million in 2022 dollars).[11]

During World War II, the number of people working at the Ingalls Shipbuilding Corporation grew rapidly until early 1943, then leveled off, before declining markedly after the war ended in mid-1945. Although the all-welded process required fewer workers than at other shipyards, the development of ten shipways at the facility fueled the demand for labor. By June 1942, the shipyard needed 5,000 workers; by February 1943, that number had doubled to more than 10,000 employees; and in early 1944, the workforce at the shipyard peaked at more than 11,000 workers. Initially, Ingalls drew from a local labor pool still suffering from the economic depression of the 1930s, but the rapidly expanding shipyard quickly exhausted that supply. As early as March 1941, many of the skilled and semi-skilled workers were in-migrants, although almost all the yard's unskilled laborers (about one-fourth of the employees) still came from the local area. By June 1942, half of all workers hired at the Pascagoula shipyard came from beyond the Mississippi Gulf Coast, although the majority still came from Mississippi. The US Employment Service (USES) provided most of the leads on potential new workers.[12]

Most of the new arrivals to Pascagoula came from rural areas. As in other war industries in the South, some of the migrants relocated to Pascagoula for only a few months, or not at all. Elvis Presley's father, Vernon Presley, from northeast Mississippi, moved his wife and son to Pascagoula to work at Ingalls in 1943 for five weeks. Others, anywhere from one-quarter to one-half of the company's workforce, commuted to work. In 1943, the Maritime Commission operated seven daily bus routes to bring workers to the shipyard, with the longest run to Picayune, 160 miles roundtrip. Others depended on private transportation. Although gas and tire rationing often made such trips problematic, on any given day, private vehicles commuting to Deep South shipyards (and other war industries) crowded the highways. In October 1943, more than 5,000 of the 22,599 workers at Mobile's giant Alabama Dry Dock and Shipbuilding Company (ADDSCO) lived outside the city. Some commuted from as far away as Greenville, Alabama, 125 miles from the shipyard. A survey by the company of a typical day in 1943 showed 657 vehicles with 4,152 passengers traveling on six different highways into the yard. When the whistle blew at the end of a shift in Mobile or Pascagoula, workers would rush out to waiting vehicles, intent on not missing their rides and getting home as soon as possible.[13]

Ingalls's managers recognized that many of the migrants coming to work in Pascagoula had never seen a big ship before, but those coming to fill skilled or semi-skilled jobs typically had received some training in shipbuilding work. Local school districts and state governments, with financing from the US Office of Education, shouldered much of the responsibility for worker training. In August 1940, a National Defense Training School opened at a Pascagoula boatyard and offered welding classes. Within a few months, the school had relocated to a temporary building near Pascagoula High School and had added classes in ship fitting, sheet metal fabrication, and loft work. By October 1942, more than 1,400 people had attended the school. Some of those students went to work for Ingalls; others found employment elsewhere. Ingalls employees often received relevant training at other locales around the state and beyond. By March 1941, the Mississippi Division of Vocational Education was offering 265 training courses in various locales. During the time when production was ramping up quickly, in 1943 and early 1944, trainees were hired before they completed their course of study.[14]

World War II provided an economic boost for Ingalls workers, as it did for other Americans. Most important, jobs were plentiful. In 1940, Jackson County had an unemployment rate of almost 15 percent. By mid-1943, practically everyone in the immediate area who wanted a job (and who had not migrated elsewhere) had one, either serving in the military or working at the shipyard or other area businesses. The Pascagoula shipyard, however, offered fewer economic benefits than other war industries. Wages at Ingalls were supposed to be set according to the rates outlined in the Shipbuilding Stabilization Committee's Gulf Zone agreement and the WMC's labor stabilization plan for the Gulf Coast region, but the company classified workers in ways that allowed it to pay them less than the established minimum hourly wages. For example, in 1943, union officials claimed that although the Mechanical Department had 312 employees and government standards set wages for mechanics at $1.20 an hour, the company had a variety of job classifications for the workers in this department. Only 88 received $1.20 an hour, while the other 224 earned less, even as little as 71 cents.[15]

Many Ingalls employees were agricultural workers taking on industrial employment for the first time, and Ingalls and his managers did not believe that most of those flooding in from the countryside represented the best class of employee. In February 1942, Robert Ingalls complained to south Mississippi congressman William M. Colmer that too many of his Pascagoula workers were not effective. Ingalls brought in speakers to bolster morale. He knew that "good men don't need it, but there are a lot who do." F. K. Etheridge, an Ingalls executive, noted in 1943 that many workers at the shipyard had a "lack of established work habits." Dallas Smith, personnel manager for the company, offered an even more negative assessment of the yard's workers. He believed that the Pascagoula shipyard had "a nucleus of fine workmen, a big group of passable workers, but 25 per cent are totally lacking in a sense of responsibility. This last group came from the swamps, pea-patches, and woods."[16]

Ingalls management complained about frequent absenteeism, although the average monthly absentee rate of between 5 and 10 percent at the Pascagoula yard mirrored that seen in other Gulf Coast yards. The causes were many. Community problems, including inadequate childcare, unreliable transportation, and housing issues, kept some away from the job. For those living outside Pascagoula, other obligations—such as maintaining a farm—led to periodic absences. Ingalls officials also claimed that some absenteeism sprang from employees trying to game the wage system, such as by working Saturdays, initially a time-and-a-half day, and then staying home on Mondays. Ingalls employed truant officers to visit the homes of missing workers who lived in Pascagoula. In early 1942, those officials found that many of the absences were due to illness, to "loafers" taking days off from work, or simply to workers pulling up stakes and leaving town without notifying the company.[17]

As factory managers had done throughout the Industrial Revolution, the bosses at Ingalls sought to discipline rural workers unfamiliar with the more regimented pace of shipyard work. To reduce absenteeism, the company formed the country's first Rickenbacker Squadron in January 1943, which awarded all employees who had a thirty-day perfect attendance record with a Rickenbacker medal. Captain Eddie Rickenbacker, a World War I pilot and president of Eastern Airlines, had become well known to the World War II generation in the fall of 1942 after he and seven other crewmen were lost at sea for twenty-four days. Rickenbacker made a tour of defense plants, including the Ingalls shipyard, in 1943 to promote the squadron idea. He told the assembled workers, "I think we would hesitate to miss work if we realized that every day we missed might cost the life of some soldier who failed to have the equipment to fight." For good measure, Rickenbacker took a swipe at labor unions. He claimed to be a "friend of organized labor," but he also declared his opposition to the closed shop as "un-American," because he believed people should only join unions if they freely chose to do so. During his tour across the country in 1943, he got the reputation as an enemy of labor. An AFL leader in Michigan said that "Captain Rickenbacker seems to have escaped the Japs only to be captured—or recaptured—by the National Association of Manufacturers." By the time of Rickenbacker's appearance at Ingalls, the absentee rate had dropped to 4 percent. Despite this decline, the absences gradually edged back up to 9 percent by the end of 1943.[18]

Ingalls used other methods to discipline workers and boost morale. The *Ingalls News*, a weekly company paper distributed to shipyard workers, contained numerous items about the need for regular attendance on the job, working hard, not wasting time, and buying war bonds, all pitched in terms of war necessity. The guest speakers the company brought in to talk with the workers emphasized how they could boost productivity by being punctual and careful. A War Department morale officer who spoke in February 1942 told the shipyard employees, "every bit of material wasted, every part you spoil, helps Hitler."[19]

Labor turnover was common at Ingalls, as it was elsewhere in the shipbuilding industry. In 1943, the US Department of Labor noted that worker turnover continued to be a serious problem at the shipyards. The WMC developed local labor stabilization plans to address the labor turnover issue in all defense enterprises. Like other plans, the one for the Mobile area, which included Pascagoula, required that employers not hire any workers unless they had been unemployed for at least sixty days, or they had a certificate of separation and availability from their former employer or the USES. Even without the problematic release/separation process, the labor stabilization plans were of limited use in actual operation. Workers came and went, and the federal government did not have the infrastructure or staff to track and monitor all the movement. Before mid-1943, in the shipbuilding industry nationwide, the labor turnover rate (the number of employees leaving a company) hovered around 10 percent monthly, but there were even larger numbers of workers coming into the industry every month. In August 1943, the US Department of Labor noted that future labor needs at Ingalls, including replacement workers, could only be met with new migrants to the area.[20]

The labor turnover problem at Ingalls had multiple causes. One reason was that the wages at the yard were lower than elsewhere and the opportunities for job advancement were fewer. As a result, some experienced workers moved to nearby shipyards, in New Orleans, Mobile, or Galveston, or even to the West Coast, to improve their bottom line. A more significant cause for the high turnover rate at the shipyard revolved around the chaotic local living and recreational conditions, a situation the Ingalls company did little to improve. In September 1943, after Monro Lanier tried to convince the Maritime Commission to convert part of a recently opened but underutilized cafeteria to a movie theater, one of the commissioners, John M. Carmody, greeted the request with criticism. He believed that "it's about time we asked Mr. Lanier and his Ingalls associates to stop crying on our shoulders and take on a responsibility that goes naturally with their job—namely, taking whatever reasonable steps are essential to create the conditions they feel are essential to attract and hold employees." Carmody suggested Ingalls do more to "develop good labor relations and community relations." To address the turnover problem and the related problem of periodic labor shortages, the company instead relied on adjustments to its operations, such as the extension of work shifts from eight to nine hours and the utilization of agricultural workers as temporary employees during the slack times in the agricultural cycle.[21]

As the local labor supply evaporated and efforts to attract workers to Pascagoula intensified, Robert Ingalls reluctantly turned to female labor. In 1940, when his workforce at the shipyard numbered approximately 1,000, only eleven women worked at the yard, all in clerical positions. At that time, the local area had a sizable supply of working women. In 1940, Jackson County had a higher percentage of working women (28 percent) than either Mississippi or the nation (both 25 percent). Many of these women toiled in local textile mills, which also expanded during the war and provided additional job opportunities for women. As wartime economic mobilization accelerated in 1941 and 1942, white women in Mississippi began taking shipbuilding training courses. The National Defense Training School in Pascagoula began accepting women for the welding course in September 1942, although other training sites in the state had begun opening those courses to women even earlier. Ingalls hired its first five women welders in mid-September 1942, all trained at the nearby Gulfport National Defense Training School.[22]

Shipyard managers initially thought that they might recruit women from among the wives of the company's male workers. Wives did join their husbands at the yard, but a significant number of those who first came to work at the shipyard were young and unmarried, typically from poorer white families and already a part of the local workforce. Among the first five women welders hired at Ingalls were the two Anderson sisters, Vera and Minnie, ages eighteen and seventeen, respectively. Before coming to Ingalls, the two women had lived with their widowed mother and three other sisters in a rented home in Gulfport. After graduating from high school at age fifteen, Vera worked briefly at a shoe store and then a garment factory. While working at the factory, she took welding classes at night. Another of the first five female welders at Ingalls, Virginia Malley, also lived with her widowed mother, who owned a house in rural Harrison County (the Gulf Coast county west of Jackson). Malley, twenty-five, was unmarried, and before coming to Ingalls she had worked at a nearby junior college museum, where she mounted insects for exhibit.[23]

This first cadre of female welders received rave reviews from their foreman. He reported that "the girls do neat work and they stick right to the job. They mean business." Within a month, Ingalls had hired ninety women welders, who hailed from twenty-two Mississippi locales, as well as from Texas, Louisiana, Alabama, Florida, Kentucky, Oklahoma, and Arizona. By the end of 1942, 5 percent of the shipyard's workforce were women, and by late 1943, women comprised 10 percent of the employees at the Ingalls shipyard (nationwide, women made up 10 to 20 percent of all shipyard workers). About 70 percent of the women worked as welders, although they took other skilled or semi-skilled positions as well and eventually labored in every department at the yard. In October 1942, the Pipe Department hired its first three female pipefitters, all married women. By early 1943, women in the department formed their own pipefitting crews, and according to the company, "They get their own pipe, carry it to the ship, saw it up, and generally do a real man's job in building ships for victory." Women workers received the same hourly pay as men with the same job classification.[24]

Not everyone approved of women workers in the shipyard industry. US Maritime Commissioner Howard L. Vickery denounced the use of women workers at Ingalls in early 1943. He contended that having men and women working together would undermine efficiency, that women might be in danger because of the "dark corners" in the shipways, and that women might want to stay on the job after the war. The Inter-Church Committee, led by J. C. Crane, pastor of the town's First Presbyterian Church, thought that the employment of young mothers with children by Ingalls Shipbuilding "has been ruinous to family discipline and to home training." The group also worried that working wives led to broken homes. In December 1943, Pastor Crane claimed that 500 families had been destroyed by "infidelity caused by stress and strain, nostalgia, bad associations, and improper environment." He recommended that if women had to work in the shipyard, then they should be segregated from the men.[25]

Although Robert Ingalls did not embrace women shipbuilders at his other locales, his operation in Pascagoula really had no choice but to use women workers. When the company first brought them on the job in the fall of 1942, it already needed 3,000 additional workers to build all the ships under contract. Because of the all-welded process used at Pascagoula, the shipyard continued to run a shortage of qualified welders for much of the war. And by the spring of 1943, the WMC concluded that "women who are not yet employed now comprise the major labor reserve for all industries." So women workers became a small but essential part of the Ingalls Shipbuilding Corporation's ongoing recruitment strategy to attract workers, especially welders. Despite the concerns of local community groups, such as the Inter-Church Committee, the company also continued to try to recruit the wives of current Ingalls employees, since hiring a second member of a household did not add further to the community problems, such as a lack of housing, caused by in-migration. Shipyard officials also recognized that, by 1943, fewer single, unmarried women were available among the pool of potential employees.[26]

Whatever personal misgivings Robert Ingalls may have had about the employment of women in the Pascagoula shipyard, he was a hard-nosed businessman first, and his company took steps to ensure that the women it hired succeeded. The company newspaper started a column, "Feminine Notes," to tout the achievements of its female employees. In November 1942, Ingalls hired Maud Ladner, a single, thirty-six-year-old former high school teacher, as Women Coordinator for the shipyard. Her job included helping female workers with safety issues, such as instructing them on proper dress for the job: "head tie or safety hat, coveralls or overalls, and oxford or safety shoes." She also counseled them about adjusting to their new work, including "about personal contacts with men" on the job. She let the women know that they could leave the job site at any time to contact her or to go to a first aid station or restroom. The Pascagoula shipyard in early 1943 also secured a $15,000 federal grant to build a "miscarriage room" at the facility, which was designed to assist pregnant workers facing health problems while on the job. Ingalls wanted his female employees to receive particular care in part because that approach ensured that he could continue to attract the women workers he needed to staff his shipyard.[27]

Proclaiming a safe working environment represented but one aspect of the recruitment strategy used by Deep South shipyards to attract additional white female workers needed for shipbuilding by the end of 1943 and into 1944. A major advertising blitz by ADDSCO in the summer of 1944 indicates the nature of the approach. The company already had a thousand female welders but needed more to meet its production targets. Advertisements in local newspapers, which only included pictures of white women, suggested that the task of welding was "no more arduous than housework" and promised "work in safe, well-ventilated areas on a job designed specifically for women." To attract female workers to the shipyard, the campaign appealed to both patriotism and economics. One advertisement that pictured male soldiers proclaimed: "WOMEN—You Can Help Our Fighting Men by Working in the Shipbuilding Industry!" Other announcements focused on the economic benefits for women who took a job at ADDSCO. An August 6 piece contained a testimonial from a woman already employed at the shipyard: "I worried about my wartime budget . . . until I started my well-paid job of WELDING at the Alabama Dry Dock and Shipbuilding Co." While never stated explicitly, the advertisements sometimes subtly suggested that the shipyard jobs for women would be temporary. A July 20 advertisement used the following headline: "Women . . . Earn a Welder's Salary Today . . . For the Plans You Have for Tomorrow!" The text of the piece elaborated on those plans, which included "a fine home, education for her children," and postwar economic security.[28]

Many married women did plan to return to the home at war's end, but not all saw their jobs as temporary. During the war, J. S. Brooks and his wife moved from Atlanta to Pascagoula, where they both worked at the Ingalls shipyard. Mrs. Brooks saw her employment as a short-term economic necessity fulfilled in a less-than-ideal setting. She told an interviewer in late 1943 that if at war's end "I had a house instead of a chicken coop, I'd rather stay home." However, Agnes Meyer, the wife of the publisher of the *Washington Post*, who made a tour of war towns in 1943, believed that many of the working women she saw in Mobile would "fight like wild animals to keep their jobs." She recognized that many of them "have been half starved all their lives," and now, with both husband and wife working, these families were "making big money for the first time."[29]

As more women entered the shipyards, the industry sought to reassure everyone that women could perform certain jobs, such as welding, at a high level. The Ingalls shipyard got a major publicity boost for the quality of work being done by its female welders, when Vera Anderson became the national women's welding champion in 1943. At the beginning of the year, the US Maritime Commission sponsored a nationwide contest to determine the country's best female welder. Anderson, who did not miss a day of work during her first five months on the job, earned a leadership position in the Rickenbacker Squadron in January 1943. In February, she won the local women's welding contest at Ingalls, earning a $100 war bond. On May 28, Anderson faced West Coast champion Hermina Strmiska, from Henry Kaiser's Oregon Shipyard. The event brought out a huge crowd of employees and company officials. The national media, including Movietone News, the Associated Press, and *Life* magazine, covered the competition with the careful attention typically reserved for major sporting events. The Pascagoula High School Band was on hand to add to the gameday atmosphere. In the first event, a two-foot vertical weld, Anderson bested Strmiska by only 3 seconds, but in the second face-off, a horizontal weld of 110 feet, Anderson finished more than 5 minutes ahead of her opponent. Judges also evaluated the quality of the work, and Anderson came out ahead in this category in both heats. She received a two-foot-high sterling trophy, as well as $300 in war bonds. In the aftermath of her victory, Anderson became a minor celebrity. In January 1944, at another event held at the Pascagoula shipyard, Anderson successfully defended her title against Edna Slocum from the Moore Dry Dock Company in Oakland, California, who had won a series of elimination contests involving 10,000 female welders at various Pacific Coast yards.[30]

Events such as the women's welding contest did more than simply suggest the work abilities of female employees. Women could do a man's job, if necessary, but these competitions, as well as others that focused more on

White women comprised an important part of the labor force at Ingalls Shipyard. Most women there worked as welders. Vera Anderson, two-time national women's welding champion, is second from the right. *National Archives (86-WWT-85-35)*

the uniquely feminine qualities of women workers, helped reassure men and the wider public that whatever jobs women were doing, they were still women, temporarily employed as just another emergency wartime measure. Indeed, Vera Anderson herself got married several months after winning her second title and left her shipyard job. She returned to Ingalls briefly in 1945, but when the war ended and her husband returned from service, she left the welding profession for good.

Other competitions, such as beauty pageants held in the shipyards and other war plants, more directly emphasized that women workers still retained their feminine characteristics. In 1944, Emma Harwell won the title of "Miss Swing Shift" at the Bell Bomber Aircraft Plant in Marietta, Georgia, where thousands of women worked assembling B-29 aircraft. An account of her victory described how quickly Harwell could transform herself from factory worker to an object of female beauty: "A quick whisk of cold cream to remove the grime and grease from her face . . . a lightning change from wrinkled work slacks to an evening gown." In addition, Deep South war industries typically focused on the female characteristics of their women employees, even when discussing their achievements. When Anderson won her 1943 contest, the *Ingalls News* described her as "slight but bright" and "comely."[31]

Not every female worker at Ingalls, of course, was a Vera Anderson: talented craftswoman, punctual, and engaged employee. As with male employees at the Pascagoula shipyard, company officials had to contend with absenteeism and high turnover among its female workers. Nationwide, the turnover rate for female shipyard workers was generally higher than for their male counterparts. However, rather than attribute the cause for high absenteeism and turnover rates among women to the larger factors that affected all workers or to the specific burdens female employees faced, male authorities tended to blame the problems on shortcomings unique to women workers. One 1944 report by welding specialist J. G. Magrath claimed that absenteeism among women employees at Ingalls was greatest among "the unmarried group, or in the young married group, where the women are working only for the 'thrill' of it," an analysis that ignored the fact that many of the young women at the shipyard needed jobs to help support themselves and their families. The WMC concluded that women shipyard workers were undisciplined, so they often quit or took "unauthorized holidays." Female workers, however, remained responsible for home duties in ways that their male counterparts did not. One anonymous female welder at Ingalls who commuted to the yard reported that she needed her job to support her two young children. Her day began at 4 A.M. when she had to get up to make it to the Pascagoula yard for her 7 A.M. shift, and she did not get home until 6:20 P.M. With essentially two jobs, it is not surprising that female employees frequently had to leave their shipyard duties, either temporarily or permanently, to attend to family matters. In addition, by 1944, many female workers, who knew they that the postwar plans of their companies did not include them, quit their temporary war jobs whenever family circumstances or obligations required or allowed them to return to the home.[32]

Black workers might have also alleviated labor shortages at the Ingalls shipyard. The company, however, generally hired Black people only for unskilled positions. At the end of 1942, Black workers made up only 10 percent of the shipyard's labor force, and 92 percent of them had unskilled jobs. Over time, Black laborers took on a few more skilled jobs at the shipyard, including as spray painters, crane operators, warehousemen, and fire crewmen, but the number of Black workers at Ingalls and the jobs they could hold there remained limited throughout the war. When the shipyard at Pascagoula began operations, local Black workers took most of the company's unskilled positions. Company vice president W. R. Guest noted in August 1941 "that sufficient colored labor [is] still available in the radius of ten miles." Within a couple of years, however, the local supply of Black men for unskilled tasks evaporated, as those not already hired moved to find war work elsewhere or join the military. By the end of 1943, the WMC reported a "critical shortage of available unskilled nonwhite labor" in the Pascagoula area, and the company began working with the USES to recruit in the interior of Mississippi for unskilled Black labor.[33]

The situation for Black women workers in the Deep South shipbuilding industry was even more dismal. At the end of 1942, only ten Black women were on the Ingalls payroll of 9,500 employees. All of them worked as maids, cleaning workspaces and common areas in the yard. A similar situation existed at ADDSCO. The company employed only a few Black women to work at the shipyard, also in menial jobs, either as maids or laborers. Andrew Jackson Higgins in New Orleans, who had already employed significant numbers of Black men, declared in 1943 that he intended to give Black women the same employment opportunities as white women. The local USES office initially stymied this initiative by failing to place women in local training classes. When Black women in New Orleans responded to newspaper advertisements asking women to apply for shipyard training, the local USES told them that "there was no provision for training Negro women." Xavier University, a Black Catholic school in the city, however, soon began a Defense Training School at the institution. Higgins Industries finally hired Marion Delahoussaye in the spring of 1944, and she became not only the first Black female welder at the Higgins shipyard but also the first Black woman in the entire South to secure a welding job.[34]

In March 1942, William M. Colmer, US representative for Mississippi's Sixth Congressional district, home of the Ingalls shipyard, sent a circular letter to the company's workers. After noting the importance of shipbuilding to winning the war, Colmer's dispatch spoke directly to the thousands employed at Robert Ingalls's company: "As a laboring man who worked his way through high school and college, as one who believes in labor and labor unions (Hitler and Hirohito permit no labor unions), as one who is a friend of labor and labor unions and wants to see it prosper, I commend you for the splendid job you are doing, and appeal to you to redouble your efforts to win the war and prevent us all from becoming the slaves of Hitler and his kind." Robert Ingalls judged Colmer's communication to his workers to be "excellent, with one exception—I think you should have deleted any mention of the Labor Unions." Ingalls did not really see the need for unions, since "the working conditions at Pascagoula are the best." In fact, Colmer shared at least part of Ingalls's negative view of labor unions. Days before issuing his letter to Pascagoula workers extolling the virtues of labor unions, Colmer proposed a bill in Congress that attacked one of labor's primary tools, the strike. Colmer's measure, which was never considered by the House of Representatives, would have ordered local draft boards to reclassify striking workers for military service and imposed penalties of up to $5,000 for anyone "conspiring for the purpose of either bringing about a cessation of the production of war materials or a slowing down of production."[35]

Like Colmer, others in the US South and beyond had complicated and often contradictory ideas about the proper role of unions in the workplace, especially as the United States ramped up production for the global conflict. Some, naturally, shared Robert Ingalls's unilateral distrust and dislike of organized labor. Others accepted the 1930s reforms that had legitimatized labor unions as essential to American prosperity. As production and jobs increased during the war, unions prospered. From 1938 to 1948, union membership in the South doubled from 500,000 to 1 million.[36] Both the American Federation of Labor (AFL) and the Congress of Industrial Organizations (CIO) shared in this growth and competed for members during the war. Although the atmosphere for union success, even in the South, had in some ways never been better, the war also led people who expressed a general support for labor, like Colmer, to condemn strikes because they delayed the production of defense-related materials, actions which seemed "unpatriotic." For others, including the workers who joined unions, the fight to secure labor's recently recognized rights, including the right to strike, if necessary, represented an important home front battle and part of the larger global struggle against totalitarianism to guarantee the economic security of average Americans.

Throughout the war, workers and labor unions faced pressures to limit any actions perceived as threatening full production for the war effort. Although the Fair Labor Standards Act of 1938 had created the first national requirements for minimum pay and maximum hours, in 1942, Congress, the president, and the war planning bureaucracy sought to place limits on overtime and holiday pay. A bill in the House sought to end overtime pay for any defense work over forty hours. This measure failed to advance through Congress, but at the same time, the War Production Board (WPB) launched a similar campaign to eliminate premium pay for holiday and weekend work. These proposals gained crucial yet partial support in September 1942, when the president issued an executive order eliminating bonus pay for weekends and holidays, on the grounds that such incentive pay "sometimes interfered with 'round-the-clock' operations." The most significant anti-labor measure during the war came after a coal strike in the spring of 1943 that idled 400,000 miners nationwide, including thousands in Alabama. In reaction, Congress passed the War Labor Disputes Act, also known as the Smith-Connally Act for its two southern sponsors, Representative Howard Smith of Virginia and Senator Tom Connally of Texas. The law placed various limits on the ability of unions to mount strikes: a thirty-day cooling-off period, mandatory notification to employers, and a pre-vote of a union's members on whether to strike, supervised by the National Labor Relations Board (NLRB). The act also allowed the government to seize and operate industrial concerns paralyzed by a strike. FDR vetoed the legislation, but Congress overrode his objection.[37]

Mississippi citizens and politicians had mixed feelings about these restrictions on labor unions and their right to strike during wartime. Some with children fighting overseas deplored strikes because they seemed to prolong the conflict. One woman from east-central Mississippi saw an essential connection between ending strikes and the time when "our boys can come home again." A man from southwest Mississippi applauded passage of the Smith-Connally Act by noting that soldiers did not strike for higher pay. Others, however, drew different conclusions. A union member from Hattiesburg noted that he had a son of military age ready "to fight for our country," but he also thought part of the fight involved preserving strong labor unions: "When we return, if we return, we will be sure of a decent living wage as long as we have unions." He also blamed most strikes on the intransigence of company executives, not workers. As Congress debated the Smith-Connally measure, a carpenter and AFL member from Meridian asked why working people had to "keep fighting to maintain our rights to make a decent living." After passage of the law, R. E. Anderson of Hopewell told Representative Colmer that he would work to "defeat every Axis-minded Congressman up for reelection" in 1944—meaning those who voted for the Smith-Connally Act.[38]

These competing ideas about the value of labor unions and their proper role during wartime loomed as the essential backdrop to the efforts to organize workers at the Ingalls Shipyard Corporation during World War II. By early 1940, the AFL's Metal Trades Department, a collective of various craft unions, sought certification from the Ingalls Shipbuilding Corporation to serve as the exclusive bargaining representative for shipyard production employees. The Industrial Union of Marine and Shipbuilding Workers of America (IUMSWA), a CIO organization, had also been trying to create a local since the shipyard opened. In addition, an independent group, the Pascagoula Marine Shipbuilding Association, worked to establish some type of workers' organization. The NLRB stepped in to adjudicate the case and decide what union, if any, should represent the shipyard workers. The Pascagoula Marine Shipbuilding Association turned out to be a small club of four men. The AFL claimed that it spoke for 500 of the company's roughly 700 workers, but it produced only 361 signed cards. The NLRB decided in March that neither the IUMSWA nor the Association had a real presence at the shipyard, so it ordered an election for workers to decide between the AFL Metal Trades Department or no union. Workers chose the AFL in a vote of 548 to 110. By July 1940, the AFL hammered out a one-year agreement with the company, which included pay increases and a grievance procedure but no guarantee of a closed shop.[39]

Soon after the finalization of the Pascagoula labor agreement, Robert Ingalls had to contend with a more serious labor struggle at his Birmingham concern. In 1937, the CIO's Steel Workers Organizing Committee (SWOC) had organized the employees of Ingalls Iron Works—almost 70 percent of them Black workers—and negotiated a contract with Robert Ingalls. SWOC's success rested in large part on claims to help Black employees advance, but the union did little in this area. By the fall of 1940, the company still classified almost all the Black workers at the company, even those performing skilled mechanic work, as unskilled "helpers." The AFL's Bridge, Structural, and Ornamental Iron Workers began organizing efforts at the company and promised to fix the classification system, get all workers equal pay for equal work, and have Black employees admitted to a company apprenticeship program.

When the NLRB ordered a new union election in September 1940, the AFL won by a three-to-one margin. As the new union representatives started negotiating with the management at Ingalls Iron Works, the company rejected the proposed reforms that had propelled the AFL to victory, instead promising an 18-cent-per-hour increase for white workers in the highest job classifications but only a 2-cent raise for Black helpers. The AFL rejected this counterproposal, and negotiations dragged on for five months. In March 1941, Ingalls officials claimed that "no raises would be granted the Negro workers." This hardline position led to a strike at Ingalls Iron Works. The company initially refused to back off from its discriminatory policy, but the NAACP contacted the Office of Production Management (the forerunner of the WPB), which sent two representatives to Birmingham. With white and Black workers presenting a united front, and with pressure from the Office of Production Management, which could possibly sidetrack or slow down the company's growing portfolio of war contracts, Ingalls quickly conceded and accepted the union's demands.[40]

The battle in Birmingham shaped Robert Ingalls's attitude toward labor at his Mississippi location. For one thing, those events may have convinced the chairman to limit, if possible, Black labor at the Pascagoula yard to prevent a replay of the successful biracial labor action against Ingalls Iron Works. The Birmingham strike also likely convinced Ingalls to try to limit union power as much as possible, despite a more ordered and structured landscape for the operation of labor organizations as war production accelerated. During 1941, labor unions reached an understanding with the shipbuilding industry. In January 1941, the AFL's Metal Trades Department struck a deal that most shipbuilders nationwide and the federal government agreed to accept. In exchange for a no-strike pledge from workers, shipbuilders agreed to provide security for unions, including a closed shop. Labor and management also agreed to hold four zone conferences to standardize wages and overtime rules. In August 1941, the AFL Metal Trades Department approved the Gulf Zone Plan, which included the Ingalls shipyard in Pascagoula. Afterward, individual shipyards began to hammer out agreements with local unions.[41]

Robert Ingalls ultimately secured a deal in Pascagoula that limited the power of the dominant labor organization at his shipyard, the AFL, which according to the federal government at the time included more than 95 percent of the shipyard's workers. As the union and the company negotiated a new contract, talks broke down because the company wanted a no-strike clause without any accompanying agreement on union security. The company argued that it could not make its employees join a union. According to labor leader H. B. Harrison, Ingalls said at the time that "he would blow the whole d___d works up before he would ever submit to union demands for [a] closed shop." From the perspective of the unions, according to a leader of the Pascagoula local of the International Brotherhood of Electrical Workers, the closed shop assured "reasonable pay, safety from injury, and Democratic working conditions." During contract discussions, the AFL shut down the shipyard with a walkout of 3,000 employees in mid-October 1941, a tactic that only reinforced the company's desire to resist union demands for a closed shop.[42]

After a three-day work stoppage, the workers agreed to return to the shipways after the contract dispute was referred to the National Defense Mediation Board (NDMB), an organization created in March 1941 by FDR to arbitrate labor-management disputes. In a November 1941 ruling, the NDMB rejected the AFL's request that union membership be a condition of employment and ratified Ingalls's opposition to a closed shop. Instead, the federal mediators relied on a compromise solution they had already imposed in six other cases during 1941: a maintenance-of-membership clause. The union could not force the company to require new workers to join the union as a condition of employment, but current union members or those who joined later had to stay with the organization to keep their jobs. As part of the final pact, the Ingalls Shipbuilding Corporation agreed to "cooperate [with] and encourage the union" and to give union men "preference" in hiring, "all things being equal and when practicable." Although these assurances from the company seemed somewhat tenuous, the NDMB claimed that the provisions "should form a basis for stable relations and guard the security of the union during the life of the contract." Unlike Ingalls, who threatened to abandon shipbuilding completely if he did not get his way, the workers at the Pascagoula shipyard accepted the agreement "in order not to hinder the defense program," according to H. B. Harrison, a leader of the carpenters and joiners at the yard.[43]

In early 1942, the WPB established a Labor-Management Committee at Ingalls, composed of one labor representative from each of the twelve crafts that made up the Metal Trades Council, as well as twelve management members. As elsewhere, this type of committee favored the interests of management rather than labor. The committee met every other week to address a number of problems at the shipyard, but as Robert Bateman, secretary of the local Metal Trades Council, explained, these gatherings addressed issues "primarily from management's standpoint." Since all but one of the unions affiliated with the Metal Trades Council did not have a closed shop—the electricians, who worked for an Ingalls subcontractor—the Pascagoula shipyard had no obligation to hire only workers affiliated with the AFL unions, and until November 1943, the company did not provide the individual craft organizations with information about hires at the shipyard. A further sign of how the company tried to ignore the union is the fact that the *Ingalls News*, a company newspaper distributed to Pascagoula employees, made few references to labor unions. Indeed, one would never realize that unions operated at the shipyard by reading the pages of this publication.[44]

Although union men at Ingalls faced obstacles, organizers for the various craft unions in the yard still managed to sign up most workers to the AFL. Union officials could not enter the yard to talk with employees, so they had to depend on the employment managers at Ingalls to send workers to the appropriate craft union after being hired. In the fall of 1942, the machinists proposed that a single person be posted near the main gate to sign up workers to the appropriate AFL union once they left the employment office, but some in the Metal Trades Council refused to cooperate. The International Brotherhood of Boilermakers, Iron Ship Builders, and Helpers of America (IBB), one of the largest AFL craft unions, had an office one block from the gate and preferred to have the employment office send new employees directly to their headquarters. In late 1943, AFL officials estimated that 75 percent of the workers at Ingalls belonged to the union, although they acknowledged this number was largely a guess, in large part because their contact with company leaders remained limited, and they did not have an accurate accounting of who worked in the shipyard on any specific date. Even if the actual number of union members at Ingalls was somewhat lower than union officials believed, the organization clearly managed to enroll a significant number of workers. This achievement was impressive, especially given the high labor turnover rates, the company's general hostility to union organizing efforts, and the not uncommon jurisdictional disputes that occurred between various craft organizations, especially involving the machinists and the boilermakers.[45]

As women entered the shipyard, the AFL also brought them into the union. The machinists, who accepted women as full members of their organization, reported that at their late November 1942 meeting, two months after the first female welders arrived at Ingalls, "7 ladies working in the Yard" had joined the Pascagoula lodge. In January 1943, the local selected two female workers, Vera Anderson and LaVerna Kuger, to attend the Southern War Labor Conference in Atlanta in January 1943, the first women delegates to attend such a conclave from "the sheet metal and construction trades." On the other hand, the relatively small group of Black workers at Ingalls had little chance to become involved with the AFL, even though during the war, southern leaders of the AFL officially pledged nondiscrimination. At the January 1943 meeting that Anderson and Kuger attended, the conference passed a resolution that declared "there should be a condition of absolute equal rights on jobs and job opportunities without any discrimination on account of race, creed or color." However, the main shipyard unions affiliated with the AFL, such as the IBB, maintained their opposition to Black members throughout the war. At Ingalls, only the AFL union representing laborers admitted Black members, and it had a separate "colored local" with little to no power to affect workplace policy.[46]

The AFL Metal Trades Council in Pascagoula never won a closed shop agreement with the Ingalls Shipbuilding Corporation during the war. Without this protection, Ingalls continued to hire non-union workers, fire union activists allegedly because of "lack of work," and lay off workers with more seniority and higher pay in favor of less experienced workers who could be paid less. The union continued to press the issue by turning to the only tool that might get management's attention: the strike, which threatened to upend tight production schedules. Despite no-strike pledges by national unions and anti-strike legislation such as the Smith-Connally Act, wildcat strikes occurred throughout the war years, including at Ingalls. These short labor actions involved relatively few workers, but each year between 1942 and 1945, there were anywhere from 2,000 to 5,000 work stoppages nationwide.[47]

At Ingalls, the battle for a closed shop intensified as the company reached peak employment and maximum production. In 1943, various wildcat strikes occurred at the Pascagoula shipyard, and the National War Labor Board (NWLB) agreed to mediate the ongoing dispute between Ingalls management and the AFL. In October 1943, the NWLB denied the AFL's request for a closed shop at Ingalls. While the federal agency refused to force the company to guarantee union security (one of the principles of the Gulf Zone agreement), Ingalls officials chided the union for defying that same agreement. Soon after the NWLB decision, the union—following the regulations of the new Smith-Connally Act—notified the Ingalls company that it would hold a strike vote. Much like the NWLB, other federal war planners sided with the company. As the AFL Metal Trades Council planned for a strike vote in late November 1943, Burton Morley, area director of the WMC, worried that "the union leaders in Pascagoula have become increasingly confident of their ability to force issues." As a result, Morley asked his superiors for permission to "take all possible steps to close referrals to jobs made vacant and to refuse releases to all strikers." Thus, if workers did approve a strike, those less committed to the union struggle would not be able to leave the Pascagoula shipyard and find other work. This kind of action on the part of the WMC was designed to dampen enthusiasm for a strike at the yard. The tactic worked, at least in the short run, as union leaders postponed the strike vote.[48]

Demands for a closed shop continued to lead to occasional wildcat strikes at Ingalls during 1944 and early 1945, and the Pascagoula Metal Trades Council tried but failed to get the NWLB to reconsider its case against the Ingalls Shipbuilding Corporation. As hopes for a new contract faded, in January 1945, the Council notified the necessary government agencies of its intention to take a strike vote. A month later, the workers decided by a count of 3,774 to 1,428 to strike. Days after the vote, the NWLB finally scheduled a March hearing to determine whether the two parties had followed the Board's October 1943 ruling, in particular the grievance procedure established in that directive. In addition to the closed shop issue and the grievance process, the union had several other long-standing complaints against the Ingalls company, including the failure to provide passes for union representatives to enter the yard, wage rates, and inadequate food service at the shipyard.[49]

On Saturday morning, February 24, 6,000 first-shift workers walked off the job. The second-shift employees did not show up for work, and by late Saturday, the workers had paralyzed the shipyard. Ten thousand Ingalls workers eventually went out on strike, making the February 1945 labor action the largest against the Pascagoula shipyard during the war. On Tuesday, local Selective Service boards in the Gulf Coast counties threatened to reclassify all striking shipyard workers younger than thirty-eight to 1-A (eligible for military service). On Wednesday, however, worker support for the strike began to erode. Fifteen hundred workers, including Vera Anderson, showed up to work, but there was no electrical power in the yard. The electricians, who belonged to the only craft organization in the Metal Trades Council with a closed shop and who did not work directly for the Ingalls Shipbuilding Corporation, refused to cross the picket lines and bring the yard back online. Administrative employees eventually restored electricity at the shipyard, and the 1,500 workers returned to work. That night, AFL leaders met with representatives from the NWLB and agreed to end the strike.[50]

Despite an impressive show of unity to gain real recognition and power for their labor organization, it was difficult for the Pascagoula workers to stay off the job for long, for exactly the reason that company officials pointed to in their efforts to delegitimize strikes: American men—fathers, sons, brothers—were dying on battlefields in Europe and Asia. Whatever the merit of the fight against the Ingalls company—and clearly most of the workers at the yard supported the union's effort to improve conditions there—workers on strike abandoned jobs essential to winning the war. But without the ability to mount a prolonged work stoppage, the AFL Metal Trades Council had no leverage to force Robert Ingalls to make substantial changes at the Pascagoula shipyard.

World War II provided economic opportunity and security after a decade of hard times for the thousands who came to work at the Ingalls Shipbuilding Corporation, mostly white people from the rural districts of Mississippi. Even at the height of the economic expansion, however, the durability of the prosperity spurred by wartime mobilization remained uncertain. In March 1944, Robert Ingalls, who served on the War Contract Termination Committee of the National Association of Manufacturers, predicted a postwar depression and thought it "folly to promise 'jobs for everybody.'" Soon after the February 1945 strike at his shipyard, with victory over Germany just months away, war orders slowed, and layoffs began at the Ingalls yard, as they did at war plants around the South and throughout the country. By October 1945, almost 90,000 shipyard workers nationwide had lost their jobs, with another 40,000 layoffs expected by early 1946. In Georgia, 35,000 workers lost their jobs in the month following V-J Day; nationwide, unemployment had climbed to 2 million by October 1, 1945, a jobless rate of just 3.5 percent, but one that had grown from 1.5 percent in August 1945.[51]

In large part, however, Ingalls Shipbuilding Corporation persevered after the war emergency passed. Robert Ingalls found ways to adapt to the changing economic landscape by adjusting the company's shipbuilding work to peacetime needs. He filled shipping orders from other countries, such as Brazil, and he added the manufacture of diesel-electric locomotives to the company's production profile without having to create new facilities. As a result, in the fall of 1945, Ingalls Shipbuilding still had 8,000 employees—a loss of 3,000 from its wartime high—a situation that looked like "substantially full employment even by wartime standards," according to one observer. Within months, however, as foreign competition recovered and as ships faced new competition from air transport, shipbuilding contracted worldwide. By March 1946, Ingalls had only 5,000 employees. When Robert Ingalls Sr. died in 1951, his son took over the Pascagoula shipyard, and in the mid-1950s, Ingalls Shipbuilding Corporation still employed anywhere between 5,500 and 7,500 workers. In the decades after World War II, the Ingalls shipyard remained Mississippi's largest employer, and today, it employs as many people as it did during the peak production years of the war.[52]

The smaller workforce of the immediate postwar period, however, looked different from the one of the war years. Most noticeably, women employees left the shipyard en masse, returning to the home or to traditional female employment outside the home. While women often gladly gave up their industrial jobs, men made clear they did not favor continued female employment in traditionally male jobs once the war emergency passed. In July 1945, one Pascagoula man wrote to Senator Theodore Bilbo and implored him to pass legislation preventing women from working in the shipyards, "so all the ex servicemen can get a job." Despite all the evidence to the contrary, the man added, "their work is no good no way."[53]

The extremely limited gains that Black men had made at Ingalls moving into skilled positions during World War II ended soon after the war. When a shortage of steel in March 1946 led Ingalls management to temporarily suspend a night shift at the shipyard, the International Union of Operating Engineers, an AFL union that represented crane operators, led a strike that eventually idled 3,000 workers. An attempt to push Black crane operators out of the union played a role in the initial walkout of fifty-one white crane operators. Union officials asked the company to put three of the white workers laid off on the day shift, but more important, they demanded that no more Black workers receive training in the crane operator craft, so that when Black operators "eventually withdrew voluntarily, white men would replace those now employed." The *Chicago Defender* called the labor action a "hate strike," and even the Ingalls company, which had an abysmal record of advancing Black employment during the war, took the high ground and claimed the union "is trying to force racial discrimination." Although the strike soon ended, the incident pointed to a further weakness of the AFL in its long fight for a closed shop and a greater say in Robert Ingalls's shipbuilding operation: racial divisions among the workers. In 1954, the Mississippi legislature approved a right-to-work law, which outlawed the closed shop and ended fifteen years of agitation over the question at the Pascagoula shipyard.[54]

During World War II, Ingalls Shipbuilding Corporation made an important contribution to the production that secured the victory of the Allies. The construction of hundreds of ships also produced huge profits for Robert Ingalls's company and provided much-needed employment for thousands of rural Southerners who had struggled economically for decades. Although the shipyard on the Mississippi Gulf Coast saw plenty of innovation during the war—in the shipbuilding process, in the use of women as essential skilled workers, in a greater presence for organized labor in the anti-union South— not all the changes outlasted the global conflict. Ingalls Shipbuilding continued to be an important place of employment for south Mississippians in the years after World War II, albeit one reserved for white males and where management made all the essential decisions about the workplace.

3
The FEPC and Black Workers

On June 18, 1942, the members of the Fair Employment Practices Committee (FEPC) assembled at the US District Courthouse in Birmingham, Alabama, to hold a hearing on employment discrimination, the first (and last) hearing the committee held in the Deep South. Merely arranging an FEPC meeting in Birmingham proved a difficult task. The southern regional director for the War Production Board (WPB), Frank Neely, balked at providing a federal facility to hold the inquiry and suggested instead "some Negro church or school." In fact, Neely refused to acknowledge employment discrimination existed in the South and suggested that the only bias he knew about was "discrimination against southern industry." He also told FEPC representatives that he feared a "racial outbreak" if the hearings were held in Birmingham. Donald Nelson, chair of the WPB, overruled Neely.[1]

Prior to the meeting, five investigators for the FEPC, two of them Black men, traveled throughout Georgia, Alabama, Tennessee, Mississippi, and Louisiana to get a sense of local conditions. They identified several companies in the Deep South that had instituted "relatively equitable" hiring practices, including Tennessee Coal, Iron, and Railroad Company in Birmingham (a US Steel subsidiary) and Higgins Industries in New Orleans. At the same time, the FEPC investigators encountered open hostility and found that many firms in the region maintained unfair employment practices. Investigators suggested that thirteen companies send representatives to testify at the hearings. In addition, the committee called labor leaders, state directors of vocational education, and other government officials to appear as witnesses at the proceedings.[2]

The three-day hearing produced a surprising amount of support for FDR's Executive Order 8802, which established the FEPC and urged the end of employment discrimination in defense industries and the federal government. Before the hearing began, the committee's executive secretary, Lawrence Cramer, a Louisiana native, expressed hope that white Southerners would embrace FDR's directive. Cramer believed that "if there could be a clearcut showing to them that 'prejudice as usual' will not win our war, it is very probable that they will be more apt to go along with our program." Indeed, because of the federal hearings, four Deep South shipyards, including the Alabama Dry Dock and Shipbuilding Company (ADDSCO), promised to follow the nondiscrimination mandate of the executive order. A major southern construction firm, as well as the Coca-Cola Company and two aircraft manufacturing concerns, made similar pledges. James V. Carmichael, the attorney for Bell Aircraft Corporation's Georgia division—at the time constructing a massive plant in Marietta, outside of Atlanta—claimed that once the company started hiring, only one standard would be used in screening potential employees: whether they had the necessary "skill, ability, and physical fitness" to do the job. "No other standards would determine the selection of our employees," Carmichael promised.[3]

The FEPC, while confidently endorsing nondiscrimination as an essential war measure, had almost no power to enforce the decree. Indeed, while most of the witnesses at the hearings vowed to end racial discrimination and to hire more Black workers, some promised continued resistance to FDR's executive order. The vice president of Gulf Shipbuilding in Mobile, which had only twenty-two Black employees (all in menial positions) among its thousands of workers, indicated that his company had no intention of obeying the FEPC directive. Despite Carmichael's pledge about Bell Bomber's future hiring practices, Georgia's vocational education director, charged with overseeing defense worker training in the state, admitted that Georgia had provided limited training for Black workers and said that "he did not want to be a party to wasting a lot of public money training folks who would never get jobs." L. M. Cooper, a leader of Mobile's AFL carpenters union, which had effectively locked out Black carpenters from the city's construction business, testified that, despite a shortage of skilled builders, "we just ain't goin' to work on the same job with Negroes."[4]

Despite the expressions of support for the FEPC coming out of the Birmingham hearings from some of the Deep South's major defense employers, Lawrence Cramer's appeal to national patriotism among white Southerners did not work. Defending white racial privilege, especially economic prerogatives, remained a much stronger sentiment in the region. *Alabama*, a newly established magazine in Birmingham, condescendingly labeled the committee "a bunch of snoopers, two of whom are Negroes." Prior to the hearings, the magazine reported derisively that the committee "will assemble in Birmingham to determine whether the South is doing right by Little Sambo." While many white Southerners simply dismissed the FEPC as unlawful federal meddling in regional affairs, southern white liberals like FEPC chair Mark Etheridge supported the federal directive to improve job conditions for Black Southerners but emphasized that change could only occur within the confines of a system of segregation. Virginius Dabney, editor of the *Richmond (VA) Times-Dispatch*, who had long called for fair treatment of Black Americans, wrote that Black efforts to abolish segregation "in the middle of a global war is the height of folly" and would lead to "violence and bloodshed." Black leaders and the Black press, however, rejected the idea that employment discrimination could end while racial segregation remained, even if some acknowledged the limited scope of FDR's executive order.[5]

The FEPC promoted the laudable objective of requiring employers to provide equal opportunities in hiring during wartime in order to maximize production for victory, but the federal directive had only a limited impact. Before the creation of the FEPC, as the United States began to mobilize economically for war in 1940 and early 1941, almost all the new defense jobs went to white Americans. Six months after the president's order, discrimination against Black workers persisted nationwide. A January 1942 survey sent by the US Employment Service (USES) to hundreds of companies with major defense contracts—seven months after the issuance of Executive Order 8802— showed that 51 percent of the employers nationwide did not (and said they would not) hire Black workers. Although Congress appropriated $60 million for the US Office of Education in 1940 to establish training programs for defense workers on a nondiscriminatory basis, in January 1942 only 194 of the 4,630 training courses nationwide accepted Black students.[6]

Over the course of the war, the FEPC made a valiant attempt to improve the situation for Black workers. The committee handled 12,000 cases and reached settlements in about 40 percent of those (20 percent in the South). Overall, the number of Black Americans working in war jobs rose from 4.2 percent in 1942 to 8.6 percent in 1945, although part of that increase could be attributed to the fact that by 1943, companies often needed any worker they could find, which mitigated any desire to maintain rigid discrimination against Black workers. The FEPC, however, never solved many of the problems Black laborers faced: they still received relatively few skilled jobs; small businesses typically still refused to hire them; and many Black employment gains occurred in industries likely to be downsized after the war emergency (such as shipbuilding or aircraft construction), which meant that war employment, even if secured, offered little long-term security. The greatest success story for Black workers during the war happened in the area where the federal government had the most control: federal jobs. The number of Black employees increased from 50,000 to 200,000.[7]

In the South, where most Black people still lived, the FEPC proved particularly ineffectual in bringing about change. White Southerners had created a system of racial apartheid designed to legally enshrine social, legal, and economic discrimination against its Black population. The South had Black citizens who pressed for implementation of the FEPC edict, though challenging white supremacy in the region entailed significant personal risks. Although a few employers in the Deep South tried to follow the federal government's nondiscrimination mandate for the workplace, most maintained discriminatory employment practices throughout the war.

A closer look at three southern companies illustrates how employers in the Deep South that made major contributions to war production managed to evade the requirements of Executive Order 8802 and to limit Black industrial employment in the region. Company leaders at both ADDSCO in Mobile, Alabama, and the Bell Bomber Plant in Marietta, Georgia, agreed to satisfy FEPC directives by providing new employment opportunities for Black workers within the established social structure. Those attempts demonstrated the limits of ending racial discrimination and boosting Black employment when maintaining racial segregation remained the primary objective. Even the segregated jobs at these companies came only after months of delays. But other employers, in places with a smaller mobilized Black community pressing for change, largely evaded FEPC oversight. Such was the case with the Ingalls Shipbuilding Corporation. Since few Black workers lodged complaints against Ingalls, and with an employer indifferent to the nondiscrimination mandate, the FEPC made little headway getting the company to adjust its employment practices. As a result, the Mississippi shipyard remained a workplace primarily for white workers throughout the war. At all three locales, a reluctance to provide adequate training programs for prospective Black employees complicated the federal effort to integrate Black workers into wartime production. Although inadequate training for Black laborers was a national problem, in the South public officials felt free to create a segregated training system for Black people that replicated the inequities in educational opportunities that had for decades defined public education in the region.

Mobile, Alabama, was one of the first locales in the Deep South to experience an economic resurgence because of war mobilization. In the year preceding May 1941, the population of the city expanded rapidly, from approximately 78,000 to 135,000, with Black residents comprising 15,000 of the new arrivals. Postal records indicated that most of the newcomers to Mobile came from rural Alabama or Mississippi. Many who moved to Mobile came to work in the two giant shipyards—ADDSCO and Gulf Shipbuilding—or to work on constructing Brookley Army Air Field. So many people came to Mobile in such a short timeframe that as early as April 1942, an unemployment problem had already emerged, despite the economic expansion, especially among unskilled workers.[8]

Black migrants arriving in Mobile faced more difficulties than white people in securing either employment or training for skilled jobs. When local National Association for the Advancement of Colored People (NAACP) leader John L. LeFlore investigated the problem in the spring of 1941, he uncovered a classic Catch-22. Officials in the Alabama State Department of Education claimed that they would open vocational training programs for Black citizens once "it can be shown that employers will accept colored craftsmen." At the same time, the management of one defense company told LeFlore that "the lack of training opportunities" was "the main problem affecting colored workers." LeFlore complained to Robert C. Weaver—a Black administrator of the US Council of National Defense—"that the federal government has not shown a determination to prevent discrimination in training and employment." LeFlore believed this situation concerned all people "who feel that America should practice as well as express in words our belief in the principles of Democracy." The Black leader received threats because he questioned the lack of defense training courses for Black Mobilians.[9]

Black men in Mobile could not even get much work on any of the many construction projects underway in the city. In the weeks prior to executive order of June 1941 establishing the FEPC, the contractor for a federally funded housing project for defense workers, the J. F. Pate Construction Company, employed ninety-six white carpenters, members of the all-white Local 89 of the International Brotherhood of Carpenters and Joiners, an American Federation of Labor (AFL) union. When Black carpenters in the city, members of the all-Black Local 92 of the same union, sought work on the job, the company said all the white carpenters would strike if any Black carpenters joined the workforce. LeFlore lodged a complaint with the Federal Works Agency (FWA), which had oversight for the housing project. After FDR issued his FEPC order, John M. Carmody, head of FWA, directed both the contractor and the white union to end discriminatory hiring and use Black builders to help construct the 500 homes. Although the company agreed to hire Black workers, the union continued to balk at the decision. The FWA eventually reached an agreement with Pate Construction that required Black workers to comprise 22 percent of the skilled labor on the housing project. Although the company soon hired a group of Black carpenters and painters, it dismissed them all within four days on the basis of "insufficient" performance.[10]

The FEPC order did little to increase defense training opportunities for Black workers in the region. On the eve of Pearl Harbor, only sixteen locations offered vocational training for Black citizens in Mississippi, and none offered the kind of training that might lead to a skilled position at the state's largest employer, Ingalls Shipbuilding Corporation. The most common course of study at these Black training locations was woodworking (offered at all of them) and blacksmithing (offered at six). In May 1942, state vocational officials had still done nothing to improve the training situation for Black residents in the state, despite prodding from the US Office of Education. Although Mobile at the time had a shortage of workers, primarily welders for the two rapidly expanding shipyards, the only training for Black welders available in the entire state was a small program at Tuskegee Institute, 150 miles away.[11]

The creation of the FEPC also had little impact on increasing employment opportunities in the shipyards for Black residents in Mobile. At the Birmingham hearings, employment policies at ADDSCO came under scrutiny from the FEPC. Fewer than 20 percent of ADDSCO employees were Black men, and all worked in unskilled positions. Committee investigators, who had worked with LeFlore to gather evidence, showed that Black employment at the shipyard had declined even as the yard expanded. Company officials limited Black hires out of a concern that if Black employment grew, white workers would quit. Since ADDSCO needed more skilled workers, the vice president of the company, John M. Griser, claimed that part of the problem lay with the fact that few Black people had "pre-training outside of the plant." When FEPC committee member Earl Dickerson reminded Griser that few training opportunities existed for Black residents in Mobile, Griser claimed that he did not realize such a problem existed. The position of the Industrial Union of Marine and Shipbuilding Workers of America (IUMSWA)—the Congress of Industrial Organization (CIO) union at the yard—mirrored that of company officials. The union seemed reluctant to have Black employees work with white personnel or to have Black laborers upgraded to skilled positions. IUMSWA officials worried that if it pressed for Black upgrading, white workers would move to the AFL, which had already unsuccessfully challenged the IUMSWA in two elections. Paul Babcock, vice president of the local union, advised against taking "abrupt measures" during wartime; instead, change had to come "quietly and peacefully, gradually, as the education progresses on both sides."[12] The standard Babcock held up depended on white citizens agreeing they would offer Black people equal employment opportunities, a change of attitude not likely to happen without coercion.

At the Birmingham hearings, ADDSCO acknowledged its discriminatory treatment of Black workers and promised to do better in the future. Company officials offered only vague assurances to abide by the federal order in the future, but the Birmingham hearings served as an upsetting wake-up call for white leaders in Alabama. To them, FDR's executive order no longer seemed merely a statement encouraging nondiscrimination in employment; it had now become nothing less than an assault on the South's entire system of racial segregation. One month after the hearings, on July 22, Birmingham attorney and political boss Horace C. Wilkinson spoke to a local Kiwanis Club and lambasted the USES and the FEPC. He warned that the latter agency wanted "to feed negroes into all grades of employment in every defense industry and place them at work at adjoining desks with white people." He also excoriated the committee for telling labor unions that excluded Black workers to end that practice and for telling white workers that "if they refuse to work alongside a negro, they will be blacklisted from all defense plants." Wilkinson suggested that white Southerners—and indeed, all white Americans—fight back. He believed "an organization should be formed so strong, so powerful, and so efficient, that this menace to our national security and our local way of life will rapidly disappear." Wilkinson reasoned that "if there is room in this country for a national association for the advancement of colored people, there is need of a league to maintain white supremacy." Wilkinson and other white Alabama leaders mailed reprints of the speech to newspapers, businessmen, and public officials throughout the South.[13]

One day after Wilkinson's speech, one of his longtime political opponents, Alabama governor Frank Dixon, seconded the objections to the FEPC. Dixon, a man described by historian J. Mills Thornton III as both a "business progressive" and an "aggressive and inflexible segregationist," released a letter to the press that he sent to the federal Defense Supplies Corporation on July 22 rejecting a state contract with the WPB. That agreement called for cotton mills operated by the state prison system to manufacture tenting material for the military, but Dixon objected to the standard nondiscrimination clause in the federal war contract mandated by Executive Order 8802. Dixon claimed that if the state signed on to the deal, the FEPC would immediately "descend upon the State with the demand that Negroes be put in positions of responsibility in that department [prison system] in approximately the same proportion that the Negro race bears to the white race in Alabama." Though Dixon claimed that Alabama wanted to do "everything it can in the war effort," the state would not put businesses "in a position to be attacked by those who seek to foster their own pet social reforms in a time of national crisis."[14]

While some of the more moderate voices in the state thought the concerns expressed by Wilkinson and Dixon were overreactions to the Birmingham hearings, many white Alabamians agreed that the two leaders had prudently sounded the alarm about a real threat to southern social relations. The *Montgomery (AL) Advertiser* claimed that the Birmingham hearings unfolded "with such calm and such reserve that there was no opportunity to become alarmed, even for professional alarmists." Without mentioning Wilkinson or Dixon by name, the newspaper opined that "the only cause for concern over questions of race in the South is the ever-present possibility that unscrupulous demagogues will attempt to capitalize on the issue for personal gain." At the same time, Governor Dixon received hundreds of letters and telegrams from around Alabama and throughout the South supporting his position. One communication came from twelve Black professionals (ministers, physicians, and business owners) in Gadsden, Alabama, who praised the governor's position, a public declaration that, according to the white press, "refuted" the notion that Blacks were denied economic opportunities. Dixon's stance also received the editorial endorsement of a wide array of newspapers across the region. For example, the *Cullman (AL) Democrat* praised the governor for his "courageous stand against a movement whose ultimate goal or attainment would be a mongrel race of whites and blacks, populating our nation."[15]

The southern white hostility to the FEPC project that emerged in the aftermath of the Birmingham hearings played a role in weakening the agency. FDR, always sensitive to southern white concerns that could threaten essential domestic and foreign policy items, did not like confrontation on racial matters. After the Birmingham hearings, white leaders in Alabama not only pledged their opposition to nondiscrimination enforcement efforts in defense employment but also claimed the entire effort represented a federal plot to end racial segregation in the region. In early August 1942, weeks after the southern backlash to FEPC efforts emerged in the Deep South, the agency, which had started out as an independent entity funded with emergency appropriations through the president's office, was moved to the War Manpower Commission (WMC). Although FDR claimed the move strengthened the agency, most observers disagreed. The FEPC would now depend on funding from Congress, which contained many powerful Southerners (and Northerners) hostile to the nondiscrimination in employment effort. Black pressure led FDR, in the summer of 1943, to transfer control of the FEPC once again, this time to the Office of Emergency Management, which put the agency back in the Executive Office of the President. The FEPC, however, never restarted its effort—on display at the Birmingham hearings—to hold entire businesses and sectors of the economy responsible for ending employment discrimination. Instead, the agency focused on resolving individual complaints, important work but not the kind of effort that could ever achieve the stated goal of equal access to wartime employment, especially in a region like the Deep South.[16]

Exactly five months after the Birmingham hearings, the FEPC announced its findings in the ADDSCO case and offered its "directions" to the company. The committee found that ADDSCO refused to hire skilled Black workers at the shipyard and did not promote Black employees already working there into skilled positions. The FEPC instructed the company to "immediately cease and desist from such discriminatory employment practices." The committee also told ADDSCO to notify employment agencies, such as the USES; labor unions; and local and state training agencies that it would not discriminate against workers based on race and would accept Black workers for all classifications of employment at the yard. The FEPC had no real power to enforce these orders, and ADDSCO did little to change its employment policies over the next six months, even though the company did hire more Black employees as production at the yard continued to expand.[17]

As the company added workers in early 1943, tensions between Black and white employees increased, but no serious problems arose as long as the company delayed the FEPC directive requiring the placement of Black personnel in skilled shipyard jobs. In January 1943, seventy Black men who had been trained as welders through federally supported programs lived in Mobile, but when these men applied at ADDSCO, the company denied them employment or hired them to work as laborers. Despite the shortage of workers at the shipyard, white rumors spread on the job that any promotion of Black workers to skilled positions would mean a reduction in white jobs. The company made no effort to squelch these reports. Finally, in March 1943, the company did upgrade some Black laborers to semi-skilled positions as chippers and caulkers.[18]

In April 1943, Burton Morley, area director of the WMC, and others at the agency had discussions with ADDSCO about a plan to create one or two segregated shipways for Black workers, which would meet, in Morley's estimation, "at least part of the urgent need for increased production through the development of higher skills among the colored group." The proposed plan specified that white employees would hold all positions as supervisors and instructors. It also pointed out that probably 500 skilled Black employees already worked at the yard (though not in skilled positions) and that if the company could not train additional Black men for skilled positions, the local National Youth Administration and the local Director of Vocational Education had signed on to provide the needed training. The company initially expressed interest in the plan, as did local CIO officials, but when the WMC tried to follow up in early May, the company did not respond. Then suddenly, on Saturday, May 22, 1943, ADDSCO sent the following communication to Morley: "We take pleasure in reporting to you that effective Monday, May 24, we are placing crews of negro welders, on the third shift, on our Ways # 1, 2, 3, & 4." After having stalled on upgrading Black workers for almost a year after the Birmingham hearings and failing to accept the WMC's plan for a segregated process of employing skilled Black shipbuilders, ADDSCO decided unilaterally to employ skilled Black welders at the yard. The company notified neither its employees nor the IUMSWA of this dramatic shift in policy, one that sparked fear among white workers at the shipyard once it became known.[19]

The twelve Black welders who arrived at 11 P.M. on May 24 to work the third shift in a segregated team completed their stint overnight without incident. But during the first shift on the following day, after word circulated that Black welders had worked on the shipways the night before, a full-scale white riot broke out. White workers began yelling racial epithets at Black unskilled laborers and the recently promoted semi-skilled Black employees. One of those urging his fellow white workers to object to the upgrading of Black workers that morning was the former CIO leader, Paul Babcock, who had testified at the Birmingham hearings. Babcock had lost his leadership position after a failed strike and apparently had wanted to undermine the new union leadership for months. Groups of white employees and company guards (many of them women) attacked Black employees with various tools and shipyard objects as they tried to exit the shipways. More than fifty were injured before forty airmen from nearby Brookley Army Air Field and a contingent of city cops arrived to quell the disturbance. Hearing of the incident at ADDSCO, the president of the local AFL Central Trades Council ordered its 7,000 Black members to leave their jobs and go home "as a protective move." City leaders also ordered all businesses selling "intoxicating beverages" immediately closed.[20]

The number of white workers involved in the riot remains unclear. The company said 500 white workers participated in the violence, but Black witnesses believed the number was ten times higher. White anger clearly revolved around the upgrading of Black workers to the position of welder. The company and the local press blamed the violence on new arrivals to Mobile, "young bucks and girls," or what the editor of the *Mobile Press-Register* described as "poor white trash" from "the poor rural sections of Georgia and Mississippi." But older, established hands also participated in the violence. One of the four people arrested after the riot was forty-two-year-old Clifford L. Williams, who was born thirty miles north of Mobile and had worked as a machinist at ADDSCO since at least 1918. Not all white workers supported the violent attacks at the shipyard. Some tried to hide Black employees in the labyrinth of half-built ships or even attempted to intervene and stop white assaults on Black workers, which led to injuries to several of the good Samaritans.[21]

In addition to the white concerns that upgrading Black employees to skilled positions would imperil white economic prerogatives, gender fears also played a role in the white violence at ADDSCO. Economic mobilization brought Black and white workers into close contact, oftentimes in situations where racial separation proved difficult to maintain. ADDSCO had recently hired thousands of white women, many of them married, as welders. The thought of putting Black men in welding jobs, where they might work alongside white women, aroused the always obsessive white fears about social integration and miscegenation.[22]

ADDSCO officials initially blamed the federal government for the unrest at the shipyard. Vice President Griser called Morley after the riot and said, "We tried to put your plan into effect, and you see what happened." The WMC, however, never suggested a unilateral and surprise upgrading of Black workers. D. R. Dunlap, ADDSCO's president, told the local newspaper that the riot occurred because the company had tried to follow the FEPC directive. He also told the regional director of the Office of War Information that the real question "was whether [the] yard was to be all white or all colored," a calculation that echoed a common refrain among white Southerners at the time that the upgrading of Black staff would cause all the white workers to leave their jobs.[23]

Despite the initial finger-pointing by company officials, within days, ADDSCO resumed negotiations with the union and federal officials (including the FEPC) to create segregated shipways. In fact, ADDSCO officials provided key support in working out a resolution of the crisis. The FEPC had already determined that Black workers in Mobile might accept segregated employment arrangements. Two days after the riot, Clarence Mitchell of the FEPC met with two Black union leaders, one an ADDSCO employee, and E. T. Belsaw, a Black community leader and dentist. Interestingly, Mitchell did not include John LeFlore, Mobile's most prominent Black activist, in this discussion. The three local Black leaders present at the meeting agreed that although a segregated compromise would not satisfy everyone, they expected that most workers would agree with the proposed solution. When Mitchell and Ernest Trimble of the FEPC met the following day with officials from the US Navy and the US Maritime Commission, the federal officials endorsed the segregation plan, citing the labor shortage and the need to use Black skilled workers to alleviate it. Morley, also at the meeting, was skeptical that Black workers could solve the skilled labor shortage.[24]

That afternoon, company representatives and union officials joined the conversation. Charles Hanson, regional representative of the IUMSWA, suggested that the company bar Black welders from the shipyard until an "educational program" could prepare white workers for the change. The Maritime Commission representative, Captain W. K. Graham, agreed with this proposal, but Mitchell and Trimble objected. And somewhat surprisingly, so did the company. Griser, referring to the critical labor shortage, agreed that the company needed Black skilled workers immediately. He proposed that segregated crews of skilled Black workmen construct the bare hulls on four shipways (ADDSCO had twelve at the time). After the preparation of a hull, the Black crews would move to another shipway, and white craftsmen would arrive to finish work on the ship the Black welders had started. The Black crews would still have white foremen. Griser asked that the FEPC "'close its eyes' to segregation for a time." He also suggested the convening of a mass meeting where the company would explain this plan to the workers. At that meeting, Griser said, any workers opposed to the plan "would be asked to leave."[25]

Over the next several hours, the parties fashioned an agreement. Morley talked to his superiors, who told him to endorse the segregated shipway plan. Captain Graham talked to his bosses at the Maritime Commission, who communicated with the White House. President Roosevelt indicated he "did not want any back-tracking on using Negro welders." At 9:00 P.M., after six hours of negotiation, all parties signed off on the four segregated ways, hull construction-only plan. Five days later, on June 2, Francis Haas, the newly appointed chair of the FEPC, approved the Mobile compromise without consulting the full committee, primarily because new members had not been appointed after the FEPC had undergone its most recent reorganization. Haas told Griser the agreement applied only to ADDSCO and warned the company that it still had a responsibility to upgrade Black workers in all positions, not just those needed for bare-hull construction.[26]

Despite their active participation in hammering out the Mobile compromise, ADDSCO officials still wanted to maintain the impression that it had agreed to employ large numbers of skilled Black welders at the yard only under duress. When Washington officials announced the Mobile agreement on Friday, June 4, ADDSCO issued a local gag order to its workers—Bulletin 86. It warned company employees not to read anything other than the company newspaper, whether at work or off-site, or face dismissal. The directive only aroused further suspicion about the negotiations and created the possibility of further violence. The effort by ADDSCO to conceal its actions lasted only a few days, as the Office of War Information published the details of the agreement on Monday, June 7.[27] ADDSCO approached the Mobile compromise in the way it did because it understood that many white Southerners— including many of its workers—would balk at a settlement that preserved segregation but not discrimination. White Southerners never aspired to implement "separate but equal." Indeed, they knew that racial segregation legally prescribed racial discrimination for every aspect of southern life, which in large part explains their unyielding support for maintaining the Jim Crow system.

Although the company feared that the FEPC might balk at a plan that maintained segregation, strictly speaking, the Mobile compromise did not violate the nondiscrimination mandate of the FEPC. The committee's executive secretary, Lawrence Cramer, noted at the time that "the FEPC has in the past refused to decide hypothetically that segregation of Negro from white workers was discrimination." Indeed, in 1942, the committee had ratified a plan of the Sun Shipbuilding Company in Pennsylvania to create a segregated shipyard for its Black workers. Many Black leaders, however, continued to argue, with unassailable logic, that segregation always meant discrimination. The *Pittsburgh Courier* thought that the agreement was "a surrender to the Nazi racial theory and another defeat for the principles embodied in the Declaration of Independence." Walter White of the NAACP bluntly told Paul McNutt, chair of the WMC, that the agreement was a "compromise with evil," one that "would be disastrous in this critical stage of war." Local NAACP leader John LeFlore seemed to accept the compromise while clearly understanding its flaws. He did not condemn the segregation part of the agreement, but he claimed the plan would only prevent discrimination if Black personnel received training in all types of shipyard work. As LeFlore recognized, the negotiated plan only called for Black employees to work on part of a ship's construction, which meant they could only perform part of the skilled duties at the yard.[28]

The white riot at ADDSCO upended production at the Mobile shipyard for almost a week. On Tuesday and Wednesday, almost no Black employees worked, and they provided crucial support roles in the production process. At a meeting on Wednesday, company and city officials urged Black workers to come back to their jobs. By Saturday, May 29, only about half of the company's employees were back at work. On May 30, approximately 400 Black workers gathered in a lot adjacent to the Davis Avenue Community Center, where FEPC representatives, union officials, and local Black leaders urged the Black employees to return to the shipyard. The next day, most of ADDSCO's Black employees did return to the yard; the rest came back in the days that followed. Some white workers continued to stay away from the shipyard until they learned the details of the Black upgrading plan, but a week after the white riot, production had generally returned to normal. State and federal troops remained in and around the shipyard for several more weeks to ensure that the peace held.[29]

With the Mobile compromise in place, in many ways, life and work at ADDSCO continued with limited change. Racial segregation remained firmly entrenched, a fact clearly in evidence on the shipways and beyond the immediate work site. ADDSCO's segregation plan did open skilled positions for Black workers at the yard—welder, burner, ship fitter, caulker, and others. By the end of 1943, three other southern shipyards had adopted a similar plan for segregated shipways: the Charleston Navy Yard, the Brunswick

Shipbuilding Company in Georgia, and Higgins Industries in New Orleans. The segregated arrangements seemed to dampen Black protest, as the FEPC received few additional complaints about racial discrimination at ADDSCO for the remainder of the war. But as Black leaders feared, the segregation compromise did not eliminate discrimination in employment at the company. Throughout the war, skilled Black workers remained confined to hull construction on shipways 1–4, which meant that certain high-paying, skilled jobs, such as machinist and electrician, remained closed to Black employees.[30]

Although the Mobile compromise limited the number of skilled jobs for Black workers at ADDSCO, the workers made the most of the opportunity. In 1943, the company and others complained about inefficient Black welders; however, by 1944, company officials recognized that the work of their skilled Black employees "compares favorably" with that of the shipyard's white skilled workforce. The accomplishments of the Black workmen on shipways 1–4 during 1944 and 1945 alleviated any lingering concerns the company might have had. One year after the racial disturbance at the shipyard, Black workers helped to break a shipyard record, completing their hull construction work on the SS *Tule Canyon* in such a timely fashion that workers finished the ship in seventy-nine days.[31]

That achievement, however, angered white workers and threatened to reignite violence at the yard. The launching of the SS *Tule Canyon*, scheduled for 11:30 A.M. on May 31, 1944, was the prearranged signal for white workers to act against Black employees and clear them from ADDSCO, according to confidential informants working for both the Federal Bureau of Investigation and the Office of War Information at the shipyard. Black workers had heard about the plan, since according to a military informant, there was "a general exit of Negro workers" from the shipway at 9:30 A.M. on May 31. The anticipated trouble delayed the launching by an hour. F. B. Spencer, general manager of the company's shipbuilding division, spoke at the launching ceremony and tried to alleviate white fears. Spencer noted that the shipyard record resulted not because Black laborers outperformed their white counterparts but because the shipway where the SS *Tule Canyon*'s hull was constructed employed so many Black welders.[32] In the end, racial segregation accelerated construction on some ADDSCO shipways, even if it limited the overall efficiency of the shipyard.

One of the most significant cases that the FEPC continued to monitor after the Birmingham hearings concerned the Bell Bomber Plant in Marietta, near Atlanta, Georgia. In February 1942, the War Department selected Marietta as one of the locations to build a new airplane for the Army Air Forces: the B-29. Beginning in the late 1930s, careful and sustained planning by local boosters—including Marietta mayor Leon Blair and his law partner and county attorney, James V. Carmichael—as well as support from future Brigadier General Lucius Clay, a Marietta native, helped convince the government to select the Georgia site. It took more than a year to construct the $50 million, government-owned plant, which covered more than 250 acres, the largest airplane factory in the Deep South. The facility had no windows (for security reasons) but did have air-conditioning. Aircraft plants, like the Bell facility in Marietta, rivaled the shipyards in the Deep South in terms of employment. At its peak, in February 1945, more than 28,000 people worked at Bell Bomber.[33]

The US government contracted with Bell Aircraft, located in Buffalo, New York, to run the B-29 operation in Georgia. Southern firms owned

Men and women work in the Metal Fabrication Department of the Bell Bomber plant during World War II. This department was one of many in the main assembly building, which covered 3.2 million square feet. *Permission of Kennesaw State University Department of Museums, Archives & Rare Books*

many of the defense industries in the Deep South, such as the shipyards in New Orleans, Pascagoula, and Mobile, while others, such as Marietta's Bell Bomber Plant, operated as satellites of businesses located in other regions of the country. Larry Bell, the founder and owner of Bell Aircraft, was one of the country's pioneering aircraft entrepreneurs. At age eighteen, Bell took a job at the Glenn Martin Company, originally located in Los Angeles. When Martin opened a facility in Cleveland in 1918, he made Bell, just twenty-four years old, superintendent of the plant, which produced the Martin B-1 Bomber, the first bomber plane built in the United States. In the late 1920s and early 1930s, Bell worked for Consolidated Aircraft Company in Buffalo, and when that company moved to California in the mid-1930s, Bell stayed behind to start his own company. He kept afloat during the tough years of the 1930s by building several planes, including the P-39 Airacobra, which became one of the primary fighter aircraft in the US arsenal prior to World War II. The Bell Bomber contract proved a boon to the company. In less than two years of production, the facility in Marietta produced 663 B-29s, which became one of the main aircraft used in the Pacific Theater during the war.[34]

From the beginning of the Bell Bomber project, Black people in the Atlanta area expressed enthusiasm for the employment possibilities, while local white officials saw the project as a whites-only jobs program. The Atlanta chapter of the National Urban League (NUL), led by William Bell, created a Council of Defense Training, which collected more than 5,000 applications for training and employment at Bell Bomber during a ten-day campaign in the spring of 1942. That effort complemented another initiative underway at the same time by Black Atlantans—a teacher salary equalization lawsuit launched by the local chapter of the NAACP in February 1942. Frank Neely, the conservative southern regional director of the WPB, called the Atlanta NUL's Bell Bomber recruitment project "an Axis conspiracy" and an effort to "create dissension and to impede the war effort." Georgia's governor, Eugene Talmadge, running for re-election at the time, told a group of Atlanta leaders in March 1942 that if Black workers did receive jobs at the aircraft plant, they would not receive the same rate of pay. Talmadge called World War II a "white man's war" and said the battle could be "won without the Negroes' help. The Negro has never done anything to help develop America so why should he be given a chance to enjoy the fruits like the white man or be given an even break."[35]

Despite its non-southern roots, Bell Aircraft shared southern attitudes on race and employment. Indeed, the aircraft industry nationwide, a relatively new sector of the American economy, discriminated against Black citizens everywhere. For example, as the industry expanded rapidly in the years before World War II, an executive of Vultee Aircraft in southern California replied to a 1940 request for Black employment from the National Negro Congress, "I regret to say that it is not the policy of this company to employ people other than of the Caucasian race; consequently, we are not in a position to offer your people employment at this time." Even after the FEPC directive, the number of Black employees in the aircraft industry increased slowly. In November 1942, non-white people made up only 3.3 percent of the workers in the nation's aircraft industry.[36]

Bell Aircraft in Buffalo hired its first skilled Black worker only in April 1942, after a pressure campaign from the NAACP. And the company continued to erect discriminatory roadblocks for potential Black employees at its Buffalo facility. Black applicants had to take a blood test (unlike white applicants), and potential Black employees could not participate in the company's on-the-job training program but had to secure outside training before applying to the company for work. It is not surprising then that Larry Bell welcomed the selection of Marietta for the southern Bell facility by noting that he was "perfectly delighted with the kind of labor you have—88 or 89 per cent pure Anglo Saxon, all good old American blood."[37]

Federal officials initially anticipated that the thousands of workers for the Bell Bomber Plant would come from the Atlanta area, which despite Bell's understanding had a non-white population of almost 35 percent in 1940. The USES estimated in March 1942 that the Atlanta area had approximately 13,500 Black citizens (10,400 men and 3,500 women) available for work, and at the Birmingham hearings, a USES official testified that its active files listed 2,200 Black men who met the basic job requirements for work at Bell Bomber. In December 1942, the WMC indicated that it was "absolutely necessary" that war industries in the Atlanta area (including at Bell) should hire from the surrounding communities to avoid any "serious housing and transportation difficulties." At that time, the WMC also indicated that Bell's plans included a workforce that would be at least 50 percent female. Three months later, the WMC estimated that 58 percent of the population in the Atlanta area did not have gainful employment and could provide the labor for war concerns like the Bell Bomber Plant. Among this labor pool, the WMC counted "housewives, the aged, the physically handicapped, the children and the part-time labor," though it made no specific mention of underutilized Black workers.[38]

From the beginning, Bell Aircraft offered vague plans to utilize Black workers at Bell Bomber. Soon after the announcement of the Marietta location for the aircraft factory, Vaughan Bell, Larry's brother and vice president of Bell Aircraft, told the FEPC's Clarence Mitchell, "Negroes definitely will be used," though he provided few details about how many or in what roles. The next month, Larry Bell elaborated on the company's plans for utilizing Black labor. Bell informed Sidney Hillman, head of the WPB's labor division, that the company would create "a suitable arrangement" to employ Black people, but one that gave "due consideration to the traditions of the South concerning the employment of white and colored workers."[39] Respecting local traditions and customs, however, ensured that racially discriminatory employment practices persisted.

The lack of training opportunities posed one of the biggest obstacles that Black citizens in the Atlanta area faced in securing a job at Bell Bomber. As in other areas of the South, state and local officials in Georgia managed the creation and staffing of the classes and largely excluded Black residents. In February 1941, only four of the fifty-five "defense training" courses in the Atlanta area provided seats for Black citizens, and those four (cement finishing, machine crating, scaffold building, and trade cooking) did not offer the kind of training that would lead to skilled jobs at a place like Bell Bomber. Georgia officials set up these specific training courses for Black Georgians because of a belief that these offerings could prepare them to take the jobs left vacant once white residents assumed war production jobs.[40]

The creation of the FEPC did little to change the training landscape in the Atlanta area. After the Bell Bomber announcement, Georgia vocational education officials announced plans to open aircraft production classes in April 1942 in as many as fifteen Atlanta locations, with the capacity to train 3,300 white men and women every ten weeks. Georgia school officials also used some of their federal monies to send thirty-seven white Georgians (but no Black people) to Buffalo to become training instructors. The failure to include Black workers in these plans had nothing to do with any special aptitude among white residents for aircraft production jobs. Richard Croop, a northern worker who came south to work at Bell Bomber, recalled that many of the white residents enrolled in the aircraft training programs were illiterate and "didn't know what a drill or drill motor or rivet gun was." Indeed, the Bell company used an advanced lofting procedure to produce completed parts for the production line, which meant that assembly-line workers needed little expertise to put a B-29 together, since the parts could fit together in only one way.[41]

State vocational officials, however, simply did not envision Black people taking war industry jobs. Indeed, without consulting with Bell Aircraft, Georgia's director of vocational education, M. D. Mobley, just assumed the company would not hire any Black workers. Federal education officials apparently had the same understanding. Ben Harris from the US Office of Education told the FEPC's John Beecher in February 1942 that Hitler and the Nazis inspired the complaints about Black defense training. Harris even rejected calling the work inequalities discrimination. He claimed that southern employment practices "were not 'discriminatory' but simply 'traditional'—it was not a matter of correcting 'discrimination' down here but of attempting to modify 'traditions.'" US Commissioner of Education J. W. Studebaker tried to clarify the federal position in April 1942 when he claimed that director Mobley would develop plans to provide training for Black Southerners in aircraft riveting, sheet metal work, fabrication, and sub-assembly.[42]

Despite Studebaker's pledge, two months later little had been done to solve the training disparity in Georgia for potential Bell Bomber employees. At the Birmingham hearings, Mobley detailed that as of June 1, 1942, Georgia had spent $1.43 million to train white defense workers but less than $150,000 to prepare Black workers for defense jobs. The state spent only $10,000 on equipment at the Black Booker T. Washington High School, the sole Black training locale in Atlanta, while spending $175,000 on equipment for defense training at the city's white schools. Mobley testified that "a constitutional limitation" required separate schools, which he offered as a reasonable justification for the discriminatory spending on defense training. After all, in the 1939–1940 school year, Georgia spent $55.56 on each white elementary and secondary student but only $16.94 on each pre-college Black student.[43] For Mobley and other state education officials, segregation necessarily entailed racial inequities.

Several months after the Birmingham hearings, Georgia established some limited training opportunities for Black residents interested in aircraft jobs. In November 1942, Georgia officials established the first Black segregated training facility for potential Bell Bomber workers (and the first for Black aircraft workers in the Deep South)—the Booker T. Washington Aircraft School. The Atlanta NUL helped recruit students for the school, which required full-time training, without pay, for three weeks. The school originally offered classes only during the day but added a night session in May 1943. Each course, however, could accommodate only seventy-five students. Most of the trainees at the Black aircraft school were women, perhaps because Bell Bomber had already announced that it anticipated using female employees for many jobs.[44]

Even though the training situation for Black Georgians improved by the end of 1942, Bell Bomber remained reluctant to utilize many Black workers at the facility, especially in skilled positions. Initially, the company either turned away or offered laborer or semi-skilled jobs to Black trainees from the Washington School who applied for skilled jobs at Bell Bomber. As in Mobile, Bell Aircraft officials feared that placing Black employees in the top-paying jobs would cause white workers to leave the company or create the possibility for white violence. James V. Carmichael, the county attorney who became the Bell Bomber Plant manager in 1944, blamed "lower type" white people, the "hill-billies of Georgia with deeply entrenched prejudice," for the company's inability to take a stronger stand in favor of upgrading Black workers.[45]

By the end of 1943 and into 1944, when employment at Bell Bomber expanded rapidly as the aircraft facility moved toward full production (not achieved until the fall of 1944), the local labor market had tightened significantly. Despite the labor shortage, Black individuals struggled to secure jobs at the Marietta aircraft factory. As late as February 1944, the company submitted employment orders to the local USES office that listed the types of jobs available "and the races desired" for each job. To fill the request for white employees made by Bell Bomber, local WMC and USES officials, despite their previous plans, allowed the company to recruit white workers from outside the immediate area. Rejected Black applicants complained to the FEPC, and committee officials objected to the outside recruitment of workers when the company refused to hire Black workers available locally—it was a clear instance of employment discrimination. The FEPC regional director in Atlanta, A. Bruce Hunt, who favored a plan of gradual integration at the giant aircraft plant, in May 1944 asked the Atlanta WMC to cut off USES referral services to Bell Bomber for labor recruits unless the positions were open to all workers, but the WMC refused to act.[46] Local labor mobilization officials did not want to impose penalties on a company merely trying to preserve local standards of race relations.

The FEPC continued to object to the hiring practices of Bell Bomber, so in July 1944, the company took action to try to dampen federal oversight. Bell

Bomber acquired a former National Youth Administration site on Roswell Road and created a separate facility—designated as Department 86—where Black skilled and semi-skilled workers would work on the construction of assemblies and subassemblies for the leading edges of the B-29 wings.[47] The segregated arrangements at Bell Bomber resembled the Mobile compromise, which tried to satisfy the nondiscrimination requirements of FDR's executive order on employment discrimination while maintaining racial segregation and white privilege.

As part of its effort to create a segregated workspace for skilled Black workers, in August 1944 Bell Bomber, with the support of the Atlanta NUL, took over the training program at Washington Aircraft School. The company provided additional equipment and began paying trainees sixty-five cents an hour (the same amount that white trainees had long received). It also screened potential apprentices at the school by giving them an intelligence test prior to admission, which allowed the company and the Atlanta NUL to develop a skilled Black workforce for Bell Bomber from the most educated segment of Black society in the Atlanta area. After August 1944, those who completed the course at the Washington Aircraft School received jobs as drill press operators, airplane assemblers, and riveters in Department 86, at a starting salary of seventy-five cents an hour. The number of Black trainees at the Washington School, however, remained relatively small compared to the number of white residents who had access to instruction in aircraft production skills. In addition, as at ADDSCO in Mobile, the segregation arrangement at Bell Bomber meant a cap on the number and type of positions available to Black skilled workers. The school closed for good in May 1945, and the company began offering a segregated in-house course for Black trainees, although by that point, full-scale production had almost ended.[48]

Department 86 eventually employed more than 500 skilled Black workers. In early 1945, Bell Bomber also created some segregated skilled departments within the main Marietta plant. For instance, the company trained Black employees for jobs in the Drop Hammer and Foundry Departments and moved the white workers there to other departments at the giant factory. Clarence Mitchell saw this procedure as "not in any sense a step toward compliance, because it cannot possibly lead to equal job opportunity." Overall, the company never had more than 800 Black workers in skilled positions, which represented about one-third of the Black labor force employed at Bell Bomber during the period of peak production. And Black workers never comprised more than 10 percent of the aircraft facility's total staff. The kitchen department was the only integrated location at the company; everything else, including water fountains, restrooms, and cafeterias, remained strictly segregated. Although the FEPC did not sign off on the Bell Bomber plan and continued to press the company on various issues of racial discrimination, the creation of Department 86 undercut Hunt's plans for integrated employment at Bell Bomber and emboldened local WMC and USES officials to continue aiding the company in its efforts to recruit more white labor from outside the Atlanta area.[49]

The small number of Black workers who did get jobs at Bell Bomber earned significantly more than Black people in the Atlanta area typically received. According to a November 1944 report from the Atlanta NUL, even menial Black workers at Bell Bomber saw more in their pay envelope than educated professionals. One Black woman with a college degree and a white-collar job, who had been making $11.50 a week, took a job as a maid at Bell Bomber, which paid significantly more. Skilled employees could make as much as $180 a month. By comparison, only a small percentage of Atlanta's Black teachers earned more than $125 a month. The economic benefits of working at Bell Bomber help explain why Black individuals who did secure a job there did not protest racial segregation at the plant.[50]

While the segregated arrangements at Bell Bomber provided economic benefits for at least some Black workers in the Atlanta area, the Department 86 solution did not eliminate racial discrimination, as even company officials readily acknowledged. When Witherspoon Dodge, who replaced Bruce Hunt as the FEPC regional director, and Dillard Lasseter, regional director of the WMC, met with James V. Carmichael in March 1945 to discuss the still-limited opportunities for Black workers, Carmichael readily admitted the company did not comply with the nondiscrimination mandate. According to Dodge, Carmichael "was quite frank in stating that the company does not intend to integrate Negro workers alongside of white employees, even though he knows and admits that he is thereby violating the President's Executive Order." Carmichael told the two federal officials that he could only take up the individual complaints pending (twenty or so) and find jobs for them "at their maximum skills." After the conference, the company also agreed to open a new job classification to Black employees: painters. However, Bell Bomber only committed to paying its Black painters $.95 an hour, even though the union wage for that job was $1.25 an hour, a rate of pay Black painters in the city of Atlanta already received.[51] As usual, racial segregation meant racial discrimination, even on a basic issue such as equal pay for similar jobs.

As at ADDSCO, labor unions at Bell Bomber, while helping overall to promote better working conditions and pay on the job, offered little help in ending racial discrimination against Black workers. Two unions operated at the Marietta aircraft plant, the AFL's International Association of Machinists and the CIO's United Automobile Workers (UAW), although the CIO represented 90 percent of Bell Bomber workers. While the Machinists did not allow Black members, the UAW officially embraced nondiscrimination. The CIO local supported the creation of the separate skilled operation on Roswell Road and helped some unskilled Black workers at the main plant receive training for upgrading their positions. The UAW local, however, despite its stated principles of nondiscrimination, generally kept its Black members at arm's length out of fear of alienating its white members. Black unionists met separately from white ones and had little say in union business.[52]

The FEPC helped create segregated skilled workspaces at ADDSCO and Bell Bomber, which provided important opportunities for Black workers in the Deep South, even if these arrangements fell far short of achieving the goal of nondiscrimination in employment in the country's war industries. In Mississippi, the FEPC had even less success, either before or after the Birmingham hearings. Like Black citizens elsewhere, those in Mississippi wanted their fair share of defense jobs. In the summer of 1941, soon after FDR issued Executive Order 8802, the War Department authorized $14.5 million to build the Mississippi Ordnance Plant (MOP), a facility near Flora, Mississippi, about twenty-three miles northwest of Jackson. The factory, which would manufacture smokeless powder bags, could employ about 3,500 workers, many of them women. Most assumed that the employees would come from four surrounding counties. Since that area had a Black population of 55 percent, Black residents of the area expected that they would find work at the plant.[53]

As construction neared completion, however, it became clear that General Tire Engineering Company, a subsidiary of General Tire & Rubber Company of Akron, Ohio, which received an $11 million War Department contract to operate the business, planned to reserve all the production jobs for white residents. FEPC officials suspected that the company had bowed to local pressures to limit Black jobs at the factory to the most menial positions. More specifically, middle-class white women worried about losing their domestic help, area farmers did not want to see the supply of "cheap day-wage farm labor" evaporate, and local business leaders had promoted the facility as a place where white women in the area could work. The USES office in

Jackson discouraged Black applicants to the MOP by telling them that "all the jobs ... are going to be given to white people," even though USES officials admitted that they had not talked to General Tire about its employment needs.[54]

As word of plans for employment at the MOP emerged, Black residents in and around Jackson mobilized to protest. On April 8, 1942, about 500 Black citizens gathered in Jackson—described as "the biggest Mass Meeting held in the State in many years." After the meeting, a committee of leaders created a ten-page document that it sent to FDR, Congress, the secretary of war, the FEPC, and other government entities. The document pointed out that Black people comprised more than half of Mississippi's population, claimed that 50,000 Black residents in the Jackson area needed work, and urged the federal government to cancel General Tire's contract if it would not abide by the FEPC nondiscrimination directive. The petition also asserted that "the Negroes are the only 100 percenters as a race group in this country today when it comes to real loyalty and patriotism." The mass meeting sparked a renewed effort by the FEPC to put pressure on the Mississippi USES and General Tire to end its discriminatory plans. After FEPC investigator John Beecher met with company officials and representatives of the USES in Jackson in May 1942, General Tire decided that "applications from Negroes will be freely accepted" and that both white and Black applicants would face the same "screening process." The company also agreed to consider creating a separate bag-loading line staffed by Black women. The USES, for its part, also promised to begin accepting Black applications for positions at General Tire.[55]

Although the FEPC seemed to have negotiated a settlement in this case—like the one it would approve in Mobile a year later—it soon became clear that the problems surrounding discriminatory hiring at the Flora bag loading plant did not end. Even as John Beecher worked out an agreement with General Tire officials and the USES, hostility toward Black Mississippians seeking work at the ammunition facility persisted. While in Mississippi working on the Flora case, Beecher held several meetings with Black citizens. At one of these events, two Jackson police detectives appeared, took down the names of everyone at the meeting, and, as Beecher reported, "indicated their own disagreement with national policy [the FEPC directive]." The agreement that General Tire worked out with the FEPC spared it from having to testify at the upcoming Birmingham hearings (General Tire was on an early potential witness list), but the company never began production in Flora. Officially, the government claimed that the MOP never opened because "more efficient plants" already existed to do a similar job. It seems unusual, however, that the government would scrap a $25 million ammunition factory because of too much production capacity during a military buildup. And in August 1942, the War Department converted the Mississippi Ordnance Plant to an Army Special Forces Ordnance Unit Training Center. John Young of the *Pittsburgh Courier* may have gotten closer to the truth of what happened to the MOP in his description of the site after he visited it several years later, in February 1945. He saw what he called an $18 million "boondoggle, [with] buildings stretched over a large area like tombstones. Machines . . . built for the purpose of sending munitions to our fighting men overseas . . . stilled by the hard hand of prejudice."[56]

The FEPC had also called the Ingalls Shipbuilding Corporation to appear at the Birmingham hearings, but no company representatives or Black complainants appeared to offer testimony. In the fall of 1941, Perry Howard, a Black member of the Republican National Committee from Mississippi, had complained to Eugene Davidson of the New Negro Alliance, a civil rights group based in Washington, DC, that the large shipyard in Pascagoula had hired hundreds of new white workers yet few Black ones. In addition, Howard noted that no welding training existed for Black people on the Mississippi Gulf Coast. Davidson referred Howard's complaint to the newly formed FEPC, which launched an investigation. The company president, Monro Lanier, told the FEPC in November 1941 that it employed Black workers at the shipyard in proportion to their numbers in the local population, relatively small compared to their numbers statewide. Lanier also blamed the AFL union at the yard for limiting training opportunities to white citizens. Other aspects of Lanier's response to the FEPC, however, suggested the company's true motives behind the failure to hire more Black workers. Lanier claimed that Black residents in the Pascagoula area "are not adapted by experience or desire to skilled mechanical pursuits." He also chided the FEPC "that great care be taken at this time to the end that no irritation or conflict be raised between the white and Colored races. This is particularly true as it applies to the South."[57]

Ingalls Shipbuilding simply preferred to maintain traditional hiring practices, which meant reserving all but the most menial jobs for white workers. Without much Black organizational support, such as a vigorous chapter of the NAACP or the NUL, or a group of Black leaders committed to pressing for change (as existed in the Jackson area), further complaints about Ingalls's hiring practices did not emerge. The FEPC had plenty of other complaints to process and try to resolve, so a company like Ingalls could simply operate below the radar of the federal nondiscrimination mandate. Beyond hiring a few skilled Black painters, the Ingalls shipyard employed a relatively small number of unskilled Black laborers at its shipyard.

When the FEPC got around to questioning the hiring practices of Ingalls as part of an examination of local USES offices in the summer of 1944, local manpower officials simply denied any wrongdoing. During the FEPC inspection, the examiner, James Tipton, discovered that the USES office had neatly divided all the open employment orders from Ingalls by race, with none of the skilled jobs, including for welding trainees, open to Black men and women. When Tipton questioned the local USES office manager, a Mr. Price, he reportedly said "that Negroes had not been referred to Ingalls Shipbuilding Corporation as welder trainees because . . . he had been advised by representatives of the corporation that Negroes were not desired in such capacities." The area field supervisor of the WMC, Charles Ballard, later "corrected" the USES official and asserted that the Ingalls company agreed that "applicants for welding or for any other occupation should not be selected on the basis of color." The lack of Black hiring in the area, according to Ballard, lay solely in the fact that no qualified Black people had applied for skilled positions at the company. As in Alabama and Georgia, potential Black employees had few opportunities to get the training that might have "qualified" them for skilled employment. In January 1944, the Pascagoula training center enrolled 883 white students and 0 Black trainees. Statewide, only 1 of Mississippi's 10 major training sites, the one in Meridian, offered a course for Black citizens that had any relevance to the shipbuilding industry.[58] Ballard's assertions notwithstanding, the Ingalls Shipbuilding Corporation clearly preferred to use white labor almost exclusively.

The gains that skilled Black workers made at ADDSCO and Bell Bomber during World War II did not last long. The last ship launched from one of ADDSCO's segregated shipways was the *Rock Landing*, on September 10, 1945. Afterward, the company laid off practically all the skilled Black employees or downgraded them to lower-paying jobs. Those welders who moved to laborer positions at the repair yard, which continued to have a significant amount of business in the postwar period, saw their hourly pay decline from as much as a $1.20 to as low as $.63. After the defeat of Japan in August 1945, the government cancelled the B-29 program, and Bell Bomber quickly shut down production and employment at the plant. The government used the massive facility as a gigantic storage shed until 1951, when it leased the building to Lockheed Corporation to overhaul B-29s. Black laborers still found limited opportunities at the refurbished plane factory, but Lockheed and the AFL's International Association of Machinists remained rigidly segregated well into the 1960s.[59]

Although the FEPC tried to alter patterns of racial discrimination in employment during World War II in the Deep South (and elsewhere), the committee faced an uphill battle as employers, labor unions, and white employees of federal manpower mobilization agencies all shared entrenched attitudes about the "proper" place of Black workers. In January 1945, WMC officials claimed that ninety essential war plants in Alabama, Florida, Mississippi, South Carolina, Tennessee, and Georgia, many associated with shipbuilding and aircraft manufacturing, faced a shortage of more than 14,000 workers. The Black press recognized the contradiction of failing to fully utilize Black workers to fully operate the country's defense industries. But white communities and federal officials focused their efforts on evading the FEPC's nondiscrimination pledge, despite the threat to America's war effort. And the failure to create a permanent FEPC at the end of the war ensured that white Southerners could promote further industrialization of the region after the war while keeping Black Southerners confined to a secondary economic role.[60]

4
"A Typical Crowded War Community": Pascagoula, Mississippi

On Thursday, December 16, 1943, the US Senate Subcommittee on Wartime Health and Education convened in the library of Pascagoula High School for three days of hearings. But only the subcommittee's chairman, Claude Pepper—perhaps the most liberal member of the South's Democratic congressional delegation—was present. The Senate had created Pepper's subcommittee in the summer of 1943 to study and investigate "deficiencies" in health and education in order "to promote the war and victory for our forces." A big concern arose from reports that 3 million men had been rejected for military service "because of mental, moral, educational, or physical deficiencies," a disproportionate number of those from the South. The subcommittee held its first hearings in Washington, DC, on the topic of juvenile delinquency. Testimony suggested that, among other factors, both a lack of educational opportunity and inadequate health facilities contributed to a rise in juvenile delinquency during the war years.[1]

Two weeks later, the Pascagoula hearings began. Subcommittee investigators had already collected information and lined up potential witnesses. Over three days, more than ninety people offered testimony, including labor leaders from the Pascagoula Metal Trades Council, federal and city officials, educators such as school superintendent Thomas R. Wells, and shipyard workers. Several Black citizens also provided information. M. L. Brown and Edward B. Wright Jr., leaders of the Pascagoula Civic Improvement Association, a Black organization formed during the war, testified, and A. N. Bennette, pastor of the town's African Methodist Zion Church, provided a statement entered into the hearing records. Although twenty-five Black citizens in Jackson County, including several who worked at Ingalls, had formed a chapter of the National Association for the Advancement of Colored People (NAACP) in early 1943, no one offered testimony on behalf of the civil rights organization, which seems to have been a clandestine group, as few traces of its wartime activity exist. Representatives from the Ingalls Shipbuilding

Company also presented evidence, although the chairman of the company, Robert Ingalls, did not appear.[2]

The witnesses recounted problems in many areas, including housing, education, health care, temporary food shortages, and an increase in crime and juvenile delinquency. Walter R. Gulley, mayor of Pascagoula and a wholesale grocer, told a reporter covering the hearings, "I don't suppose you'll find things worse anywhere in the whole country than you will right here." Yet throughout the proceedings, Claude Pepper tried to reassure city residents that the location had not been singled out because it "was a bad community or that it was particularly in need of any remedial measures." Rather, the Florida senator emphasized that the town was "a typical crowded war community," and the investigation hoped to establish facts that would illuminate a national problem.[3] The difficulties that Pascagoula faced as a result of wartime mobilization had deep roots in a region that had paid relatively little attention to social welfare issues in the preceding decades. In many cases, wartime mobilization merely worsened existing difficulties, and finding solutions to these problems proved only partly successful.

For one thing, the town's primary employer, Ingalls Shipbuilding, did little to ease the troubles created by the rapid expansion of the gigantic shipyard. At the Pascagoula hearings, Senator Pepper indicated that Robert Ingalls would help address the town's problems, an opinion the senator based on a meeting he had with the industrialist while in Mississippi. Newspaper columnist Drew Pearson, however, claimed that when the two men met at the Ingalls shipyard, the senator expressed shock at Ingalls's anti-FDR attitude, which included asking Pepper to "lead a revolt of Southern Senators against the Administration." At the time, the Ingalls company had recently launched a nationwide recruitment campaign for additional shipyard workers, and Robert Ingalls believed the hearings had given his business a "national black eye." Robert Feltus, staff director for Pepper's subcommittee, thought Ingalls really feared bad publicity from the hearings and associated newspaper stories. In the opinion of Feltus, Ingalls remained "unwilling to establish minimum health and welfare standards even at government expense."[4]

Beyond the fact that the town's largest employer offered little assistance to address the problems that accompanied economic mobilization, other factors also played a role in limiting solutions. Although the federal government provided help during the war years to address the most pressing needs created by mobilization in Pascagoula and elsewhere, the federal resources allocated remained relatively small, especially compared to the billions in federal expenditures allocated for constructing and operating war plants and military facilities. At the same time, any attempt to sort out the problems created as southern communities like Pascagoula mobilized for war had to contend with the entrenched negative attitudes that rural migrants held toward the federal government and urbanization. Finally, equitably resolving the stresses placed on wartime society remained impossible because of white Southerners' unwavering commitment to white supremacy.[5]

Wartime economic mobilization created a housing shortage. Nationwide, perhaps 9 million people who relocated to work in war jobs required housing. The Lanham Act of 1940 provided federal funding for housing and other needs of communities affected by wartime changes, and between 1940 and 1945 the federal government spent $2.5 billion on new housing. The National Housing Agency, created in 1942, coordinated the building of 800,000 units during the war. Federal officials disagreed, however, on what type of housing to construct. Some wanted to use the opportunity not only to solve the immediate housing crisis created by wartime expansion but also to pave the way for long-term, permanent solutions to housing problems faced by many areas. Others, including many private real estate brokers and bankers, favored the creation of more temporary housing, so as not to compete with private builders and sellers once the war emergency passed. In the end, the latter option won the day, and during the war, the federal government focused mostly on providing temporary structures. That decision may have more efficiently (and cheaply) solved the immediate housing shortage of the war years, but it led to negative postwar consequences. The nature of World War II home building contributed to a severe housing shortage at the end of the war. In the late 1940s and 1950s, private developers—assisted by the federal government—launched a suburban housing boom that eased this housing crisis but also created new environmental challenges and further entrenched the racial segregation that had long characterized US housing markets.[6]

A housing crunch already existed in the rapidly growing town of Pascagoula and the wider Jackson County area by the time the Ingalls Shipbuilding Corporation launched its first ship in the summer of 1940. The town had 1,544 dwellings, while the rest of the county had another 3,907 houses. As workers flocked to the area, they set up housekeeping in trailers, tents, and houseboats or congregated in existing homes. In October 1940, Robert Ingalls complained to his congressman, William Colmer, that the company faced a problem in retaining workers because of inadequate housing. He pleaded that "ship builders who are presently contributing to the

Thousands of rural migrants moved to work in Mobile's two shipyards during World War II, but housing was soon in short supply, so people sheltered where they could. These families lived in small trailers in Spanish Fort, across Mobile Bay from the shipyards. *Courtesy of the Doy Leale McCall Rare Book and Manuscript Library, University of South Alabama*

defense program under their own financial power [men like him] should and must be protected in this situation." Two months later, the US Navy began construction on almost 700 "semi-permanent" frame houses. Each structure, built on concrete piers on large lots, had asbestos shingle siding, asphalt roofs, screened porches, electric refrigerators, gas ranges, space heaters, and hot water heaters. After they were completed in August 1941, the US Maritime Commission managed the properties for a time before turning the operation over to the Federal Public Housing Authority (FPHA), but the development continued to be known as the Maritime Housing Project (MHP). Compared to the housing constructed later in the war in the Pascagoula area, the MHP offered deluxe accommodations for Ingalls's workers.[7]

However, this initial foray of the federal government into the Pascagoula housing market generated controversy. As construction on the MHP neared

"A TYPICAL CROWDED WAR COMMUNITY" 97

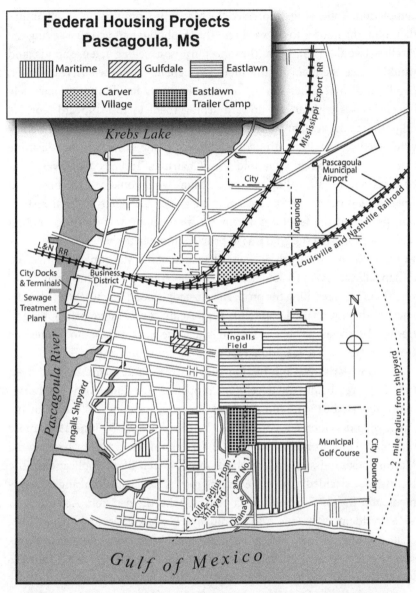

The federal government built five housing projects in Pascagoula during World War II, all roughly one mile from the Ingalls Shipyard. Two of the housing areas—Gulfdale and Carver Village—were for Black workers. Though located separate from the white housing projects, the Black lodgings were of an equal or better quality than the white dwellings. *Source: Box 26, Senate Subcommittee on Wartime Health and Education, Records of the US Senate, Record Group 46, National Archives, Washington, DC. Map created by Jeffrey Patton*

completion, Robert Ingalls pressed the Maritime Commission to sell, rather than rent, the houses to his workers. The shipbuilder argued that selling the dwellings would accomplish "the same purpose as selling defense bonds" and would enable the plant to hire more permanent employees. A year earlier, Ingalls and some other Pascagoula entrepreneurs had built approximately fifteen houses with an eye toward selling them to the shipyard workers migrating to the area, but almost none of the purchasers worked at the shipyard. Even so, Ingalls continued to lobby for home sales with the Maritime Commission leadership. He told Vice Chairman Thomas Woodward that he could locate "a hustling real estate man" who would sell the houses to "men of good character and earning capacity." Although no legal restriction prevented the federal government from selling war housing, renting made more sense if the goal was to provide immediate shelter for migratory workers in war industry. E. S. Land, chairman of the Maritime Commission, told Ingalls that even if it sold the homes to his employees, nothing could prevent them from reselling the properties to people not doing war work. Ingalls rejected this rationale. Despite his supposedly conservative principles and free market ideals, he believed that if "a defense worker ceases to be one, the Government may, at its option, repossess the house and resell it."[8]

The US Maritime Commission moved to exclude Black tenants from the MHP even before the development opened. The Lanham Act had originally allocated $12 million for Black housing, including 100 units in the Pascagoula development constructed by the US Navy. By June 1941, more than 400 white workers had applied for one of the new houses, but the Maritime Commission had received only fourteen Black applications. The commission decided to turn the entire project into a white housing development, and Ingalls Shipbuilding concurred with the decision. According to Vice President W. R. Guest, the company's Black workers already had adequate housing, and any additional units "could be of a very inexpensive construction and located in the area where colored people now live."[9] In other words, the MHP was too good for Ingalls's Black employees—who at the time were mostly locals. In addition, the housing would not preserve segregation between the races.

Black shipyard workers, however, objected to the decision to convert the entire MHP to a white neighborhood. Edward B. Wright Jr., who worked as a porter at Ingalls Shipbuilding, disputed the claim that all area Black residents had adequate housing. Wright claimed that many Black employees were eager to move to the new houses, for "in doing so they will rise to a higher, more sanitary, and a more progressive standard of living." Nevertheless, the Maritime Commission refused the original Black applicants and others and promised instead the development of a fifty-home project "in the negro section between Moss Point and Pascagoula." The move to block wartime housing projects for Black defense workers also occurred elsewhere in the United States, including in Arkansas, Virginia, and most notably, Detroit. There, white residents objected to the creation of the Sojourner Truth Housing Project, designed for Black war workers, and the controversy led to a racial confrontation in February 1942 that resulted in more than forty injuries and hundreds of arrests.[10]

By March 1942, Ingalls officials believed the state of local housing had become "a very acute problem." By the end of the year, Pascagoula's population approached 20,000, a fourfold increase over the prewar count. Those numbers continued to grow in 1943 and into early 1944, when the Ingalls shipyard reached its peak wartime employment. As additional workers moved to the Pascagoula area to work at Ingalls, the federal government constructed housing in 1942 and 1943. The additional structures primarily housed Ingalls's white shipyard workers, and by the end of 1943, federal housing projects could accommodate more than 13,000 white residents.[11]

The Eastlawn Housing Project, a term used to describe all federal housing developments for white tenants other than the original MHP, eventually provided a variety of accommodations. More than 750 one-room apartments had two beds, two chairs, and a hot plate, an appliance that "was designed only for getting breakfast," according to local FPHA housing manager Harrison Otis. Eastlawn also contained more than 1,000 temporary houses of various sizes (one-, two-, and three-bedroom). In addition, Eastlawn had a trailer park consisting of 450 used trailers, which according to Otis badly needed paint and waterproofing. Depending on the size, each trailer could accommodate four to six people. Some families squatted in the park, using tents as shelter. The Eastlawn Trailer Camp had men's and women's bathhouses, each with showers and toilets. Five dormitories in Eastlawn offered 360 single-occupancy rooms, with one building set aside for single women workers, but few workers wanted to live there. In late 1943, only ten women lived in the women's dorm, and overall, one-third of the dormitory spaces remained unoccupied. Rental rates ranged from $5 a week for a dormitory room or a small trailer to $48.50 a month for a three-bedroom, furnished house in Eastlawn; monthly Ingalls's wages ranged from $120 to $192 for most workers. Private homeowners who rented out extra rooms provided some limited supplemental living options.[12]

The Ingalls company favored temporary and "lower price housing," since many of its workers did not earn premium wages, and the federal government obliged. The US Maritime Commission provided a lump-sum contract for the construction of Eastlawn and did not require inspection of the work during or after completion of the project. As a result, the housing proved less than ideal. The houses in Eastlawn were heated with gas, but the gas lines were poorly designed and small, so the system could not adequately warm many of the dwellings. In addition, the builders located the heating vents in the ceiling, which limited the effectiveness of the system. The entire project had almost no outdoor lighting: only five streetlights in the apartment/dorm section and none in the single-family housing area. Although the federal government began work in late 1942 on a citywide sewer system in a town that primarily used septic tanks, which quickly became overburdened with the influx of war workers, that project was not completed until 1944. Without adequate pumps, sewage rose to the surface on many of the housing plots. For more than a year, in one section, sewage ran into a fifteen-foot open ditch that drained directly into the Gulf of Mexico, damaging a valuable state-owned oyster reef just offshore. The city did not pick up garbage from the area regularly. And instead of sidewalks, the Eastlawn area had shell walks, which tended to damage shoes, a rationed item. The apartments did not have electric refrigerators, and ice deliveries to the neighborhood occurred only three times a week. None of the housing in Eastlawn had phone service, which meant that tenants had a twenty-minute walk if they needed to make a telephone call.[13]

Tenants complained about the conditions in Eastlawn, and when the federal manager failed to respond, they formed the Eastlawn Tenants' Association in the spring of 1943, led by H. M. Bloomer, a pipe fitter at Ingalls who lived in one of the apartments. The group initially received a somewhat dismissive response from the local federal housing manager, but in August 1943, a new FPHA manager came to Pascagoula, Harrison Otis, originally from Wisconsin. Although he proved more responsive to the tenants' concerns, change happened slowly. Otis secured a contract to start fixing the heating problems, although tenants still complained that it was "a botched-up job." In the fall, when the weather turned cold, 1,000 tenants signed pledges to withhold rent payments until the FPHA fixed the heating problem. Several hundred tenants ended up carrying out a rent strike in

October and November 1943. By mid-1944, federal and local officials had fixed the heating and garbage problems, but many of the other deficiencies in Eastlawn remained unsolved. In addition, even after the new citywide sewer system came online, the town's waste runoff problems persisted. Federal planners designed the new system for a population of 15,000, and by the summer of 1944, Pascagoula's population had already grown to twice that number.[14]

The poor conditions that existed in Eastlawn contributed to an occupancy rate in the development that rarely reached 100 percent, despite the massive in-migration of white workers. Other factors also played a role. The one part of Eastlawn that always remained full was the trailer park, which seemed to appeal to country folk used to minimal accommodations and unwilling to pay much for rent. When an interviewer asked one man with a large family crammed into a trailer why he did not move to a larger house, he replied, "What's good enough for the boys in Africa is good enough for me." At one point in 1943, the FPHA announced plans to discontinue trailer housing, but after an uproar from the residents, the agency rescinded the order. In addition, many Ingalls workers continued to make long commutes because they preferred to stay in their rural neighborhoods (like the residents of northeast Mississippi who commuted to Grenada or Muscle Shoals for war jobs) and do some farming in their "spare time." Some workers who did move to Eastlawn tried to preserve a semblance of the farm in the city. People planted Victory gardens, and many kept chickens, ducks, geese, and pigeons. In March 1944, Otis responded to "chicken complaints" from some tenants, who disliked "the flies, odors, noise, clutter, mice and stray hens that frequently accompany poultry raising."[15]

The federal government also built housing for Black defense workers in Pascagoula. In the early 1940s, Black residents in the town, as in other Mississippi communities, had substandard housing. Local Black neighborhoods had few streetlights and inadequate sewer systems. Paved roads stopped on the edge of the Black housing areas. In early 1942, A. D. Stewart, regional director of the Farm Security Administration (FSA), described the housing for Black residents in Pascagoula as "squalid, unsanitary hovels." Initially, war mobilization provided little incentive to improve Black housing in town, since Ingalls Shipbuilding Company employed few Black workers. However, as the shipyard grew and as job opportunities for Black workers improved nationwide, Ingalls found it harder to rely on the local Black labor pool for its growing unskilled labor needs.[16]

To entice local Black citizens to stay in Pascagoula and to attract some Black migrants to town required adequate housing, and by the end of 1942, federal agencies had established two Black housing projects. The FSA spent approximately $135,000 to build fifty five-room temporary houses, which opened in the spring of 1942, in a project known as Gulfdale. Each dwelling, built on a 50' × 90' lot, had two bedrooms, a combination dining room/kitchen, a living room, and a bathroom. Black defense workers paid $15 a month rent for the houses. The FPHA added forty-eight efficiency apartments and a thirty-six-room dormitory to the development later in 1942. Another Black federal housing project, Carver Village, located adjacent to the Louisville and Nashville Railroad in northeast Pascagoula, included one-, two-, and three-bedroom houses, all red hollow tile construction. Each dwelling had a gas range with oven, an electric refrigerator, and a hot water heater. The development even had real sidewalks between the houses. The 225 permanent residences rented at $20 to $25 a month, depending on size.[17]

The federal housing built for Black workers proved better in many respects than that provided for white employees, and the new dwellings, even the temporary ones, represented a significant upgrade over the town's existing housing stock for Black residents. When investigators for the Wartime Health and Education Subcommittee toured local federal housing projects in November 1943, they described Carver Village as having "an extremely tidy appearance." Those African Americans lucky enough to secure a spot at Gulfdale or Carver Village clearly had lodgings better than those for Black residents in the rest of Pascagoula. In fact, already insufficient Black housing in the town became even more unlivable as the wartime population swelled. At one location in 1943, three Black families lived in a four-room house. In another Black dwelling, a married couple and two single men shared a spare bedroom that had two beds. M. L. Brown, who became chair of the Pascagoula Civic Improvement Association, said that when he first moved to Pascagoula, he lived in a four-room cottage with thirteen other people, with "all practically sleeping over one another."[18]

Other Deep South war communities did even less to address the housing needs of African American war workers. In May 1943, Black workers comprised almost 20 percent of the 41,000 employees in Mobile's two shipyards, but as a Bureau of Agricultural Economics (BAE) official noted in October 1942, "practically no provision for the increased housing needs of the Negroes has been made." Indeed, among the thousands of dwellings then under construction by the federal government, the units set aside for Black workers numbered fewer than one hundred. As a result, new Black arrivals in Mobile typically boarded with established residents. In Marietta, Georgia, African Americans made up about 10 percent of the Bell Bomber plant workforce of almost 30,000, but the city made no effort to provide new housing for Black residents. The federal government built about 2,000 housing units in the town during the war, all for white workers. Private construction in the town, which expanded its city limits by 50 percent during the war, provided additional homes for Bell Bomber's white workers. Mayor Leon Blair noted that Marietta tried to control and plan the growth associated with the location of the huge airplane factory in town in a way that would preserve "a clean city, clean physically and morally." In part, Marietta officials achieved that objective by limiting the new housing built in Marietta during the war. Instead, Bell Bomber relied on a sizable commuting workforce, including many of the Black employees. The fact that the town had a trolley link to nearby Atlanta made employment of large numbers of commuters more feasible than in many other areas.[19]

The Pepper hearings in Pascagoula focused particular attention on how the wartime economic boom affected health care in the area. The Wartime Health and Education Subcommittee explicitly sought to determine how deficiencies in providing health services to poorer Americans everywhere and in certain parts of the country, such as the South, adversely affected the country's economic and military mobilization. In the process, the hearings offered a glimpse of the Deep South's ongoing health challenges, in some cases made worse by economic mobilization, as well as the impact of federal endeavors during the war years to improve medical services in the region.[20]

Despite almost a decade of health reform provided by various New Deal programs, health services in south Mississippi, as in the Deep South as a whole, still lagged behind the level of care in other parts of the country. At the Pascagoula hearings, Dr. L. C. Spencer, medical director at Ingalls Shipyard, who had also worked in Louisiana and Georgia, estimated that less than 10 percent of Southerners received adequate medical care. Compared to the rest of the country, the South had a shortage of both doctors and hospitals. The South's shortage of doctors, already critical before the war, only worsened during the conflict. By 1943, most counties in Mississippi had a doctor-to-patient ratio above 1:3,000, considered an "emergency" by public health officials. In Jackson County, the ratio approached 1:3,500. At least three Mississippi counties (Carroll, Kemper, and Walthall) had dramatically high ratios, greater than 1:15,000 in 1943. In addition, the state, with a million Black residents, had only fifty-eight Black doctors.[21]

In the early 1940s, the US Public Health Service (USPHS) considered the minimum safe hospital service as 4.5 beds per 1,000 population. In 1941, Mississippi had the fewest hospital beds (1.5 per 1,000 people) of any state in the nation. The almost total lack of hospital facilities for Black citizens in the state skewed that statistic substantially, as white patients had 2.4 beds per 1,000 people, while the corresponding ratio for Black Mississippians stood at 0.7 per 1,000 residents. In 1942, only forty-seven of the state's eighty-two counties even had a hospital, including Jackson County, which in 1931 had built a thirty-five-bed facility in Pascagoula. Even so, with the rapid growth of the county's population beginning around 1940, the county's only hospital offered only 1.6 beds per 1,000 citizens in 1942.[22]

During the war, the federal government invested funds to bolster health care across the country. The Lanham Act provided for the construction of additional hospital facilities, and Pascagoula received money to construct an addition to the city hospital, which more than doubled its size. The project provided for forty new beds: thirty-two for white patients and eight for Black residents. Continuing the practice begun during the New Deal, federal health care reform during the war typically improved services for both Black and white Southerners, though on a strictly segregated basis. Completed in the fall of 1943, the new addition created a hospital with a seemingly adequate capacity for the city's growing population. In December 1943, the expanded facility had an occupancy rate of 60 percent. The federal government also constructed an infirmary in the Eastlawn Housing Project in early 1943 and built two small infirmaries in the Black federal housing areas in 1944. Between November 1942 and December 1943, as the number of people coming to the shipyard community exploded, the number of doctors in the county increased from five to twelve. Despite the extra medical help, it remained difficult for area residents to see a doctor. Many recent migrants to the shipyard town were frustrated enough with the physician service available in Pascagoula that they returned to their home communities to seek medical attention for themselves or their families.[23]

With the passage of the Emergency Maternal and Infant Care (EMCI) program in 1943, the federal government offered pregnant women married to most servicemen a new and important (though short-lived) health benefit. It was available to the wives of men in the four lowest ranks in both the Army and Navy (87 percent of all enlisted men). The Children's Bureau of the US

Department of Labor distributed the funds as state grants, which allowed prenatal and postnatal care, as well as hospital services, for women who gave birth to 1.2 million American children (one of every seven) between 1943 and 1949, when the federal funding ended. The EMCI encouraged more women to give birth at hospitals, a national trend underway since the 1920s, but one less pronounced in more rural parts of the nation, especially among Black women. In Mississippi, in 1944, 70 percent of women still gave birth at home, although 70 percent of those who took advantage of the EMCI program that year chose a hospital delivery. Although Pascagoula was a war production town rather than the site of a military camp or base, many of the women in the area, including some who worked at the Ingalls shipyard, had husbands in the military and could participate in the EMCI program. During the first eight months of the program in 1943, fifty-six of the fifty-nine Pascagoula women who participated in the program accepted hospital care as part of their birthing plans. Public health officials in Mississippi believed that the significant move from midwives to hospitals alone improved the care that pregnant women received and reduced the state's high infant mortality rate.[24]

The federal funding for hospital construction and to support the EMCI demonstrated the benefits of national health reform efforts, but a more ambitious federal proposal during the war to improve health care for all Americans failed to gain traction. In the summer of 1943, congressional reformers introduced the Wagner-Murray-Dingell Bill, which proposed—for the first time—a national system of health insurance. While proponents of the bill thought that wartime idealism would help their cause, strong opposition from doctors and their professional organization, the American Medical Association, prevented passage of the measure.[25]

Public health officials recognized the value of compulsory health insurance, but they also acknowledged the power of the opposition to such a program. Dr. Felix J. Underwood, head of the Mississippi State Board of Health, testified at the Pascagoula hearings and explained to Senator Pepper that even with adequate health care facilities, many poor Mississippians could not pay for health services. Underwood thought that existing insurance programs worked well but helped relatively small numbers of people. He also understood that the proposal for a system of national health insurance faced robust opposition from doctors. Senator Pepper wondered if the federal government could create a system that would not "run afoul of the prejudices of the medical men and certain laymen," perhaps a class-based, tiered system of paying for health care: free health care for the poor, a group insurance plan for the middle-class, and private payment for the wealthy.[26] The creation of a comprehensive system of national health insurance, on the scale of a program like Social Security for retirement benefits, however, would continue to elude the efforts of reformers well into the twenty-first century.

Federal assistance in other areas, such as housing, also provided help with medical outcomes in war towns. For example, at the time of World War II, despite significant public health efforts in the preceding decades, hookworm remained a problem in parts of the South. A population with children who often went barefoot, as well as the presence of unsanitary outhouses, continued to provide a welcome environment for fecal-borne intestinal organisms that infected poorer Southerners with the disease. In December 1943, the Jackson County Board of Supervisors estimated that only 2 percent of rural dwellings had "sanitary privies." The rest of the houses in the county either had no outhouses or unsanitary ones. A survey of the county's white schools in April 1942 determined that more than 40 percent of the county's white children had hookworm; one rural school had an infection rate of 92 percent. While the county made little progress eradicating hookworm during the war years, Pascagoula largely brought the disease under control, primarily because of the federal housing projects. Though still inadequate, the waste disposal improvements that accompanied this construction, and the creation of a citywide sewer system, generated more hygienic conditions. Even the Eastlawn Trailer Park had toilets connected to a sanitary sewer. All these improvements reduced the conditions in which hookworm could thrive in the city of Pascagoula.[27]

Ingalls shipyard, with its massive federal contracts, provided additional health services for its employees, although the company's health care operation remained less than ideal. Ingalls had a medical outfit that included three first-aid stations, as well as a larger infirmary, which could perform minor surgical procedures such as suturing wounds. Four doctors staffed the health facilities. In November 1943, almost half of the medical department's cases involved eye problems, either foreign particles in the eye or flash burns caused by the welding equipment. Proper safety eyewear could have prevented many of these injuries, but both the flaunting of safety procedures by workers and a weak integration of the medical department into the company's operations diminished the necessary safety protocols. Many shipyard workers refused to wear the proper eyewear available; they also frequently shunned the respirators the company provided to protect against the fumes from lead-based and zinc chromide paint. At the same time, the medical and safety departments at Ingalls did not work together, and neither reported directly to the company's top management, which meant that their issues did not always receive priority attention. Dr. Spencer estimated that he spent 75 percent of his time "fighting management"; he had to navigate four layers of management to reach Robert Ingalls. Because of the organizational structure of the company, the medical department had little input on several issues that affected worker health: basic sanitation, first-aid instruction, and food-handling standards.[28]

Because of the way Robert Ingalls arranged his contracts with the US government, utilizing lump-sum payments, he never considered adopting the kind of generous health services provided to workers by some other shipbuilders, such as California's Henry Kaiser, or by other Deep South companies, such as Tennessee Iron and Coal Company in Birmingham and Standard Oil in Louisiana. Indeed, Ingalls sought to keep the medical expenses of the company to a minimum to boost his bottom line. In a state with no workman's compensation law (the only one in the country without such a statute), Ingalls employed a large staff of insurance men to make sure that the company did not pay for any injuries that resulted from employee carelessness or an accident that happened outside the workplace. In his interview with the Pepper subcommittee's investigators, Dr. Spencer recounted one case where he had put a cast on a worker, but when one of the insurance men determined the next day that the employee's injury was "non-industrial," Spencer was ordered to remove the cast.[29]

Despite the overall positive changes to health care that federal support brought to southern war towns and the entire region, as in other areas of life Black Mississippians received few of the benefits. M. L. Brown, a leader of the Pascagoula Civic Improvement Association, claimed that Black residents admitted to the "negro ward" at the city hospital received "very poor" service. In addition to the limited number of beds at the hospital reserved for Black people, nursing support for Black patients remained inadequate, according to Brown. In addition, the county had no Black doctors, although a few Black physicians worked elsewhere on the Mississippi Gulf Coast. Black leaders in Pascagoula tried to entice a Black doctor to relocate to the shipyard town, even securing the promise from the federal government of a free apartment in the Gulfdale development, but those efforts proved unsuccessful. Although white doctors treated Black patients, physicians typically saw them only after all white patients had received attention—much like the Black experience at consumer outlets—treatment that Brown called "out and out discrimination." In addition, the county health department did not conduct the kind of regular sanitary inspections of Black-owned eating establishments that it did for white cafés, a situation that endangered the health and safety of Black patrons.[30]

Two diseases of poverty, syphilis and tuberculosis, that afflicted Black Southerners disproportionately received sustained attention from wartime health systems. Despite the overall success in reducing the incidence of these maladies in the South, treatment for Black people remained incomplete. In the early twentieth century, syphilis affected Black people more often than white citizens. When the army started drafting men in 1940, tests revealed that almost 30 percent of Black soldiers (most from the South) had syphilis, while the rate of infection among white GIs was less than 5 percent. The USPHS had begun a major campaign to combat venereal disease in the 1930s, with much of this effort concentrated in the South. Their work included the deplorable Tuskegee study, which denied treatment to a group of Black syphilitic men in Alabama for forty years—without their knowledge—to study the effects of the disease if left untreated. During the war, the USPHS increased its efforts to find and cure syphilis patients, working through state health departments. In Mississippi, the USPHS provided about two-thirds of the funding for the state's syphilis treatment program. By 1943, the syphilis infection rate in Mississippi had declined to 12.5 percent for Black citizens and 1.5 percent for white residents, although it remained higher in Pascagoula. Ingalls's doctors and Jackson County health officials estimated in May 1943 that the syphilis infection rate among the "shipyard population" may have been close to 15 percent.[31]

Syphilis treatment in Mississippi disadvantaged some of the poorest sufferers from the disease, including many African Americans. In Pascagoula and elsewhere along the Mississippi Gulf Coast, local public health offices, to placate local physicians, would not treat syphilitics unless an area doctor had certified that the patient could not pay for treatment from a private physician, which could cost up to $200. This required extra step in Pascagoula and the surrounding area to receive free care for syphilis discouraged some poorer people from seeking treatment. Workers at Ingalls, largely white, faced the same policy. When the company asked the public health department to set up a syphilis treatment clinic in the shipyard, the agency, consistent with its policy in the community at large, declined, "because of deference to local physicians." At the same time, the cost-conscious Ingalls management refused to take on this burden when the health department declined to act.

Irresponsible thriftiness by Ingalls and the timidity of the local health department diminished the campaign to control the often-debilitating disease.[32]

Tuberculosis was a major cause of death among Black Southerners in the first half of the twentieth century, and during World War II public health officials made important advances to treat the ailment, including in some southern states, such as Alabama and Louisiana. Mississippi, however, with an incidence of tuberculosis among the Black population three times greater than that of white residents, focused most of its resources on treating white patients. The state had built a tuberculosis sanatorium in Simpson County at the end of World War I. In the 1940s, the institution had 500 beds for white patients, but only forty for Black ones. Part of the disparity stemmed from the fact that for any patients unable to pay for a stay at the sanitarium, their home counties had to pay $1 per day for their care at the institution. At the Pascagoula hearings, Felix Underwood, state health director, admitted that "we are not proud of what we are doing for the Negro in this State in tuberculosis control," but the war did little to change the diagnosis and treatment of the disease among Black Mississippians. About 80 percent of tuberculosis patients survived with timely hospitalization, but since Black residents in Mississippi faced greater difficulties securing a bed at the state sanitorium or even their local hospital, they continued to die at a much higher rate from the disease. Between 1940 and 1942, Jackson County, a white-majority county, had thirty-five cases of tuberculosis among white people and nine within the Black population. Of that number, seven white patients (20 percent) and six Black ones (66 percent) died.[33]

Beyond health issues, the rapid population growth in Pascagoula taxed the city's public education system. During the war years, the local white public schools quickly exceeded their capacity. During the 1939–1940 academic year, the Pascagoula city schools served 925 children (807 white, 118 Black), well below the capacity of the existing school buildings. The town had two elementary schools and one junior/senior high school for white children, as well as a "trades building" for vocational education. Altogether, the four buildings could accommodate almost 1,500 students. By the beginning of 1941, however, members of the city school board worried about a coming "catastrophe," as school enrollment had already increased more than 20 percent in 1939 and 1940. By November 1943, an additional 2,211 white and 125 Black students attended classes in the public schools. The increase in white school enrollment numbers might have been even greater without the city's housing shortage, which did not begin to subside until the completion of several federal housing projects in 1943. Before then, many Ingalls workers refused to bring their families to Pascagoula, deciding instead to find temporary quarters in town or simply commute to work in the shipyard.[34]

By the end of 1943, most of the white schools operated on a split shift to accommodate the new students. The white elementary schools started operating two sessions (7:30 A.M.–12:30 P.M. and 12:45 P.M.–5:30 P.M.) in October 1941, followed by the junior high school (grades seven and eight) with the beginning of the 1943–1944 school year. This arrangement meant that young children often had no adult supervision for much of the day. Even with the shortened school day, absentee rates rose among children older than ten. Some stayed home to care for younger, preschool siblings while both parents worked. Others took jobs, not at the shipyard, but in positions at gas stations, cafés, and stores vacated by older teens and young adults who had moved on to war work or military service. For migrants from the rural South, this kind of contribution to the household economy was quite common. In addition, junior high school boys sometimes became indifferent to school, already thinking about the day when they could enlist and join the war that dominated every conversation and seemingly every other aspect of daily life.[35]

The town's high school for white students did not face the same overcrowded conditions, primarily because many high-school-age pupils quit attending school, and some of those who moved to town never enrolled. Nationwide, by April 1944, 3 million children between the ages of fourteen and seventeen worked either full-time or part-time. And by the 1943–1944 school year, high school attendance nationally had declined by 1 million students. Ingalls shipyard had a policy to employ no workers younger than sixteen, but some of their high-school-age workers still attended school and worked a full eight hours (typically the second shift). In a small number of cases, boys as young as thirteen worked at the shipyard and tried to attend school. Local newspaper editor Easton King claimed that when Superintendent Thomas R. Wells discovered these cases, "he raised hell about the situation" with the Ingalls management, which claimed the young workers had "been able to hoodwink" the company about their age. Some sixteen- and seventeen-year-old boys working at Ingalls had moved alone to Pascagoula from the rural districts. Many of them had received industrial training back in their home locales from agencies such as the National Youth Administration, and several of them secured housing in Pascagoula's federal dormitory project. Local welfare officials described them as a "restless, aggressive, lonesome, homesick outfit."[36]

As war mobilization progressed, the district had trouble recruiting and retaining an adequate teaching corps. The Pascagoula schools, like other school systems, experienced rapid turnover among teachers, primarily because of greater opportunities for white women in higher-paying war work or government jobs. Before the war, white teachers received, on average, $900 per year, a relatively high salary for a teacher in Mississippi and across the rural South. By the 1943–1944 school year, that average salary had risen to more than $1,100, yet it could not compete with the pay at Ingalls, where even "inexperienced youngsters" could make almost $1,500 a year. Given this reality, the turnover rate among teachers in the Pascagoula schools during the war approached 50 percent a year. As a result, the school district abandoned its qualification standards for teachers. By the end of 1943, Pascagoula employed many who did not have college degrees, who had no teaching experience, or who came out of retirement to take instructional positions.[37]

Black schools did not experience most of the problems faced by the city's white schools, which led some observers to claim that the city had exemplary race relations. With few opportunities available for Black workers at the Ingalls shipyard, the Black population in the area grew at a smaller rate than the more sizable white migration to Jackson County. When Agnes Meyer visited Pascagoula in 1943, she noted that "Pascagoula is the only city, North or South, in which I found the civic leaders, the social workers, and the private citizens co-operating, not only to meet, but to anticipate the needs of the Negro population." Much of that conclusion rested on what she observed and heard about Black education. Superintendent Wells had boasted that "the Negro was planned for all the way through on a percentage basis.... We have a deep conviction in our educational system that we cannot go much higher socially and educationally unless we lift our Negro citizens proportionally." Meyer pointed to a new Black school recently built and to the lack of split sessions for Black children as signs of Black progress in the town. Yet her analysis ignored several realities about Black education there.[38]

Even though Black residents of Pascagoula did have a new and spacious school, it had replaced a wholly inadequate building and still preserved a second-class setup for Black education. The new school had only six rooms to accommodate all the Black students in the community. Though the building could hold as many as 180 students, it did not have enough rooms to conduct a real graded school, with a separate space for each of twelve grades; it also did not have a library, a standard component of the white schools. The former Black school became a vocational center, which also housed the lunchroom and kitchen to serve Black children, but unlike the white vocational program, the Black one had little equipment and did not offer any courses in skills that might be useful to potential shipyard workers. At the same time, Black teachers received as little as $450 a year, significantly less than their white counterparts. There was less turnover among the Black teaching corps, but only because other economic opportunities for Black workers in the area, including at the local shipyard, remained severely limited.[39]

The rapid influx of school-age children—primarily white—into Pascagoula seriously strained the already limited public education. No state or local funds existed to help Pascagoula school leaders with the extra buildings and equipment needed as the white student population swelled, and federal monies represented the only realistic financing source. The school district already carried bonded debt close to the maximum allowed under state law. In addition, increased economic activity only marginally increased the local tax base, especially since the Ingalls Shipbuilding Corporation had received a five-year tax exemption as part of the Mississippi Balance Agriculture with Industry program that brought the company to Pascagoula. Despite the city's overheated economy because of war mobilization, local tax revenue available to the public schools increased less than $13,000 between the 1940–1941 and 1943–1944 school years. Using federal funds provided by the Lanham Act, the city did construct two new, white elementary schools, both of which opened in early 1944, although the new buildings did not eliminate the crowded conditions in the white schools. Lanham Act funds also provided additional operating funds for the Pascagoula schools.[40]

During the war years, the US Congress considered other measures to provide federal funds to aid public education, but racial concerns blocked these efforts, as they had ever since the nineteenth century. In April 1941, Democratic senators Elbert Thomas of Utah and Pat Harrison of Mississippi introduced a bill to provide $300 million to the states to meet "financial emergencies in education and in reducing inequalities of educational opportunities." The bill, as many before it, renounced "federal control over the educational policies of States and localities," although it did require a "just and equitable" distribution of funds in states with racially segregated school systems, without a reduction in existing state support for Black schools. More than three-fourths of the proposed funds would have gone toward expenses such as raising teacher salaries and hiring additional teachers. Under the planned distribution, Mississippi would have received almost $13 million, Georgia more than $15 million, and Alabama more than

$16 million. As a point of comparison, the state appropriation for public education in Mississippi in 1942 was only $7.24 million. The size of the federal aid package would have transformed education in the Deep South at a time when some districts, especially those near war industries or military camps, faced difficult challenges.[41]

The Thomas Education Bill made little headway during the 77th Congress (1941–1942). Teachers strongly supported the legislation, but the measure generated some opposition from those concerned about adding further to the growing federal debt but especially from southern leaders worried that the law posed a threat to racial segregation. During the 1942 governor's race in Georgia, Eugene Talmadge, running for re-election, said he thought the federal funds would lead to "co-education of the races, . . . something Georgia don't stand for." By the time Congress reconsidered Thomas's education bill in February 1943, wartime mobilization had further stressed the funds available to effectively operate public schools in Pascagoula and many other communities. Additional salary dollars to hire and retain teachers represented the most pressing problems. H. M. Ivy, the superintendent of the Meridian public schools and chairman of the Legislative Commission of the National Education Association (NEA), told Senator Theodore Bilbo that Mississippi needed federal funds to "stem the tide of capable teachers leaving jobs in our State." At hearings on the legislation in April, numerous southern educational leaders testified about the urgent need for federal funds to rescue public education in the region. White teacher organizations in southern states mobilized to promote passage of the federal aid bill. Both the NAACP and the American Teachers Association, a national organization of Black teachers, also urged adoption of the legislation.[42]

Despite all the support for the federal aid to education measure, including from southern senators who agreed to support the original nondiscrimination requirement for the distribution of federal funds, the bill went down to defeat after a more direct challenge to the South's system of racial segregation came up during the 1943 floor debate. In October, after five days of discussion, Senator William Langer of North Dakota proposed an amendment prohibiting racial discrimination not only in the administration of federal funds provided for in the bill but also in any state funds appropriated for education. The southern delegation unanimously opposed the amendment, but it passed, in part through the support of some Republicans who hoped to kill the Thomas bill for other reasons, such as an objection to excessive federal spending. Southerners then joined with other opponents of the bill and sent the legislation back to committee, where it never re-emerged. White Southerners could not abide any federal effort to force them to use their own resources to fund Black education at the same level as white schooling. Even H. M. Ivy agreed that white Southerners could not accept the much-needed federal funding for public education under these conditions. Although legislators attempted to pass federal legislation to aid education once again in the US Senate in 1945, that effort never advanced beyond committee deliberations.[43]

When Southerners in rural districts thought about the problems war towns in the region faced because of rapid economic mobilization, they did not worry about inadequate housing, insufficient health care, or deficiencies in public education. In fact, compared to national standards, rural communities of the Deep South lagged the rest of the country in the provision of such services, and despite the rapid growth and chaos of many war towns, housing, health care, and education there often outpaced such facilities in rural areas. The seeming moral decay associated with life in war towns troubled rural Southerners the most, based on what they heard from their neighbors who returned home either temporarily or permanently from these locales. A store owner in Iuka in northeast Mississippi believed that the extra wages earned by war workers led them to "drinking bouts & all night gambling, which [they] did little of before they got into big money." Specific examples of war worker returnees could provide a cautionary tale that reverberated through rural communities. A white farmer in the northeast Mississippi county of Tishomingo related to a BAE interviewer in 1944 the story of a neighbor's son who had spent two years working in Mobile. The young man had returned home to Tishomingo with two children, after "his wife ran off with another man." According to the farmer, the man spent his days after returning "drunk all the time." Given such experiences, the farmer believed "it's no wonder the Revival Preachers are all preaching against going to war work & begging people to coax their relatives back before they all go to Hell."[44]

Other rural Southerners had more general concerns about the problems associated with urban areas. A large plantation owner in Lafayette County in northeast Mississippi claimed many residents stayed put in the area rather than seeking a better job in a war town because wives oftentimes discouraged the move, as they "don't want husbands & children to be exposed to [the] wickedness of big cities." An FSA supervisor in Lafayette County simply believed that cities were "usually very evil places."[45] While generally not as bad as rural folk imagined, life in war towns did expose rural migrants to a different way of life, with a wider range of experiences—many considered immoral—that frequently strained traditional social relations.

One of the negative aspects often associated with urban life was crime, but despite the increasing urbanization associated with World War II economic mobilization, the crime rate nationally declined during the war years for almost all types of offenses. Nevertheless, as people crowded into Pascagoula to work at Ingalls and elsewhere, in houses and apartments and trailers, with strangers for neighbors, even sporadic instances or reports of violent crime confirmed the migrants' worst fears about an urban underworld. In June 1942, someone broke into a Catholic boarding school and several other residences in the Pascagoula area and cut the hair of young girls while they slept. Later that month, someone assaulted and robbed Terril Heidelberg, the young son of a local judge, and his wife in their home. A few days after the attack on the Heidelbergs, the Pascagoula newspaper headline announced: "CRIME WAVE HERE DEVELOPS INTO VIRTUAL REIGN OF TERROR AS YOUNG COUPLE IS BRUTALLY BEATEN AT HOME, ROBBERY ATTEMPTS CONTINUE TO INCREASE." The following year, reports of two violent crimes that occurred within a span of six weeks shocked the local community. At the end of August 1943, a twenty-year-old white widow who worked at a café (only identified as Mrs. Gibson) claimed that one of her Black co-workers, Johnnie Richardson, raped her in the middle of the night in the room where she lived in the back of the restaurant. Then, in mid-October, a passerby discovered the murdered body of thirteen-year-old Nellie Opal Ricks twenty feet off South Pascagoula Street. Her family had recently moved to town from rural, east-central Mississippi. She was last seen attending a movie in town two days earlier.[46]

White Pascagoulians assumed that drifters or African Americans committed these crimes. The series of stealth hair-cuttings and the attack on the Heidelbergs occurred so close together in time that many assumed a single individual committed the crimes. During the hysteria that followed these events, a Pascagoula police officer shot an unknown Black man in the back when he ran away after being told to halt. No one ever identified the victim, a young man in his twenties. Eventually, the authorities arrested and convicted William Dolan for the offenses. Dolan had once lived at Pelham's Point, an area near the Pascagoula River and Ingalls Shipbuilding, home to squatters living in a variety of makeshift housing: tents, Quonset huts, and other temporary shelters. Dolan said he was from New York City, and he had apparently traveled around the country doing various jobs before marrying a woman in south Mississippi. In the weeks after Nellie Opal Ricks's murder, the police questioned several white men but released them. Then, in February 1944, the police arrested a twenty-one-year-old Black man, Henry Lee Wiley, for "accosting a white woman." According to Wiley's attorney, the authorities put the young man "through the third degree for several hours," and he eventually confessed to killing Ricks. Despite doubts about Wiley's confession, a local, all-white jury convicted him of the crime, and the state executed him in December 1944.[47]

The alleged rape case occurred in a café that housed several individuals; Mrs. Gibson shared one of the boarding rooms with another woman. Gibson claimed that she awoke to find a man in her room but said she could not identify the man or even determine his race. Her roommate never awoke during the incident, and Gibson did not initially report that a crime had occurred. A woman in a trailer park next door to the café, however, had seen a man entering a window in Gibson's room and leaving an hour later. The woman recognized the individual as Johnnie Richardson, a Black cook at the café. She called the police, and when an officer arrived, Gibson claimed that a man she could not identify raped her. While searching the premises, the officer found a used condom in Gibson's bed. The police arrested Richardson the next morning as he arrived at work. Highway Patrol officers took him to Jackson later that day—to prevent a feared lynching—and the patrolmen reported that Richardson confessed to the rape during the trip. At trial, a jury convicted Richardson and sentenced him to death. On appeal, however, the Mississippi Supreme Court granted him a new trial. At the second trial, the prosecution presented essentially the same case, and the jury issued the same sentence. Due to the intervention of the NAACP and the American Civil Liberties Union, however, the court granted a motion to resentence and changed the punishment to life imprisonment in Parchman Penitentiary.[48]

The incident involving Johnnie Richardson and Mrs. Gibson demonstrated that the kind of Jim Crow justice that had prevailed in Mississippi and the rest of the South for decades continued to operate during the war years. Richardson received a death sentence (twice) and went to the penitentiary for violating the unforgiveable sin of southern life: a Black man having any kind of relationship with a white woman, even a consensual one, as the affair between Richardson and Gibson almost certainly was. Almost nothing about her rape charge made sense. Gibson could not identify Richardson, although a neighbor watching from her trailer at night had no trouble recognizing the cook. Gibson's roommate did not wake during the commission of a sexual assault feet away. Richardson was such a considerate rapist that he thought to wear a condom. Richardson strolled into work the morning after the alleged incident with no seeming fear of apprehension by the law. Even such a staunch defender of the racial status quo as the Mississippi Supreme Court, when sending the Richardson case back for a retrial, observed that "the testimony of the prosecutrix is so highly improbable as to be scarcely believable, except, of course, to one who would simply prefer to believe it."[49] That attitude essentially sealed Richardson's fate. In a war community populated largely by white migrants from the rural Deep South, outsiders of all kinds, and especially Black people, became easy scapegoats for the worst calamities that punctuated life in a village crowded with strangers.

Beyond occasional violent incidents (or rumors of violence), the most noticeable break in the social fabric in war towns like Pascagoula was the problem of juvenile delinquency. Nationwide, an increase in criminal violations, mostly misdemeanors, among young people occurred in war towns. In the fall of 1943, the Children's Bureau of the US Department of Labor issued a report that examined juvenile courts in cities with a population greater than 100,000 (significantly larger than Pascagoula) and found a 16 percent increase between 1940 and 1942 in the number of cases coming before these courts. A follow-up report in 1943 recorded an additional 31 percent growth in the juvenile delinquency rate. The increase involved all age groups above fourteen and both genders and was greater among white than Black youth. The offenses of vagrancy and prostitution and other sex offenses comprised the biggest increase in criminal detentions among girls. For boys, the largest growth in arrests involved charges of drunkenness and disorderly conduct.[50]

Commentators at the time and scholars later attributed this rise in juvenile delinquency to a variety of factors: "crowded living conditions" in war industry towns and near military camps; less parental and teacher oversight of children because of war work and military service—the rise of the "latchkey child"; more employment opportunities and additional disposable income for teenagers; inadequate educational, health, and recreational facilities in war towns; and the rise of a distinct "teen culture," where the opinions of peers began to carry more weight than traditional sources of authority, such as parents, schools, and churches.[51]

As in other war communities, young people in Pascagoula engaged in behavior during the war years that shocked their elders, not to mention rural

Mississippians who heard stories about life in war towns. In May 1942, Judge L. C. Corban commented that prostitution and juvenile delinquency in the town had "increased alarmingly." Most of the cases involved disorderly conduct and drunkenness. A report made by the Senate subcommittee's investigators of a tour they took of local roadhouses with Easton King and his wife suggests the extent of the problem. The excursion included a visit to three different drinking establishments on Saturday night, December 4, 1943. The last stop was the Airport Inn, just north of Pascagoula. The Inn was hopping that night, with about 100 people present, "including girls 13 or 14 years of age, leaving the place to return later" (the report implied that they were leaving the bar to engage in sexual activity). The report of the visit to the Airport Inn also described "visible drunkenness" among a "half dozen lower teen-age girls," as well as three or four boys of the same age.[52]

The ready availability of alcohol contributed to the juvenile delinquency problem. Even though Mississippi officially remained a dry state during the World War II years, the counties on the Mississippi Gulf Coast had always openly sold liquor, and bars—many of which also served as gambling parlors—flourished in Jackson County. Ingalls Shipbuilding complained that cafés near the shipyard sold liquor, so employees sometimes worked shifts under the influence of alcohol, "which mitigated strongly against peak production of the ships so badly needed for war." J. C. Crane, a Presbyterian minister in Pascagoula, believed that "Joe's beer joint" was "the first and only 'institution' to reach" war workers during their off-hours. Local law enforcement did little to enforce the state liquor laws. When the Senate investigators and the Kings left the Airport Inn in December 1943, they noticed a lawman watching the revelry, although he gave no indication that he would take any action to shut the party down or curb underage drinking.[53]

Beyond an easy supply of alcohol and ineffective law enforcement, some in Pascagoula blamed the juvenile delinquency problem on working mothers who left children unattended. Reverend Crane, spokesman for the town's Inter-Church Committee, claimed that some working mothers left their children wherever they could while working, such as at movie theaters, and "sometimes they forget to come for them." That charge was a common one. At the Pascagoula hearings, witnesses recounted instances of young children left unattended while both parents—or single mothers—worked. A survey of the families at the town's white elementary schools found that almost one-third of the families that had working mothers had no plan to deal with their children after school, "other than to let them play around the neighborhood."

In many cases, working families left their youngsters in the care of only slightly older children.[54]

One possible solution to the juvenile delinquency problem was to create more recreational opportunities for young people and give them something to do when adults had to work. Pascagoula, however, had little to offer in this area when economic mobilization began, and with more pressing concerns during the war—such as housing and education—improvements of the situation came slowly. At the end of 1943, the town still had no public playgrounds or library, no gyms, and no bowling alleys. The city had leased the one public park in town, on the beach, to the Army in 1941 for use as a "recreation camp" for soldiers. Pascagoula did have two movie theaters, with a combined capacity of 1,300 seats for white patrons and 200 seats for Black moviegoers, and both cinemas were "constantly crowded to capacity." The city also had a swimming pier on the beach and a golf course, both reserved for the exclusive use of white citizens. The Ingalls company created the Ingalls Athletic Club to promote team sports among its workers and even built a $30,000 baseball stadium, but these efforts did nothing to create recreational opportunities for most of the town's young people. The federal housing projects also had rooms set aside for recreation, although in the case of the one at Carver Village, it had no recreational equipment.[55]

In the fall of 1943, Mayor Gulley convened a committee of local leaders to survey the recreation situation in town and make recommendations. The following February, the town created a Recreation Commission, which submitted two applications worth almost $200,000 to the Federal Works Agency (FWA). The money would fund seven playgrounds and two recreation centers (two of the playgrounds and one of the recreation centers for Black residents). These projects did not receive approval until late in 1944, but the US Maritime Commission also created a recreation center in the Eastlawn Housing Project, which expanded the leisure options for the white residents who lived there.[56]

Since many women needed to work, providing help with childcare represented another possible solution to the problem of unsupervised children. Although the federal government allocated resources for childcare centers during the war, federal support for such services proved uneven. The Works Progress Administration (WPA) had provided childcare services during the Great Depression, largely as a relief effort to support out-of-work teachers. In 1942, the WPA expanded its work in this area to support the war effort as more women entered the workforce. The FWA also began to allocate millions of Lanham Act funds for childcare centers in towns with war industries. By mid-1943, more than 3,000 childcare centers with the capacity to tend to more than 180,000 children had received funding from the federal government. The federal support of childcare operations through the Lanham Act required a 50 percent match from local governments, typically raised by charging fees to the parents who utilized the childcare services. The attempt to create group childcare facilities had numerous opponents, including officials of several federal agencies, the NEA, conservative religious and political leaders, and many working mothers.[57]

A bill introduced in 1943 by Democratic senator Elbert Thomas of Utah sought to replace the Lanham Act funding with a separate $20 million appropriation to support individual, rather than group, childcare. States would have to request the funds and match any federal dollars with an equivalent in state resources. Designed to preserve traditional family arrangements, Thomas's bill would also reduce federal expenditures on childcare and make it easy to dismantle federally supported childcare when the war ended. The bill passed the Senate but died in a House committee. After the defeat of the Thomas bill, Lanham Act funding for childcare increased throughout the remainder of the war, eventually serving 600,000 children over the course of the war, although the federal government began to phase out this support almost as soon as the war ended.[58]

Pascagoula benefited from the federal efforts to create childcare facilities, although federal resources did not meet all area needs. At the end of 1943, the town had one facility for white youth, equipped to handle thirty children but with an enrollment of eighty. The school system also ran an operation to look after children between the ages of six and twelve, but that facility, designed for only about five youngsters, quickly became overcrowded. Lanham Act funding in late 1943 allowed for the creation of two new daycare centers for white kids, which provided spaces for more than 300 additional children. Those facilities became available in 1944. In October 1943, a small nursery school opened in Carver Village, although it only had spaces for thirty Black children. Since the Pascagoula childcare centers charged a fee ($3 per child per week), many rural migrants balked at paying for the service. According to Superintendent Wells, most of the new residents in town working at the shipyard did not "see the value of putting that much money into care for their children." Recognizing that Black workers earned less than white ones, Wells knew that the childcare fees represented "an even more important factor [in limiting childcare enrollment] with the Negroes than with the whites."[59]

At the conclusion of the Pascagoula hearings, Pepper sounded an optimistic note. He believed the city had a fine "spirit of cooperation," and with help from the federal government, "we can all work together for the good of the community and particularly in order that war production in this fine shipyard may be unimpaired by any remediable shortcomings." Local citizens and the federal government did try to resolve the problems created by wartime economic mobilization, although they received little help from the Ingalls Shipbuilding Corporation, and entrenched rural and racial prejudices often hindered potential solutions. Even so, federal efforts produced a few lasting changes in the town. By the early 1950s, over a thousand housing units built during the war remained in use. The town also had several new recreation facilities, built near the end of the war, as well as a new water and sewer system for the town. Perhaps most notable, the federal government's construction of public schools in Pascagoula during the war gave the town "the most modern school plant in Mississippi," according to one account. Even though the war had brought turmoil, Pascagoula emerged from the conflict with at least some new assets, which helped to improve postwar life for many of the town's citizens.[60]

PART II
MILITARY MOBILIZATION

5
Military Mobilization and Black Troops

Destined for Jackson, Mississippi, the Southern Railway train pulled out of Union Station in Washington, DC, early on the Fourth of July 1942. Like all Southern Railway trains traveling in the South at that time, this one was segregated by race, with one coach for Black passengers and eight or nine cars set aside for white travelers. The train carried soldiers, Black and white, headed for training in the numerous military camps that increasingly dotted the southern landscape. S. D. Redmond, a lawyer and physician from Jackson, rode in the "colored" coach. He took his breakfast in the train's only dining car at 8:30 that morning as it passed through southern Virginia. When he returned for lunch later in the day, however, the dining car staff denied him service. Redmond, along with the other Black civilian and military passengers, had sandwiches and coffee delivered to them in their overcrowded, separate car at 2:00 P.M., the first food of the day for most people in the compartment. A Black waiter explained the railroad company's dining room policy to Redmond: the staff had orders "not to serve Negroes south of Virginia, and damn few in Virginia."[1]

Redmond had little trouble qualifying as one of the "damn few." By any standard in almost any society, he had a truly exceptional biography. Born in a log cabin in rural Mississippi, the child of formerly enslaved people and sharecroppers, Redmond rose to become a medical doctor, a lawyer, a banker, and a successful businessman. His first wife, the daughter of Mississippi's Hiram Revels, the first African American to serve in the US Senate, died tragically young. Redmond remarried, this time to the daughter of a Black member of Alabama's Reconstruction legislature. In 1919, Redmond went to France as a delegate of the Pan-African Congress and as a correspondent for several Black newspapers covering the Versailles Peace Conference. He spent most of his life in Jackson, Mississippi, though he practiced law for a time in the early 1930s in the nation's capital. In Mississippi, Redmond survived several attempts to disbar him, as well as a federal indictment for selling patronage jobs (as a leader in the all-Black faction of the state's Republican Party). He also occasionally received grudging respect from the state's white establishment, even addressing a joint session of the state legislature in 1924. At his death in 1948, Redmond had an estate valued at more than $600,000 (almost $7 million in 2022), making him one of the wealthiest Black men in the country.[2]

Redmond complained to the Southern Railroad Company about the treatment he and his fellow Black passengers received on his Independence Day trip. They had to travel on a segregated, filthy, crowded car with limited access to food and drink. In a time of war, Redmond pointed out at least two problems with such unequal treatment. First, Redmond asserted that the railway's "method of handling the Negro public of this country over your vast system will destroy more Negro morale in a minute than we can build up in a year." Redmond also recognized the inefficiencies inherent in trying to provide segregated services, particularly problematic given the war emergency: "organizations like yours sitting on the wheels in this war, . . . are serving as just so much dead weight, . . . at a time when the very existence of this country hangs in the balance." The president of Southern Railway answered Redmond's criticisms by claiming that "it is our established policy to treat every patron, regardless of race, with courtesy and consideration, and with due regard to the laws of the states through which we operate." For travel in the American South, that meant separate and unequal accommodations for Black Americans.[3]

The Black soldiers crammed into that Southern Railway coach with Redmond, traveling south to complete their military training, arrived at facilities that brought a host of people together: Northerners and Southerners, Black and white. All of them lived and worked in the same space, and all of them looked for recreation and respite from the rigors and monotony of military training in neighboring communities. Like the Southern Railway, the US Army preserved racial segregation at its military facilities, but the military also had to abide by federal nondiscrimination mandates. As a result, the army had different standards about how to enforce or implement racial segregation on its bases than those used by white Southerners—in part to reduce the inefficiencies Redmond spoke of or for reasons of military necessity. The military made no attempt to enforce nondiscrimination directives in nearby communities, and as a result, racial segregation did more than dampen "Negro morale." The population centers that surrounded southern military installations became sites of racial conflict. The presence of Black soldiers in the region during both the Spanish-American War and World War I had also sparked racial tensions, but Black GIs training for military service in the South during World War II, whose numbers dwarfed those of previous conflicts, threatened the region's racial status quo in unprecedented ways.[4]

During World War II, perhaps 80 percent of all Black recruits trained in the South, as the region became a major location for the establishment of military training camps. Overall, the federal government invested more than $4 billion in military facilities in the region (36 percent of the national total). The South had several things going for it: good climate, large tracts of unoccupied or sparsely populated land, and a powerful congressional delegation. But the boosters of southern communities also lobbied to get these installations in their backyards. In Hattiesburg, Mississippi, local businessmen organized a "Camp Committee." It offered cash inducements and gave or leased land to the federal government to convince it to build a major army training facility at the location of the former Camp Shelby, a World War I post. During World War II, the site became one of the army's largest training facilities, with a capacity to accommodate 86,000 soldiers. Built at a cost of $24 million, Camp Shelby reopened in October 1940, one month after the nation instituted its first peacetime military draft. In southwest Mississippi, local businessmen and politicians similarly began agitating in late 1940 for the army to build a facility in that isolated corner of the state. The army eventually located Camp Van Dorn on a 42,000-acre site in Wilkinson and Amite Counties, near the small town of Centreville. The encampment could potentially house more than 40,000 men.[5]

Although white Southerners actively sought the location of federal military camps in their states, they opposed the training of Black troops at these facilities. During the first half of 1942, when military training accelerated rapidly, Deep South officials appealed to military leaders to reconsider decisions to station Black soldiers in their region. In April 1942, when the Mississippi governor reported that the military would send not only Black enlisted men, but Black officers, to the state, the entire US House of Representatives delegation from Mississippi petitioned Army Chief of Staff George C. Marshall to reverse the action. Black officers both upset white notions that Black people were only fit for servitude and raised concerns that Black officers might embolden the Black soldiers under their command to riot against white authority. When white citizens near Huntsville, Alabama, learned in the summer of 1942 that Black troops would arrive at a nearby camp, they told the War Department that they preferred no Black soldiers in their majority-white district. As an alternative, they urged "that by all means see that the negroes sent here are from the South and not from the North." In

August 1942, US Senator John Bankhead of Alabama had a well-publicized exchange with Marshall, in which Bankhead requested that all Black military personnel be trained outside the South. The Army Chief of Staff ultimately rejected Bankhead's request, citing "the dictates of military necessity" as the army's chief concern.[6]

White Southerners could not keep Black soldiers out of the South, but they advocated strongly that the military preserve racial segregation. The federal government agreed, as it had no desire to lead the way in reforming southern social mores. Many of the top military brass, including Secretary of War Henry L. Stimson and Army Chief of Staff Marshall, shared the deep-rooted racial prejudices of white Southerners. President Franklin D. Roosevelt also favored the maintenance of racial segregation. The president, however, was more sensitive to pressure from a northern Black population increasingly mobilized politically, and thus took small but significant steps to bolster the status of Black soldiers in World War II. In advance of the 1940 presidential election, Roosevelt, under prodding from Black leaders such as A. Philip Randolph, head of the Brotherhood of Sleeping Car Porters, and Walter White, executive secretary of the National Association for the Advancement of Colored People (NAACP), authorized the creation of a separate Black air force unit—the Tuskegee Airmen—and appointed a civil rights advocate and judge, William Hastie, as Civilian Aide on Negro Affairs to the Secretary of War. Hastie had previously worked in the Roosevelt administration as an assistant solicitor in the Department of the Interior. In 1937, he had become the first African American appointed to the federal bench when FDR tapped him to serve on the federal district court in the Virgin Islands.[7]

Even more important, the US Congress and the president approved the Selective Service and Training Act of 1940, which officially disavowed racial discrimination: "in the selection of men for training and service ... there shall be no discrimination against any person on account of race or color." The statute did not, however, directly attack racial segregation. Indeed, a month after the bold declaration of the draft law, the War Department reiterated that its policy was "not to intermingle colored and white enlisted personnel in the same regimental organizations" since the policy of racial segregation "has proven satisfactory over a long period of years."[8] Thus, the military's stance on the eve of America's involvement in World War II suggested a complicated and unattainable standard: racial segregation without discrimination, similar to the principle outlined in the creation of the Fair Employment Practices Committee a year later.

As military mobilization began, discrimination against Black soldiers in both service and training proved routine. The army had to build its Black units virtually from scratch. In the summer of 1940, fewer than 5,000 Black men served in the army, and the service had only five Black officers: three chaplains and Colonel Benjamin O. Davis and his son, a lieutenant. When conscription began, Black enrollment lagged until the army could create new Black units. Even after the army formed segregated organizations, Black conscription continued to trail white enlistment, due in large part to the fact that Black Southerners suffered from substandard health care and limited education, which made many of them "unfit" for military service, according to existing military standards. When Judge Hastie complained in the weeks before Pearl Harbor about the small numbers of Black men inducted into the military, George Marshall advised the War Department to point out to the judge that it "cannot ignore . . . that either through lack of educational opportunities or other causes the level of intelligence and occupational skill of the negro population is considerably below that of the white."[9]

The slow incorporation of Black men into the armed forces also drew the ire of white Southerners, who vacillated on the question of Black people and military service. On the one hand, many white Southerners deemed Black men incapable of anything but the most menial military positions. At the same time, the fact that the realities of southern life disqualified a sizable number of Black citizens from military duty and imposed an extra service burden on white men potentially created racial problems at home once the "white protectors" of the southern way of life deployed. As congressmen from the Deep South campaigned for re-election in the summer of 1942, they heard complaints from their constituents about the unequal induction of the races, about Black people bragging about avoiding military service by claiming illiteracy, and about rumors of planned Black uprisings. The military moved to reassure white Southerners that they could solve the problem of unequal enlistments. Indeed, in August 1942, the army began "accepting illiterates at a controlled rate," in the words of Robert Patterson, under secretary of war, a change that did increase the number of Southerners—Black and white—qualified for military service. Even so, the Black proportion of the army never reached its share of the national Black population during the war.[10]

Discrimination against Black soldiers in training further complicated the logistics of building a biracial, yet segregated, army. Soon after the draft began, the War Department claimed it would enroll Black fighters in all segments of the army. The War Department and most white Americans, however, thought Black men incapable of combat service. A nationally syndicated cartoon drawn in October 1942 by Jack "Herc" Ficklen, an army captain from Texas, vividly reflected that pervasive white attitude. The caricature depicted a Black soldier who had tied his razor onto the end of his rifle standing next to a white officer with a puzzled look on his face. The caption, "But I lost my bayonet, suh," suggested that African Americans lacked the intelligence to accomplish the basic duties of soldiers. The International Workers Order, a communist-affiliated fraternal order, called the piece "extremely harmful to national unity and a malicious slander to fifteen million Negroes who have pledged their support to our Nation's war effort." Though the army did create a few new Black combat units, the number of Black enrollees assigned to these remained relatively small.[11]

Enrolling and training Black soldiers on a nondiscriminatory basis proved a challenge because the military remained committed to respecting "accepted social customs." For example, in transportation, a real disconnect existed between military policy and southern segregation practices, which created unnecessary problems for Black GIs. The army's official transportation of personnel policy after the United States entered World War II mandated transportation service "without regard to segregation of races," as Under Secretary of War Patterson explained to NAACP executive director Walter White in the summer of 1942. Presumably, the army wanted to avoid the wasted time and effort needed to re-create the often-complex local rules of racial segregation that ordered the use of buses and other vehicles in the southern states: moving signs demarcating white and Black sections, preserving customs about where and when Black riders should enter a conveyance, and policing when Black patrons had a right to sit down and when they needed to stand. In actual practice, however, government-run transportation remained, for the most part, racially segregated, especially in the South. In some cases, the military simply operated separate white and Black buses in the region. The army, however, typically contracted with local companies to handle its transportation needs, especially for routes between its installations and civilian communities. In those instances, as Patterson told White, "Members of the armed forces are bound by all existing civil laws"—that is, the local practices of racial segregation.[12]

A Black soldier training in a southern camp might have a different experience on government-run transportation and civilian conveyances, even if both preserved segregation. The trips on public transportation run by civilians opened Black GIs up to one of the most confusing, frustrating, and potentially dangerous features of segregation in the region. As historian Robin D. G. Kelley has observed, during World War II, buses in the Deep South were "small war zones." Throughout the South during the war, the NAACP received numerous complaints about the problems Black soldiers encountered as they attempted to maneuver around the region on public conveyances. Some faced eviction or attack by white transportation employees annoyed for any number of reasons by Black men and women in uniform. And in many southern communities, white bus drivers carried guns. In August 1942, a Mobile, Alabama, bus driver (a recent migrant from south Mississippi) shot one of his passengers, Henry Williams, a Black private from Birmingham. Many of the bus drivers in the city were recently arrived from the rural areas "where traditionally intense anti-Negro feeling has prevailed," according to a Bureau of Agricultural Economics report. Local officials arrested the bus driver, but he never stood trial. Most white Mobilians simply assumed the bus driver who killed Williams had a "justifiable" reason for killing the soldier. NAACP leader John LeFlore organized a boycott of the bus company but called the action off after the company agreed to disarm its drivers.[13]

Although the military's transportation problems involved logistical factors other than race, Black soldiers still tended to suffer the worst treatment. The Tri-State Bus Company had the contract to provide transportation between Camp Shelby and Hattiesburg. The company never had enough buses running for anyone, especially on weekends, but it operated twenty-eight buses for white GIs and only three for Black men. Army officials sought to alleviate some of the transportation shortage by conveying soldiers, especially Black ones, back and forth to Hattiesburg, but the lack of adequate busses still affected Black GIs more than white ones. And when on civilian buses, Black soldiers clashed regularly with white bus drivers, who sought to maintain local segregation traditions unfamiliar to many of the Black riders. The transportation problem in Hattiesburg proved so severe that, in several cases, Black soldiers from Camp Shelby seized buses to expedite their transportation options.[14]

In many cases, the military simply replicated the racial segregation common to American society. Military planners laid out new military camps with white and Black areas, much like the segregated small towns and cities of the South and the Black metropolises of the North at the time. Each area had its own housing, recreation facilities, and post exchange (PX). Traditional markers of segregation, like those found in many southern locales, abounded on army posts in the Deep South. At Camp Stewart in Georgia, classrooms, theaters, and bathrooms displayed white and "colored" signs. At Camp Shelby, a PX open to all soldiers sported a sign, "Whites please use front door." Local white civilians ran most of the PXs reserved for Black soldiers, and service at these white-run facilities varied. Generally, the Black section of most camps could be found on the edge of the installation, typically far away from the headquarters and main parade ground. Commanders at some locations, such as Camp Gordon, near Augusta, Georgia, reinforced racial segregation by issuing orders designating certain sections of camp as "off-limits" to white soldiers or "colored."[15]

Even though the military maintained racial segregation and enforced traditional aspects of social relations on many fronts, it had neither the time nor the resources to vigilantly guard the color line, at least not with the ardor white Southerners expected. In some cases, individuals on army posts interpreted the nondiscrimination directive in ways at variance with local racial mores. When Claude Montgomery Jr., from the Mississippi Delta, trained at Camp Shelby in 1943, he was standing in a long line at an installation theater with other Black soldiers waiting to buy a ticket. Montgomery recalled that a white solder tried to avoid the line and went directly to the ticket booth. The female attendant told him, "You're in the Army now. You've got to get back in line like the rest of them."[16] Though this incident represented only a small denial of white privilege, it portended a major reordering of southern social relations for those actually involved in the episode.

In some cases, the military clearly deviated from local segregation customs. At Fort Benning, near Columbus, Georgia, the army began training Black and white officer candidates in the same units in 1940, the military's first real experiment with racial integration. Black and white officers attended classes together, slept in the same quarters, and ate together. The War Department made the decision largely on practical grounds, specifically the small number of Black men selected for officer training. By the end of 1942, the army had enrolled only 800 Black soldiers in Officer Candidate School (OCS), 0.2 percent of the more than 450,000 Black soldiers enlisted in the military at the time. At the same time, OCS had trained 72,200 white GIs, 1.5 percent of the white military population. White Southerners complained bitterly about this relatively minor yet blatant violation of the color line. Pete Jarman, an Alabama congressman, decried the "unnecessary and uncalled for mixing of the races" at Fort Benning. He disliked the fact that "Negroes and Whites are

After the graduation ceremony of the 16th Officer Candidate School class at Fort Benning, Georgia, May 1942, these new second lieutenants put on their brass bars. The Officer Candidate School at Fort Benning was desegregated in 1940, one of the first attempts by the US military to racially integrate its personnel. *National Archives (111-SC-137679)*

housed in the same barracks, use the same showers, lavatories and drinking fountains."[17]

Some types of segregation typically found in Deep South communities proved difficult to replicate. For example, the military made little effort to segregate its medical facilities. Most camps had only one hospital. While some medical facilities maintained segregated white and Black sections—such as the one at Fort McClellan in Alabama—that arrangement did not always prove practical or efficient. At the hospitals at Camp Shelby and Keesler Field in Mississippi and many others in the Deep South, medical personnel merely assigned patients to the next available bed, regardless of race. These integrated arrangements shocked white Southerners who observed them in their backyard. Abner Spiers of Picayune worked at Keesler Field and complained that "the damn Negro is bed by bed in the same ward with white soldiers." When one of Georgia's US senators, Richard Russell, complained about the integrated arrangements at the army's Lawson General Hospital in Atlanta, the War Department responded that it had observed "no manifestation of racial or color problems" at the facility and "there has been no evidence of friction between members of the hospital staff and Negro patients." The War Department official even cited the nondiscrimination provision of the Selective Service Act of 1940, telling Russell that "under the law, it [the War Department] cannot discriminate."[18] That was the official policy, although for Black soldiers, especially at military outposts in the Deep South, instances of racial discrimination and racial violence abounded, both within and outside the camp.

White Southerners—and indeed, white Americans more broadly—succeeded in holding the line on retaining a segregated military. The training of Black and white troops at the same army camps, however, unleashed a battle over the racial segregation the military had refused to abandon, yet officially pledged to replicate in a "fairer" manner. In short, the federal government's policy of segregation without discrimination placed racial questions into stark relief during World War II. White Southerners stiffened their resolve to preserve the kinds of racial separation they had carefully crafted, a system not designed to be free of discrimination. At the same time, the federal government's somewhat lukewarm support for nondiscrimination—but support nonetheless—provided an opening for Black Americans to challenge the racial status quo in the Deep South. Black soldiers from the North seemed especially keen to exploit the gap between federal rhetoric and southern practice. But some Black Southerners in the military also joined the fight against the South's particularly insidious and inequitable system of racial segregation.[19]

Even before America's official entry into World War II, racial problems developed in and around military posts in the Deep South. The arrival of thousands of Black troops at Fort Benning in late 1940 and early 1941 led to an outbreak of racial violence there. On March 21, 1941, several white military police (MPs), including Robert A. Lummus, got into an early morning altercation with several Black GIs from the 48th Quartermaster Regiment, including Lawrence Hoover, from Columbus, Ohio, and his new friend, Albert King, a native of Columbus, Georgia. At some point during the incident, the nineteen-year-old Lummus killed the twenty-one-year-old King, shooting him five times. The physical evidence suggested that the last four shots struck King in the back while he lay prostrate on the ground. The MPs also badly beat Hoover. It remains unclear exactly what happened that morning. The MPs claimed that King and Hoover started a fight, Hoover resisted arrest, and Lummus shot King while he tried to escape custody. Other witnesses disputed this account and suggested the MPs had attacked the Black soldiers after pulling them off a bus and claiming they were causing a disturbance. Three months later, a military court-martial acquitted Lummus. Judge Hastie vigorously protested the proceeding, since it had accepted "in its entirety the utterly specious and wholly unbelievable testimony of Sgt. R.A. Lummus and ignores the physican [sic] evidence of the wounds inflicted by him." The Department of War, however, pronounced the matter closed.[20]

Like King, Lummus was a Georgia boy who had grown up near Macon, where his father worked as a cotton mill foreman. By the mid-1930s, the family had moved to Cusseta, less than twenty miles from Fort Benning. Lummus joined the army before the fall 1940 draft began and ended up at Fort Benning with the 66th Infantry. In April 1940, almost all the men in Lummus's barrack were white boys from the South. The demographics of the booming camp, however, had already begun to change, as the army designated the camp a national training center in 1939. After the draft started, troop numbers at Benning rose rapidly and included increasing numbers of both white Northerners and Black soldiers from all over the country. Lummus likely viewed Lawrence Hoover as an outside agitator, but he certainly expected Albert King to understand and abide by the existing racial hierarchy. These racial expectations of white Southerners—combined with the federal experiment to build a biracial army in the Deep South based on a less rigid form of segregation than typically found there—may have cost King his life on that March morning.[21]

One week after Lummus killed King, the camp found out about another murder of a Black soldier on post. An engineering unit marching in one of the isolated, wooded parts of Fort Benning came upon the dead body of Felix Hall, still in uniform and hanging from a tree with his hands tied behind his back and a bullet in his head. A nineteen-year-old private from Montgomery, Alabama, and a member of the 24th Infantry, Hall had volunteered in August 1940. Officials estimated that Hall had died weeks earlier (no one had seen him since mid-February), and the FBI came in to investigate what looked like a lynching of a US soldier on a US Army installation. Military leaders, however, offered some alternative and unlikely explanations for the incident: that Hall committed suicide (a seeming impossibility with one's hands tied behind his back) or had died as part of a sex crime. The FBI report, not released publicly until decades later, suggested several other possible reasons for the murder: Hall had fought with a white mill operator at the sawmill where the army had assigned him to work (in itself an odd deployment of military personnel); he had wandered into a white non-commissioned officer housing area of the camp, where white men who suspected Black "Peeping Toms" in their neighborhood had killed him; or he had shown too much interest in white women.[22]

Despite the leads produced by the FBI's investigation, which suggested a racially motivated killing, no one was ever charged with Hall's murder. The bureau seemed reluctant to vigorously pursue any potential suspects. The army, for its part, did everything possible to downplay the obvious conclusion that white people on or near one of their posts had lynched a Black service member. Although the story failed to gain much traction in the white press, Black Americans knew a lynching when they saw one and pointed out that the crime damaged the federal government's efforts to unify the country as war became imminent. As Roy Wilkins, the NAACP's assistant secretary, told FDR in April 1941, the "attempt to dismiss this [Hall's murder] as suicide, or a whitewash of the whole situation, would be a further blow at the morale of colored Americans who are being urged daily to give unstinted support to the national defense effort."[23]

The lynching of Hall failed to register in the national white mind. After all, most white killings of Black people in the Deep South at the time went unpunished. King's murder had received even less notice than the Hall lynching. The murder in May of a Black civilian ninety miles south of Fort Benning took a parallel course. A white employer accused Robert Sapp of stealing, and the employer and two other men brutally beat Sapp to death with a club and a machine belt. Existing white attitudes, which devalued Black lives, helped the military dodge a public relations disaster. The army contained the public inquiry into Hall's lynching, but the boiling racial tensions at army camps all over the region did not go away.[24]

The army did not endorse white Southerners' approach to dealing with Black soldiers, especially given its stated policy of nondiscrimination. Indeed, it soon took some halfhearted steps to eliminate the most visible and overt signs of racial discrimination, at least within the confines of its own facilities. Early on, the army tried to crack down on the offensive language that white officers and enlisted men used to refer to Black men. In a February 1942 directive, the War Department reminded all commanders of the following army regulation: "superiors are forbidden to injure those under their authority by tyrannical or capricious conduct or by abusive language." By way of clarifying this existing regulation, the order stated that "the use of any epithet deemed insulting to a racial group should be carefully avoided."

That order represented a bold declaration, but different commanders—and not just in the South—applied and implemented this command in numerous ways, dependent on their own beliefs and temperament. Some carefully followed up on the instruction. The commander of the 28th Infantry, training at Camp Livingston in Louisiana, issued an order in June 1942 that stated that "the word 'nigger' is a provocative word when used in speaking to or about colored soldiers." The commander's instructions included orders that "this word will not be used in this Division at any time." Not all army leaders, however, enforced these directions as vigilantly. A Black soldier from New York at nearby Camp Claiborne reported in May 1943 that white officers still regularly used the offensive term.[25]

The army's failure to control offensive language highlighted the fact that, despite the military's nondiscrimination policy and whatever incremental steps it might take in this direction, these efforts did not always change the hearts and minds of the men who wore the uniforms. Moreover, the army sometimes contributed to racial tensions on post through implementation of its own half-baked assumptions. For example, a significant part of the ongoing racial conflict within southern camps sprang from the army's preference to have white, southern officers lead Black units. Army leaders believed these men had a better understanding of how to "handle" Black men. The idea, fallacious on its face, made no sense in relation to Black troops from the North, who had little inclination to offer the kind of deference that southern white men typically expected from Black men. A group of northern Black soldiers training at Louisiana's Camp Claiborne claimed in March 1943 that "our conditions are worst [sic] than a dogs are here. These Southern whites that is commanding are terrible."[26] Within the gates of its facilities, the army had the authority to enforce segregation without discrimination, but its efforts in this area remained inconsistent and often ineffective, in part because of the racist assumptions of white military personnel.

Off-post, the army took no action to impose its nondiscrimination policy. Indeed, it maintained that its soldiers had to follow local segregation laws and southern customs when they entered southern communities. That decision ultimately undermined the military's halting efforts to enforce nondiscrimination initiatives at its installations. Southern communities did not adjust existing racial arrangements to accommodate the army's Black recruits. Although all soldiers needed a break from the grind of military training, that reprieve proved difficult for Black trainees in the Deep South."[27]

As war mobilization ramped up, southern towns eagerly sought Army camps for the economic benefits, but they initially thought little about town-camp relations. Southern white leaders also assumed that Black soldiers would adhere to the same Jim Crow laws and customs as local Black residents. In Hattiesburg, the town fathers who pressed so hard for the reestablishment of Camp Shelby made few preparations to provide recreational opportunities for any soldiers—Black or white. Part of the problem was that the camp and the town saw an influx of soldiers before the national United Service Organizations (USO) formed and before federal agencies had time to plan and build recreation facilities for the military. If these shortcomings affected all servicemen, they hit Black soldiers particularly hard. Like other Deep South communities, Hattiesburg maintained strict racial segregation. The Black section of the town, the Mobile Street District, could not handle the sudden population influx. According to a 1942 report of the Office of War Information, most Black soldiers described the Black district as a "hell hole" that offered "little more than bad bootleg whiskey, high prices for whatever you buy, a group of contentious men who resent soldier attentions to their women, and an excellent chance for venereal disease."[28]

All the problems associated with the army's embrace of southern segregation and local racial customs in civilian areas became clear in Alexandria, Louisiana, soon after the United States entered the war. Located in the central part of the state, thirty miles from Colfax, the site of a vicious white massacre of eighty Black men during Reconstruction, Alexandria became the civilian hub for three area Army camps (Claiborne, Livingston, and Beauregard) and three Army airfields, all within a twenty-mile radius of the town. These facilities trained 50,000 white troops and more than 15,000 Black soldiers. Alexandria experienced a doubling of its population in the early 1940s, growing to more than 50,000 people by the time the United States ramped up its mobilization in the wake of Pearl Harbor. The Black section of Alexandria, a four-block district surrounding Lee Street, was known as Little Harlem, which one Black recruit training at Camp Claiborne described simply as a "ghetto."[29]

A major racial disturbance occurred in Alexandria on Saturday night, January 10, 1942. That incident, however, did not happen in a vacuum. Military mobilization, well underway for almost a year, only increased the racial violence that had regularly roiled the town for decades. Local Black newspaper editor Georgia Johnson claimed that violence against the town's Black population had long been a fact of life. Such treatment, she wrote, "was imposed upon the civilians, so when the men in service came, it went on." The *Chicago Defender* claimed that Alexandria had "been known unfavorably insofar as its race relations are concerned and its policemen have a reputation for brutality and meanness." As in other Deep South communities, the white citizens of Alexandria viewed the Black soldiers who congested their town and who hailed from all over the country as outsiders and as a threat to the racial status quo.[30]

January 10, 1942, was much like any other Saturday evening in Little Harlem since the army had arrived. Thousands of Black servicemen from the nearby camps crowded into the area. Perhaps a similar number of Black civilians joined the soldiers in the four-block district. The mass of humanity milled in the streets and visited the one theater and fifteen eating and drinking establishments in the area. Around 8 P.M., an argument erupted outside the Ritz Theatre, when a Black GI got into a beef about the admission price at the establishment. The soldier became sufficiently belligerent that a Black MP placed him under arrest. At that point, a white MP intervened and demanded control of the prisoner. When the Black MP refused, the white MP, according to one account, said, "Nigger you can't arrest no one, we white people run this town." Black soldiers began to argue with the white MPs trying to seize the prisoner, and the MPs called the provost marshal, Ray McKnight, who had lived in Alexandria for a dozen years and had married a local woman. The provost marshal, who commanded MP units, issued a general riot call, sent in a detachment of sixty white MPs, and called on the local and state police for reinforcements. White press accounts later claimed a white MP from Wisconsin started the initial confrontation, though Black press accounts said that the white MP who created the commotion hailed from Mississippi, part of a detail that "had been carrying on a systematic program of abuse against colored soldiers for months, subjecting them to every form of indignity."[31]

Wherever he was from, the white MP who started the conflict in Little Harlem had discharged his firearm at the unarmed Black soldiers gathered around him, but the scene really descended into bloody violence only after the local police arrived. As the MP unit called into the area by the provost marshal started trying to round up Black GIs at gunpoint to get them to the bus station and back to Camps Livingston and Claiborne, the local police arrived with guns blazing. Chaos ensued. Some Black soldiers, though unarmed, tried to resist the white lawmen, but most fled, with white MPs and white police in pursuit. A Black resident of the neighborhood described one of the many encounters that evening between white lawmen and Black soldiers. While sitting on his porch, the civilian claimed, "I saw two white M.P.s coming down the street. They leaped over my hedge and hid when they saw a colored soldier approach. I distinctly hear one of them say, 'Here comes a d__ n__r soldier now; let him have it.' They started shooting point blank at him as he fled, with the pair in hot pursuit, pumping their revolvers. I don't know whether they struck him or not."[32]

When the smoke cleared, thirteen Black servicemen had suffered gunshot wounds and seventeen had received beatings that required medical attention. The Alexandria police, led by Chief George C. Gray, apparently were responsible for most of those injuries. The military's investigation of the incident found that all the gunshot wounds came from .38 caliber guns or shotguns, both of which the police officers carried. The report concluded that while "a show of force may have been justified to disperse the exciting [sic] crowd," the injuries in Alexandria resulted from "civilian policemen and one military policeman [who] indulged in indiscriminate and unnecessary shooting." Various sources at the time, including several Black soldiers and James B. LaFourche, the public relations director for the NAACP's Regional Conference of Southern Branches, based in New Orleans, reported that as many as ten people died during the Alexandria disturbance. The military denied these claims. The belief that Black soldiers died in the Alexandria racial uproar, however, has long persisted, particularly in subsequent oral histories, not only among Black residents of Alexandria but even in the recollections of some white law enforcement officials.[33]

White lawmen not only sought to subdue Black soldiers and send them back to camp but also terrorized the Black civilians of Little Harlem. A complete accounting of the civilians injured and the homes and businesses damaged is hard to come by, since the army and most press accounts offered little comment on this part of the Alexandria episode. One of the first outside groups to come to Alexandria to investigate the city's racial disturbance did report on the larger attack on Black Alexandria that night. A group of actors and writers from the Stage and Screen Division of the Fight for Freedom Committee arrived just days after the violent episode. This contingent included actor Burgess Meredith and screenwriter Ben Hecht. The committee of artists reported that "hundreds of Negro civilians in the city of Alexandria were beaten by police authorities, rounded up and forced to remain inside their homes." At least one Black civilian, Mary Frances Scales, a twenty-two-year-old waitress working at Hunt's Grille Cafe, suffered a gunshot wound during the event. When the shooting erupted in Little Harlem, Scales tried to run back to her rooming house, but a stray bullet struck her in the hip. Civilians brought her back into the restaurant, and although the city police refused to call an ambulance for her, Black MPs transported her to the hospital. At least one other Black woman received a beating from a state police officer, an incident known only because it resulted in the only white injury during the two hours that white officials rampaged through Black Alexandria. For several months after the January 10 incident, white mobs reportedly continued to harass Black civilians in the town.[34]

In the aftermath of the Alexandria unrest, the army confined Black soldiers from Camps Livingstone and Claiborne to their posts, at least temporarily. The army also sought to keep the Black press, the only news outlets with any sustained reporting on the racial troubles that had rocked central Louisiana, out of the area. Some white residents feared Black soldiers might return to the city to retaliate—armed this time. Rumors circulated that Black GIs had claimed as much as the MPs escorted them back to their camps on the night of January 10. At least one story asserted that military commanders placed restrictions on the Black soldiers at one of the camps because, upon their return to camp, they broke into an installation arsenal to collect firearms. In the aftermath of the Lee Street disturbance, the army even briefly disarmed the white MPs who patrolled Alexandria. After ten days of restriction, Black soldiers could leave camp, although Little Harlem remained off-limits for two months. Even then, many of the Black men decided to take liberty elsewhere, traveling more than two to three hours away to either Baton Rouge or New Orleans. As a result, both Black and white businesses in Little Harlem suffered. In the end, racial animosity erased at least part of the economic benefit of locating army posts near Alexandria.[35]

As the events in Alexandria demonstrate, Army MPs regularly occupied the frontlines when disputes broke out between Black soldiers and white civilians. White MPs sometimes used excessive force when carrying out their duties, especially when dealing with Black soldiers. Complicating matters, the MPs had contradictory orders when mediating racial disputes in the South. The army supported both nondiscrimination and respect for local discriminatory laws and customs. In some cases, MPs refused to uphold the inequitable treatment of Black citizens practiced by white Southerners. In April 1942, Black soldiers from the air base near Columbus, Mississippi, went to town to play baseball with Black civilians. At some point a fight broke out, and when a Black soldier pulled a knife on a white officer trying to stop the ruckus, the local constable arrested the enlisted man and hauled him before the city marshal. Before local authorities could impose punishment, however, a white MP intervened in court, and according to a local white lawyer, "showed decided signs of upholding the negro because he had on a uniform." As the lawyer reported to Mississippi Senator Theodore Bilbo, "This condition cannot be tolerated."[36]

For the most part, however, white MPs deferred to local segregation law and practice. Civilian lawmen in the South—overwhelmingly white—had traditionally offered rough treatment for Black Southerners who stepped out of line on a variety of issues, both major and trivial. Indeed, many communities in the Deep South had long histories of law enforcement brutality toward Black people.[37] In Hattiesburg, which did not have a MP detachment detailed to the town when Camp Shelby opened, the local police initially handled all law enforcement matters involving military troops. As a result, in the summer of 1941 several Black soldiers from Camp Shelby reported that the local cops had "brutally beaten" them. Throughout the South, run-ins between white lawmen and Black GIs led to a variety of situations that diminished the options for Black servicemen on leave from their military duties. The army banned 1,000 Black airmen stationed at the airfield near Meridian, Mississippi, from the town in the spring of 1942 after what a local minister described as "a misunderstanding between the civilian police and the Negro soldiers." Hearing of the ban, the preacher noted that "the morale of these soldiers is very low." In July 1942, local police in Columbus, Georgia, arrested several Black soldiers from Fort Benning. The men did a stint in the town jail, and the police officers also later put the Black GIs to work cleaning the town's streets. Around the same time, soldiers from Camp Gordon claimed that the local police in nearby Augusta not only stopped them and issued random beatings but also monitored and disrupted their contact with local Black women.[38]

Black soldiers often saw little difference between their fellow white soldier wearing the MP armband and the local backwoods southern sheriff. As a Black soldier from Brooklyn stationed at Camp Claiborne put it, the MPs were a "deputized Dixie mob." In an effort to reduce racial tension in Black neighborhoods that Black GIs frequented, the army utilized Black MPs, even in Deep South communities. Black soldiers perceived discipline from such military policemen differently. As one pointed out in 1942, "Those colored boys beat hell out of the troops too, but somehow it don't make you quite as mad as it does when the white boys do it." Even though Black MPs often patrolled the Black districts of southern towns and disciplined Black soldiers, Black soldiers in MP units had little power to act when disputes occurred between Black soldiers and white civilians or white MPs. In many cases, local white officials succeeded in disarming Black MPs. In Alexandria, they had initially received pistols, but after white residents objected, the army took away their guns. By the beginning of 1942, they patrolled the town with only batons. As late as 1944, Black MPs in Alabama at Mobile's Brookley Army Air Field carried no weapons. Unlike white MPs, their Black counterparts were not always regular outfits; rather, the army often cobbled Black men together from various units for temporary police duty.[39]

Even with these constraints imposed on Black MPs by the army, Deep South communities refused to recognize that they had any authority, which severely limited their ability to do their jobs. When a group of Black soldiers from Camp Gordon had a run-in with the Augusta, Georgia, police in June 1942, the Black MPs knew they could do little to shield Black soldiers from the abuse of local law enforcement. The police had stopped five Black soldiers for a seemingly random reason, lined them up against a wall, and started hitting them with their blackjacks. To the amazement of other Black soldiers observing this police brutality, Black MPs stood across the street and watched. When the white policemen moved on, the Black MPs crossed the street and took the injured soldiers to the post hospital. Had they tried to intervene to stop the beating, however, the racial violence on the streets of Augusta would surely have escalated.[40]

Indeed, Private Raymond Carr, a Black MP from Louisiana's Camp Beauregard, lost his life in Alexandria in the fall of 1942 after challenging a white Louisiana state trooper. Carr was a local boy. He had completed only the fifth grade, and before enlisting in the army in the summer of 1942 he had worked as a hoe man in a sugarcane field in south Louisiana and as a shrimp dock worker. Soon after midnight on November 1, Carr and a fellow Black MP, John Spears, a draftee from Florida, patrolled Alexandria's Black downtown district. The two MPs came upon a Black couple engaged in a dispute, and the woman tried to get the MPs to intervene. Since the quarrel did not involve military personnel, Carr and Spears demurred. Two Louisiana state troopers arrived on the scene, and an argument broke out between the MPs and the state lawmen. The state policemen decided to arrest all four of the Black folks. The MPs refused to submit to arrest and claimed that leaving their post would make them subject to possible court-martial. While the MPs and state police bickered, the arguing couple slipped away unnoticed.

The troopers left but soon returned with reinforcements, both to search for the couple and to arrest the Black MPs. Spears surrendered, but Carr continued to argue with one of the white state police and eventually tried to run away. Trooper Dalton McCollum caught and shot the unarmed Carr, who died three days later.[41]

In the aftermath of this incident, the military requested the arrest of McCollum. Nine eyewitnesses described the killing as a "cold-blooded murder," and Carr confirmed these accounts to nurses at the hospital as he lay dying. The assistant superintendent of the state police, L. A. Newsome, told the commander of Camp Beauregard, Colonel K. F. Hanst, that he would not arrest a state trooper for shooting a Black man. The army's official investigation concluded that "an American soldier on his official post of duty was shot down in cold blood, without any provocation whatsoever." Noting that the state refused to endorse a prosecution of Carr's killer, the army investigator suggested that the incident "be handled vigorously or the Army will be subjected to just criticism for its failure to protect its men killed on duty without any justification."

The military tried to pressure the US Justice Department to intervene in this matter. Assistant Secretary of War John J. McCloy told the US attorney general that if the federal government took no action to bring Carr's killer to justice, then "I fear that many Negro soldiers, particularly, and not alone those from the North, will be infected with growing apprehension that as soldiers they can expect no protection from abuses on the part of State and local law enforcement officers." When a Louisiana grand jury failed to indict McCollum, the NAACP claimed that "it is difficult to believe that our democracy has a chance of survival as long as it is unable to punish an individual who kills a United States soldier while on duty pursuant to orders of the War Department." Despite the urgings of the army and the NAACP, the US Justice Department refused to act to bring McCollum to justice.[42]

In response to racial unrest in the Deep South, local communities did take some small steps to improve conditions for the Black fighting men stationed nearby. For one thing, white Southerners embraced the work of the USO, created to serve "the religious, spiritual welfare and educational needs of the men and women in the armed forces and defense industries, and in general to contribute to the maintenance of morale in American communities." Three days after the Lee Street melee in Alexandria, local white citizens endorsed the creation of a Black USO center, which opened in February 1942. The following month, the USO opened a facility for Black GIs in Hattiesburg's downtown Black district. The institution provided many amenities: meeting rooms, an auditorium, showers, a kitchen, reading and writing rooms, and a free banking service. By March 1944, the USO had 239 operations in 92 communities in Louisiana, Mississippi, Alabama, and Georgia. At least 10 percent of those, located in the larger towns in the region, catered to Black servicemen.[43]

Although Black USO centers in the Deep South provided much-needed recreational facilities for Black soldiers, white citizens sought to maintain tight control over the activities of these establishments. For example, in Hattiesburg, a management committee composed primarily of white businessmen and led by Frank M. Tatum, whose family had a major timber operation and ran Willmut Gas & Oil, controlled the operation of both the white and Black USOs in town. The management committee created a Black advisory committee made up of local Black residents, but it had little to no say in most matters of importance. The army and navy YMCA provided the staff and funding for the Black East Sixth Street USO, and the national YWCA also provided some funding and an assistant director to help with programming and services for the wives and children of Black servicemen.

The YWCA appointed Aquilla Matthews to this latter position in Hattiesburg. A light-complexioned woman with degrees from both Northwestern and Columbia Universities, Matthews quickly fell out of favor with the town's white leaders for several of her actions. She helped organize a local affiliate of the Women's Federated Club movement and offered the USO facilities as a weekly meeting spot for the group. She also arranged for a speaking appearance at the Black USO in July 1942 by Mary McLeod Bethune, the noted educator and activist who served as director of the Division of Negro Affairs in FDR's National Youth Administration. Bethune spoke to a gathering of more than 2,500 and reminded the assembly that "united effort and equal opportunity for participation in all phases relating to human welfare and the war program are the pleas of the Negroes of America." Despite Bethune's moderate message, whites in Hattiesburg—according to a local Black resident—blamed Matthews for bringing in a "detestable, uppity Negro, coddled by Roosevelt's New Deal" to address a Black crowd in Hattiesburg.[44]

A month later, members of the management committee informed the YWCA that Aquilla Matthews's work was unsatisfactory and that she needed to be removed from the Hattiesburg USO. The YWCA asked for details about Matthews's allegedly unsatisfactory job performance and noted that the

YWCA "have had no reports up to this time which would give us any facts on which to base judgment." Frank Tatum responded that the committee's assessment that Matthews's "services are unsatisfactory, and she does not cooperate with the other directors and workers in carrying on the activities" was reason enough for dismissal. Local white opinion suggested that the main complaint about Matthews was that she acted "too white for a Negro in Hattiesburg," according to an unpublished investigative report by the Office of War Information. The YWCA pointed out that the Hattiesburg Management Committee did not control the selection and payment of USO workers, but Tatum said the organization would need to accede to the committee's personnel decisions. The YWCA, however, did not back down. It recalled Matthews to New York, and it also removed all the furnishings and equipment the organization had provided to the East Sixth Street building and promised to cut off all future support to both of Hattiesburg's USOs. The Black Advisory Committee cautiously crafted a petition protesting the removal of Matthews. The document stated that "we, as a committee, appeal to you—not demanding, not asking, but begging for advice as to what can be done to reinstate the work of the YWCA." Tatum declined to even present the petition to the entire management committee, although several months later, Hattiesburg leaders reached a compromise with the YWCA, which brought the organization back to the city.[45]

For many of the thousands of Black soldiers at Camp Shelby, all of them in support units of one kind or another, Hattiesburg's tiny Black quarter and relatively small USO facility offered few attractions and too many restrictions. As one Black GI noted, "When I leave camp I keep right on to New Orleans. Unless I can't help myself, I am never caught in Hattiesburg. It's hell." Elsewhere, Black soldiers on leave generally sought to bypass smaller communities near their training stations for larger towns farther away that had more substantial Black business and entertainment districts. Most Black GIs stationed at Camp Van Dorn made only one trip to the small but rapidly expanding village of Centreville.

Even Black people from other parts of the South did not always recognize the local segregation customs of the small town: each race had a separate side of the downtown streets to use; some businesses catered to Black people on segregated terms while others strictly prohibited their presence. In addition, many of the white civilians carried guns. As one northern soldier in the 512th Quartermasters noted, the white residents "seem to want a pitched battle with Negro soldiers." When Black newcomers to the area inevitably violated the racial rules, white locals lashed out with violence, much as they would have with any area Black person who stepped out of his "place." As a result, Black soldiers from Camp Van Dorn often took their leave at other locales farther away—Natchez (small yet relatively cosmopolitan), Baton Rouge, and New Orleans.[46]

As racial troubles broke out in southern communities near military installations in the first two years after mobilization began in the fall of 1940, the War Department considered altering how it assigned Black soldiers to training facilities. In May 1942, the War Department crafted a directive that called for the training of northern Black soldiers in the North and southern Black troops in the South, whenever possible. However, when Judge Hastie's assistant, Truman K. Gibson, reviewed an early draft of the document, he predicted that the instruction would create "practical administrative difficulties." He also pointed out that a geographic segregation of Black GIs would not end the racial tensions that had rocked the South. Despite claims by white Southerners that northern Black soldiers caused all the problems, Gibson's analysis noted what the military brass already knew: "in nearly every case [of racial incidents] Southern Negroes have been involved." The adjutant general of the Army, Major General J. A. Ulio, told Gibson that the directive would merit only "secondary consideration; the needs of units must control assignments regardless of locations."[47]

Early in World War II, the military largely tried to ignore the racial problems that training a biracial fighting force near southern communities created, even though its own policies played a key role in sparking that turmoil. The military had promoted racial unrest by officially embracing a less discriminatory form of racial segregation yet subjecting its Black recruits to the harsh realities of segregation in southern locales. The disconnect between military rhetoric and military action infuriated Black soldiers who came south from other regions (although southern soldiers also recognized the contradictions). In January 1942, Roy Wilkins explained to Secretary of War Henry Stimson how the army disregarded its nondiscrimination policy to create racial conflict in the South:

> The Army has adopted and is enforcing a social pattern in keeping with the mores of the small communities adjacent to the Army camps. The Army has taken thousands of Negro men from northern and eastern states and placed them in localities whose traditions and practices are designed deliberately to humiliate and insult them, and even to maltreat and kill them. Not only

does the War department take these men to these kinds of communities, but the military police, upon the slightest pretext, solicit the active assistance of civilian police, who have no regard for Negroes as men, or citizens, or soldiers of their country, and who shoot them down without hesitation.[48]

Wilkins understood that these racial problems would not go away if the military supported southern-style segregation in any instance. Even "if the Negro soldiers in their separate units were treated with absolute equality," he wrote, the military would still need to insist "bluntly and unequivocally that all soldiers of the United States must be treated in the same manner by communities near which they happen to be encamped." Like S. D. Redmond, Wilkins knew that the racial unrest and violence rolling over the Deep South damaged Black morale, not just among soldiers but beyond the army and beyond Dixie. As Wilkins told Stimson, "The morale of Negro citizens is already dangerously low, all optimistic reports to the contrary. Colored people are infuriated over the physical violence done to their soldiers. They are bitter and resentful."[49] Wilkins's clear analysis of the problem fell on deaf ears. As the summer of 1943 approached, the racial tensions surrounding military installations building since the fall of 1940 crested and exploded in the Deep South.

6

The 364th Infantry Regiment, Camp Van Dorn, and the Crisis of 1943

On Sunday, May 30, 1943, not far from the main gate of Camp Van Dorn, an army fort near Centreville, Mississippi, a local white lawman shot and killed William Walker, a Black private in the 364th Infantry Regiment. The unit had arrived at Camp Van Dorn only four days before this slaying occurred, a brief period marked by racial disturbances both within and outside the camp. The 364th had previously faced difficulties at earlier postings in Louisiana and Arizona. In the aftermath of Walker's death, unrest in the camp briefly spiked, which led to rumors of widespread violence and mayhem taking place at the camp. These rumors spread among the white civilians in the small town of Centreville—almost adjacent to the facility—and beyond. Decades later, tales about a massacre of Black soldiers at Camp Van Dorn in the fall of 1943 emerged. These massacre rumors, which continue to circulate, sprang from white anxieties about local Black activism during the civil rights era and have no validity. Unfortunately, they have obscured a more important story about the difficulties faced by a Black combat unit training in the Deep South during World War II.

To fully understand the killing of William Walker at Camp Van Dorn, the incident must be placed in its proper context. During 1943, racial tensions related to war mobilization—both economic and military—peaked nationwide. One of the largest racial commotions of 1943 occurred in June in Detroit, a city that experienced a rapid influx of both white and Black citizens (many from the South) to provide labor for the "Arsenal of Democracy." Earlier in June, in Los Angeles, military personnel attacked young Mexicans, "zoot-suiters," in a week of violence that led to hundreds of injuries and more than one hundred arrests. The white riot at the Alabama Dry Dock and Shipbuilding Company in Mobile occurred the week before the Walker killing. In the Deep South, during the weeks surrounding the killing of Private Walker, major racial conflicts erupted in the areas around several other army installations in the region, including Camp Stewart in Georgia and Camps

Home Front Battles. Charles C. Bolton, Oxford University Press. © Oxford University Press 2024.
DOI: 10.1093/oso/9780197655610.003.0007

McCain and Shelby in Mississippi. Other rumors of racial trouble in the area circulated during the same period. In early July, reports of an anticipated race riot in Atlanta led to a call for mothers to keep their children indoors after dark. Part of the story involved untrue claims that Black and white workers at the nearby Bell Bomber Plant had already engaged in "bloody conflict." Altogether, national press outlets noted more than 100 racial incidents in the South between March and December 1943.[1]

The military had created the 364th Infantry Regiment when it split the 367th Infantry Regiment into two regiments. The 367th, one of three separate Black infantry regiments created in 1940 as part of the army's effort to expand the opportunities for Black soldiers to serve in combat roles, originally organized at Camp Claiborne, Louisiana, in March 1941, largely with men from Florida, Mississippi, and Louisiana. Some of these soldiers may have been in Little Harlem during the Alexandria racial trouble of January 1942. In the spring of 1942, after the army divided the 367th, Black draftees from the North made up many of the replacements who joined the newly formed 364th Regiment. Thus, the unit had men who came from all over the country. The Black soldiers of the 364th trained with inadequate equipment, and a sparsely outfitted service club for the enlisted men offered little respite during off-hours. The unit had only six Black officers at the time, and according to Truman K. Gibson, assistant civilian aide to the secretary of war, these second lieutenants "were smeared by the post's commanding officer as troublemakers."[2]

Like other Black soldiers in the Deep South, the men of the 364th faced their share of troubles with white civilians. In May 1942, a white woman staying at the Camp Claiborne Guest House accused three members of the 364th of raping her. The men claimed the woman consented to the sexual activity. In a long, drawn-out proceeding, in which the National Association for the Advancement of Colored People (NAACP) came to the men's defense, a military court-martial—based on inconclusive evidence at best—convicted the three men and sentenced them to death. President Franklin D. Roosevelt later commuted their sentences to life, and the army paroled all three men in 1947.[3]

In June 1942, the 364th moved to the army's Southern Land Frontier in Arizona at a time when an enemy attack in the West still seemed like a possibility. Detachments of the regiment guarded the country's border with Mexico, area air bases, and the city of Phoenix. The work was hard; conditions in their base of operations, Camp Papago, ten miles outside of

Phoenix, were primitive; and adequate clothing and shoes were in short supply. The regiment's Black chaplain, Captain Elmer Gibson, as well as a relative of a Pennsylvania soldier in the regiment, complained to members of Congress that the unit's top white commanders, Colonel Fred Wickham and Lieutenant Colonel Hugh Adair, engaged in violent and racist behavior. Gibson later claimed that the rape allegations in Louisiana had "stirred our Commanding Officer [Wickham] and the majority of our Officers who were southern to the highest pitch," leading to "unreasonable disciplinary measures [and] punishments not according to regulation." The specific complaints included accusations that Wickham put men in the camp stockade for minor offenses, such as reporting late for duty. Once there, prison guards reportedly woke the men at night and forced them to run around the grounds while shooting at their feet, and sometimes they worked the soldiers through the night. In addition, the prison cells had no beds.[4]

The harsh treatment of prisoners on post led to a near-riot at Camp Papago on November 13, 1942. After a group of soldiers at the camp theater heard shots coming from the nearby stockade, they went to investigate. As the soldiers shouted at the guards for information about the gunshots, a group of the prisoners came out toward the fence and egged their fellow soldiers on, telling them, "You men on the outside should do something about this." The gathering of soldiers outside the fence eventually grew to two or three hundred. Colonel Wickham arrived on the scene, and along with other officers, tried to get the Black soldiers to disperse. Unable to calm the crowd, which became increasingly angry while listening to the complaints of their incarcerated brothers, someone ordered the use of tear gas to disperse the soldiers from the area of the stockade.[5]

The charges lodged against the white commanders of the 364th must have had some merit, for after an investigation, army officials recommended that the unit receive new leadership. Before the War Department took any action, however, a tragedy occurred. On Thanksgiving night, November 26, members of the 364th got into a violent fight in Phoenix with a group from the 773rd Military Police (MP), a Black company. The squabble grew out of a long-standing conflict between the men of the two units. The feud may have, in part, involved a dispute over civilian women. Robert Thomson, a white lieutenant in the 364th who came from Virginia, later remembered that "members of the 364th had been developing relations with the women in the Black/Mexican portion of Phoenix prior to their duty in the Arizona desert. When they returned to Phoenix, they discovered that the MPs had become rivals for the same women." Whatever the cause of the friction between the two groups of soldiers, the animosity worsened in the days leading up to Thanksgiving Day. On Monday, the men of the 364th who had been assigned to MP duty in Phoenix received notification that the 773rd would be taking over many of their tasks, including the "walking patrols" in the city. On Thanksgiving night, at the Savoy Café, when a disturbance broke out—one that MPs from the 364th might have easily diffused—a member of one of the new 773rd patrols discharged his weapon and injured one of the men from the 364th. A throng of soldiers from the Black regiment quickly gathered outside the restaurant. The 773rd shut down the Savoy, as well as a nearby Black United Service Organizations facility where another group of soldiers had begun to congregate, and ordered the men to the bus station to return to Camp Papago.[6]

Word soon reached the camp about the events in Phoenix: a story circulated that the 773rd was attacking and killing the enlisted men of the 364th. That rumor enraged many of the men in the regiment, including some who had formerly performed MP patrol duty in the city. An unknown number of soldiers left the camp and made their way back to Phoenix to confront the 773rd. Beginning shortly after midnight, a three-hour pitched battle raged in a twenty-eight-block area of southeast Phoenix. Civilian police and 400 soldiers eventually quelled the disorder, and in the process, detained more than 150 Black soldiers and civilians as possible participants in the incident. When the fighting ended, fourteen people had suffered gunshot wounds, three of those fatal: a white MP, a Black soldier, and a Black civilian.[7]

Armored MP vehicles patrolled the streets of Phoenix for almost a week after what some began calling the Phoenix Massacre, and for days afterward, turmoil raged in the 364th. Many men in the unit went AWOL for several days. The army court-martialed twenty-seven members of the regiment and eventually convicted fifteen of them, handing out sentences from twenty-five to fifty years, and in one case, that of Private John Sipp, a death sentence. Some of these men had clearly participated in the Phoenix gun battle, although it proved difficult to know precisely what role any of them played in the hostilities that Friday morning. Some of those convicted, however, apparently never even made it into Phoenix on Thanksgiving night.[8]

The army's official investigation of the Thanksgiving incident in Phoenix blamed the disturbance on poor discipline and morale, as well as "a failure of leadership." Before the Thanksgiving weekend ended, the military had addressed the latter issue by appointing a new commander of the 364th: Lieutenant Colonel John Forest Goodman, who would lead the unit for the remainder of the war. Goodman soon restored discipline among the men of the 364th. According to Irvin Wiley, a private in the outfit, Goodman "took this regiment under his wing during the Phoenix Thanksgiving Day disorder, and guided them through a maze of criticisms, accusations, and extremely low morale." The army also moved to update the regiment's substandard camp facilities. The regiment had no trouble on or off the installation for the remainder of its tour in Arizona.[9]

In early 1943, the 364th received new orders: move to Camp Van Dorn in Mississippi to train for eventual assignment to the European Theater of Operations. Some soldiers in the regiment thought that the army sent the 364th to the Deep South as punishment for the troubles in Arizona, but little evidence exists for that claim. Army units constantly moved during the war for different training or assignments. In April 1943, army leaders concluded that the "long retention [of the 364th] at this station is likely to produce a deterioration in its present efficiency." The military had other reasons for the transfer. By 1943, protecting America's borders no longer required the manpower originally envisioned by war planners. The army needed combat units for the European theater and had vague plans to eventually use even the few Black contingents like the 364th, but it required further training to prepare for that mission. Most southern training facilities had unused capacity.[10]

The arrival of the 364th in southwest Mississippi was big news among both the Black soldiers already stationed at Camp Van Dorn and the white civilians of the area. Although some had undoubtedly heard about the racial disturbance in Phoenix, the real novelty was that the 364th Regiment was a Black *combat* unit. Rumors had spread among whites throughout southwest Mississippi that this Black outfit might seek revenge for previous wrongs done to Black soldiers. White residents might have assumed that a Black combat unit would retaliate more readily than the Black service units that had trained at the camp since its opening in November 1942. The addition of the 364th to the population of Camp Van Dorn also significantly increased the number of Black soldiers at the facility; the almost 3,000 Black men of the regiment joined perhaps 6,000 Black soldiers already at the camp. And unlike the other Black units at Van Dorn, the 364th also had Black officers—thirty-nine of them, mostly second lieutenants. When the first of the two troop trains carrying the 364th stopped at McComb, forty miles from Centreville, the unit's commanders refused to let the soldiers off the train. According to Samuel D. Smith, a Black corporal from Michigan, "the town people [of McComb] were hostile." As the train rolled through Centreville on the way to Camp Van Dorn (a spur line ran straight from downtown Centreville into the camp), white MPs lined the tracks, armed with machine guns. As the men unloaded the train's supplies, a fight broke out between a white private and one of the new arrivals of the 364th, although an officer broke up the fisticuffs before things went too far.[11]

Some of the men in the 364th had already decided that they would not adopt a submissive posture or follow the rigid, discriminatory racial segregation practiced in the rural southwest Mississippi army camp or the neighboring community. The night after the first men of the 364th arrived at Camp Van Dorn, May 27, many of them went to the Black service club. They got in trouble with the Black hostess and a Black sergeant, who was the ranking officer at the club, over uniform violations, bringing beer from the one of the post exchanges (PX) into the building, and being "rude" to the hostess. The new arrivals did not appreciate the effort by the Black non-commissioned officer to enforce military discipline after-hours. They were combat soldiers, after all, training for deployment to Europe. The sergeant ran the men of the 364th out of the club. Other men from the 364th, joined by some soldiers from the 518th Quartermaster Regiment, entered one of the white theaters on the installation. At first, no one stepped forward to enforce the typical exclusion of Black patrons, but then, about halfway through the picture, the lights came on, and someone ordered the Black soldiers to leave, which they did.[12]

Other members of the 364th ignored an order to avoid Centreville and headed to the village. There, they met a hostile civilian population. Townspeople, backed by the white MPs from Camp Van Dorn, determined to keep the soldiers of the 364th out of their community. As one member of the regiment from Georgia, Clarence Jones, remembered, the "local people as well as the Military Police did all they could to keep the colored soldiers from having anything to do with the local colored people, saying that 'the northern Niggers would spoil the local colored people.'" Unsubstantiated rumors of soldiers going into Centreville and not returning existed before the arrival of the 364th and continued afterward. Lieutenant Thomson recalled the killing of one soldier on May 27; he reportedly wanted "to test the system" in town. The Black press reported that the next night a local taxi driver killed another Black soldier who wandered into Centreville.[13]

On the evening of May 28, after the remainder of the 364th arrived, another attempt to challenge segregation occurred at one of Van Dorn's PXs.

THE 364TH INFANTRY REGIMENT 155

The camp had both Black and white PXs, of unequal quality. The two Black PXs had limited stock, slow service, and crowded facilities (together, the two PXs now served 9,000 soldiers). Some of the white PXs, such as the one for the white 99th Infantry, had outdoor beer gardens. According to the FBI, a group of soldiers from the 364th entered one of the white PXs and insisted on service. The exchange officer, a Captain Tyson, responded by closing the facility. Major General Virgil Peterson, the army's inspector general, later claimed that the shuttering of the store resulted from the "profane, disrespectful and threatening conduct" of the Black soldiers. Another army investigator, C. C. Park, labeled the soldiers' conduct before the 8:15 P.M. closure as "on the verge of becoming boisterous." Both descriptions, however, represented euphemisms for Black activism, as neither man mentioned the segregation challenge described in the FBI report. After Tyson announced the store's closure, the Black men of the 364th threw beer bottles at the officer and eventually stormed the PX, looted items, and damaged the facility. They then quickly retreated, escaping before the MPs arrived.[14]

The next night, Saturday, May 29, about seventy-five men from the 364th took their most provocative action since arriving in southwest Mississippi. Ignoring orders to avoid Centreville and heading up the spur line toward the small town, the Black soldiers encountered an angry and armed group of local citizens, led by Centreville police chief Robert J. Knighton, a man characterized by one Black member of the 364th at the time as someone "who molests, threatens and intimidates the men when they are off military reservations." An army investigator later claimed that the Black soldiers "marched around town in formation and used indecent and profane language in the presence of those they encountered," before being stopped by Knighton and his "deputized citizens armed with shotguns." Other accounts suggest that the Centreville men halted any advance by the Black GIs before they got very far into town and did any marching. In any event, the very fact of Black combat soldiers descending on tiny Centreville in an organized group of any kind clearly frightened the town's white citizens. Although Knighton reportedly tried to arrest the Black soldiers, the provost marshal from Camp Van Dorn, having heard about the brewing confrontation, arrived with a contingent of MPs before the lawman and his "deputies" could take the soldiers into custody. Army officials sent the men back to camp but did not punish those who had disobeyed the Centreville off-limits order.[15]

The next day, Van Dorn MPs patrolled the perimeter of the camp, hoping to keep unauthorized soldiers from leaving the installation and preventing a potentially violent confrontation like the one narrowly averted the night before. At 4:30 in the afternoon, two white MPs came upon five soldiers from the 364th just outside the camp. The men did not have passes to be off-post and several of them had uniform violations. One of the MPs, Charles Hix, hassled the men about these breaches of military discipline. Hix, a twenty-three-year-old draftee from the Atlanta area, who had worked as a sales-clerk in a grocery before the war, had a reputation of treating Black soldiers roughly. In March 1943, Hix had worked on the Centreville-to-Vicksburg train when he encountered Sergeant Harvey Watkins, a Black New York soldier from Van Dorn's 512th Quartermaster Regiment. Watkins did not have a pass to go to Vicksburg; he boarded the train at the last minute to try to talk one of his men out of going AWOL. Hix asked to see Watkins's pass with a "Hey, soldier." Watkins objected that Hix failed to recognize his rank. As the two men started to argue, Hix quickly brought out his blackjack and started to beat the Black sergeant. An army investigation later admitted that Hix "may have resorted to the use of his club sooner than was necessary." Hix and his fellow MP wrestled Watkins to the end of the train, where they continued to beat him for "resisting arrest," as both MPs later claimed, a justification the army accepted. At the Gloster stop, the two MPs turned Watkins over to the town marshal. The Black soldier had numerous cuts and bruises on his face and head, as well as a wrist sprain.[16]

Six weeks later, when Hix ordered the Black soldiers of the 364th to fix their uniforms, William Walker, a private from Chicago, argued with the MP and refused to comply. Perhaps Walker had heard of Hix's reputation and wanted to stand up to the white MP. When Walker refused to follow Hix's command, the MP grabbed his blackjack and got out of his jeep. A fight broke out between the two men and Walker gained the upper hand. Walker's companions and Hix's MP partner, Private Leslie Milburne, a twenty-two-year-old white Tennessean, stood by and watched the struggle. Although armed, Milburne made little effort to stop the fight. Local law enforcement, who also wanted to keep Black soldiers out of town, arrived at the scene after the fight had started. All accounts suggest that Hix asked the lawmen to help him—the Black witnesses said that Hix specifically asked Centreville Police Chief Knighton to shoot Walker. The white and Black accounts of what happened next diverge significantly. Knighton, Sheriff Richard Whitaker, and Deputy Sheriff Claude Henderson said that Walker charged the sheriff, who shot the Black private as he ran toward him. Interestingly, Milburne said he "could not tell if the soldier was taking after the Sheriff or not."[17]

The Black soldiers present claimed that Knighton shot Walker without provocation. They also said that after Hix shot Walker, the MP clubbed the Black soldier with his blackjack. The four other Black soldiers scattered, although the oldest of the group, thirty-one-year-old Morgan Franklin, from the Mississippi Delta, did not get far before Knighton beat him and then made him gather up Walker's body for transport to the nearby Camp Van Dorn hospital. Hix drove the jeep to the hospital (with Milburne and Franklin aboard), but Walker died on the way, less than fifteen minutes after the fight began. The .45 caliber bullet had ruptured his inferior vena cava, the large vein running through the middle of the body.[18]

Federal officials largely accepted the white lawmen's version of Walker's killing. Investigations by the military and the FBI concluded that Sheriff Whitaker had justifiably shot William Walker for resisting arrest. Yet the sheriff (or the Centreville police) had no real authority to intervene with deadly force in this tussle between two soldiers (one a MP), which is perhaps why the white civilian lawmen claimed that Hix had requested assistance and that Walker had charged at them. Walker's military death certificate contradicts a key component of the official account of the incident, stating that the soldier died of a "gunshot wound, entrance right flank, exit left flank then lodging in the inner aspect of left elbow over olecranon [point of the elbow]." Such a wound suggests that the victim had not run toward the shooter, but rather, stood sideways to his assailant. Perhaps this discrepancy explains Private Milburne's reluctance to confirm the testimony of the other white witnesses on the key point that Walker charged at the sheriff (though Milburne corroborates much of their remaining story). Whether Whitaker or Knighton shot Walker remains unclear, but both disliked Black soldiers.[19]

And what about Charles Hix? Did he ask the white lawmen to shoot Walker? Such a request seems plausible, coming from someone who had an apparent dislike of Black men in uniform. When talking with investigators after the incident, Hix littered his speech with the racial epithet "nigger." Even Whitaker and Knighton, in their accounts, used the more benign "colored" to describe Walker and the other Black soldiers. At the post hospital, according to Morgan Franklin, the Black GI dragooned for ambulance duty, Hix reportedly told another MP, "I just got me another nigger and now I reckon I get my transfer."[20]

Within an hour, word of Walker's death had spread throughout Camp Van Dorn. When one of the battalion commanders, Lieutenant Colonel Charles W. O'Bryant (a former high school principal from Kansas), arrived outside the barracks of Walker's unit, he found a crowd of Black soldiers, noticeably upset and talking excitedly to the company commander, Captain Charles L. Ellis Jr. O'Bryant urged the men "to have confidence in Colonel Goodman" to investigate Walker's death and then told the soldiers to disperse and return to their barracks, an order they obeyed. About fifteen minutes later, however, a group of soldiers broke into the company supply room. They apparently wanted to gather weapons to avenge their comrade's death. By the time O'Bryant and Ellis made it to the supply hut, perhaps 100 soldiers mulled around the area; the officers could not positively identify those who had broken into the storeroom, which had several weapons missing. Hearing of this incident, Colonel Goodman ordered the firing pins removed from all rifles and guards placed at weapon storage areas throughout the regiment's buildings.[21]

Over the next couple of hours, sporadic violence broke out around the camp. Some Black enlisted men fought with the men safeguarding the weapons, while other Black soldiers randomly attacked white soldiers at various points around the installation. Hundreds of men from the 364th, joined by some soldiers from the 518th, gravitated to the nearby Black PX and took over the building, kicking the white employees out of the store. After the PX manager reported the takeover, a Black MP unit arrived to restore order. Dating back to the unit's Arizona days, the men of the 364th had little respect for Black MPs. The Black troops attacked the MPs' vehicles and crowded in on the Black police unit. One of the Black MPs fired two shots, one of which inflicted a non-life-threatening thigh wound to Private Raymond Johnson.[22]

As this scene unfolded, Colonel Goodman arrived. He had garnered widespread respect among the soldiers in the regiment since he had taken over the outfit after the Phoenix troubles. One corporal from the regiment called Goodman "a champion of the colored soldier." His actions that evening perhaps prevented the anger of his men from deteriorating into a deadlier affair. According to Private Wiley, Goodman climbed to the porch of the PX and asked one of the men of the 364th to join him. Goodman put his arm around the soldier and said, "My children, for to me, you are my children, color doesn't mean a damn to me, and I love every one of you. I am not much of a Christian, but I want each one of you to say the Lord's Prayer along with me." Goodman's words calmed the men and restored order to the 364th. The colonel instructed the men to return to their barracks, and they complied. Perhaps indicative of the belief at the time among the 364th's officers that the events on post during the evening of May 30 represented a serious but understandable and controllable commotion was the fact that none of them bothered to identify the soldiers who participated in the night's turmoil. The overall commander of the post, Colonel R. E. Guthrie, described the events of that evening as "a little emotional disturbance among colored troops."[23]

The next day, Memorial Day, racial tensions continued to simmer at Camp Van Dorn, and white fear grew in nearby Centreville. A group of heavily armed white soldiers rode into the 364th's area on Monday morning. Corporal Anthony Smirely of the regiment's H Company described the white detachment as consisting of "four (4) Armored scout cars, each with about ten M.P.'s armed to the teeth." The white patrol left the area only after Colonel Goodman reportedly threatened to arm the men of the 364th. Many of the Black soldiers believed camp leaders wanted to put them under guard in their own camp, but it is unclear on whose orders, if any, the white detachment descended on the Black regiment's encampment.[24]

Also, on Monday morning camp leaders had to respond to the white outrage that had initially erupted in Centreville on Sunday night and continued to grow the following morning. White locals believed a full-scale riot by Black troops had occurred at the camp. Many of these white Mississippians may have initially thought the killing of Walker, to keep a Black soldier in his place, meant little (after all, local law enforcement had long killed Black men for little or no reason without any consequence). Hearing of the angry reaction to Walker's murder among Black soldiers, however, local white citizens became alarmed. Army leaders met with the white citizens of Centreville and neighboring communities, along with local law enforcement, including Sheriff Whitaker and Chief Knighton. An army investigator described local citizens as "very much exercised over the situation, [they] have armed themselves so as to protect their lives and property and are definite in their insistence that the 364th be transferred to another station." The FBI reported that "the Sheriff is apprehensive of a race riot" if the 364th remained at Camp Van Dorn.[25]

The mayor of Centreville, Omer Carroll, had already conveyed the same messages in telegrams to Governor Paul B. Johnson and US Senators Theodore Bilbo and Jim Eastland. Carroll requested "that steps be taken to have 306th [sic] Infantry colored" moved by the War Department to a "northern station." Carroll claimed the unit had provoked "race riots and openly boast they have come here to clean out Mississippi." In the days that followed, the local white press attributed the "clean out Mississippi" statement to the men of the 364th upon their arrival in Mississippi, but the first direct evidence of such language comes in the mayor's telegrams. Indeed, one army investigator viewed these press statements as one of the major causes that heightened racial tensions among area civilians. White residents began using the phrase after Walker's death and the subsequent Black anger at the installation in the aftermath of that killing. This language reflected white fears about an impending race riot and offered a justification for the request to remove the 364th from the area.[26]

Fears and rumors about mass racial violence and murder at the camp soon extended well beyond southwest Mississippi. In McComb, the local white newspaper noted that in the days following Walker's death, "many wild rumors floated about . . . rumors of men being killed by the scores and of women being molested." The paper, however, reported that the stories were "greatly exaggerated." The night after the Walker shooting, a woman in New Orleans, 130 miles from Camp Van Dorn, sent the army's adjutant general this brief, cryptic telegram: "Militia Needed at Camp Van Dorn Mississippi, Colored Soldiers Being Massacred, Trouble." Black soldiers also sensed growing danger. Much like the aftermath of the Phoenix Massacre, several soldiers from the 364th went AWOL as racial tensions rose in southwest Mississippi. Clarence Jones, who soon turned himself in to military authorities in Atlanta, explained that he left the camp on June 3 "because of the cruel treatment which the members of our Regiment received from the Military Police and civilian authorities at Centreville."[27]

Beyond Camp Van Dorn, racial violence directed at Black soldiers occurred during the same period at other locales in the Deep South. On the same day as Walker's murder, a white MP shot and killed a Black soldier on furlough from Camp McCain in central Mississippi as he passed through the town of Duck Hill, eight miles south of camp. The killing occurred because of a rape scare in the area. In late April, military officials at the camp placed the town off-limits to Black troops after an elderly white woman in the town accused a Black man in uniform of raping her. The woman said she woke up and found a Black man in her bed. She died soon after, from the "shock" of this encounter, according to local district attorney and future Mississippi governor, J. P. Coleman, "although [her] death was attributed to other causes," the politician admitted. Two days earlier, a white woman had claimed that six Black soldiers had gang-raped her on a road near Duck Hill. She said the Black men held off, at gunpoint, a white soldier with her at the time. Although local officials and camp investigators interviewed 1,500 Black soldiers, neither the woman nor the white soldier ever identified anyone involved in the incident.[28]

In the weeks that followed, Black GIs from Camp McCain had several other run-ins with civilians in area communities, where the locals viewed them as suspicious "outsiders." The Black soldiers at Camp McCain eventually got tired of the abuse they suffered at the hands of white civilians in the area. In June, a group of them had written the army's inspector general and claimed that "the truth of the matter is no action on the part of the Colored soldiers off of the Post warrant any cruelty from a people they are risking their lives to protect." Weeks later, a group of Black GIs from the camp took weapons from the supply hut, went to the edge of Duck Hill on the Illinois Central Railroad, and shot up the town. No one was injured, but the soldiers did a significant amount of property damage. The army court-martialed thirteen soldiers from the 470th Quartermaster Truck Regiment for the attack on Duck Hill; the court convicted seven of those tried, and each received sentences of five to fifteen years at hard labor. Five of the seven convicted soldiers came from the South. No white citizens in the area ever faced charges for the abuses they had heaped on the Black soldiers at Camp McCain.[29]

Further south, on June 6, Black servicemen on leave from Camp Shelby got into a confrontation with a highway patrolman, a white civilian, and two white soldiers on Mississippi's Highway 49. This incident led to a brief panic among the white citizens of the nearby small town of Collins. Black soldiers from the 735th Sanitary Company spent their Sunday off playing a baseball doubleheader in the town of Sanatorium. Between games, they borrowed a civilian truck to travel south to Mount Olive to pick up some bootleg liquor. Soon after heading back to Sanatorium, a highway patrolman stopped the truck and ordered the soldiers out of their vehicle at gunpoint. The lawman, however, accidently dropped his gun into the truck, and one of the soldiers, perhaps already intoxicated, picked it up. At that moment, a passing Tri-State bus stopped at the scene, and the driver and two white soldiers got out to assist the officer. A brief gunfight followed, in which—amazingly—only one soldier was slightly injured. The patrolman, assisted by the white passersby, eventually arrested the fifteen soldiers. MPs from Camp Shelby later took the soldiers into custody. When word of this incident spread to the nearby village of Collins, a small group of armed citizens gathered to "protect" the town, which remained on alert throughout the day and into the evening, when an armed civilian tried to stop another Black GI driving through Collins.

When the Black driver refused to get out of his car, the white man shot him in the leg.[30]

Three days later, at Camp Stewart in south Georgia, a contingent of Black troops engaged in three hours of sporadic fighting with white MPs. One of the white MPs was killed and four were injured. Members of two white battalions eventually ended the disturbance. Rumors that white soldiers or MPs from the post had murdered a Black soldier and raped and killed his wife apparently sparked the attack, but racial animosity had been brewing in and around the camp for weeks. The War Department had received numerous complaints about conditions at Camp Stewart and the surrounding civilian areas. Many of these criticisms came from the families of soldiers from a cadre of the Black 369th Coast Artillery Regiment, recently transferred from Hawaii to Camp Stewart and embedded among existing units to help with anti-aircraft training. Relatives of soldiers in the 369th, composed largely of former New York National Guard troops, organized a letter-writing campaign in April and May 1943 that alerted army officials to the potential problems. Between May 8 and May 15, the War Department received more than 400 letters, some originally sent directly to President Roosevelt. William D. Alford, a resident of New York City, asked that something be done "about Nazi-held Georgia and other Nazified states, and we want it done now. We cannot longer support a war against Nazi ideals abroad, while at the same time, being the victims of the same ideals here at home."[31]

Responding to the charges, the military sent Brigadier General Benjamin O. Davis, the highest-ranking Black officer in the military, to investigate. Born in Washington, DC, in 1880, Davis served as an officer in a volunteer corps during the Spanish-American War. He later joined the regular army and served as a second lieutenant in the Philippine-American War in 1901–1902. In the 1920s and 1930s, Davis moved up the officers' ranks while holding various positions, including professor of military science at Tuskegee Institute in the early 1920s and commander of the 369th New York National Guard in the late 1930s (later reorganized as the 369th Coast Artillery Regiment). As World War II approached and the army expanded, Colonel Davis seemed poised to become its first Black general. Though Davis was initially passed over for promotion, President Roosevelt approved his promotion to brigadier general in October 1940, largely in response to Black pressure, prior to the 1940 presidential election, to end discrimination in economic and military mobilization. During the war, in part to avoid having

Davis command white soldiers, the army stationed the Black general as a staff officer in the army's Office of the Inspector General, where until 1944 he primarily conducted investigations about the conditions of Black soldiers training at locales throughout the United States.[32]

Davis's report detailed the problems at Camp Stewart, including the widespread use of segregation signage, inadequate recreation facilities for Black troops, and discriminatory treatment by white MPs toward Black soldiers. One Black GI stationed at Camp Stewart—the nephew of a prominent Black Republican from Mississippi, Perry Howard—recently discharged from the army because of his advanced age, described his departure from Camp Stewart to General Davis as a release from a "concentration camp." The nearby village of Hinesville offered few services for Black troops and often treated Black men in uniform with outright hostility. Davis heard widespread complaints from Black soldiers about the paucity of transportation options to get to Savannah, as well as problems within Savannah itself: inadequate or overpriced lodgings and food provided for Black soldiers, "abusive language and unnecessary roughness" by both the civilian police and the MPs, and the frequent arrest of "women accompanied by colored soldiers" on suspicions of venereal disease. While the Camp Stewart racial incident took place on-post, the racial unrest at the training center in south Georgia had roots in the treatment Black troops received at the hands of area white civilians—much like the conflicts surrounding other Deep South military installations occurring at the same time.[33]

The dissatisfaction among Black soldiers at Camp Stewart extended beyond the soldiers who had come from the 369th, and as at other locations, involved both non-Southerners and Southerners. Although families of men from the 369th had complained the loudest about the problems at Camp Stewart, members of this unit played no role in the battle with the white MPs. Indeed, later reports found that most of those involved in the June 9 fight came from the 458th Antiaircraft Artillery Battalion, while some were from the 100th Coast Artillery Regiment, a unit composed in large part of men from the South. In the end, the army's official investigation blamed the Camp Stewart incident on "long pent-up emotions and resentments" among Black troops, but the report also noted, despite this conclusion and the actual evidence, that the problems resulted from the decision to train northern Black men in the South, as well as the "average negro soldier's meager education, superstition, imagination and excitability." The army court-martialed a group of Black soldiers identified as leaders of the attack on the white MPs.

It also gradually—and without any fanfare—reduced the number of Black troops at the facility from 15,000 to 5,000.[34]

Back at Camp Van Dorn, in early June, two separate army investigations examined the recent racial disturbances: one conducted by Colonel C. C. Park, the Third Army's inspector general, and another by Colonel J. R. Burney, of the army's Office of the Inspector General. Park recommended that the three battalions of the 364th be turned into service units and each sent to a separate camp. He also recognized that inadequate PX and theater facilities at Camp Van Dorn had contributed to low morale among Black soldiers at the camp and recommended improvements. Finally, he suggested that the MPs "be instructed to identify and report those guilty of minor violations of regulations as to uniform, bearing, and courtesy, and to avoid use of physical force" when possible. The Third Army's commander, Lieutenant General Courtney Hodges, rejected the recommendations to remove the 364th from its post, break the regiment up, or change its mission. Colonel Burney presented the results of his investigation to the head of the army's ground forces, General Leslie McNair. Burney also recommended that the 364th be transferred to another location, but McNair rejected that suggestion. The general had received other such requests from local communities in the past, and he had no intention of letting civilian pressure dictate military logistics. However, McNair did order that the 364th be confined to post and deprived of "all privileges until such time as it will disclose its real trouble-makers and has demonstrated its worthiness to enjoy the rights of other organizations."[35]

By the time McNair issued his directive on June 8, the process of placing blame for the events of May 30 had already begun. Investigator Park arrived on June 1 and started interviewing witnesses, with the help of what he labeled "responsible commanders in the 364th." Park noted that many of the white officers of the regiment did not seem that interested in enforcing discipline. Commander Guthrie had initially downplayed the events of May 30 as a "little emotional disturbance," but he soon changed his opinion under prodding from Park. The camp commander told the investigator that nine white officers "had lost confidence and perspective": two of the regiment's three battalion commanders, including Lieutenant Colonel O'Bryant; three company commanders, including Company A's Captain Ellis; and two captains on the headquarters staff.[36]

Most of the white officers of the 364th apparently did have an atypical "perspective" for white officers. The white leaders of the 364th treated their Black subordinates with respect, dignity, and understanding, unlike those who typically led Black troops. Corporal Smirely, writing on May 30 to the editor of the *Philadelphia Tribune* to complain about the treatment he and his fellow soldiers were receiving at the hands of Centreville's white civilians and Camp Van Dorn's white MPs, made a special point of noting that "the white officers of our Regiment are about the best there are." A Black officer in Lieutenant Colonel O'Bryant's battalion described him as "a fine officer, fair, square and non-prejudiced." Just before the 364th left for Mississippi, O'Bryant, after listening to complaints about the anti-Black attitudes of one of the captains under his command, engineered the captain's transfer from the regiment. Commander Guthrie's list of untrustworthy white officers in the 364th included Colonel Goodman. Park recommended that the army relieve Goodman of his command "without prejudice." While Park may have thought Goodman too lenient toward the men in his regiment and unwilling to enforce strict discipline, the colonel had effectively gained the trust of the Black men under his command (somewhat rare during World War II) and had effectively calmed a potentially violent outburst in the aftermath of Private Walker's death.[37]

By June 6, military officials had arrested twenty-one enlisted men and confined them to the stockade for their involvement in the events that transpired on May 30. Eventually, in July 1943, seven of these men faced a court-martial for breaking into the weapons storeroom of Company A. All were convicted, despite little direct evidence of who committed the crime; the court condemned at least some of the accused based simply on their presence at the scene (even though scores of others present faced no charges). The convicted men initially each received a sentence of fifty years at hard labor in the Atlanta Federal Penitentiary, a punishment later reduced to fifteen years. An army board of review overturned the conviction of one of the seven, Private James L. Brown. Like many others, Brown had been at the scene, but the evidence showed he went to the supply room to keep a friend of his out of trouble and had, in fact, disarmed this friend during the incident and turned the stolen rifle over to an officer.[38]

General McNair initially wanted to tell the people of Centreville that the town would remain off-limits to the 364th "until such time as the citizens themselves request that the ban be lifted." Inspector General Peterson convinced McNair of the inadvisability of that action as one that would unnecessarily tie the army's hands in the future. Peterson had earlier reaffirmed his belief, after a 1942 incident in Arkansas, that Black soldiers had to have access to civilian communities. The Kentucky officer believed in the "necessity that soldiers, white or colored, be afforded protection when on a pass in a civilian community." Though they were not permanently banned from Centreville, the army confined the 364th to camp for more than a month. General McNair also proposed an intensified training regimen for the 364th, to "keep the men exceedingly busy." At one point, the citizens of Centreville, fearing an all-out attack by the Black combat unit in their midst, asked that the 364th be disarmed. Commander Guthrie rejected that solution, an impractical one for a combat organization in the middle of training for possible overseas deployment. Guthrie told local white officials that "to disarm the troops who are being trained for combat duty would be a disgrace to the United States," a statement that earned him rave reviews in the Black press.[39]

The army also sent a Black private, George Kennedy, as an undercover investigator to Camp Van Dorn three days after Walker's death. It wanted Kennedy to ascertain if the recent events at the camp had "resulted from the work of subversive influence." After ten days embedded in the regiment, he found no subversives at work, although he did discover that several men in the regiment's Company E sold bootleg whiskey. Kennedy also blamed much of the 364th's troubles on its officers—Black and white—who failed to enforce discipline in the ranks. In his estimation, the regiment's enlisted men were a "group of undisciplined delinquents." A second undercover investigator who infiltrated the 364th five months later, Homer Scretchings, largely confirmed Kennedy's report about lax discipline, which he labeled a "local command problem."[40] Neither investigator found an out-of-control riotous Black unit or one intent on terrorizing local white citizens.

Undercover investigator Kennedy predicted "further disturbances" among the Black troops at Camp Van Dorn, and an event in early July, according to some accounts, seemed to confirm that fear. Because many Black soldiers, including those in the 364th, remained confined to camp, the hostess of the Black service club arranged a dance at the installation for July 3 and bussed in about 200 Black women from Baton Rouge and Natchez for the affair. A huge crowd of Black soldiers—not just those from the 364th—showed up, more than organizers of the event had anticipated. With 2,000 people packed into the hall, an officer from the 364th announced that everyone would need to leave the dance hall and enter again after purchasing a ticket.[41]

The men refused to leave, and after Black MPs proved unable to clear the gathering, regimental officers summoned the white MPs. Black soldiers started to fight with them, so a lieutenant colonel called in a unit from the 99th Infantry for assistance. According to one Black GI present at the dance, the 99th Infantry arrived with "rifles, pistols and mounted machine guns." However, the public relations officer for Camp Van Dorn, who termed the events at the service club a "slight disturbance," noted that most of the soldiers had left the area by the time the men from the 99th arrived on the scene. In the end, no one fired a weapon, and no one got hurt. The organizers halted the dance and the Black soldiers returned to their barracks peacefully, though disappointed at the canceled social engagement.[42]

The army continued to monitor the situation at Camp Van Dorn, and by late summer, despite the continuing hostility between Black troops and the neighboring civilian area, conditions at the camp had improved for Black soldiers. Acting on Colonel Park's June recommendations, General Hodges directed the Camp Van Dorn commander to enhance camp accommodations for Black trainees and reign in the MPs. Third Army Headquarters, less than a week after the turmoil at Van Dorn, instructed regimental commanders to arrange separate bus service for Black soldiers traveling to Natchez, McComb, and Baton Rouge. In response to General McNair's directive, Colonel Goodman oversaw the stepped-up training of the 364th, which helped to boost morale in the ranks, even though the officers initially had the men train with rifles without firing pins and with bayonets removed. As late as mid-October 1943, the regiment remained on track to complete its training and head for a combat assignment in Europe by spring 1944.[43]

Another army investigator, Colonel Lathe B. Row, a career military officer, visited Camp Van Dorn in September 1943. He presented a much different picture of the 364th from that painted by the three investigators who had visited the camp in the days following Walker's killing. Row reported that other than the events at the end of May, "serious breaches of discipline appear to have been few considering the large number of troops stationed at the camp." He also praised the work of Colonel Goodman. Row did hear Black servicemen express "considerable resentment toward Jim Crow laws and the attitude of white civilians." He concluded that the hostility of area civilians and the large number of Black soldiers made future racial unrest likely. Row recommended the deployment of the 364th overseas as soon as possible. Later military analyses echoed Row's conclusion. Responding in February 1944 to an inquiry by Mississippi congressman Thomas Abernethy, Under Secretary of War Robert Patterson claimed that the army fully investigated the May 1943 incident at Camp Van Dorn and judged the event "isolated in nature rather than a reflection of a general lack of discipline."[44]

In 1998, a former banker from south Mississippi, Carroll Case, published a book claiming that he had uncovered shocking evidence about a 1943 massacre of Black soldiers at Camp Van Dorn. In the early 1960s, Case heard "hushed rumors" about a mass killing of Black troops during the war. Then, in 1995, others offered Case further details. A former soldier stationed at the camp, Bill Martzall, asserted that in the fall of 1943 he and fellow white MPs, acting on orders from their superiors, slaughtered more than 1,200 Black soldiers, members of the 364th Infantry Regiment. Local residents, including Luther Williams and W. M. Ezell, confirmed this story. If true, this incident, notwithstanding the decades-long era of Black lynchings, would represent the worst racial atrocity in twentieth-century US history.[45]

As Case's story circulated, the US Army began a sixteen-month investigation into the author's claims. The army created a database of the more than 3,800 men who served in the 364th at Camp Van Dorn and found military separation records for all but twenty. Researchers discovered nine of those missing individuals in other records: death certificates or VA claims after the war. The army also claimed it had information about the eleven remaining men—proving they had continued to serve in the military after the 364th left Camp Van Dorn in December 1943—but privacy regulations prevented the service from revealing further details. The army report of 1999 concluded that Case's book was full of "inaccuracies and a lack of supporting evidence."[46]

It later turned out that Case's primary informant, Bill Martzall, was not even at Camp Van Dorn during at least part of the time he reported first-hand observations. Martzall offered details about the July dance incident, even though he did not enter the Army until two months later. He claimed he had served as part of the MP contingent called in to help clear the dance hall that night. The tale he apparently heard months after the event, and then recounted to Case decades later, was that the dance took place at the white service club, and the Black 364th broke into this whites-only event, one with white women present. In addition to getting the facts of the dance completely wrong, the intelligence officer for Camp Van Dorn in July 1943, J. B. Meriwether, noted at the time that "there was nothing racial about the [dance] incident at all." Along with a memory that had Black soldiers trying to crash a social event to dance with white women, Martzall also told Case that his MP unit had heard that men from the 364th " 'had caught a pregnant white woman and sliced open her belly with a knife, took the baby out and stomped it.' " In addition to Martzall's ludicrous and fantastic recollections, W. M. Ezell later recanted part of his testimony. The army's investigation, however, did not quell the rumors fanned by Case. The NAACP asked the US Justice Department to open an independent investigation. That second investigation never happened, and suspicions about what happened at Camp Van Dorn continue to linger.[47]

In his book, Carroll Case pointed to army records that recounted several racial conflicts involving the 364th Infantry Regiment, including the one in Arizona in 1942. Racial unrest shook military installations around the United States during World War II, and in many ways, the troubles the 364th Regiment encountered at Camp Van Dorn in 1943 represented the all-too-common difficulties that Black men had faced since they began training for wartime service, especially in the Deep South. Yet Case implied that the US Army deliberately eliminated a troublesome Black infantry unit and then covered up the massacre for more than four decades.[48] There are several problems with this thesis. First, had the army tried to rid its ranks of Black soldiers who white civilians considered "troublemakers," the body count would have numbered far more than 1,200. Second, army racial policy during World War II was at odds with local racial customs in the South, and this disjuncture created much of the racial turmoil that surrounded army posts. In fact, the white officers leading the 364th were perhaps more sympathetic to the army's nondiscrimination approach than those training almost any Black unit during World War II.

To be sure, the army was not blameless for the problems the 364th encountered at Van Dorn. The army's decision to station a Black combat outfit with a large number of northern recruits at an isolated camp in the backwoods of the Deep South—a locale with a tradition of white racial violence directed toward keeping Black people "in their place"—demonstrated the army's inability to grapple with or understand the racial tensions fanned in part by its own hands-off nondiscrimination policy.[49] If a massacre had occurred in southwest Mississippi, however, it would make more sense that white civilians would have committed the crime, rather than military personnel acting under orders from their superiors.

So, given the general racial unrest and violence that consumed army installations and surrounding communities, especially in the South (and especially in spring and summer of 1943), why did four days of racial unrest and the killing of one Black private at Camp Van Dorn by a white lawman lead to persistent rumors of a mass murder of Black troops during wartime in the Deep South? The army's investigation of Carroll Case's massacre story suggested that the tale may have grown out of a later incident: a shootout between Black soldiers that took place in 1944 in the same area of the camp that the 364th vacated at the end of 1943. No one died in that event, but local people might have heard the gun battle and seen the evidence of the firefight in the bullet holes that pockmarked camp buildings.[50]

The massacre rumor, however, may have also started as a white fantasy: a yarn that resonated with white civilians in the area. Case first heard the massacre account in 1962. Someone told him about a large number of Black soldiers killed near Centreville during the war, "stacked on boxcars and hauled off in the night on a train." The person telling the story said, "This was the way that the people of Centreville handled the situation, and [it] may become necessary to do that type of thing again with things looking like they were during the [civil rights] movement."[51] Similar feelings may have provided the germ for the massacre tale back in the 1940s. Local people then disliked the stationing of Black combat troops near their town. They particularly detested the fact that members of the 364th seemed intent on challenging racial segregation—an attitude in part encouraged by the army's nondiscrimination policy. When Sheriff Whitaker or Police Chief Knighton shot Private Walker, they did so in the name of restoring racial order in their bailiwick. The disturbances that occurred at Camp Van Dorn in the aftermath of the Walker shooting suggested that the 364th would not easily be cowed. That defiant attitude sent local white citizens into a panic. If all was right in the world, white men would not have to stand by while Black men flouted racial customs and perhaps threatened the very existence of white supremacy.

White residents in Centreville may have wanted to kill all those troublesome Black combat soldiers training just outside their town—just as they wanted to kill Black civil rights "agitators" decades later. Some within the army, such as MP Charles Hix (and perhaps MP Bill Martzall), did what they could to keep Black men in check. But for the most part, white Southerners remained powerless to stop the actions the army had already taken in the 1940s to weaken the existing racist order. The federal government, while still supporting racial segregation, had a different vision of how segregation should operate—more fairly, without the blatant discrimination that defined southern race relations. Remembering a massacre of the men of the 364th by the very institution that threatened to undermine long-established social relations, even if it never occurred, may have eased the psychic pain white men and women felt as the army and the federal government laid siege to their racially controlled world. Those feelings would only grow over time as the federal government increasingly moved to support the Black freedom movement.

Perhaps as disconcerting as the inaccurate memories of the 364th as a troubled regiment murdered by the US military was the organization's actual experience and fate. After the 364th trained for deployment to combat duty in a war zone for much of 1943, the army changed the orders for the regiment in the fall of 1943, largely due to the tumult—real and imagined—the regiment had experienced in both Arizona and Mississippi. Black combat troops were controversial in the 1940s. A controversial Black combat unit was perhaps not the best choice for a battle assignment. That was the thinking of the general who made the decision about the 364th's next move. Major General Ray Porter, the War Department's assistant chief of staff for organization and training and an Arkansas native, actually favored sending Black units into combat, but he concluded that "the 364th Inf. does not appear to fit into any practical scheme.... Many officers have rated the regiment as a menace.

Boxing champ Joe Louis visits members of the 364th Infantry Regiment in the summer of 1945 in the Aleutian Islands, where the unit was sent after the troubles it encountered at Camp Van Dorn in Mississippi. Louis is second from the left, front row standing. To his right on the front row is the regiment's chaplain, Elmer P. Gibson. *Courtesy of the State Archives of North Carolina*

Perhaps it is wise to trade it to Alaska for a good white regiment & seek to have some other Negro unit sent to combat." So Porter slotted the 364th for overseas duty: but in Alaska, not Europe.

The regiment left Camp Van Dorn on Christmas Day 1943 for the Pacific Northwest and eventual deployment to the Aleutian Islands—technically a "combat zone" but clearly one on the fringes of the actual fighting. It remained there for the duration of the war, under Colonel Goodman's leadership, and by all accounts, performed well in carrying out its assigned duties. In the end, however, the racism of some army officials and the hostility of white Mississippians relegated a well-trained Black combat unit to the sidelines in the fight against the Axis Powers. As Clyde Blue, who served alongside the 364th at Camp Van Dorn, later remembered, "A real gung-ho group with esprit de corps to spare were junked." Lieutenant William Price, one of the 364th's Black officers, agreed: "I was with three different infantry regiments and in my opinion the 364th was head and shoulders above all of them. These were men who stood together under good or adverse circumstances. That the government chose to be punitive in their dealings with this group was its loss, for the 364th was a first-class fighting regiment of black enlisted men."[52]

As Truman Gibson later recalled, even without a massacre, the 364th faced numerous hurdles, and ones that proved quite typical for Black troops during World War II: "inadequate training, second-class facilities, racist officers, poor discipline, abuse by civilians, kangaroo courts-martial, and murder." In World War II America, Black soldiers, including those in the 364th Infantry Regiment, discovered that maintaining racial privilege took precedence over fighting fascists.[53] After the turmoil in the Deep South during 1943, however, the US military started to take its nondiscrimination charge more seriously. What happened at Camp Van Dorn and elsewhere in the Deep South in the spring and summer of 1943 shaped how the US military approached the issue of training and utilizing a Black fighting force for the remainder of the war.

7
A Conservative Revolution

Between November 25 and December 22, 1943, Reverend J. L. Horace, pastor of Chicago's Monumental Baptist Church, president of the Illinois Baptist Convention, and a World War I veteran, toured nine army camps and their surrounding communities in Louisiana, Mississippi, Alabama, and Georgia. The Fraternal Council of Negro Churches, which represented eleven denominations and more than 6 million members, sponsored Horace's southern trip. Following the disturbances involving Black troops at Deep South army camps in the spring and summer of 1943, northern Black churchmen and other concerned citizens offered to investigate the problems facing Black soldiers in the South.

At a Chicago mass meeting in June 1943, organized by the National Negro Council and the Chicago Citizens Committee of 1,000, a resolution was passed asking President Roosevelt to send five leading Black pastors to investigate the recent troubles at Camp Van Dorn and Camp Stewart. The War Department rejected this request, telling Edgar J. Brown, director of the National Negro Council, that "it is not the policy of the government to grant authority to any civilian organization to visit military reservations to conduct investigations." Military officials also noted that the army already had inquiries underway to determine what had occurred at these two camps.[1] So Reverend Horace conducted his own survey of Deep South camps and the surrounding communities without the official sanction of the military.

Although Horace did not visit Camp Van Dorn or Camp Stewart, he did travel to Camps Livingston and Claiborne in Louisiana, Camps Shelby and McCain in Mississippi, and Fort Benning in Georgia, as well as four other military installations. He heard about and observed many of the racial problems that had plagued camps in the Deep South since military training began. Although the military did not authorize Reverend Horace's tour of southern army camps, in January 1944, he personally delivered the report about his trip to John J. McCloy, assistant secretary of war, perhaps better-known as one of the so-called Wise Men who shaped post–World War II foreign policy, an American High Commissioner of postwar Germany, and an early president of the World Bank.[2]

McCloy had worked on the issues surrounding the use of Black troops since August 1942 when the War Department appointed him chair of the Advisory Committee on Negro Troop Policy, often called the McCloy Committee. In its first year of operation, this body did little to try to solve the military's racial problems, perhaps reflective of disinterest in the matter on the part of McCloy's boss, Secretary of War Henry Stimson. After the racial upheavals of 1943, Stimson privately blamed the incidents on "certain radical leaders of the colored race," who wanted to use the war emergency to obtain "race equality and interracial marriages." McCloy was no racial liberal, but he had more sensitivity to racial inequities than Stimson. McCloy also came to believe that racial segregation hamstrung the War Department's effort to use its human resources in the most efficient way possible. And after the events at Camp Van Dorn and Camp Stewart (and elsewhere), he began urging more substantive action to resolve racial tensions within America's armed forces. Over the next two years, in what historian Todd Moye has called a "conservative revolution," McCloy and others within the military leadership of the United States took increasingly bolder steps to enforce the army's official policy of nondiscrimination toward Black soldiers. White Southerners responded with fear that certain racial apocalypse loomed on the horizon.[3]

The racial unrest in and around army camps in the Deep South in May and June 1943 increased racial worries among white citizens. Days after the killings of Black GIs near Camp Van Dorn and in Duck Hill, Mississippi, an attorney in the Mississippi Delta town of Greenville, Charles W. Wade, predicted "terrible trouble" unless the federal government did something "to quiet" Black Americans. Wade believed "there has come the time when white domination must be protected and vigorously asserted." Two months later, District Attorney J. P. Coleman described the mood in central Mississippi as "tense." Indeed, he told Congressman Thomas Abernethy that he "would not be surprised to hear of white citizens oiling up their private artillery and using it. Nothing but their intense loyalty to their country prevents their doing it. If these negros [sic] were not in the uniform of the United States, they would not last until the water got hot."[4]

Many white people, ignoring their own role in fanning racial unrest around military posts, blamed the northern Black press for the eruption of racial disorder in their areas. Since the beginning of the war, Black newspapers had pointed out the contradictions of fighting the Nazis with a

Jim Crow army. In early 1942, the *Pittsburgh Courier* had launched its Double V Campaign, which emphasized that, for Black Americans, World War II was both a fight against fascism abroad and a battle against racism at home, a message adopted by a variety of northern newspapers. The Black press also regularly reported on Black soldiers, both celebrating their achievements and condemning their treatment, particularly in southern training camps. Military leaders disliked the criticism. John McCloy believed that the Black press unnecessarily highlighted the "alleged mistreatment" of Black soldiers. Members of the Roosevelt administration, including the president himself, considered moves to censor the Black press, although Attorney General Francis Biddle refused to pursue such efforts.[5]

In the summer of 1943, conservative white newspapermen, such as the nationally syndicated columnist Westbrook Pegler, faulted Black journalists for inciting the racial incidents in America's war towns. Pegler charged "the popular Negro press of this country" with "recklessly, violently, and persistently preaching race hatred." At the same time, white Southerners sought to silence the Black press, which had provided the only sustained coverage of the clashes that had recently occurred in the region. Military leaders at both Camp Shelby and Camp Stewart banned Black newspapers, including the *Pittsburgh Courier*, the *Chicago Defender*, and *The People's Voice*, from their facilities. White officials also halted the sales of Black publications in communities near military stations, and individuals with any association with the northern news outlets came under scrutiny. In July 1943, the police in Hattiesburg told local distributors of Black newspapers to halt sales.[6] If the northern Black press was guilty of anything, it was of vigilantly reporting on the problems associated with mobilizing a biracial army pledged to support nondiscrimination in a segregated setting—stories the white press ignored or mentioned only in passing.

While white Southerners in 1943 sought to contain what they viewed as a brewing race war in their midst, Black leaders nationwide urged the federal government to do more to protect Black GIs in the South. William Hastie, who had, in a major rebuke to the Roosevelt administration, resigned as civilian aide to the secretary of war in January 1943 over what he termed "reactionary policies and discriminatory practices" in the Army Air Forces, described in mid-June 1943 the precarious position of Black soldiers in southern communities: "the Negro soldier finds himself not only outside the protection of the law but even the object of lawless aggression by the officers of the law." Judge Hastie suggested that "Americans must be told plainly that public manifestations of race prejudice cannot and will not be permitted to impede the Nation's struggle for victory and a free world." He even called for making all civilian communities "off-limits" to both white and Black soldiers until local officials "shall take all responsible steps to protect all men in uniform against lawless violence and abuse." Hastie noted that such action might lead to real change, once southern towns and cities calculated the economic losses associated with the absence of all soldiers from their communities. Roy Wilkins, assistant secretary of the National Association for the Advancement of Colored People (NAACP), agreed with this analysis. He told the new civilian aide to the secretary of war, Truman Gibson, that everyone knew the problems but "that little or no attempt has been made to adjust these matters with white people giving in on some of their prejudices." In fact, he claimed, that white officials only proposed solutions that "will not 'disturb' white people."[7]

In Reverend Horace's report on southern army camps, he had presented the War Department with a stark choice: "Southern communities should be made to respect Negro soldiers or they should be moved to places where they do not have to live in constant fear." The War Department apparently did not have the practical ability or the administrative will to implement the first option (one favored by many national Black leaders), and military necessity seemingly prevented the latter course. At the same time, the military continued to claim its commitment to the policy of nondiscrimination. As J. A. Ulio, the army's adjutant general, told one Southerner complaining about a violation of southern "traditions," military rules remained clear: "it is not the policy of the Department to permit discrimination against any soldier because of race, creed or color."[8]

Military leaders ultimately ignored the fears of white Southerners and heeded some of the concerns of Black leaders by gradually stepping up efforts to enforce the principle of nondiscrimination. Army Chief of Staff George Marshall took up the issue of "Negro Troops" with his commanding generals in early July. In a memo largely prepared by John McCloy and his advisory committee, Marshall described "riots of a racial character" that had occurred at Camps Van Dorn and Stewart and elsewhere as following a definite pattern: they began because of "real or fancied incidents of discrimination and segregation," and then when the military took no corrective action, gossips and rumors turned small incidents into serious problems. These racial incidents stemmed from a failure of leadership, especially the need for "continuous and vigorous action to prevent incidents of discrimination and the spread of inflammatory gossip." To solve these problems, Marshall called for the enforcement of military discipline among all soldiers, along with the provision of "adequate facilities and accommodations" for Black troops. Finally, the chief of staff noted that "good order between soldiers and the civilian population is a definite command responsibility," although he offered no suggestions on how to enforce such a directive in the Deep South. An order issued by the War Department at the same time directed that commanders take "rigid precautions" to secure weapons and ammunition on army installations, a mandate seemingly intended to prevent the access to arms and ammo by potentially riotous Black soldiers.[9]

Marshall's orders remained vague enough that commanders at Deep South army camps could interpret them in ways that generally maintained the racial status quo. At Camp Stewart, the new commanding general, E. A. Stockton Jr., created what he called the "Educational Program for Colored Troops" in late July 1943. The program, detailed in a twelve-page booklet and distributed to all Black GIs at the camp, organized a series of training sessions for officers and NCOs of Black units at the camp, which included instructions to convey the lessons to the Black soldiers under their command. Much of the Educational Program focused on encouraging officers to exercise greater control over their Black soldiers and to have Black GIs understand and obey orders; avoid rumors; and ignore perceived racial discrimination, or, as the program instructions put it, "avoid babying himself with the belief that every little inconvenience he suffers is racial discrimination."[10]

While the Camp Stewart Educational Program reiterated the official army policy that "there will be no discrimination between white or colored" soldiers, it proposed to address the directive from General Marshall to maintain "good order between soldiers and the civilian population" by instructing Black soldiers to meticulously follow the area's discriminatory segregation laws. Stockton told his officers to inform their men they had to obey Georgia law: "it is your duty to do exactly as the laws say, and to accept the customs of the people, while you are in Georgia. Be polite and respectful in any talk you may have with white people. Don't try to start conversations with white strangers. Stay out of white places and sit where you are supposed to sit on trains and buses." The *Atlanta Constitution* called the Educational Program "words of wisdom" and suggested the document become "required reading, of every Negro in every southern camp." The *Baltimore Afro-American*, on the other hand, thought the Educational Program demonstrated that General Stockton shared the attitudes of "some of the leaders of the countries who comprise the Axis powers." Luther Francis Yancy Jr., a cartoonist at the paper, characterized the Educational Program as reminding Black men in uniform to "accept segregation," an attitude General Stockton equated to observing "the Golden Rule."[11] Stockton's Educational Program did not offer a realistic way to address the racial discord that characterized southern army camps. His approach to solving the conflict between white civilians and Black soldiers consisted largely of telling the latter to keep their mouths shut and do whatever white people told them.

By the beginning of 1944, within army leadership competing ideas existed about the causes of racial problems in and around army camps—especially in the South—and how to resolve these tensions. The counterintelligence section of the army blamed the problems on the stationing of northern Black troops in the South and the lack of inadequate entertainment/recreational facilities in southern Black communities. The counterintelligence evaluation also faulted the Black press for calling for "a non-segregation policy in the Army," a stance it believed the Communist Party and the Fair Employment Practices Committee (FEPC) fostered. With this analysis, only two solutions existed: move northern Black soldiers out of the South and/or improve post recreational facilities for Black servicemen so they would not need to go to "the localities in which they are stationed." Both the McCloy Committee and the Personnel Division of the army had a different assessment. Both urged more concrete actions to solve the racial difficulties faced by the military: improvements for Black officers, including opportunities for advancement; early deployment of Black combat troops; further directions concerning the use of recreational facilities on army camps; and "instruction of military police in handling negro offenders."[12]

Over the next six months, the army unevenly moved to implement these recommendations. In January 1944, the War Department revised its policy on the "Promotion and Assignment of Negro Officer Personnel." Essentially, the military eliminated previous restrictions placed on Black officers. The new rules allowed the assignment of Black officers to any units with Black troops and applied the same promotion policies to all officers, which removed the previous requirement that white officers always outrank Black officers in any unit. The new policy opened more positions for Black officers and increased the possibility for promotions beyond the rank of second lieutenant. In August 1942, the army had only 817 Black officers; three years later, when the war ended, the army had commissioned more than 7,700 Black officers. Thirty-four of those held the rank of colonel or lieutenant colonel.[13]

Despite this policy change and its very real effect on improving the lot of Black officers, local command decisions could still thwart the army's well-intentioned reforms. In May 1944, the army sent eleven Black officers (one first lieutenant and ten second lieutenants) to Camp Shelby as personnel consultants for a Special Training Unit. Such outfits provided targeted instruction for illiterate soldiers; non-English speakers; or those classified as Grade V, the lowest performers on the army's aptitude tests. After soldiers went through this program, the army judged them eligible for regular service, gave them a special assignment, or discharged them from the service.

The Camp Shelby Special Training Unit had five battalions—three Black and two white—of about 1,000 soldiers each. The officers and teachers in the white battalions were all white. To perform their jobs, the Black personnel consultants, though assigned to Black battalions, needed to have contact with white officers and teachers; however, the Black officers had to conduct their business through the white personnel consultant, who would then convey all matters to the white officers and teachers in their battalions. When the Black officers complained about the situation, General George Halloran, the commanding general, threatened them with a court-martial. After the army investigated and confirmed the practices reported by the Black officers, General Halloran admitted the stance toward these soldiers violated War Department directives and promised to take "corrective action . . . to remedy all deficiencies."[14]

As in previous American military conflicts, the issue of assigning Black units for combat duty had percolated since the beginning World War II. The principle of nondiscrimination in the training of soldiers established in the Selective Service and Training Act of 1940 led the army to organize Black combat units from the earliest days of mobilization. However, by mid-1943, the military had made only minimal use of these troops in actual fighting. Although the McCloy Committee recommended in July 1943 that "Negro combat troops be dispatched to an active theater of operations at an early date," in the fall of 1943, reports surfaced that the military had transferred the men in several Black combat units, including two battalions of field artillery and one tank destroyer battalion, to service units at the completion of their combat training. The army had also reassigned the 364th Infantry Regiment at Camp Van Dorn, which had prepared for a combat mission for much of 1943, to a non-combat role in Alaska.[15]

In February 1944, however, the War Department quietly distributed a pamphlet to its officer corps titled "Command of Negro Troops." It called racial segregation in the military a necessary, though inefficient, system but also reaffirmed the nondiscrimination principles of the Selective Service act. In the document, the War Department specifically rejected the notion that Black men were inherently unfit for combat duty. As the pamphlet proclaimed, "Good soldiers are made, not born." Rejecting existing theories of racial inferiority, the publication asserted that "there is not one piece of research which proves that Negroes are, as a group, mentally or emotionally defective by heredity. All peoples seem to be endowed by nature about equally with whatever it takes to fight a good war . . . and most of the less mentally alert in either race can be made to learn and to fight if properly led." The War Department acknowledged the inefficiency of underutilizing Black manpower in the army and charged its officer corps (still largely white) to "reduce such waste by remembering that effective command cannot be based on racial theories."[16]

This new thinking represented a dramatic about-face for the military. Two years earlier, military leaders had claimed that "the lower average intelligence of colored selectees is an obstacle to broad employment of colored soldiers throughout a modern, highly mechanized army." Beginning in March 1941, the War Department had given all army inductees the Army General Classification Test (AGCT), which the military called an intelligence test, but which, in fact, measured educational level. Many Black people, especially those from the South, had limited educational opportunities, which skewed the results concerning educational attainment in favor of white soldiers. Indeed, of the army enrollees tested between March 1941 until December 1942, two-thirds of Black GIs scored in the bottom rating, or Grade V, compared to 15 percent of white GIs. Since far fewer Black people had enrolled in the army, the overall percentage of soldiers slotted in the lowest grade stood at 19 percent (roughly 385,000 men out of almost 2 million who had joined the service). In March 1943, the army decided, somewhat arbitrarily, that combat units could have no more than 6 percent Grade V soldiers, and after April 1, 1943, it planned to reject all selectees beyond a 6 percent quota in the Grade V class.[17] That action made the organization of all-Black combat outfits virtually impossible.

Of course, had the army decided to integrate its ranks, the desired mix of soldiers with differing educational levels would have posed fewer problems. Instead, to maintain the requirement that Black men be enrolled in the army in proportion to their percentage of the population yet placed in segregated units, the army proposed to "double" its call of Black soldiers to get a higher percentage of Black men scoring in the top four grades. The army believed that northern Black recruits would score highest on the AGCT, which, according to its analysis, would benefit society at large. Army planners noted that southern states would like this plan because it "will return to them the rural Negro—needed on the farms and not, generally speaking, a source of racial friction—and will take away Negroes from the cities where, on the whole they are employed at less essential tasks." The army, however, never implemented this plan, and by February 1944, with the release of "The Command of Negro Troops," the service declared that the AGCT "is not a test of intelligence." Rather, the army now called the test "a roughly accurate measure of what the new soldier knows, what skills he commands, and of his aptitude in solving problems."[18]

Not everyone welcomed the War Department's reassessment of the mental abilities of Black soldiers and their suitability for combat duty. To promote its new thinking, the War Department purchased 55,000 copies of a pamphlet, "The Races of Mankind," written by two Columbia University anthropologists, Ruth Benedict and Gene Weltfish. The army planned to use the pamphlet in its orientation courses for new inductees. The thirty-three-page green booklet, intended to reject Nazi Master Race theories, claimed that science showed the artificiality of racial distinctions and demonstrated the existence of "one human race," in which "all peoples" were "much the same." When word about the War Department purchase of the Benedict/Weltfish pamphlet became known in early March 1944, the chair of the Military Committee of the US House of Representatives, Andrew J. May of Kentucky, threatened to expose what he described as the true motive of the publication: "to teach racial equality, especially the equality of whites and negroes, to the troops."

Senator Theodore Bilbo of Mississippi railed against the logical outcome of this teaching: "that every form of segregation should be eliminated from the American way of life." Bilbo, May, and other southern white leaders found "The Races of Mankind" especially troubling because it claimed that life circumstances, rather than inherent racial characteristics, determined intelligence. Benedict and Weltfish pointed to World War I "intelligence tests," which showed that Black Northerners had scored higher on average than white Southerners—a difference the authors attributed to the South's less-developed educational system. The War Department ultimately decided not to use the pamphlet, although it claimed that decision came before the House committee raised its objections.[19]

In the end, the War Department did little to put more Black soldiers in combat roles. On the same day the War Department issued the "Command of Negro Troops" pamphlet, the McCloy Committee recommended "that, as soon as possible, colored Infantry, Field Artillery, and other combat units be introduced into combat." As McCloy later explained to Secretary of War Stimson, "With so large a portion of our population colored, with the example before us of the effective use of colored troops (of a much lower order of intelligence) by other nations, and with the many imponderables that are connected with the situation, ... we must, I think, be more affirmative about the use of our negro troops. If present methods do not bring them to combat efficiency, we should change those methods." Stimson reluctantly accepted the Committee's recommendation but stalled on implementing the plan. By June 1945, just 12 percent of Black soldiers served in combat outfits; almost 48 percent of all white GIs fought in such units.[20]

The issue of inadequate recreational facilities and transportation options for Black GIs represented perhaps the most severe problem the army needed to resolve regarding its southern camps. In July 1943, in the aftermath of the racial incidents convulsing the South, Truman Gibson told the War Department that transportation and recreation issues "were the basic causes of low morale and interracial clashes in the South." The army had issued an earlier order concerning post recreation spaces, a directive largely ignored. The March 1943 order required, for any camps that included "units of two or more races," that "recreational facilities, including theaters and post exchanges, will not be designated for any particular race." While the Black press hailed the new policy as a "sign of real progress," few enlisted men (and even many officers), especially in the South, seemed aware of this instruction from the adjutant general. The bold-sounding policy of March 1943 also had an escape hatch. The new rule included a clause that allowed the assignment of specific recreational spaces to individual units, and since all units remained segregated, real integration could be avoided when desired. The army had previously stated that government transportation ran on a nondiscriminatory basis, although in operation, that policy had generally meant separate buses for Black and white soldiers.[21]

By the end of 1943, army leadership recognized the ineffectiveness of the March 1943 directive and searched for a solution. The McCloy Committee debated whether to clarify the existing policy or issue a stronger, clearer mandate. When the War Department issued a new directive on July 8, 1944, it did a bit of both. In a mild rebuke of those who had ignored or had not enforced the original order, Adjutant General J. A. Ulio claimed that although "in general the spirit" of the order had been followed, "occasional reports indicate that practices exist on some installations that are not in harmony with its provisions." The new directive then proceeded to try to close the major loophole in the March 1943 policy. While maintaining that a camp exchange or movie theater could still serve specific units, the new order clearly stated that "personnel will not be restricted to the use" of an exchange or theater assigned to them, "but will be permitted to use any" such facility on post.[22]

Ulio's statement also contained a particularly forceful proclamation on the army's transportation rules, which clarified existing policy. High-profile incidents involving noted Black athletes and the military in the days and weeks prior to the July 8 order had further highlighted the problems surrounding bus segregation and Black soldiers in the South.

In April 1944, two famous Black boxers, Joe Louis and (Sugar) Ray Robinson, members of the army's morale boxing team, struggled to get a segregated bus at Camp Sibert, Alabama, to Birmingham. The two fighters eventually decided to call a taxi for the trip and sat down to wait for their ride in the "white" waiting room at the camp bus station (the installation had a white and Black waiting area, but only the white area had a phone). When a white MP ordered the boxers out of the white space, Louis objected. The heavyweight champion said he had "religiously respected" segregation laws in southern communities "but did not have to stand for jim crow on army territory." And just two days before the Ulio order, Jackie Robinson, a noted football and track star and a member of the 761st Tank Battalion training at Fort Hood, Texas, got into an altercation with a white bus driver. The army later court-martialed Robinson for disobeying the orders of a superior officer. A military tribunal acquitted Robinson—who would desegregate Major League Baseball three years later. Issued in the shadow of these incidents, Ulio's July 8 instructions provided that all government-owned, or operated, transportation would "be available to all military personnel regardless of race." And perhaps most important, the directive instructed commanders to enforce the anti-segregation policy, "regardless of local civilian custom."[23]

As army commanders in the Deep South gradually implemented the July 8 instructions, word got out to surrounding communities, and southern white leaders condemned the order. In late August, six weeks after the army had promulgated the July directive, Alabama's governor, Chauncey Sparks, became aware of the implementation of the anti-segregation order at Maxwell Field in Montgomery. On August 23, camp leaders had ordered an end to racial segregation at the camp PXs, and some of the white civilians working at the stores quit their jobs. Sparks fired off a telegram to President Roosevelt and claimed the order "breaks down an essential principle of race relationship in the South" and "grievously handicaps efforts to bring about better race relations." Rosa Parks, who ten years later became famous during the Montgomery Bus Boycott, worked at Maxwell in 1944 and rode a desegregated trolley at the installation after the implementation of the army's anti-segregation order. She later recalled that "Maxwell opened my eyes up. It was an alternative reality to the ugly policies of Jim Crow."[24]

Other Deep South leaders objected to the army's anti-segregation instruction. Representative John Rankin of Mississippi opposed the measure on the floor of the US House of Representatives. Rankin claimed that "it attempts to wipe out segregation throughout the South" and "would probably precipitate race riots and other racial disturbances at a time when they would do the country the most harm." The *Jackson Daily News* called the July 8 directive "the worst boner pulled by the war department during this present world conflict." Robert Patterson, under secretary of war, responded to southern critics by noting "there has been no change in the War Department's practice concerning segregation of races." He described the July 8 order as reiterating existing policy, in place since the beginning of the war, "that all soldiers, regardless of race, be afforded equal opportunity to enjoy the recreational facilities which are provided at posts, camps, and stations."[25]

Patterson correctly characterized the July 8 publication as a restatement of existing military policy—maintaining segregation while eliminating discrimination—first enunciated in the 1940 Selective Service Act. Despite the attempt to reassure southern leaders like Sparks and Rankin that nothing had changed, they rightly perceived the July 8 directive as a renewed—and more vigorous—effort by the military to enforce the nondiscrimination principles it had professed throughout the war, actions that might permanently transform the South's racial arrangements. Indeed, the army seemed prepared to try to abolish racial segregation in most areas under its control, except the organization of individual units. And going forward, the army did more than it had previously to eliminate racial segregation within military camps. Even so, opportunities abounded for the continuation of separation policies. For parts of camp not specifically covered by the July 8 orders, such as officers' clubs, Jim Crow remained intact. Even in those spaces specifically singled out in the new instructions, such as theaters, seating continued to operate on a unit-by-unit basis. So, since individual corps remained organized by race, technically integrated theaters preserved separate seating areas for Black and white soldiers.[26]

Even with clearer, more forceful directions from the army brass on eliminating racial segregation on post and in military transportation, enforcement ultimately depended on local commanders. Based on complaints received by the NAACP, it seems clear that local military leadership resisted implementing the anti-segregation order at numerous military installations, in the South and beyond. At Fort Benning, Georgia, home to more than 10,000 Black troops in the summer of 1944, the fort's leaders hesitated to disseminate the July 8 instructions. On August 12, two Black officers, who had heard about the new policy, went to the main (white) PX to buy cigarettes. The white manager, following existing custom, refused to serve them. When the officers complained to Post Headquarters, camp leaders claimed that they had "inadvertently" failed to notify the PX manager about the July 8 order. During an inquiry into the incident, an army investigator concluded that one of the Black officers "will cause racial trouble when given a chance" and tagged him for continued surveillance. Within two weeks, installation commanders had informed the entire camp about the "new" anti-segregation policy. As at Maxwell Field in Alabama, white civilian personnel at Fort Benning complained about the "unjust, strife-creating, trouble-making racial equality" order. On August 30, Colonel John P. Edgerly, leader of the camp reception center for inducting and classifying new Black soldiers, gathered his Black officers, NCOs, and "key negro enlisted men" to talk to them about the anti-segregation directive. Some at the meeting told the Black press that Edgerly claimed the new instructions would not lead to any changes and reminded them that "this is Georgia." He also reportedly said, "I hope you will not try to carry out this order at Fort Benning . . . for if you should it will cause trouble."[27]

The War Department took little action against post leaders who failed to enforce the anti-segregation orders. After Walter White, director of the NAACP, called on the War Department to investigate the situation at Fort Benning, Assistant Secretary McCloy promised to investigate and to punish Colonel Edgerly if he had refused to carry out army policy. After a study of the matter by the inspector general of the Fourth Service Command, McCloy concluded that Edgerly had done nothing wrong. McCloy also determined that the allegations of the Black soldiers who had complained about Edgerly and his remarks were "considerably distorted from the facts." Whether or not Colonel Edgerly ever suggested that he planned to ignore the army's non-segregation order, racial segregation clearly continued at Fort Benning. Black soldiers tested the new standard at various white spaces at the installation, but white officials turned them away. In January 1945, a Black lieutenant, David A. Blake, went to the bowling alley on post. The white civilian manager told him that he could not use the facility, but Blake bowled a few frames before leaving. He returned the next evening with five enlisted men from a Black quartermaster truck company. This time, the manager did not try to stop the men from bowling, but when they began to play, the German prisoners of war who served as pin boys refused to reset the bowling equipment on their lanes, a fitting collaboration between Nazis and white segregationists to thwart Black activism seeking to enforce a US-backed anti-segregation effort. Months after the war ended, in November 1945, a Black soldier stationed at the fort claimed that "segregation at Fort Benning is complete."[28]

Although the July 8 order boldly proclaimed an end to segregation on government-owned or operated transportation, the instructions changed little in the Deep South, since the army contracted much of the bus service between camps and nearby communities to private civilian companies. In fact, the directive may have exacerbated racial tensions on southern transportation serving army facilities, particularly since commanders at southern military installations gave conflicting descriptions of the new policy. Racial confrontations on Deep South buses sometimes became deadly, especially because white bus drivers often ruled their vehicles as personal fiefdoms in the Jim Crow South. In late 1944, a Black sergeant boarded a bus in Hattiesburg. All the seats reserved for Black riders were occupied, while most of the "white" seats remained empty. Another Black soldier moved the Jim Crow sign separating the two sections forward a row to provide a seat for the sergeant. Seeing this literal attempt to adjust the color line, the bus driver screamed, "Put that Goddam sign back." The sergeant, seeking to avoid trouble, went to move the sign back to its original location. As he did, the bus driver critically shot him. Both Black and white witnesses described the shooting as "unprovoked," but the bus employee clearly thought any challenge to racial segregation on his bus required a vigorous defense.[29]

Despite the racial reforms promoted by the War Department during the first half of 1944, racial segregation and discrimination continued at southern military facilities throughout the war. Two major racial incidents involving Black servicemen in the Deep South during 1944 illustrate the larger contours of the ongoing difficulties. In late May 1944, Black airmen at

Brookley Army Air Field in Mobile, Alabama—a repair, supply, and training facility for the Army Air Forces—engaged in a shootout with white MPs in the Black section of camp. No one died, though a Black sergeant, shot eight times, sustained serious injuries. The incident inflamed racial tensions in a southern port town already consumed by racial animosity, site of a major racial disturbance a year earlier. The army court-martialed and convicted nine Black privates for involvement in the May 1944 shooting. Three months later, at Camp Claiborne in Louisiana, a similar scene unfolded. Black troops engaged in a gun battle with white soldiers and MPs in the Black housing area of the post. Several soldiers, Black and white, suffered relatively minor injuries. Claiborne officials court-martialed fourteen Black soldiers and convicted all but one of the men.

In 1944, Black servicemen at Brookley Field remained strictly segregated by race. Housed in a separate area of the camp in substandard barracks surrounded by barbed wire fence, Black airmen reportedly had to obtain a pass to enter the white area of the military facility. They had access to only one PX. According to John LeFlore, the leader of the Mobile NAACP branch and chairman of the organization's Regional Conference of Southern Branches, both Black military personnel and Black civilian workers at Brookley faced "gross discrimination and abuse" from white locals and white MPs. Black troops had requested more Black MPs and the arming of the ones already on duty, like their white counterparts.[30]

The May 1944 incident at Brookley began just before midnight on the 24th, when a white man employed at Alabama Dry Dock and Shipbuilding Corporation, Marshal LeRoy Holp, who moonlighted as a supplier of bootleg liquor for Black airmen, got into a fight with some of them. The Black servicemen claimed he had insulted a Black woman, which led to the assault. Holp claimed the Black men robbed him, a story he soon relayed to the white MPs. Accompanying Holt to the scene of the fight, near one of the gates to the camp, the MPs found forty Black airmen waiting for a bus to downtown Mobile and ordered them back to their barracks. A reinforced team of MPs then decided to take Holt to the Black housing area of camp, presumably to identify his assailants. Black troops later claimed the white MPs failed to properly identify themselves with the sentry to the all-Black, fenced-off section of the base, and when the white MPs tried to enter anyway, shots were exchanged. Other Black servicemen soon broke into a weapons storeroom and secured guns and ammunition. When the MPs arrived in the Black section of camp, a firefight broke out between about seventy-five Black airmen from the 437th Aviation Squadron and the 4906th Army Air Force Base Unit Aviation Squadron and the white MPs. In an hour of shooting, the combatants fired about 1,000 rounds of ammunition.[31]

When the gun fight began, two white captains and a Black sergeant went to a nearby ammunition dump and sought to remove the material to a different location, as a way of perhaps limiting the confrontation. One of the white captains asked the sergeant, Wellington Abrams of Washington, DC, to locate a jeep to help move the ammo. While doing so, the MPs shot Abrams, mistaking him for one of the Black antagonists. Abrams suffered serious wounds but ultimately recovered, and he became the only major casualty in the Brookley gun battle. Interestingly, the white press mistook the light-skinned Abrams for a white officer, featuring him two days later in a picture on the front page of the *Mobile Register* laid up in the base hospital as a hero in the fight against Black rioters. The incident at Brookley only ended with the arrival of the commander of the Mobile Air Service Command, General James A. Mollison, a career army officer, originally from Kansas. The general, who obviously had the respect of the Black airmen, entered the battle scene unarmed and convinced them to lay down their weapons, reminding them that "this is not the conduct of good American soldiers." Mollison ordered all Black servicemen confined to base, while promising "impartial justice" for anyone involved in the episode. Not all white officers took the same approach. Colonel Donald Hudson, another Brookley commander, berated an assembled group of Black airmen soon after the melee, telling them, "You men think you can come down here and change customs of the South, but the army will win in the end."[32]

In late June 1944, the army moved to punish nine privates from the 437th and the 4906th for the racial incident at Brookley. Lieutenant Colonel William McCaw, a former Dallas district attorney and Texas state attorney general, led the army's prosecution. The army's case seemed weak. General Mollison's investigation concluded that the supposed incident that precipitated the fight between Black troops and the white MPs—the robbery of Holp—never occurred. A Board of Officers also found that a more serious incident did not occur because "many of the soldiers in the two organizations are of excellent type and character." At the same time, investigators did not think that the military (including the MPs) bore any responsibility for what it perceived as a Black mutiny. Although the army acknowledged that about seventy-five Black airmen took part in the pitched battle with the MPs, the military only charged nine men. The primary evidence against those? Someone had seen them with a gun during the early morning hours of May 25. That comprised the testimony of one prosecution witness, Black sergeant Curtis Nunnally, whom army authorities had initially arrested for participating in the incident. The military court convicted all nine of the privates and sentenced them to hard labor for terms of sixteen to twenty-five years. Despite Colonel Hudson's claim that Black soldiers from outside the South represented the cause of all the trouble, at least five of those convicted of charges stemming from the Brookley disorder hailed from the South or the border South.[33]

As in Mobile, the area surrounding the military facilities near Alexandria, Louisiana, had continued to simmer with racial tension and intermittent racial violence ever since the upheaval that rocked Alexandria's Little Harlem in January 1942. In the first half of 1944, unknown assailants had killed three Black soldiers within ten miles of Camp Claiborne; Black GIs assumed white individuals had murdered these soldiers. The alleged rape of one white woman and the alleged assault of another enraged local white communities near Camp Claiborne. Since Reconstruction, rumors and unproved charges of Black men raping or assaulting white women had fueled white violence against Black men and served as a primary justification for white supremacy and lynching. On August 14, the sheriff of Rapides Parish launched a search for the Black assailants and requested bloodhounds from Angola State Prison to help with the effort. Some soldiers from the camp assisted with the hunt, soon joined by "hundreds of white citizens" from Forest Hill and Glenmora, two nearby communities. The white civilians, who patrolled the area for the next two days, threatened to shoot any Black soldiers they encountered. White officers who later testified at a court-martial described the situation as "groups of armed civilians prowling near the Military Reservation." One report claimed that the white patrollers tried to stop any vehicles leaving the installation to search for Black GIs, and some Black soldiers claimed that they saw white civilians with guns and dogs on post, though the army denied these accounts.[34]

The border between military post and southern community, which delineated the operation and limits of Jim Crow justice, had remained tenuous throughout World War II, but for Black soldiers at Camp Claiborne in August 1944, that line now seemed porous. As one put it, "This camp isn't run by government regulations, its controlled by the state of Louisiana and white civilians." Rumors spread. The FBI described one report that claimed a white mob with bloodhounds had tracked the alleged rapist to the Black area of camp and lynched him. On August 16, after two days of armed white civilians circling the camp, another story spread that one of the white posses had killed four Black soldiers in the camp's isolated bivouac area. This tale may have started because of the actual killing that day of a Black serviceman at Camp Livingston, another army installation in the Alexandria area. MPs there shot Ralph Stewart, a private from Pennsylvania, reportedly for trying to drive a stolen truck through a camp fence.[35]

Whether or not Black soldiers at Camp Claiborne heard about the killing of Private Stewart remains unclear, but the report that white people had killed four of their comrades set off a violent chain of events. Late on the night of August 16, thirty to forty Black GIs from three engineer service units descended on Regimental Headquarters to inquire about the rumored killings. White officers said they would investigate and ordered the men back to their area. Another group of soldiers from these units, perhaps numbering 200, went to the supposed crime scene, but white officers turned them away. Early on the morning of August 17, Black soldiers, still agitated about the supposed murders, secured weapons as part of a continued effort to discover if local white citizens had killed Black GIs. White officers, worried about the unrest among their men, went to check the various weapon storerooms and discovered guns and ammunition missing. At one location, Black soldiers fired on white officers inside one of the supply dumps. Several Black enlisted men and white officers received minor injuries. Black soldiers later claimed that they acted in self-defense. They believed white civilians planned to attack and kill them, a reasonable assumption given the armed and enraged white gangs operating around the camp in the previous days.[36]

The army arrested between twenty-five and forty Black soldiers and eventually court-martialed fourteen of them. Military tribunals convicted all but one, and those found guilty received sentences from nine years to death (for a soldier who struck a white lieutenant with a gun), although an army board of review reduced the death sentence to forty years' imprisonment. Those convicted came from all over the country, including the South. One soldier found guilty, Charles B. Coleman, claimed that he and many of the others court-martialed "were seemingly picked at random from the different organizations (colored) at Camp Claiborne." As the court-martial proceedings were underway, the army arrested Lee R. Davis, a Black GI from Mississippi, who later confessed to both sexual assaults. Walter White, the longtime executive secretary of the NAACP, doubted the "accuracy and validity" of the confession; while admitting that Davis might have committed the crimes,

White also noted that "I have long since learned to be highly suspicious of such confessions in the South."[37]

While the army punished at least some of the Black soldiers engaged in mutinous behavior on August 17, it also brought in a new commander for the camp, who arrived seven days later—Brigadier General Louis F. Guerre, a former head of the Louisiana State Police in the 1930s. On his arrival, Guerre reportedly told a group of white officers that the military sent him to Camp Claiborne to straighten out existing racial problems. He immediately moved to disarm the Black units involved in the disturbances. Guerre shared the typical racial views of white Southerners at the time, so it remained unlikely that he could address the real problem that led to the riot of Black soldiers— the distrust and animosity that existed between Black GIs and white soldiers and civilians. As a result, racial conflict continued. On September 2, the white manager of the Black PX attacked two Black soldiers with a hammer. The next day, a white lieutenant in one of the engineer service units involved in the recent troubles shot and killed Private Leonard P. Washington of New Orleans; the lieutenant claimed Washington attacked him.[38]

The incidents at Brookley Field and Camp Claiborne highlighted the realities of life for Black soldiers at military installations in the Deep South in 1944, after almost four years of training Black troops in the region. Despite the army's anti-segregation efforts, southern military facilities remained deeply separated based on race. In addition, white MPs continued to cause problems for Black soldiers in southern camps. The fact that white MPs at Brookley took the side of a somewhat sketchy white civilian against Black comrades-in-arms led to the shooting outbreak at the base. White officers also did not necessarily drop their racist mindsets—despite directions from the top military brass—a situation not confined to the Deep South.

For every General Mollison, there seemed to be a General Guerre, and Black troops remained at the mercy of the racial attitudes of their (largely) white officers. As for the court-martial system, the army used it to punish some—or any—Black soldiers for incidents in which they clearly broke discipline and endangered lives, but for which the identification of all—or any—of the guilty parties remained impossible. The system remained particularly unfair because it punished Black soldiers affected by incidents at least in part caused by the military's inability to enforce the nondiscrimination principles it espoused. At the same time, white soldiers typically received no punishment for their part in creating and inflaming racial tensions within the army, a further measure of the limits to the military's commitment to the principle of nondiscrimination. Finally, despite claims at the time, and later, the dissatisfaction of treatment in the South was not limited to Black GIs from the North; the World War II military experience also emboldened some southern Black soldiers to fight against southern racial discrimination.

Both incidents also revealed that white civilians in the Deep South remained exceedingly hostile to the Black servicemen in their midst, even after more than three years of war against Nazism. The military's increasing support for anti-segregation measures within its facilities—though unevenly enforced in the Deep South—further contributed to a confusing pattern of race relations in and around southern camps. When Lou Layne, a Black NCO from New York City stationed at Fort Benning, requested a transfer out of the South in June 1944, he summed up what he perceived as the competing racial standards he encountered: "While we know there is no such thing as discrimination and prejudice on army posts, it cannot be denied the treatment accorded Negro soldiers in the South at the hands of civilians is far from ideal." Since not all white soldiers embraced the military's stricter nondiscrimination standards, efforts to improve the training conditions for Black soldiers faltered. And the ongoing tensions between Black GIs and southern communities, a problem that had plagued the mobilization and training of a biracial fighting force in the South since the beginning of the war, proved intractable. The army never entirely abandoned the idea that limiting the number of Black troops placed in the South represented the only real solution to the problem. In October 1944, General Brehon B. Somervell, head of the Army Service Forces, ordered a study to see how many Black units in the South the army might shift to northern camps, a possibility already unsuccessfully explored by the War Department earlier in the conflict. This new effort also went nowhere, but the fact that the army still considered this kind of racial reassignment as potentially necessary suggested the seriousness of the problem and the difficulty in finding a solution.[39]

By 1945, the military had sent a Black combat unit, the 93rd Infantry Division, to fight in the Pacific, and another, the 92nd Infantry Division, to the battlefields of Italy. Squadrons of the Tuskegee Airmen had flown missions in North Africa, Sicily, and Italy. In the fall of 1944, the all-Black 761st Tank Battalion, Jackie Robinson's old outfit, joined General George Patton's Third Army and fought in northern France, in the Battle of the Bulge, and on into Germany. Out of necessity, in late 1944, the army integrated some Black service troops into the infantry; they fought during the Battle of the Bulge and afterward in Germany.[40] All these deployments challenged basic understandings in the white South about Black inferiority and the ability of Black men to perform any soldiering task white men could. White Southerners quickly fastened on any reports of Black failure on the battlefield to generalize about the unsuitability of Black men to participate in the fight against fascists.

Ironically, Truman K. Gibson provided some of the initial ammunition for southern critics of Black combat troops in Europe. The War Department sent him to the European theater in February and March 1945 to investigate reports about the lackluster performance of the 92nd Infantry Division. A national publication, Newsweek, had called the 92nd "luckless" and claimed that the outfit had produced more "disappointment and failure than of anything else." Specifically, the newsmagazine had charged the division's Black soldiers as "trigger-happy" and quick to retreat under fire.

After two weeks in Italy, Gibson held a press conference in Rome. He admitted that Black troops often did seem to "melt away" or engage in "more or less panicky retreats" when confronted by the enemy, but he suggested that any shortcomings among the men of the 92nd said nothing about the overall courage of Black soldiers and their ability to fight. While pointing out that white units faced similar issues, Gibson admitted the 92nd seemed to have more of these problems. He blamed the discrepancy not on racial differences but on the peculiarities of training a racially segregated army. Unlike white draftees, the military did not always place Black servicemen in units best suited to their abilities. The army sent Black men to the 92nd because it was a Black outfit. Some did not even receive preliminary basic training before arriving. In addition, almost 20 percent of the soldiers of the 92nd fell into Grade V. The army had developed a program to provide specialized training to these often-illiterate soldiers, but since the 92nd had organized before the creation of this program, many Grade V men of the 92nd had not benefited from the additional training.[41]

Gibson's analysis simply suggested that the army needed a better program for training Black soldiers in segregated units. Others saw the problems more as an intractable outcome of a segregated military. The liberal New York newspaper PM, after investigating the reported issues surrounding the 92nd Division, reminded its readers that "the 92nd Division is a Jim Crow outfit with all the faults inherent in Jim Crow." Most notably, it had a white command that doubted the abilities of its Black cadre from the start. White officers "who believe Negroes are inferior to whites" doomed the 92nd to perform poorly. Soldiers from the unit told the PM reporter that Major General

Edward M. Almond (a Virginian), commander of the 92nd, told his troops that "the Negro press had demanded combat duty for Negro soldiers—and now they were going to get it." The soldiers believed the general told them that "they were given combat duty as a penalty for the aggressiveness of the Negro press." The Black GIs also complained that when relieved of front-line duty to rest, their leaders sent them to areas with recreational facilities "off-limits" to Black soldiers. The NAACP, in an editorial in *The Crisis*, pointed out that separate training in the United States did not represent the ideal form of instruction for foreign combat: "It must be remembered that these men were beaten up by bus drivers, shot up by military and civilian police, insulted by their white officers, denied transportation to and from the post, restricted to certain post exchanges, and jim-crowed in post theaters." After this treatment, it seemed unfair to expect the Black soldier to " 'join the team' after a little pep talk and give a superlative performance."[42]

Gibson's report on other parts of his European trip received less attention. After talking with Allied commanders about the use of mixed Black/white units in the fighting on the Rhine River, Gibson stated that these troops gave "the lie to any charge that Negroes cannot and will not fight." At an early April press conference upon his return from Europe, Gibson concluded that any differences between white and Black soldiers in combat zones "are not due to racial characteristics but to such factors as training, motivation, and environment." Despite Gibson's firsthand evaluation, which basically condemned the army's policy of racial segregation while celebrating the few exceptions to that dominant military model, the NAACP's board of directors approved a vote of no confidence in Gibson. The organization did not like that Gibson had offered any criticism about the performance of Black combat troops in Europe and that he did not always express a more straightforward condemnation of segregation.[43]

Soon after Gibson's initial report from Italy, white segregationist political leaders in the Deep South seized the opportunity to disparage Black fighting men. Judge Horace C. Wilkinson, founder of the League of White Supremacy, gave a speech in the spring of 1945 to the Birmingham Civitan Club, titled "Preserve White Supremacy," in which he claimed that it was "foolish for the white man to count the Negro as a combat asset." Wilkinson explained to the city's civic leaders that "it is no reflection on the Negro to say that he cannot be made a combat soldier; neither can a mule, and yet a mule plays an important role in military and civilian life." An even more notable attack on Black soldiers came on June 29. During a filibuster in the US

Senate against the creation of a permanent FEPC, Senator James Eastland of Mississippi turned his attention to the matter of Black combat soldiers. With only six or so senators in the chamber but a gallery full of mostly Black visitors, Eastland—"flailing his arms and jerking his tie askew"—proclaimed that "the Negro soldier was an utter and dismal failure in combat in Europe." Speaking specifically about the 92nd Division, the senator maintained that "it had the best training of any division in the American Army" but still failed to perform well under fire. Eastland also claimed that he was "not prejudiced against the Negro," a remark that drew laughter from the largely Black audience present.[44]

Many other people rejected Senator Eastland's slander of Black troops. The Supreme Commander of the Allied forces in Europe, Dwight D. Eisenhower, had already done so two weeks before Eastland's outburst. Speaking at a press conference in Paris, Eisenhower remarked, "I have seen Negro soldiers in this war, and I have many reports on their work where they have rendered very valuable contributions and some of them with the greatest enthusiasm. In late November, when we were getting short of reinforcements, replacements, some 2,600 Negro soldiers volunteered for front-line service and they did good work." Other American military leaders, such as Brigadier General Charles Lanham, echoed this evaluation. Much of the southern press also recoiled at Eastland's rhetoric. The *Macon (Ga.) News*, which reaffirmed that it held "no brief for the Negro beyond insisting that he receive fair treatment and due credit for his loyalty and patriotism," called Eastland's speech "a disgraceful performance that ought to shock, sadden and make ashamed every Southerner who loves his country." Despite the blowback, Senator Bilbo doubled down on his Senate colleague's remarks ten days later when he told the press that "Negro soldiers have caused the U.S.A. to lose prestige all over Europe.... They will not fight. They will not work.... They are guilty of more than half the crimes in the Army." Bilbo's remarks received the same reviews as Eastland's, including from Black servicemen serving overseas.[45]

Even those white Southerners who thought the remarks about Black soldiers from Mississippi's senators went too far still believed the War Department's racial reforms posed a threat to the long-term viability of racial segregation. As the war ended, white Southerners tended to greet every violation of southern racial mores within the military with alarm. In July 1945, P. H. Sanders expressed outrage to Bilbo after hearing that the navy placed Black and white sailors in the same companies at the Great Lakes Naval Station near Chicago, including his son and eighteen other Mississippi boys.

The navy had desegregated its training of officers at Great Lakes in late 1944, four years after the army took the same action. When a navy man complained in August 1945 about the mixing of races aboard his cargo ship, Bilbo seemed to encourage violence on an active-duty vessel when he reminded the sailor that since the war had now ended, he could "take a stand for your rights or, should I say, your natural protection as a white man."[46]

In some cases, white Southerners had rejected the "true faith" of racial segregation after a stint in the military, a situation that offered further proof of the dangers associated with the War Department's racial policies. James P. O'Bryan from Meridian, Mississippi, joined the navy and served alongside Black sailors. O'Bryan admitted that "it was not easy at first to eat, sleep and wash by them." But his attitude changed over the course of his service, at least in part because the rules and customs of southern segregation did not shape his contact with Black seamen. O'Bryan ultimately concluded that "the Negro in this war has proven himself entitled to the benefits of democracy above and beyond the call of expectation. If this be denied, then we are frauds." Another white Mississippian, Willie Jones, who fought in Europe, claimed he "hated Negroes" when he entered the army. Yet, after fighting alongside them in 1944 and 1945, he believed his Black comrades deserved the freedom they were fighting for in the war. He claimed that "a lot of southern GIs feel the same way."[47]

Although white Southerners frequently believed that the military's wartime racial policies threatened the region's racial arrangements, the War Department never mounted a frontal attack on southern segregation during World War II. Indeed, immediately after World War II ended, when the War Department revisited the issue of how best to utilize Black troops in the future, it recommitted to the policy of nondiscrimination but did not recommend an end to racial segregation. In September 1945, Secretary of War Robert Patterson, acting on a recommendation from John McCloy and Truman Gibson, created the Gillem Committee.[48]

Over the next four months, a group of generals, two from the South, interviewed more than fifty individuals and examined numerous documents. Many of the military witnesses expressed negative views about Black soldiers. For example, General Almond, commander of the 92nd Division, told the board that Black men could not "be made into good infantry soldiers or even satisfactory ones." Others, such as army Inspector General Virgil Peterson, blasted the performance of Black officers in the war but admitted that "the Negro officer will not disappoint if he gets equal training to whites." The board also interviewed several Black civilians, including William Hastie and Truman Gibson (the past and present civilian aides to the secretary of war), as well as Walter White and Charles Houston, both national NAACP leaders. All except Gibson urged an immediate end to racial segregation in the military; Gibson favored a gradual end to the policy. The board also looked at white survey opinion on the question of a mixed fighting force. The relatively small number of white soldiers who had fought alongside Black GIs in Europe at the end of the war overwhelmingly saw little wrong with an integrated military, while more than 60 percent of white soldiers who did not have such experiences—regardless of where they hailed from—favored preserving segregation. The final report, released in April 1946, offered vague statements about utilizing Black manpower in the event of another war "without regard to antecedents or race" but proposed that the army limit Black soldiers to 10 percent of the army and avoid placing Black units near communities that might object to their presence. Beyond recommending the integration of some overhead units, the Gillem report supported a continuation of racial segregation in the military.[49]

Judging by the conclusions of the report, one would think that the military did little to challenge southern race relations during World War II. However, the War Department's support for the principle of nondiscrimination, though often flawed in conception and unevenly enforced, provided an alternative vision of race relations on southern soil throughout the conflict. During the war, most white Southerners rejected any suggestion by the military to reform the southern system of racial segregation. After the war, military racial policy would continue to evolve. White Southerners in the Deep South, who saw firsthand during the war years how the federal government, through its military, promoted nondiscrimination, were not surprised. The World War II military posed a substantial threat to the South's discriminatory social system, and most white Southerners worried that future encroachments on southern racial norms by the federal government would follow.

PART III
SOUTHERN POLITICS

8
Ellis Arnall: Southern Liberal

On March 25, 1943, as American forces battled the Germans in Tunisia and the Japanese off the coasts of New Guinea and Australia, leaders of seven southern states met in Florida's State Capitol building in Tallahassee for the eleventh annual Southern Governors Conference. Early in the proceedings, the chairman introduced the newest and youngest member of the group, Governor Ellis Arnall of Georgia, a short, round, balding man, only thirty-six years old. The governor immediately took up the issue that had led to the founding of the southern governors group back in 1934: unequal freight rates. Railroads had long charged different freight rates for trains in the Northeast—known as Official Territory—and the rest of the country, including the South. Arnall advised his fellow chief executives that a season of war offered the perfect time to ramp up their fight to rectify this long-festering problem. Arnall proposed that as American soldiers battled "to obtain fair treatment for small nations, minority groups, all over the face of the world. . . . The time has come for us to insist, here in the South, that discrimination against the South be eradicated." The Black press in the Georgia capital city quickly seized on the language Governor Arnall used to describe the South's plight. Cliff Mackay of the *Atlanta Daily World* observed that "freight rates is [sic] not the only discrimination that is harmful to the South." Mackay thought that Arnall and other southern leaders "might point out that all discrimination is wrong, whether sectional or racial."[1] The governor, however, spent his wartime political career studiously avoiding any connection between economic and racial discrimination.

In his remarks at the governors' conclave, Arnall also alluded to the next presidential election, still almost twenty months away. He told his southern brethren that on the freight-rate issue, he (and Georgia) "are going with the one who will offer us the most. We are going to be hard-boiled about it and cold-blooded about it, and I hope you fellows join us." Louisiana's governor, Sam Jones, who was also at the conference, had published a piece just weeks earlier in the *Saturday Evening Post* in which he also questioned the future loyalty of the Solid South to the Democratic Party. Jones complained that "the present Democratic leadership has done considerable bellowing about underprivileged groups. What about underprivileged sections?" He believed that only "one thing can save the New Deal Democratic Party—that is, a complete reversal of attitude toward the South."[2]

President Franklin D. Roosevelt, attuned to the political winds as always, heard these complaints from his own party blowing in from the South. On April 13, the president boarded a train for Mexico to meet with President Manuel Ávila Camacho. FDR, however, took a circuitous route through the US South, stopping at various war towns and military installations. He did not arrive in Monterrey until April 20, although the public received no details of his detour until he arrived in Mexico. Along the way, the president met with restive southern governors, and he convinced at least some of them that he still had the South's best interests in mind. Governor Arnall had the longest visit with Roosevelt. The two men met at Fort Benning, watched some troop training, and then headed to the president's retreat in nearby Warm Springs for several more hours of conversation. At the end of their conference, the Georgia governor believed FDR had promised to help the South.[3] President Roosevelt's meeting with Arnall in the spring of 1943 cemented FDR's alliance with a southern political leader not obsessed with states' rights and race, but rather, one focused on the more palatable ground of promoting southern economic progress.

The relationship between FDR and Arnall had begun a year earlier, during the 1942 Georgia gubernatorial campaign. Arnall ran as a progressive alternative to the incumbent, Eugene Talmadge, a staunch defender of southern traditions and institutions and an ardent opponent of the New Deal. President Roosevelt backed the challenger, who hailed from the town of Newnan in Coweta County, in the Georgia foothills. Arnall came from the town's business elite (his father was a prosperous merchant), but rather than enter business, he chose politics. When he was twenty-five, Coweta County elected him in a landslide to serve in the state legislature, where the lawmaker became the floor leader for Governor Talmadge's program. Arnall, however, soon distanced himself from the conservative Talmadge faction of Georgia politics and gained a reputation as a progressive and reformist legislator. After an anti-Talmadge ticket won the statehouse in 1936, Governor E. D. Rivers appointed Arnall to the position of state attorney general in 1939. Despite his progressive reputation, Arnall maintained some conservative credentials, especially on matters of race. As attorney general, he confirmed the constitutionality of both the poll tax and segregated schools.[4]

Arnall's adoption of the progressive mantle in the 1942 gubernatorial race proved relatively easy, given Talmadge's actions in the runup to the campaign. After his 1940 election, Talmadge eliminated the offices of controller general and state treasurer to take control of state finances. He also gained control of the State Board of Education by stacking it with his political appointees. Then in May 1941, a recently fired University of Georgia education professor, Sylla Hamilton, charged that her dean, two years earlier, had proposed the establishment of an off-campus teacher training institute for both Black and white pre-service teachers. Although the university never built the center, Governor Talmadge fastened on the story and demanded that the dean, Walter D. Cocking, and another administrator, Marvin S. Pittman, president of Georgia State Teachers College (now Georgia Southern University), either resign or be fired. The governor charged the two academics with promoting racial equality and looked for further evidence—real or manufactured—to make his case. One of Talmadge's supporters even tried to bribe a photographer to doctor an image to show Dean Cocking shaking hands with Black men recently drafted into the army. At a hearing in June, the state higher education Board of Regents rehired Cocking in an eight-to-seven vote and delayed a hearing on Pittman's case.[5]

Talmadge did not let the matter rest. He may have sensed that opposition to FDR would no longer be a winning issue, especially as mobilization for war began; a focus on the tried-and-true race issue and how mobilization for war threatened established race relations might better ensure his political success. So the governor continued his attack on the dean. He moved to engineer the removal of three Board of Regents members who supported Cocking with new members who shared the governor's fears about the "foreign" Cocking (originally from Iowa). Attorney General Arnall weighed in on Talmadge's meddling in Board of Regents' decisions, calling him an "imitation Hitler." When the reconstituted Board took up the matter of Cocking and Pittman at its July meeting, in a ten-to-five vote, the trustees backed the governor and dismissed both men from their positions.[6]

An outcry to the firings quickly followed. National Association for the Advancement of Colored People (NAACP) director and Georgia native Walter White, in a letter to the editor of the *Atlanta Constitution*, claimed the action would "hold us up as a nation to ridicule in other parts of the world" and would "destroy [the] faith of twelve million Negroes in the democratic processes." In the months that followed, the Southern University Conference, a regional alliance of the South's major colleges, dropped the University of

Georgia from membership. Seven hundred University students responded by traveling to Atlanta to hang the governor in effigy at the statue of Populist hero Tom Watson on the Capitol grounds. In addition, the Southern Association of Colleges and Secondary Schools pulled its accreditation of ten of the state's colleges and universities, and thousands of Georgia students began to make plans to go elsewhere for their education.[7]

Amid this fallout to Talmadge's firing of the two professors, Arnall announced in November 1941 that he would enter the Georgia governor's race. Talmadge's bungled handling of the higher education issue allowed the attorney general to pitch his campaign as one of democracy versus tyranny, as a "crusade to uproot dictatorship here and to redeem the reputation and honor of our state." As the Democratic primary campaign heated up in early 1942, Talmadge continued to highlight the race issue, undercutting Arnall's ability to portray himself as a democratic champion. In February 1942, a Black junior high school teacher in Atlanta, William H. Reeves, backed by the Atlanta chapter of the NAACP, filed a teacher salary equalization lawsuit against the local school system. In 1941–1942, on average, a white teacher in Atlanta made 49 percent more than a Black teacher there ($2,324 versus $1,556). State school officials complained that a statewide teacher salary equalization program would cost the state $1 million. Governor Talmadge, however, focused on a more fundamental threat posed by the lawsuit. He believed that equal pay for Black and white teachers would lead to attempts "to admit the Negroes to all of our schools and public places." In April, the governor claimed that if Reeves's litigation succeeded, the state would simply replace Black teachers with white ones, even though such a move would have cost as much as equalization. That same month, the Georgia Teachers and Educational Association, which represented 7,000 Black educators in the state, passed a resolution at its annual meeting condemning the governor's "use of the Negro as a 'red herring.'"[8]

Arnall tried to downplay the racial issues favored by the Talmadge campaign. At a speech at Fort Valley, Arnall said, "The race issue is not only false; it is bunk." He accused the Talmadge forces of "stirring up ... racial hatred" simply to win the election. Talmadge countered that he was fighting a real threat to white supremacy, not one artificially created, but rather, "raised in Washington and projected into every state in the South." He identified as a specific concern the nondiscrimination demands of the US military and the Fair Employment Practices Committee (FEPC), which amounted to a "struggle to fasten racial equality upon the South." Arnall continued to try to make the gubernatorial choice a referendum on Governor Talmadge's shortcomings, especially his "destruction" of the higher education system and his "dictatorial" tendencies. Ninety percent of the state's press backed Arnall. Ralph McGill, editor of the *Atlanta Constitution*, talked about the need to end corrupt government and compared the gubernatorial primary battle to that of the Founding Fathers opposing the king of England. Talmadge, as if to confirm the charges that he acted like a dictator, called for a change in libel laws "to protect officials and all other persons from wanton attacks in the press." McGill also pressed for "the right to a free ballot," an amazingly ironic plea from a white leader in a state where one-third of its citizens could not vote in the whites-only Democratic Party primary election, which represented the only one that really counted in the one-party state.[9]

Despite Arnall's efforts, he could not banish discussion of racial issues during the campaign. Indeed, in mid-July the arrest of the world-renowned Black tenor Roland Hayes and his wife, Alzada, in Hayes's hometown of Rome, Georgia, after an altercation over segregated service at a local shoe store, focused international attention on racism in Georgia. On a sweltering Saturday morning, Alzada Hayes and her daughter Africa went into the Higgins Shoe Store to buy some tennis shoes. They sat down in the white area of the store, and when, in the usual manner, a store employee rudely told them to move to the back of the store, Alzada made a comment about the clerk needing to join Hitler. The salesclerk ordered the Hayes women out of the store, and after Roland heard about the confrontation, he got into an argument with the police on the street outside the store. The police beat Roland and then arrested him and his wife. When word spread around Rome about the incident, many white residents regretted that a famous native son had received such rough treatment, but they blamed Alzada Hayes for the trouble, since she refused to act in a manner appropriate to a Black woman—obey a white man trying to enforce the customs of racial segregation. On the campaign trail, Arnall remained silent about the events in Rome, while Talmadge used the incident to defend segregation. The governor issued a statement supporting the local police and warning Black people who did not like the state's laws "to stay out of Georgia."[10]

A month before the election, Talmadge amped up the racial rhetoric and finally forced Arnall to demonstrate his white supremacy bona fides. In early August, apparently acting at the suggestion of the governor and with the implicit approval of the US Army, the head of the Georgia State Guard, Colonel

Lindley Camp, issued "alert" orders for possible "subversive activity" among the Black population and the potential for "racial conflict." The orders specifically raised the prospect that the state's white women faced imminent peril and needed protection (safeguards obviously not needed or available to Black women such as Alzada Hayes). Camp noted that "there have been an unusual number of assault cases and attempts to assault white ladies." At the time, the US Department of Justice denied that it had received any reports of "subversive influences in Georgia," and the Atlanta Police Department reported that both assaults and attempted assaults "are the lowest in years." At a speech in Chatsworth in north Georgia, Arnall ridiculed Talmadge for manufacturing a racial crisis in the state, but he also felt the need to reassure his audience that white supremacy remained beyond danger. Arnall claimed that "we don't need any governor to keep Negroes out of our white schools.... We know how to handle the Negro problem. Why, if a Negro ever tried to get into a white school in the section where I live, the sun would not set on his head. And we wouldn't call on the governor or the State Guard." Later, after a radio address, thinking the broadcast had ended, Arnall opined more crudely: "Any nigger who tried to enter the university would not be in existence [the] next day. We don't need a governor [or] sheriff to take care of that situation."[11]

Arnall's comments raised concerns among his more moderate supporters. Dorothy Tilly, a leader of the Atlanta chapter of the Commission on Interracial Cooperation (which became the Southern Regional Council in 1944), understood that Arnall was "playing politics," but she worried that "his remarks make it appear that he condones lynching." Tilly and other southern white women, working through several organizations, had argued against the oft-cited rationale for mob violence against Black men—protecting southern white women. She and other churchwomen convinced Arnall that his remarks would cost him votes, so he issued a statement that opposed "mob violence in all its insidious forms." Ralph McGill also met with Arnall and cautioned him against making racially inflammatory statements. Although he reassured his most liberal white supporters that he was not a violent racist, Black leaders remained unconvinced. Eugene Martin, an officer of the Atlanta Life Insurance Company on Auburn Avenue (and brother-in-law of national NAACP director Walter White), believed that Arnall did not have "the Christian manhood to say one word in the matter of treating the Negro fair, but has come out for lynch laws just like Talmadge." Martin saw the election as "a choice between two evils, Talmadge being possibly the worse of the two." Of course, Martin and most other Black Georgians had no chance to make a choice in the contest.[12]

Arnall won the election, and much of the national press, Black and white, believed that his victory meant a more enlightened future for Georgia. The *New Republic* judged the election a victory for "progressives," though it admitted that Arnall "did not conduct his campaign on so high a plane as might have been wished." Even the Black press believed the election signaled fundamental change; the *Pittsburgh Courier* claimed that Talmadge's defeat proved that the "race issue is dead in Dixie" and the *Chicago Defender* labeled the outcome "a remarkable victory for democracy." For many national observers, Arnall looked so good because Talmadge appeared so bad. As *The Nation* put it, "Arnall is to be preferred to Talmadge, but this is surely a new low in compliments."[13]

The new governor did bring progressive change to the state on several fronts. With a liberalism somewhat unique for a statewide leader in the Deep South during World War II, Arnall quickly established his progressive and reform credentials after he assumed office in January 1943. It had taken FDR a hundred days to win his first series of New Deal victories in 1933, but Arnall needed only twenty-four days to get the Georgia legislature to adopt his entire legislative agenda. Ten bills, most designed to undo Talmadge actions, passed unanimously. Legislation reshaped the state boards that managed higher education and the public secondary and elementary school systems and insulated them from future executive control. As a result, accreditation for the higher education institutions was quickly restored. Another bill eliminated the practice of gubernatorial clemency for felons, and still others prevented the governor from removing state officials, such as the state treasurer, and created a new State Finance Commission to help the governor on budgetary matters. Months later, in a special session, the legislature passed a law reforming the state's prison system, which not only addressed a humanitarian problem but saved the state money.[14]

Talmadge left Arnall with a budget deficit of $35 million, so he also moved rapidly to hold the line on government spending. Facing the loss of about one-third of state revenue, primarily because rationing reduced gas taxes, in February 1943, Arnall issued an executive order requiring that state agencies cut expenditures as much as possible. He urged each state department "to voluntarily cut every possible expense. . . . Jobs must be held to a minimum. No expanded services will be tolerated." By the summer of 1943, these economizing measures helped Arnall trim $8 million off the state debt, and the state had almost retired the debt by the end of his term. At the same time, throughout his administration, Arnall managed to increase government spending, but without raising tax rates—one of his campaign pledges—because of increased tax revenues generated because of new, war-related economic activity. Much of this new money went into education: the public schools, the college/university system, and teachers' salaries. Between 1942 and 1946, education spending in the state almost doubled.[15]

Although the Arnall administration brought significant progressive reforms accompanied by fiscal responsibility, racial realities in Georgia did not change. Segregation, disfranchisement, and racial violence (or its threat) continued to order the lives of Black Georgians.[16] Even minor challenges to racial segregation related to war mobilization enraged white citizens. In November 1943, the FEPC opened a regional office in Atlanta in the Forsythe Building, an eight-story structure occupied solely by white federal government workers. As word spread that the FEPC might hire Black employees to work in a building that had no segregated restroom facilities, the Atlanta City Council leapt into action and passed a resolution calling for closure of the FEPC office and asking that the director leave town. After the office hired a Black secretary in January, white workers, city leaders, and a US congressman launched a new round of complaints, including to Arnall, who claimed he had no power to act. The uproar evaporated only after the building's owner constructed separate bathroom facilities for Black workers.[17]

The new governor did not encourage racial violence directed toward Black citizens, but he took little affirmative action to end the problem, even against violent, anti-Black government officials. Soon after Arnall assumed office, a sheriff in southwest Georgia, M. Claude Screws, and two other lawmen killed a Black man, Robert Hall, after he dared to use the legal system to try to recover a pistol he claimed the sheriff had stolen from him. After Hall's lawyer sent Screws a letter about the matter, the sheriff arrested Hall on a trumped-up theft charge. After the three white men took Hall into custody, they literally beat him to death on the courthouse square in the small town of Newton. The Arnall administration claimed it could not intervene but did support an investigation by the US Department of Justice, which eventually led to a conviction of Screws and his two accomplices on federal charges of violating Hall's civil rights (a decision overturned in 1945 by the US Supreme Court).[18]

As the flap over the opening of the Atlanta FEPC office and the Hall killing suggest, Arnall tried to avoid racial issues as much as possible. Arnall's biographer, Harold Henderson, concludes that the governor had an "enlightened view of race relations," at least by the standards of white Georgians at the time. Unlike Talmadge, Arnall did not use damaging racial rhetoric to inflame racial passions, and Black Georgians appreciated that difference. After he gave a speech in November 1944 to the Catholic Laymen's Association of Georgia in which he proclaimed that "I hate intolerance and prejudice," the *Atlanta Daily World* editorialized that "it is a heart-warming experience for all Negroes in the state to know that now, unlike the past, their Governor will have no truck with bigotry, prejudice and intolerance." And Arnall did favor improving the lot of Black Georgians by making separate but equal fairer. As he told the *Christian Science Monitor* in June 1944, "We want the Negro to get better wages, to have better homes, to improve his standard of living. It is foolish for anyone to think otherwise. The more prosperous the Negro is, the better off all of us are."[19]

Despite these sentiments, Arnall's actions did not always translate into ending the discriminatory treatment that characterized racial segregation in Georgia. Three months after Arnall's election, the Atlanta Board of Education, after stalling to resolve William Reeves's teacher salary equalization lawsuit, fired him—supposedly for "health reasons"—temporarily ending the challenge to equalize teacher salaries. Within a month, however, another plaintiff, Samuel L. Davis, a teacher at Booker T. Washington High School, stepped forward to file a similar complaint, backed by both the Atlanta chapter of the NAACP and the national organization's Legal Defense Fund. The attorney for the board of education initially told the federal district court judge that "even if the government ruled that salaries paid to Negro teachers were unequal and unfair to those paid to the whites, nothing could be done about it." Indeed, the school board had no intention of providing equal salaries to Black and white teachers. It soon moved to eliminate its salary schedule and then declared the problem solved because it now paid teachers "on an individual basis."

Ending the reporting of salaries based on race, however, did not provide extra wages for Black educators but merely obscured the ongoing disparities. The Davis case languished in court proceedings for almost a decade before a dismissal of the action. Although Arnall had no role in the Atlanta case, his administration never took any specific action to equalize education expenditures in the state. The governor did support funding that increased teacher salaries overall, but at the end of his term in 1947, the gap statewide between Black and white teacher salaries had grown slightly from the 1943 levels, and in 1945, total state spending on white education—despite an overall increase in education spending—remained three times greater than that for Black education.[20]

Arnall's position on race mirrored that of the federal government, with its nondiscrimination mobilization directives, and reflected a consensus that emerged during the war among many white Americans. As historian Glenda Gilmore noted, by 1944–1945 "racism had become un-American," and "most white Americans outside the South had accepted tolerance for racial and ethnic minorities as a civic value, even if they still were perfecting its practice." Even if white people did not overtly advocate for an end to racial segregation, those outside the South had come to embrace the notion that extreme discrimination against groups like African Americans had no place in a country waging war against racism and totalitarianism. Some rank-and-file white Southerners, and certainly white moderate/liberal organizations in the region, shared these sentiments. In a survey conducted by Sara Kennedy for the NAACP in the fall of 1942, she found that white folks in Alabama and Mississippi supported the provision of both additional education funds and better legal protections for Black citizens, although the white residents surveyed did not want "to change the segregation laws and customs." Groups like the Southern Regional Council and the Southern Conference for Human Welfare (SCHW) also did not support racial desegregation, although they did seek improvements in various areas of Black life—a stance historian Harvard Sitkoff labeled "a liberalization of race relations without meaningful change." Black Georgians, however, understood the limits of Arnall's liberalism on the race issue in a society where Black people held no political power. As Atlanta NAACP leader A. T. Walden noted at the time, Arnall was "as liberal as it is possible for a white man to be and hold office in the South."[21]

Much of Arnall's reputation as a progressive on race came from his efforts at voting reform, although he never really championed the right to vote for Black Georgians. During his first year in office, Arnall proposed a state constitutional amendment to change the voting age from twenty-one to eighteen. In promoting the measure, the governor often used stories of young Georgians fighting overseas. The slogan for the campaign became "A man old enough to fight is old enough to vote." Georgia voters agreed and in August 1943 ratified the amendment by an almost three-to-one majority, which made Georgia the first state to enfranchise voters younger than twenty-one. Since the state's poll tax law applied the levy only to those between the ages of twenty-one and sixty, the new voters, potentially 165,000 of them, did not have to face that obstacle to cast a vote in the state. The reform also presented the possibility of increasing the state's voter rolls by almost 40 percent (from 425,000 to 590,000). It also raised Arnall's national profile, as did his support for providing new opportunities for Georgia servicemen and servicewomen to cast a ballot.[22]

In late 1943, the US Congress could not agree on provisions to provide a more effective mechanism for members of the armed services to vote in federal elections, largely because of objections from southern lawmakers that such an effort violated states' rights. In the aftermath of the deadlock in the national legislature, many states moved to consider legislation to allow their own servicemen and servicewomen to vote. As with the eighteen-year-old vote, Georgia led the way. Governor Arnall called the Georgia legislature back into special session in early January 1944, and it quickly passed a bill easing voter registration procedures for members of the armed forces and eliminating the poll tax ($1 a year) for those in the military. Although Walter Winchell claimed in his popular national radio broadcast that the action opened Georgia voting to all the state's citizens, the reality for Black citizens was more sobering. Arnall obliquely made clear that Georgia's "soldier vote" bill would not eliminate racial restrictions on Black voters when he clarified that "the legislation would not increase the number of persons eligible to vote above the number that would be eligible if they were at home instead of abroad or in a training camp."[23]

In other words, nothing in the Georgia military voter law changed the fact that most Black Georgians could not exercise their basic franchise rights. In 1940, only 3 percent of Black people in Georgia were registered to vote. A study conducted that year by the SCHW concluded that Georgia prevented most Black people from voting "by the simple device of excluding him from the primaries," as well as "routine discrimination" against Black Georgians who attempted to register to vote. As the reality that the state's new vote law for members of the armed forces would not change voting rights for African Americans became clear, Black men and women in Georgia challenged the notion that the legislation represented an effort to promote American democracy. The Atlanta branch of the NAACP sent the governor and legislative leaders a telegram noting that Georgia had 100,000 Black men and women in uniform. The group reasoned that "there is no discrimination in the sacrifice which every member of the armed forces is required to make for his country," and "there should be no discrimination in the right to participate in the determination of the kind of government for which he (the Negro service man) may have to die." This statement reflected the growing political mobilization of Black Georgians. During the war years, Black activists in Georgia, particularly in Georgia's larger cities, such as Atlanta, Savannah, and Macon, increased their organizing efforts—often working through groups such as the NAACP and the National Urban League—to challenge racial discrimination and Black disfranchisement in the state.[24]

Despite strident complaints from Black Georgians, Arnall initially showed no interest in eliminating either the poll tax or the white primary in the state, although national efforts to abolish both moved forward during the war. National reformers began seeking a federal anti–poll tax law in 1939, and in 1940, the National Committee to Abolish the Poll Tax estimated that the tax disfranchised 11 million Southerners, 60 percent of those white. Since southern politicians faced relatively few voters, they tended to easily win reelection. In fact, in the early 1940s, 40 percent of congressmen serving for more than twenty years came from the southern poll tax states. Not surprisingly, these congressmen led the effort to block the federal challenge to the poll tax and other racial reforms during the war. The fight against the white primary played out in the federal courts, after a Black dentist in Houston challenged the Texas white primary, eventually resulting in the 1944 decision *Smith v. Allwright*, in which the US Supreme Court ruled the practice unconstitutional. The FDR administration, however, did not actively seek to enforce the decision. Although the president considered supporting an Alabama voting rights suit after the Supreme Court ruling, he ultimately decided to take no action because of fears that pressing the Black suffrage issue would cost him southern votes in the upcoming 1944 presidential election. At the same time, southern states railed against *Smith v. Allwright* and argued that their Democratic primaries were "private" affairs and thus not subject to state oversight. Arnall viewed these national efforts to attack the white primary and the poll tax as counterproductive. In June 1944 he observed that "the recent decision of the Supreme Court of the United States giving the Negro the right to participate in primaries of the Democratic Party was a blow to liberalism."[25]

For Arnall, the solution to the race problem, as he had announced to his fellow southern leaders soon after his election, lay not in empowering Black citizens but in improving the economy of his state and region. He focused specifically on fixing the country's railroad freight rate system, which charged shippers different prices in the Northeast and the rest of the country. The Interstate Commerce Commission (ICC) estimated that in 1943, southern freight rates stood 3 to 5 percent higher than those in Official Territory. As a result, the Georgia governor concluded that ending this differential would aid smaller businesses in his state and would transform the regional economy, and with it, the racial problems that had plagued the South since the Civil War. As he told *PM* reporter Kenneth Stewart in 1946, "Eliminate the discrimination against our section and race tensions will be eliminated."[26]

Southern politicians had complained about discriminatory freight rates in the region since the mid-1930s. They had won some limited backing for their protests from both President Roosevelt and the ICC, as well as key politicians from other sections of the country, such as US Vice President Henry Wallace of Iowa, who believed that discriminatory freight rates led to a second-class economic status for both the West and the South. Despite the opposition to the existing system, little changed in the late 1930s and early 1940s, in large part because shippers and heavy industries in these regions favored the status quo.[27]

Unlike other southern governors, who had only groused about the unfairness of differential freight rates, Arnall decided to take more direct action. In May 1944, he filed suit in the US Supreme Court against twenty railroads for conspiring to maintain discriminatory freight rates in Georgia and the rest of the South. The complaint asked for more than $60 million in damages for Georgia and for individual shipping firms. Questions arose immediately about whether the nation's highest court had jurisdiction over such a dispute and whether the ICC represented the more appropriate forum to decide such a question. Southern carriers and Arnall's fellow chief executives disapproved of the lawsuit, but the Roosevelt administration ultimately endorsed the action. The Supreme Court heard oral arguments in the case on January 2, 1945, and Arnall appeared for the plaintiffs, the first time a sitting governor had argued a case before the US Supreme Court.

Rather than stand at the podium as petitioners traditionally did, Arnall paced back and forth, as if addressing a Coweta County jury back home. He claimed that a "conspiracy and coercion" by the railroads "has an adverse effect of far-reaching impact in the economy of Georgia and the South." The railroads responded that the ICC should adjudicate such matters and that the court had no business refereeing this dispute. Two months later, in a 5–4 decision, the US Supreme Court ruled in favor of Arnall. Justice William O. Douglas, writing for the majority, acknowledged that the court could not set or alter railroad rates, since that function belonged to the ICC, a government agency Congress had created. But Douglas claimed that "if the alleged combination is shown to exist, the decree which can be entered ... will eliminate . . . the collusive practices which the antitrust laws condemn." In May 1945, the ICC issued an order calling for uniform railroad rates. Although the ICC delayed implementation of the directive for two years, the agency's decision effectively ended the freight-rate case.[28]

From the beginning of his fight to end discriminatory freight rates, Arnall had imbued the effort—and his other attempts to promote economic development—with the power to solve the many problems Georgia and the South faced, including the so-called race problem. As historian Bruce Schulman notes, Arnall became the first of the South's "development-oriented politicians," who used the economic development issue as "an escape route, a tunnel out of the tyrannous grip of the race issue that had so long afflicted southern politics." One month after Governor Arnall sued the railroads, he held a press conference where he trumpeted all the support he had received for his action and urged all those who wanted to help Black citizens to join his crusade. Arnall concluded that "when you remove the economic barriers—discriminatory freight rates—you will have enough jobs for white and black and you remove the cause of discord." The governor suggested that an improved southern economy would allow southern governments to improve schools and health conditions for all its citizens, Black and white.[29] Arnall's explanation for the ills of the South resonated at home because it placed all the blame for these problems on external factors, specifically the economic discrimination the region had suffered from the North. Such a calculus, however, failed to consider that the South's weak economy resulted in large part from the region's own discriminatory actions to preserve second-class status for the region's Black people.

Governor Arnall's support of voting reforms and his fight against freight-rate differentials brought him to the attention of the nation as a prominent southern liberal. His support of President Roosevelt and Vice President Wallace during the 1944 presidential campaign further burnished that reputation. Arnall played a small but significant role in the 1944 presidential drama. For months leading up to the national Democratic convention, questions had swirled around whether FDR would run for an unprecedented fourth term. After the 1942 Georgia gubernatorial election, Arnall and the president had struck up a friendship. In late June 1944, FDR met Arnall at the White House and told the Georgia governor that he had a duty to seek the presidency again because of the war. Roosevelt also told Arnall that he wanted Wallace as his running mate, even though it might "cost the ticket a million votes" and asked the Georgian to support Wallace. When Arnall left the White House, he relayed all this information to the press, in a statement FDR had obviously approved. Two weeks later, FDR officially announced his 1944 candidacy for president.[30]

By the time of the 1944 Democratic Party convention, much of the white southern Democratic political establishment had turned against the national party—but not Arnall or most of the southern population. More than 80 percent of all Southerners in the Deep South supported FDR heading into the November election. Following the convention, Arnall established closer ties with Wallace, although he lost the vice-president nomination in a contested convention vote to Harry S. Truman. In August, Wallace, who did not really know Arnall well, visited the Georgia governor in Atlanta, where the two men played tennis and talked politics, cementing what became a close friendship. Six months later, Arnall offered strong support for Wallace in his controversial confirmation fight to become secretary of commerce. Also, in August 1944, the Georgia governor made another trip to the White House, and the Georgia politician's audience with the president sparked rumors about a possible cabinet position for Arnall should FDR win in November. The Georgia governor denied that he had discussed such matters with the president, although years later he claimed that Roosevelt said he planned to offer him the post of attorney general. In the fall, Arnall became the most prominent southern leader campaigning for FDR's re-election. A week before the November election, Arnall made a swing through Tennessee, Minnesota, Oklahoma, and Missouri. In addition to rounding up votes for FDR, Arnall's trip also enhanced his own reputation outside of Georgia. At the end of a speech in Chattanooga, Tennessee, many in the crowd of 2,500 rushed to the stage to shake his hand. One observer claimed, "That young man is going to be a national leader, you just watch him."[31]

As Arnall's national stature grew, he warmed to the idea of further voting reforms. In early 1945, he pushed forward a plan for the state of Georgia to abolish the poll tax. The 1945 session of the Georgia legislature considered a host of changes to the Georgia constitution recommended by a constitutional revision commission created by Arnall in 1943 and chaired by the governor. The commission had not made elimination of the poll tax one of its proposed changes, and Arnall had not pressed for such a change during the commission's deliberations. However, after the legislature convened in January 1945, he told the assembled lawmakers that he favored abolition of the tax. He further informed them that if they did not make the change, he would eliminate the levy by executive action after the legislature adjourned.

While the legislators initially balked at Arnall's threat, many soon realized that if he ended the poll tax by fiat, he would get all the credit among newly enfranchised voters in the 1946 elections. So, in early February, the Georgia legislature passed a poll tax repeal bill, which Governor Arnall promptly signed. The new Georgia constitution, ratified by voters in August 1945, eliminated the poll tax provision, but the document still included "a genuine literacy test for voters," which, Arnall claimed, "safeguards the ballot box in Georgia."[32]

Arnall also suggested that in abolishing the tax, "Georgia spoke today for democracy." Progressives, North and South, agreed with this narrative. Scores of progressive and liberal individuals, including southern newspaperman Harry M. Ayres, historian Charles Beard, American Civil Liberties Union director Roger Baldwin, and Mary McLeod Bethune, head of the National Council of Negro Women, signed on to "A Tribute to Governor Arnall of Georgia." The statement claimed the politician's career "symbolizes the arrival of the people to power and gives earnest of an unshackled and progressive South." The repeal of the poll tax in Georgia, however, represented little effective change for Black voters. Many white Southerners knew that the white primary and literacy tests, rather than the poll tax, represented the most important mechanisms for blocking Black votes. Poll tax reform in Georgia primarily benefited the many poor whites disqualified by the levy. Indeed, suppressing the white vote had made it difficult for southern politicians like Arnall to challenge political machines, such as the Talmadge organization in Georgia. One legislator from Dougherty County in southwest Georgia estimated that repeal would add 25 percent more white voters to the rolls.[33]

The federal challenge to the white primary represented more of a racial minefield to navigate. Arnall initially tried to downplay the importance of the *Smith v. Allwright* decision, but within a week of the ruling, white Democrats urged the governor to call a special session of the legislature to repeal Georgia's primary laws to "beat" the decision. Arnall demurred, saying the new Georgia constitution would resolve the problem. At the same time, the US Supreme Court decision energized Black Georgians. By the end of April, NAACP leader A. T. Walden and the editor of the *Atlanta Daily World*, C. A. Scott, had opened a Black "voting school" in the city, which taught Black citizens how to register to vote. They also organized the Fulton County Citizens Democratic Club. Thousands of Black citizens went to the county courthouse to enroll. White county officials did not block these efforts but made sure to separate potential Black voters from white ones by putting up a sign at the courthouse, "Register Here Colored Only." Scores of Black Georgians also registered to vote in the state's other urban areas. All hoped to cast a ballot in the Democratic primary scheduled for July 4, 1944. In Georgia and beyond, white moderate/liberal organizations, including the Southern Regional Council, the Southern Baptist Convention, and the SCHW, as well as several white newspapers—including the *Atlanta Constitution*—recommended that white Southerners abide by the court decision.[34]

The Georgia Democratic Party, however, decided otherwise. On June 7, a subcommittee of the party's executive committee claimed that the court's decision did not apply to Georgia and recommended that the party continue to follow the existing primary rules that limited voting to "white electors who are Democrats." Black leaders across the state protested the subcommittee's action. Those in Atlanta urged a reconsideration. But the full committee confirmed the subcommittee's decision. Dorothy Rainey, a member of the committee, and the wife of Glenn W. Rainey, a Georgia Tech professor and prominent white liberal, offered the lone dissent. Mrs. Rainey claimed she wanted "to live up to the finest tradition of the South and of my country and to the universal teachings of Jesus." She also suggested that "it is now clear that if America remains a democracy, operating under laws of fair play and equal opportunity, the Negro who is qualified to vote is going to be given the vote." Other white liberals also lamented the decision. Alma Metcalfe, a faculty member at Atlanta's Agnes Scott Women's College, asked readers of the *Atlanta Journal*, "Is it not strangely ironic that the front page of Wednesday's *Journal* filled with news of the invasion of Europe by which we hope democracy will be preserved, should carry one discordant item indicating how little we value democracy at home: 'State Group Bans Negroes in Primary?'"[35]

White political leaders, including Governor Arnall, did not embrace this patriotic logic concerning Black voting. Lon Duckworth, the chairman of the Georgia Democratic Executive Committee, told Black insurance man Eugene Martin off the record that he favored allowing "representative Negroes" to vote in the party primary, but he also noted that if he made such a claim publicly, he "would be dead in Georgia politics." He urged Black citizens to challenge the white primary law in court to force the state to change. Arnall likely shared this attitude, in part because he continued to face pressure from white conservatives to hold the line on Black disfranchisement. In mid-June, the Municipal League of South Fulton County, an organization based in a white conservative stronghold in Atlanta, told Arnall and state legislators to develop a plan "to protect the purity of the traditional white primary" or resign their positions. So Arnall supported the decision of the Democratic Party Executive Committee and affirmed his devotion to the white primary.[36]

Following the decision by the Georgia Democratic Party to bar African American voters from the July primary, Black leaders from eleven counties, many with organizational backing from the Atlanta NAACP chapter, met in Macon and organized a statewide Association of Citizens' Democratic Clubs. At this meeting, activists debated what strategy to pursue concerning the July 4 election. Some favored a token vote, which would lay the groundwork for a court challenge—as Democratic Party chairman Duckworth suggested—without creating major, disruptive episodes. C. A. Scott later explained to the NAACP's Thurgood Marshall that "we did not want to risk incidents in view of the pending national election." Interestingly, potential Black Democratic voters had more concerns about party unity during the presidential campaign than did many of the actual white Democratic voters across the South. Others at the Democratic Clubs meetings believed all Black Georgians who had managed to register to vote should go to the polls and try to cast a ballot in the Democratic primary. On election day, Black voters in several cities and towns, including Atlanta, Savannah, Macon, Columbus, Albany, Moultrie, and Sylvania, attempted to vote, but white citizens turned them away from the ballot box. Election officials typically claimed that they did not have any Black voting registration lists. Although thousands of Black men and women had registered to vote in 1944, election officials never forwarded those names to the polling stations.[37]

After the election, Black activists in Georgia faced another choice of strategies to force the state to follow the *Smith v. Allwright* ruling. Black leaders in Atlanta, working through the NAACP, collected evidence of voter disfranchisement and sought support from the US Department of Justice to file a criminal lawsuit against Fulton County election officials. The Justice Department launched an investigation but decided not to act. Black activists in Columbus, however, decided to proceed on their own. In August 1944, Primus King, a Black minister and barber in Columbus, along with two other Black citizens, with backing from the local NAACP chapter, sued members of the Muscogee County Democratic Executive Committee in federal court. At least one member of the Democratic committee, Theodore J. McGee, wanted to accede to the Black demands. He urged Governor Arnall to capitulate voluntarily, reasoning that it would do "so much more to create understanding and good will" than a court fight. The governor rejected that strategy. He instructed his attorney general to aid the local Democratic Party in its defense, noting that "the matter at issue in the Muscogee county suit is of great import and importance to the people of Georgia." It was certainly a crucial matter to white Georgians. Lon Duckworth, the Democratic Party chairman, told US Justice Department investigators that the state could not easily change its primary rules since they had "been in existence for time immemorial" (for forty-four years, as the white primary was adopted only in 1900). The *Macon Telegraph*, in June 1945, claimed the Black efforts to challenge the white primary were "not sincerely intended to elevate the Negro, but rather to create agitation and unrest as part of the general scheme to discredit the American system of government and open the way for Communist rule."[38]

As the Primus case made its way through the legal system, Georgia leaders tried other forms of resistance. The new state constitution approved by the Georgia legislature in early 1945 eliminated all references to party primaries. Speaker of the House Roy Harris admitted the action gave the state "the utmost elasticity" in evading court efforts to abolish the disfranchising mechanism of a white primary. Georgia voters ratified the new constitution in August 1945, but later that year, federal judge T. Hoyt Davis in Macon ruled that Black citizens could vote in Democratic primaries. Although the state constitution no longer referred to party primaries, Judge Davis ruled that "whenever a political party holds a primary in the State, it is by law an integral part of the election machinery," and therefore, open to all registered voters. Some of the white Georgia press and some white Georgians applauded the decision. The *Columbus Sunday Ledger Enquirer*, the *Macon News*, and the *Atlanta Journal* all endorsed the verdict. Ora Eads, a clerk at a Goodyear store in Atlanta, wrote in a letter to the editor of the *Atlanta Constitution* that she believed the court decision "will do much to establish justice and promote the general welfare," since "the right to vote is fundamental." Much of the white political establishment, however, would not concede defeat, and Arnall, for his part, successfully urged the Muscogee County Democratic Executive Committee to appeal the ruling.[39]

Despite his sustained opposition to ending Georgia's white primary, the governor continued to attract attention in 1945 as someone who promised a more progressive path for the postwar South than typical southern states' rights defenders had long offered. His economic ideas, along with his opposition to the poll tax and his apparent acceptance of the principle, if not the reality, of Black voting, seemed enough to draw plaudits from national observers. The *New Republic* in February 1945 viewed Arnall as "a sign of political things to come. Arnall is lining up with the people who want what he wants for the South, industrialization, and the expanding prosperity for all the people that this can mean when properly directed." Nationally syndicated newspaper columnist Drew Pearson dubbed Arnall "the South's greatest leader since the Civil War." In the spring and summer of 1945, he embarked on a national speaking tour to spread the word about his new brand of southern progressive leadership, an undertaking that by August 1945 had earned him $20,000 in lecture fees (more than $300,000 in 2022 dollars). FDR did not name Arnall as attorney general during his abbreviated fourth term (he died in April 1945), but the new president, Harry S. Truman, did consider the Georgia governor for the same post, although he ultimately gave the job to Tom Clark of Texas.[40]

In June 1945, Arnall had to clarify his racial views in a somewhat reactionary way while in Louisville, but this act did not diminish his standing as a model representative of white southern liberalism. Prior to a speech to Kentucky Democrats on Jefferson Day, Arnall talked with reporters at a press conference at the Louisville City Hall. A Black journalist, Hortense Young, asked the governor about the opportunities for Black men and women in Georgia. The governor claimed Black people in his state had "equal opportunity for education, income, and the right to vote just as any other citizen." When pressed about racial segregation, Arnall shot back: "What the hell difference does it make if you sit down and eat with Negroes, visit with them in their homes, talk with them?" One of the local white papers, the *Louisville Times*, mischaracterized this comment as evidence that Arnall had no problem with racial segregation, although he meant to suggest that racial segregation was a non-issue. As Arnall had already stated many times, economic improvement would solve any racial problems and would produce the "equal opportunity" goals he laid out for Georgia's Black population. In a statement issued the next day, Arnall made sure to clarify his racial stance. He claimed that "we of the South do not believe in social equality with the Negro" and that "we in the South by heritage and by tradition believe that segregation is conducive to the welfare of both the white and colored races." He also expressed opposition to the FEPC as "unworkable and an irritant to harmonious race relations."[41] In short, if economic improvement represented the answer to the "race problem," Arnall basically asked Black Georgians to trust white Georgians to treat them fairly, even though nothing in the state's history of race relations suggested that such trust was justified.

Despite this bump in the road, Arnall's national star continued to rise. In late July, *Collier's* magazine published his article "Revolution Down South," which presented Arnall's economic agenda for solving the South's problems and reiterated his stance that "the so-called race question is an economic one, not social." He failed to mention that he wanted to preserve racial segregation, other than a vague dismissal of "social equality," which he equated with "racial intermarriage." Instead, Arnall emphasized that "the ten million Negro citizens of the South . . . are a part of the South, and their economic welfare is a part of the section's economic welfare." The piece was so convincing as a roadmap to solving southern ills and evasive enough on racial matters that it received approval from the northern Black press, which seemingly forgot about the Louisville dustup involving Arnall a month earlier. The following week, *Life* magazine published a glowing profile of Arnall (condensed in *Reader's Digest* in October), which claimed that the Georgia politician "has lifted his state from the benightedness of Tobacco Road to the position of runner-up to North Carolina for the title of 'most progressive state.'" Arnall continued to be courted for prominent positions beyond the governor's mansion, both locally and in the Truman administration. Arnall turned down an offer from the University of Georgia to serve as its chancellor, as well as a request from President Truman to become US solicitor general.[42]

As World War II ended, Ellis Arnall had one year left on his four-year term. In just three years, he had engineered significant changes in Georgia. His actions, however, did little to alter the second-class status of the state's Black population. If national observers overlooked this shortcoming in their chorus of praise for the Georgia governor, that perspective spoke to their own limitations in understanding how much the war had altered Black expectations for substantial alterations in existing race relations. Indeed, on matters of race, Arnall's liberalism differed little from that of most of his liberal counterparts in the South and beyond. But as the events of 1946 would demonstrate, his liberal approach to southern leadership led to opposition on multiple fronts.

9
Theodore Bilbo: Southern Reactionary

On March 22, 1944, as the Eighth Army Air Force continued its bombing campaign in Germany, Theodore G. Bilbo, Mississippi's senior US senator, addressed a joint session of the Mississippi legislature. "The Man," as the senator was commonly known in Mississippi, had driven the 1,000 miles from the national capital to Jackson in his gray Cadillac to make an eighty-minute speech, which served as the opening salvo of his 1946 re-election campaign. During his talk, the sixty-six-year-old Bilbo, a short man with a bit of a potbelly who often wore red ties adorned with his trademark diamond horseshoe stickpin, both praised President Franklin Roosevelt and railed against a perceived federal attack on white supremacy during the war years.[1]

After recounting his own achievements as a former governor of Mississippi and summarizing the course of the war to that point, Bilbo indicated his strong support for the as-yet-undeclared FDR in the 1944 presidential election. While acknowledging the questionable actions of some of the president's "associates," Bilbo argued that putting Republicans in charge would only make matters worse, and the country needed Roosevelt to win the war. Bilbo conceded that the growth of the federal war bureaucracy posed a danger to "our dual system of government"—one that maintained states' rights—but he believed that Americans would preserve that system.[2]

Bilbo spent the bulk of his talk outlining the threats created during the war to the southern way of life, or what the *New York Times* described as "waving the flag of 'white supremacy.'" He criticized proposed federal anti-poll tax legislation as unconstitutional and referenced his recent appointment as chair of the Senate's District of Columbia Committee to bemoan the possibility of Black suffrage there. Taking aim at FDR's Executive Order 8802, which created the Fair Employment Practices Committee (FEPC), Bilbo correctly noted that while the directive "has not been successfully enforced in the war industries in the South," it had integrated federal offices in the nation's capital, where "whites and Negroes work in the same rooms, the same offices, eat together at the same cafeterias, use the same rest rooms and recreational facilities." The Congress of Industrial Organizations (CIO) had even opened an integrated military service club in the city, a development that foreshadowed for Bilbo the specter of miscegenation, the inevitable result of racial segregation's abolition. To address these efforts to weaken white supremacy, Bilbo proposed the "voluntary resettlement of America's 12,800,000 Negroes in their fatherland, West Africa." He claimed that 3 million Black Americans had already signed on to his plan, first introduced in Congress in 1939. As chairman of the District of Columbia Committee, Bilbo had already proposed a resettlement plan for Black residents there. He wanted to move the "slum dwellers" of the city to the farms of Kentucky, Virginia, and Maryland, which needed farm laborers. He said at the time that the relocation of Black citizens of the District to nearby rural districts would get them prepared to return to Africa.[3]

Bilbo closed his oration with a plea to hold the line on racial segregation: the "people of the South must draw the color line tighter and tighter, and any white man or woman who dares to cross that color line should be promptly and forever ostracized. No compromise on this great question should be tolerated." The senator then demonstrated the necessary mindset by throwing the first stone, lobbed at Louise Perry, a speech teacher at Delta State Teachers College in Cleveland, Mississippi. Originally from Missouri, though educated in Louisiana and North Carolina, Perry had taught at Delta State for only six months. According to Bilbo, based on a complaint he had received from three Delta State students, Perry had advocated Black equality in her classroom. The teacher denied the allegations, and a committee of the Mississippi Board of Trustees of State Institutions of Higher Learning launched an investigation the next day. Within a week, the committee cleared the educator, finding "the evidence inconclusive and the charges not sustained."[4]

Bilbo viewed the vigilance he asked of his fellow white Southerners as necessary in a world where white privilege seemed increasingly under siege. Unlike Ellis Arnall in Georgia, who saw the war as an opportunity for the South to advance economically and socially, Bilbo saw the war years as presenting existential dangers to southern mores. During World War II, Bilbo and other white Southerners focused on "defending White democracy." The nondiscrimination stance of the federal government, expressed in FDR's Executive Order 8802 and the Selective Service and Training Act of 1940, as well as in renewed national efforts to pass anti-lynching and anti–poll tax legislation, posed challenges to the South's system of race relations. These federal initiatives, as well as the general sense that the United States entered World War II to preserve and promote democracy for all, helped create an atmosphere where Black activism—even in places as hostile to Black freedom as Mississippi—could begin to flourish. While other southern politicians during World War II sounded alarm bells about the increasing threats to racial norms, Bilbo became the most outspoken doomsayer. Indeed, by the end of World War II, his defense of white democracy had become so extreme and seemingly "un-American" that it inspired a national anti-Bilbo movement.[5]

In the 1930s, Black activists and their white allies had pressed for an end to the poll tax. During the late 1930s, Bilbo himself had supported repeal of the voting tax in his own state, primarily because the levy disfranchised many of his poor white supporters and because he believed other disfranchising measures, such as the so-called literacy test—actually a mechanism for local voter registrars to disqualify whomever they chose—did more to prevent Black citizens from voting in Mississippi elections. Indeed, a combination of disfranchising tactics had kept Black voters to a bare minimum in the Magnolia State since the state's 1890 constitutional convention. In 1940, the state had only 2,000 registered Black voters, a mere 0.4 percent of those eligible. The US House of Representatives overwhelmingly passed a poll tax repeal measure in October 1942. During debate on the measure, House supporters appealed to patriotism and democracy, while opponents bemoaned the attacks on white supremacy. The chamber's only Black member, Arthur W. Mitchell of Illinois, claimed that if a Black man were "good enough to wear the uniform of his country, if he is good enough to shed his blood for this country, then he is entitled to vote in peacetime as well as in wartime." By contrast, Pete Jarman, a congressman from Alabama, called the legislation an attack "on white supremacy in which we have every reason to take much pride. We of the South are proud indeed of the purity of the blood that flows through our veins."[6]

The poll tax abolition bill, however, went nowhere in the US Senate, thwarted by what Ira Katznelson has called a "southern cage" that enveloped national politics on matters of race. Southern senators, led by Bilbo, mounted a filibuster to prevent consideration of the legislation. Bilbo told the press that he could talk for thirty days if necessary. Although he privately termed the legislation "the communistic negro-loving poll tax repeal bill," Bilbo's public opposition in the Senate focused more on reasons that had less to do with race. Bilbo and other southern senators called federal action against the poll tax a threat to states' rights principles and America's "dual system of government." Bilbo's defense of states' rights, however, seemed to conflate the South's position in the US Civil War with the conflict underway against the Axis powers. He told supporters, "I am as much a soldier in the preservation of the American way and American scheme of Government as the boys who are fighting and dying on Guadalcanal. Our soldiers are fighting the enemies who would destroy our scheme of Government on the outside, while I am fighting the enemies who would destroy our scheme of Government from the inside." After seven days of filibuster in November 1942, senators agreed to hold a cloture vote to end debate. That measure failed by a vote of forty-one to thirty-seven, but since the 77th Congress soon ended, poll tax reform died in 1942.[7]

During World War II, the American people disagreed about the need for poll taxes. Opinion polls showed that two-thirds of all Americans and one-third of white Southerners in poll-tax states supported the elimination of the voting levy. However, those white Southerners (and some other white people around the country) who supported the effort of Bilbo and his Senate colleagues to oppose efforts to repeal the poll tax in 1942 held passionate opinions about resisting the federal reform. W. M. Burt, who worked at the War Department's ordnance training center near Jackson, Mississippi, and whose only son served in the US Army Air Forces, supported Bilbo's fight. Burt believed "that if we win this War against the Germans, Italians, and Japs, and yet have this Poll Tax bill rammed down our throats, we of the South will have won only HALF a victory, and the remaining half will have to be won all over again." Charles Fox, a medical doctor in Southampton, Pennsylvania, agreed with Bilbo's states' rights arguments concerning the poll tax. The doctor thought that when the federal government told states what they could do "in all the details of government—then we have lost our democracy." Liberal organizations, such as the National Committee to Abolish the Poll Tax, labor unions, and national civil rights groups, mobilized in 1942 to eliminate the poll tax. Many white citizens, even in the South, especially disagreed with the Senate tactic of the filibuster to oppose the anti–poll tax bill. Sam Franklin Jr., a white minister in the Mississippi Delta, disliked the Senate action because it reduced "the solemn legislative procedure of our democracy to the level of a farce," which only bolstered "fascist and nazi criticisms of government by the people."[8]

Although congressional opponents reintroduced anti–poll tax legislation several times over the next few years, the measure met the same fate as in 1942. In June 1945, the *Jackson Daily News* called the repeated efforts to repeal the poll tax an "annual mockery," with no chance of passage. Indeed, the House approved anti–poll tax legislation three times between 1943 and 1945. Many House Republicans joined with House Democrats in supporting the measure, in part because they knew that Senate Democrats would kill the bill, but only after a prolonged fight that highlighted the growing split between northern and southern Democrats. When the 1943 bill came up for debate on the Senate floor in May 1944, opponents offered 1,000 amendments, part of a prearranged deal in which everyone knew their roles: southern Democrats could filibuster and rail against the bill for a week; proponents of the legislation would then offer a cloture amendment they knew would fail; and finally, all parties would agree to move on to other legislative business.[9]

Bilbo played a key role in the Senate speechifying against the poll tax. He regularly professed his willingness to mount a record filibuster, if necessary, though everyone in the Senate knew such heroics remained unnecessary given the choreographed proceedings. The Mississippi senator offered not only arguments against the legislation but also readings from the Sears Roebuck catalog and an amateur stand-up comedy routine. In April 1944, the Senate had delayed its scheduled filibuster against the anti–poll tax bill to allow Bilbo "a chance to get adjusted to his new store teeth." The Mississippi senator's filibuster antics became something of a national joke. In January 1945, *The New Yorker* noted that "the annual battle over the poll tax will probably begin some time in the spring. Already lines are forming, strategy is being mapped, and Bilbo is clearing his throat." Yet the Mississippi senator also continued to receive serious criticism about wasting the time of the US Congress during a national emergency with his long-winded opposition to repealing a tax on voting that he personally opposed. Bilbo, however, turned these critiques back on his detractors, faulting them for "pushing this piece of Negro-sponsored, unconstitutional legislation" and distracting Congress from more essential matters.[10]

Beginning in 1944, Bilbo and most other white politicians in the Deep South also mounted sustained opposition to the FEPC, especially after liberal members of Congress and civil rights activists proposed that the Committee become a permanent government agency. During consideration of 1944 and 1945 appropriations for the FEPC and its long-term future, southern Congressmen, in alliance with political leaders from other parts of the country, attacked the fair employment committee. During debate on the FEPC appropriation in late June 1945, Bilbo launched a surprise two-day filibuster, a move that temporarily delayed consideration of the massive War

Appropriations Bill, which bankrolled sixteen wartime agencies still vital to the ongoing military conflict against Japan. The Mississippi senator attacked those who supported the creation of a permanent FEPC as "cheap Red Communists." Bilbo also launched a personal attack on Eleanor Roosevelt, the widow of FDR, who had died in office in April 1945. Bilbo claimed that the Roosevelt children might have turned out better if she had given them the same attention she did to "trying to force recognition and social equality for the Negro in America."[11]

Although the FEPC had proved generally ineffective at ending racial discrimination in the southern workplace, despite the wartime labor emergency—a fact Bilbo acknowledged in his 1944 speech to the Mississippi legislature—the prospect of a permanent FEPC encouraged a tightening of the "southern cage" in the Senate like no other issue. Even southern liberals, such as Governor Ellis Arnall of Georgia, opposed a permanent FEPC. Ignoring the possible economic benefits for a South freed of a system of discriminatory employment, Arnall complained that a permanent FEPC would be "a racial irritant and do more damage than good." Bilbo and other southern leaders, many of whom also had reputations as economic liberals, opposed the FEPC because they believed it represented a threat to racial segregation. Yet weeks earlier, the agency had made its position clear on this matter in hearings before the Senate Committee on Appropriations. Malcolm Ross, chairman of the FEPC, testified that the committee "has never taken the position that segregation per se is contrary to the provisions" of FDR's fair employment executive order. Indeed, the committee had carefully avoided any direct challenge to racial segregation in the South—or anywhere else—when enforcing Executive Order 8802.[12]

Despite the strong wall of opposition to the FEPC from southern leaders, as with the poll tax issue, white popular opinion remained divided. To be sure, plenty of white Southerners (and white people beyond the South) supported Bilbo and other southern legislators in their fight against the fair employment agency. In June 1945, a woman from the Mississippi Delta told Bilbo that the FEPC represented "nothing but a vicious scheme aimed at the South's color line, but camuflaged [sic] with a pretense of applying to all colors and classes." She thanked the senator for saving "the white people of America from becoming a jaundiced skin, frizzled headed batch of mongrels and our civilization from sinking into stagnation and race decay."[13]

Not all Southerners, however, demonized the FEPC and called for its elimination. The Southern Conference for Human Welfare, a southern liberal organization, launched an "emergency appeal" in June 1945 to save the FEPC appropriation, and within forty-eight hours the organization assembled a petition with 1,640 signatories. At the same time, the group's Georgia affiliate, the Committee for Georgia, collected 672 signatures in a separate petition. Both documents contained the names of Black leaders but also the signatures of a variety of white supporters of the FEPC, especially ministers and educators but also some businessmen.[14]

The Georgia petition, which called racial and religious bias inherently "fascistic," particularly incensed Bilbo. He publicly complained that "the great majority" of the Georgia signers represented "negroes, Jews and Quislings of the white race, [who] hail from the City of Atlanta, the hot bed of Southern negro intelligentsia, communists, pinks, reds and other off-brands of American citizenship in the South." Although most who signed the Georgia petition did come from Atlanta, they were not radicals. Rather, as one of the petition's organizers, Armand May—a white, Jewish businessman in Atlanta—explained, "We are not advocating anything revolutionary, only evolutionary, and doing it in the normal American way by an appeal to reason instead of prejudice." Bilbo told one of the other organizers of the Georgia petition drive, William Holmes Borders, a Black preacher in Macon, that he had no problem with "the principles of equality, justice, fair dealings and guarantee of the rights of the individual citizen regardless of race, creed, color, religion or national origin." Bilbo believed that federal legislation could not achieve such goals; rather, they "must be brought about by the processes of education, training and culture."[15] Bilbo's proposed remedy, however, had done little to achieve the lofty goals he cynically claimed to support.

Even if abolition of the poll tax or the operation of the FEPC did not pose an immediate cure for Black disfranchisement or racial segregation in the South, these federal actions, with their promises of nondiscrimination, threatened to undermine the ability of white Southerners to preserve a system of white privilege. Southern leaders had to look no further than the FEPC itself to understand how the nondiscrimination ideal might destroy the South's racially discriminatory arrangements. As the congressional debate over the FEPC raged in the spring of 1944, Deep South politicians became obsessed with the racial makeup of the FEPC staff. Mississippi congressman Thomas Abernethy told a member of the committee that it was "discriminating against the white race" because it had "an inequitable pro rata distriubtion [sic] of employment of the races" within its own offices. Bilbo raised the same issue on the Senate floor, asking how Malcolm Ross could promote the elimination of discrimination when he "so brazenly discriminates against the white race by making the personnel of a committee of about 115, two thirds Negroes and only one third white," in a country where Black residents made up only about 10 percent of the population. Connecticut senator John Danaher suggested that Chairman Ross might have just selected those he thought most qualified for the jobs. Bilbo expressed shock at this explanation, telling Danaher that if he, "as a white man, is willing to admit that no members of his race are qualified to fill these positions, then I have nothing further to say."[16] Oddly, in an effort to maintain white prerogatives, Abernethy and Bilbo professed support for a system of racial quotas, which if actually applied in Mississippi, would have dramatically improved the economic opportunities available for the state's Black citizens.

Federal actions that challenged established race relations also emboldened Black activists in Mississippi. Although Bilbo always claimed he did not see the poll tax as essential to disfranchising voters in Mississippi—since other tactics could handle that task—he knew that at least some Black citizens in his home state had become more vocal in clamoring for voting rights during the war. In the summer of 1942, during the US congressional elections, a few Black voters, especially in places like Jackson and Meridian, attempted to cast ballots in the Democratic, or "white" primary, but local election officials turned most of them away. Following the election, Carsie Hall, president of the Jackson branch of the National Association for the Advancement of Colored People (NAACP), asked the national organization for assistance in filing a voting rights suit against Mississippi. While white leaders in the state generally played down Black voting attempts, the head of the state Democratic Executive Committee, Herbert Holmes, was worried enough that he issued a statement post-election complaining about federal intrusion in the state's voting affairs: "We don't need the Federal government to tell us who shall vote in our primary elections."[17]

Concerns regarding Black voting in Mississippi continued throughout the war years. During the campaign for governor in the summer of 1943, all four candidates decried the federal government's meddling in the state's racial affairs. One of the losing contenders, Lester Franklin, told white Mississippians during the campaign that "regardless of what Congress does with the poll tax issue now before Congress, Mississippi Negroes are not going to belly up to the polls and take charge of the elections in this state, while I am your Governor." After the US Supreme Court's *Smith v. Allwright* decision in April 1944 outlawed the white primary, Democratic chairman

Holmes told his fellow white Mississippians that "the Supreme Court or no one else can control a Democratic primary in Mississippi." As elsewhere, however, the ruling energized Black activists in the Magnolia state. Black Mississippians attempted but generally failed to vote in municipal and federal elections in several locations around the state during the 1944 primaries. But in November 1944, the newly formed Mississippi Progressive Voters League, led by T. B. Wilson of Jackson, held a statewide meeting of Black voters, which in part discussed filing a lawsuit against the state's Democratic Party. During the war years, in addition to the emerging voting rights struggle, new or strengthened chapters of the NAACP formed across the state, not just in Jackson, but in Natchez, Pascagoula, McComb, and Meridian.[18] Given the increase in Black activism in Mississippi and elsewhere in the South during World War II, any attack on local white control of the election process posed a threat to white supremacy.

As in Georgia, Black educators in Mississippi pursued an equalization campaign. In the fall of 1941, months after the creation of the FEPC, the Mississippi Association of Teachers in Colored Schools, the Black teacher organization in the state, created a legislative committee to "use whatever method is available to law-abiding citizens in a democracy to secure better educational opportunities for our children and better salaries for our teachers." Although the state superintendent of education warned Mississippi educators not to file a lawsuit against the state, they secretly raised funds for a teacher salary equalization suit, and along with other Black leaders, they continued to press for equalization more broadly in the state's education system. A statewide mass meeting of Black citizens held in February 1944 sent a petition to the governor and state legislature, which pointed out that the state spent more than 90 percent of its education budget on white schooling in a state in which Black people made up almost half of the population. The group complained that this arrangement prevailed even though "a Negro soldier is called every time a white soldier is called to shoulder his gun, face the enemy, and offer to make the supreme test, yet this colored soldier in the fox holes of New Guinea and before the withering fire of the German Howitzers and shell fire must reflect upon the fact that at home . . . he is only about a tenth rate citizen." Mississippi's grossly unequal funding for Black education, as detailed in the petition, convinced even the state's arch-conservative Speaker of the House, Walter Sillers, that Mississippi leaders had a "responsibility to the inferior race" to improve Black schooling. The governor, Thomas Bailey, a relative racial moderate and former educator, responded to the Black complaints by appointing a special committee in 1944 to study the state's education system, and then supported its recommendations for a broad program of educational equalization during the 1946 legislative session.[19]

As Bilbo fought against federal initiatives such as anti–poll tax legislation and the FEPC, he frequently intimated that such measures would only lead to an increase in racial violence, especially once the war ended. In July 1943, following the racial incidents at Camp Van Dorn and Camp McCain, Bilbo told a group of white citizens in northeast Mississippi that there would be "more trouble with the negro when this war is over. The situation grows worse every day and we might as well fortify ourselves if we are going to maintain white supremacy in the South." The following spring, in his speech to the Mississippi legislature, Bilbo predicted that at the end of the war, Black soldiers would return home "filled and poisoned with political and social equality stuff." As a result, he expected a situation in which "hell breaks out all over this country." Many of Bilbo's constituents shared his fears. A white woman in McComb complained in the spring of 1944 that "the negroes are getting to be a menace to our towns. . . . If something is not done to correct the negro situation, some of our good white men and also some good negroes are going to get killed." Bilbo told the woman that "all we can do right now is to keep up the fight for race integrity and white supremacy, 'load our guns' and stand our ground."[20]

Racial violence had long plagued the South, and any perception that the war promoted Black success particularly excited white individuals determined to keep their Black neighbors subjugated. On March 26, 1944—just days after Bilbo's speech to the Mississippi legislature—a six-man, white mob killed Isaac Simmons, a prosperous sixty-six-year-old Black farmer and preacher in southwest Mississippi. Simmons owned a 220-acre farm, mortgage-free, that contained both valuable timber and potentially prized oil deposits. He had inherited the land from his father. The first sizable oil field had been discovered in the state in 1939, and by 1944, the state already ranked twelfth in the nation in oil production. A white neighbor, Noble Rider, had made it clear that he wanted the Simmons land, so Simmons went to Jackson and secured the services of a lawyer to confirm he had clear title to the property. A month later, Rider and five other men abducted Simmons and his oldest child, Eldridge, who lived with his father and helped operate the place. One of the white men then shot the elder Simmons. The mob beat up Eldridge but let him go, with an ultimatum: abandon the Simmons property and remove the two tenants on the place. Eldridge, fearing for his life, followed these orders; he found new locations for his tenants and moved himself and his family to New Orleans. He also reported the crime, although an Amite County grand jury failed to indict the murderers.[21]

While Bilbo talked about the potential need for violence to keep Black people in their place, he had another "solution" to avoid a coming race war: remove Black Americans from the country. Various colonization schemes for relocating African Americans in the United States to Africa or some other place had existed since the earliest days of the republic. Black nationalists in the nineteenth and early twentieth centuries, such as Henry McNeal Turner and Marcus Garvey, had embraced the idea that for Black people in the United States to achieve real freedom, they had to abandon the United States and settle in Africa. In April 1939, Bilbo introduced legislation in the US Senate, which he claimed would lead to "the orderly, friendly, and voluntarily [sic] resettlement of the Negroes of this country in Africa." He maintained that Black Americans worried about racial "amalgamation and the production of a mongrel race" as much as he did. This realization came through his work with the Peace Movement of Ethiopia (PME), based in Chicago and led by Mittie Maud Lena Gordon, a former Garvey supporter. Bilbo claimed that the PME had collected 2.5 million signatures on petitions supporting repatriation to Africa. The PME touted inflated numbers for its petition drive, and Bilbo further overestimated Black support for a repatriation program, claiming at one point that 75 percent (8 million) of African Americans wanted to move to Africa.[22] Ironically, Bilbo admitted that widespread and sustained racial discrimination against Black men and women represented the reason that Black citizens needed to leave the United States, a state of affairs he had long supported and bolstered.

Bilbo proposed to pay for his plan by receiving 400,000 square miles of land controlled by France and England adjoining Liberia in exchange for the cancellation of a portion of the two countries' World War I debt. In the senator's scheme, that territory would eventually become part of the country of Liberia, or what the senator described as Greater Liberia. The two European countries would also provide supplies to the Black migrants in an additional swap for further credits against their outstanding financial obligations to the United States. Bilbo's legislation never made it out of committee but continued to attract support from Black nationalists. In March 1941, J. R. Stewart, Marcus Garvey's successor as president general of the

Universal Negro Improvement Association, told a Chicago audience that although he disliked Bilbo personally, he approved of the Mississippian's proposed legislation. The *Militant*, a socialist newspaper, lamented at the time that "the Garvey movement, which once attracted the hopes of so many millions of Negroes, is now acting as the tail to the kite of America's outstanding exponent of 'Negro inferiority.'"[23]

During the war, Bilbo frequently claimed that he would reintroduce his Back-to-Africa legislation, but he never did. Both privately and publicly, however, the Mississippi senator continued to tout the plan as the "one solution to the race question in America." He also promoted this "solution" to future race problems during his frequent speeches against efforts to repeal the poll tax and abolish the FEPC. In June 1944, as part of the southern fight against continued funding of the FEPC, Bilbo ended a speech in the Senate with a tirade laced with racial epithets directed at Black Americans. He concluded that "so long as the Negro is a political factor, we shall continue to have bloodshed, riots, race troubles, and other disturbances and we shall have this kind of damn-fool legislation." Bilbo's Back-to-Africa bill went nowhere, but his idea appealed to a segment of white Americans throughout the country. A recently retired major from the US Army told Bilbo in the spring of 1944 that his Greater Liberia proposal offered innumerable advantages for "the Caucasian race." The removal of Black people would create a white utopia, according to the former soldier: "Tolerance, cooperation and the spirit of neighborly love among all our people would increase and true and unhampered democracy would be the ultimate result."[24]

Whenever he spoke about his Back-to-Africa plan during the war, Bilbo continued to assert that millions of Black Americans supported the proposed massive postwar migration. While the cause had its Black enthusiasts, America's involvement in World War II strengthened Black opposition to Bilbo's Back-to-Africa plan. Even before the United States entered the conflict, in the summer of 1941, the Mississippi senator had to cancel a scheduled speech at a mass meeting in Harlem celebrating Marcus Garvey's birthday because of Black antagonism. Billed as the "Principal Speaker" and the "Author of the Famous Greater Liberian Act" for the event, Bilbo traveled to New York City to appear on the program. He decided not to attend, however, after a "citizens committee" that represented forty-five religious, fraternal, and labor groups in Harlem, along with the National Negro Congress (NNC) and the NAACP, organized picket lines outside the venue for the occasion. Prior to the event, the citizens committee sent a telegram to Bilbo warning him that "when tempers are short because of anxiety over national and world affairs any person with your anti-Negro record and reputation" should not come to Harlem, "lest there be unpleasant consequences." At the last minute, the senator canceled his appearance, citing "important business in Washington" that required his attention.[25]

After the publicity following Bilbo's 1944 speech to the Mississippi legislature, James Hatchett, a Black sergeant stationed in England, lashed out at the senator's Back-to-Africa stratagem, perhaps speaking for thousands of Black men and women in uniform around the world. The sergeant reminded Bilbo that "we are Negro Americans fighting for the cause to let each man, regardless of Race or Color, have his freedom. . . . America is our home." He suggested that if Bilbo had problems with the United States, perhaps he should return "to his own Fatherland, which, I don't believe is the United States of America." Hatchett ended his missive with a series of pointed questions about Bilbo's favored solution to what he perceived as America's number-one home front problem, including "Is Senator Bilbo supporting Hitler or President Roosevelt?" and "Are we fighting for race superiority or democracy?"[26]

In answer to the first question, Bilbo could point to his long-standing support of the US president. Indeed, despite his vigorous opposition to federal initiatives deemed dangerous to the white South, the Mississippi senator continued to back FDR, including the president's unprecedented bid for a fourth term. By the spring of 1944, much of the Mississippi political establishment (all of whom were Democrats in the largely one-party state), as well as Democrats in most other southern states, wanted to dump FDR, unless white Southerners received assurances that the federal assaults on white supremacy would cease. In Mississippi, Democratic county chairmen urged the faithful to "get in this fight for FREE, WHITE DEMOCRACY in Mississippi with everything you've got and give the new-dealers an honest-to-goodness licking in your precinct conventions." Anti-FDR Democrats did prevail, and they controlled the state convention when it met in early June 1944. The state party authorized the delegates chosen for the national Democratic Party convention to vote for any candidate they deemed appropriate if the national Democrats did not offer certain protections for the white South.[27]

Bilbo, who skipped the state party meeting, disagreed with any effort to undermine Roosevelt's renomination. Bilbo knew that the vast majority of white Southerners supported the president. So Bilbo believed that the strategy pursued by the Mississippi Democratic Party would "repudiate the will of the majority of the people of Mississippi." In addition, he recognized the futility of opposing Roosevelt's 1944 presidential bid. By the time the Mississippi Democrats met, delegate counters had already calculated that FDR had the votes needed to receive the Democratic nomination. Bilbo thought that opposing the president's likely re-election would only hurt the state. He did not think the Republicans offered a viable alternative to the national Democrats, whatever their potential shortcomings as defenders of white supremacy. He announced that he would quit the national Democratic Party if it endorsed the repeal of the poll tax or embraced "racial social equality," but he deemed the common complaints about a growing federal bureaucracy "Republican propaganda." In the end, Bilbo preferred FDR over "having some damn Republican from New York [Thomas Dewey] in the White House." Indeed, the Republican Party had adopted a more specific and stronger civil rights platform plank than the vague statement endorsing racial equality embraced by the national Democrats at their convention in the summer of 1944.[28]

Regarding Sergeant Hatchett's second question, Bilbo would have answered that his plan for a complete separation of the races would preserve both democracy and racial purity. He sincerely believed that if Americans understood the facts, then they would all join his cause and support his plan to remove Black people from the United States and set them up in a new location in Africa. As he often made clear, only those ignorant of his ideas could possibly oppose them. To that end, beginning in 1943, Bilbo made plans to write a book laying out the case for African American repatriation to Africa. He started collecting and reading books on race, including those written by Black authors. In the fall of 1945, he explained his motivation in pursing the book project to Earnest Cox, another outspoken white supremacist. Bilbo told Cox that if white people correctly understood what he called "the ever-perplexing race problem," then they would want to take action to solve it.[29]

Bilbo eventually tasked a young aide with the actual drafting of his book. Evelyn Gandy of Hattiesburg, who had worked on Bilbo's 1940 senatorial campaign as a nineteen-year-old, graduated from Ole Miss Law School in 1943 and then resumed working for the senator as a legislative assistant based in Mississippi. By the beginning of 1945, Gandy was working full-time on the book manuscript. Bilbo corresponded regularly with Gandy and sent her suggestions about what to include in "our book." For example, in June 1945, the senator asked Gandy to edit some of the chapters she had already written. The senator hoped to complete the project by the end of 1945, so he could use it as a campaign document for his 1946 re-election contest. Despite Gandy's efficient work, Bilbo could not find a publisher and eventually had to self-publish his magnum opus, *Take Your Choice: Separation or Mongrelization*.[30]

Because of the delay in publication, the book did not appear until 1947, shortly before the Mississippi senator's death. The volume laid out in alarming language what he deemed the danger that faced white America in the postwar world. Bilbo preferred a civilization "blotted out with the atomic bomb than to see it slowly but surely destroyed in the maelstrom of miscegenation, interbreeding, intermarriage, and mongrelization." After an extended discussion of the peril posed by race mixing, the book explained that separation was the only "proper solution to the race problem" and closed with a description of his plan for Black resettlement in Africa. Gandy received no acknowledgment for ghost-writing the book, an omission that served her well in the future. She had political ambitions of her own, and although people knew about her association with Bilbo, no one ever acknowledged that she had authored his overtly racist book, which would have likely ended a political career that peaked after the civil rights movement transformed Mississippi's political landscape. In fact, Mississippians, including large numbers of Black voters, elected Gandy lieutenant governor in 1975 (she was the second woman to hold statewide office in Mississippi).[31]

Even before World War II, Bilbo had a reputation as a racist southern demagogue, but during the war he became even more shrill in his opposition to all efforts to weaken racial segregation and white supremacy in the South and the nation. But by 1944, after more than two years of fighting openly racist and totalitarian regimes, public expressions of racism in the United States seemed "un-American" and faced increasing criticism, especially outside the South. After Bilbo's speech to the Mississippi legislature in the spring of 1944, the national media tagged him as one of the most extreme white segregationists in the country. In Washington, DC, a coalition of church groups, women's organizations, and Black organizations and leaders, calling themselves the Sponsoring Committee to Oust Senator Bilbo, adopted a resolution asking the US Senate to remove Bilbo as chairman of the District of Columbia Committee. Katherine Shryver, executive secretary of the National Committee to Abolish the Poll Tax, called Bilbo's speech "vicious and un-American." A Black soldier stationed at Key Field Army Air Base in Meridian, Mississippi, heard the senator's speech on the radio and wrote to ask him to reconsider his position. The solider told Bilbo that "we men of color who are giving our all for democracy (not white supremacy) are trying to make this world a better place in which to live." A men's Bible class from St. James Presbyterian Church in Harlem complained to FDR that Bilbo—"one of the most reactionary, undemocratic, Negro-hating senators from the deep South"—had endorsed the president for a fourth term. The churchmen felt that Roosevelt should make a "speedy renunciation of this specious brand of political support."[32]

Bilbo's speech, however, also brought praise from white people who believed that his call to vigilance in maintaining the color line was an essential home front battle. W. H. Rucker from the Mississippi Delta appreciated Bilbo's address to the Mississippi legislature, although he did not like the senator's support for FDR. Rucker believed that the *Smith v. Allwright* decision, announced less than two weeks after Bilbo's speech, confirmed the racial dangers described in his remarks. Rucker claimed that his Revolutionary and Confederate ancestors had fought for their rights, "and I have a rifle I might use now for freedom." In Tulsa, Oklahoma, attorney Phil Davis praised the senator for his "fundamental understanding of the relation of the race question to the preservation of civilization and the adequate protection and nurture of the Christian faith." He agreed with Bilbo that "an aggressive, offensive movement in defense of the purity and supremacy of the white race must be inaugurated without any delay."[33]

A more sustained attack against Bilbo, from multiple fronts, exploded in the summer of 1945. In July, during Senate debate of the charter of the newly created United Nations, Bilbo complained about "the monotony of the discussion which has lasted so long today" and interrupted the proceedings to present a letter from a Brooklyn woman who objected to the senator's recent filibuster against the FEPC. Josephine Piccolo, an Italian immigrant who had lost a brother fighting in Germany, said that she found "it very hard to believe that you are an American citizen and much, much harder to believe that you are allowed to enter the doors of the United States Senate." Bilbo presented his response, which began "My Dear 'Dago.'"[34]

It soon came to light that Bilbo had denigrated other Americans in his recent correspondence. Dolly Mason, who led the Women's Auxiliary of the CIO in Detroit, received a "My Dear Nigger Friend" letter. Bilbo later claimed that the term he used to address Mason was not "an insult but more a word of endearment because we all like a real 'nigger' friend." Leonard Golditch of New York City, executive secretary of the National Committee to Combat Anti-Semitism, got a response letter from Bilbo addressed "Dear Kike." The letter to Golditch suggested that Jews "sponsoring and fraternizing with the negro race . . . will get a very strong invitation to pack up and resettle in Palestine," a repatriation plan for Jews to match the one he had already proposed for African Americans. At a time when Americans had just learned the magnitude of Hitler's genocide of European Jews, Bilbo used incredibly insensitive language to describe what would happen if Congress passed legislation for a permanent FEPC: "the great mass of the American people would revolt and figuratively liquidate every member of their groups [Jews and African Americans]."[35]

Bilbo's rhetoric aroused a firestorm of opposition, especially outside the South. Newspapers and radio broadcasts denounced the Mississippi politician as undemocratic and un-American. The popular Walter Winchell pummeled the senator in his weekly broadcast. The radio station WOV in New York broadcast an interview with Josephine Piccolo, titled "The Reply," in both Italian and English. In the weeks that followed the revelations about Bilbo's correspondence with his fellow Americans, national Black organizations mobilized to voice their concerns and called for his censure or impeachment. The NAACP asked its branches to organize a letter-writing campaign to Democratic Party leaders. The NNC, which had already started an "Oust Bilbo" campaign to have the senator removed as chair of the District of Columbia Committee, called on its members "to initiate or join campaigns in your state to put pressure on your two Senators to call for the impeachment of Bilbo." In early August, the Chicago chapter of the NNC handed out 20,000 anti-Bilbo leaflets at the Negro Baseball League All-Star game and later collected 10,000 signatures for a Bilbo impeachment petition.[36]

A host of other groups, mostly in the Northeast, joined the effort to draw attention to Bilbo's racism and discredit him as an acceptable member of the US Senate.[37] Northern politicians responded to this outpouring of opposition to Bilbo with their own denunciations of the Mississippi senator. Both candidates in the New York City mayoral race, William O'Dwyer and Jonah J. Goldstein, called for an "end to Bilbo and 'Bilboism.'" Likewise, both of New York's US senators, Democrats Robert F. Wagner and James M. Mead; New Jersey's Republican US senator H. Alexander Smith; and two members from New York's US House delegation, offered rare public condemnations of a Congressional colleague. Soon after, Senator Robert A. Taft, the Republican leader from Ohio, labeled Bilbo "a disgrace to the Senate." He also revealed to the press that he and other senators had discussed initiating expulsion proceedings against Bilbo, although they recognized the impossibility of getting a two-thirds vote in the chamber to remove him. Taft also believed that any attempt by the US Senate to officially censure or get rid of Bilbo would only bolster the Mississippi politician with his base back home. Indeed, Bilbo told the *New York Times* a few days after Taft's attack that he would seek re-election to the US Senate in 1946. He said he would continue his fight against the FEPC, efforts to repeal the poll tax, "and other anti legislation introduced by the Yankees."[38]

Bilbo's rantings against racial and ethnic minorities also disturbed many veterans, soldiers, and their families. The American military represented perhaps the most racially inclusive institution in the country at the time, and it had just won a decisive victory over totalitarian foes. Bilbo's attacks on racial minorities seemed a repudiation of all the sacrifices made by military personnel. Some people with military ties sent the senator unsigned letters with their own negative forms of address, including "Dear Runt" and "Dear Nazi scum." One veteran said he would like to share a foxhole with Bilbo for two minutes, "just to show you what a dear 'Dago' I would make." Thirty-four crew members of a merchant marine ship still on duty in October 1945 called Bilbo "white trash" and "a busy little bee in the interests of fascism." The sailors criticized the senator for "fomenting the same problems at home which were the cause of this second great war abroad."[39]

In September 1945, Bilbo received a gentler admonition about his recent racial slurs from a Gold Star mother from Texas. In June 1945, Paul Bell, the son of an oil company electrician in Houston, died fighting with the 96th Infantry Division at Okinawa. His mother sent Bilbo some things to read about her son, whom she said was "neither a 'Kike' nor a 'Dago.'" The items included a document produced for her son's memorial service, in which she and her husband questioned why soldiers were coming back to the United States "to unfair treatment because of race or creed, by those who in their narrow ignorance forget that the four freedoms are for ALL MEN?" In his response to the grieving mother, Bilbo tried to be sympathetic, but he could not resist trying to show her the error of her ways for ignoring his concerns about the purity of white blood. Bilbo asked Mrs. Bell "to stop and think before you permit your grief to carry you so far that you destroy the very thing that your Son died for—the American way of life," or more accurately, the white American way of life.[40]

Some military personnel did draw the same lessons from World War II as Senator Bilbo and did not believe the conflict had anything to do with promoting racial equality. In August 1945, amid the home front brouhaha over the senator's use of discriminatory language directed at American ethnic groups, white and Black soldiers clashed in occupied Italy. In Viareggio, the headquarters town of the largely Black 92nd Division, white officers in the unit and some Italian men objected when Black officers, some accompanied by white women, tried to patronize one of the division's officers' clubs (one that had traditionally catered only to white officers in the division). The white soldiers—reportedly led by officers from the Deep South—at one point improvised a song with the lyrics, "We want Bilbo." Other white officers in the club demanded that any glassware used by the Black officers "be washed in a special solution." After fighting broke out in the club, a white colonel, the ranking officer present, managed to restore order and prevent a full-scale riot. A second incident in the town occurred at an Italian nightspot, when Black enlisted men tried to enter the establishment, which had traditionally been reserved almost exclusively for white GIs. More fighting broke out there, which led to a few arrests and several minor injuries.[41]

Bilbo's response to the cascade of criticism included a combination of defiance and denial. The day before the Japanese surrender, in a seeming ploy to undercut arguments that he supported totalitarianism, Bilbo announced proposed legislation for a $1 million reward to capture Adolf Hitler alive. Many in the United States doubted that Hitler had committed suicide and believed the German leader remained alive. In September, Bilbo also issued a letter to every member in Congress justifying his rhetorical approach that had caused such a firestorm of reproach. He claimed people had "deliberately twisted, distorted and misrepresented" his "honest convictions." He said he had never used racial slurs to attack any specific group. Rather, he asserted that he "was only castigating certain individuals regardless of 'race, creed, color or national origin' because of their advocacy of what in my opinion are the most vicious and un-American legislative concepts." He later explained to a correspondent that the "legislative concepts" he opposed included those "attempting to destroy our dual system of Constitutional Government and to make of us a mongrel Nation."[42]

The initial flood of agitation against Bilbo in the summer of 1945 was intense, but it might have died down but for the actions of one military man—a disabled veteran from New York City named Edward Bykowski. The son of Polish immigrants, Bykowski grew up in the East Village of Manhattan. He worked as a hospital drug clerk before the war, and he enlisted in the navy in August 1940. Assigned to duty as a pharmacist's mate on the USS *Vincennes*, Bykowski saw action in the Doolittle raid, the Battle of Midway, and the Battle of the Coral Sea. During the Battle of Savo Island (part of the

Guadalcanal campaign), Japanese torpedoes hit the *Vincennes*, and it sank in less than half an hour. More than 300 sailors died. As the ship went down, Bykowski tried to gather up the supply of morphine to tend to the wounded. In the process, shrapnel struck him, which fractured his left leg in four places. As he struggled to reach the ship's main deck, a final Japanese torpedo hit the ship and threw him 250 feet in the air, but fortunately, clear of the sinking ship. Bykowski's injuries left him permanently crippled. He spent the next three years in a naval hospital. In 1944, *Reader's Digest* ran a story that detailed Bykowski's heroics.[43]

Soon after he had returned to his home in Queens in the summer of 1945, Bykowski read the papers describing Bilbo's ethnic slurs. He decided to go to Washington, DC, to talk to the Mississippi leader. Bykowski believed if Bilbo had more information about the rainbow of humanity that fought for America in the world war, the senator would certainly realize the error of his ways. In the Pacific, Bykowski had served alongside Italians, Jews, and Blacks. When Bykowski arrived in Washington on Friday, August 24, Bilbo had left town for the summer break. The New York veteran, a tall, skinny man, set up a personal picket in front of the Senate Office Building. He carried a sign that read, "Was this in vain? Tell it to me, Bilbo—I fought for democracy." The Capitol police forced him to leave, so he moved his protest to the senator's DC residence a few blocks away. He held vigil each day for about three hours, which represented the limits his disabled body could endure. The press initially took little notice of Bykowski's crusade. Although Black journalists showed some of the earliest interest in covering the story, they were essentially barred from a scheduled press conference in early September at the segregated Raleigh Hotel, where Bykowski stayed. When Bilbo returned to work on September 5, he avoided the lone protester in the morning and quickly got in his car to go to the Capitol for the day. After more than two weeks of pounding the pavement, seemingly in vain, Bykowski returned to New York.[44]

Though discouraged, Bykowski did not end his protest. Bilbo continued to lash out at anyone who criticized his inflammatory rhetoric on race. When he responded to a group of soldiers that condemned his language and called them "four dirty and cowardly so-called military men . . . sickening and offensive to all clean and decent human beings," Bykowski decided to renew his campaign against the Mississippi senator. He returned to DC in mid-October. Before he left, a mass "Oust Bilbo" rally held in Manhattan attracted 1,200 people. The rally began with Bykowski leading a line of protesters that included Dolly Mason and Josephine Piccolo, as well as a string of merchant seaman, veterans, and a WAVE. When Bykowski resumed his picketing outside Bilbo's residence, he had reinforcements. The size of the picket line varied day to day. At times, Mason, Piccolo, and Leonard Golditch joined the protest, as did various groups of soldiers and veterans. Two of the Black veterans that participated in the protest came from the Deep South, one, from Jackson, who had fought with the navy for three years during World War II as a warrant officer, and the other, from Birmingham, who had served the navy for two years in the same role as Bykowski, as a pharmacist's mate. Many of the protesters carried the increasingly iconic "Oust Bilbo" signs. The Mississippi senator began to travel with two bodyguards, and he generally avoided the demonstrators by ducking into an alley and using a basement entrance to his building.[45]

The protest in front of Bilbo's Washington residence continued for the remainder of 1945. This second act, however, had the backing of an increasingly organized national effort to impeach Bilbo. By the time Bykowski's second round of picketing began in October, the NNC's campaign against the senator had shifted into high gear. The Washington chapter of the NNC actively engaged in lobbying organizations to send telegrams to senators, worked to get veterans' organizations to help with the picketing of Bilbo's residence, conducted fundraising for Oust Bilbo efforts, and called on union members in the national capital to man downtown street corners to collect Bilbo impeachment petitions. The Chicago NNC chapter had Oust Bilbo booths set up around the city to collect signatures on petitions. In December, a Veterans-Citizen Committee formed in Washington, DC, and started its own national petition drive against Bilbo's continued service in Congress. Protests in other northern locales involved a variety of activist groups. At the beginning of December, more than a dozen groups, including the NAACP, the American-Jewish Congress, and several union organizations organized an anti-Bilbo mass meeting in Philadelphia.[46]

Although opposition to Bilbo became intense in the North in the second half of 1945, in the white South, few criticized his racially insulting rhetoric. A group of Methodist women from nine southern states meeting in North Carolina in August 1945 issued a statement condemning not only Bilbo but also Mississippi's other senator, Jim Eastland, for their "abusive attack" on Black Americans. A handful of southern newspapers also censured Bilbo. The *Macon (Ga.) News* opposed the Mississippi senator by reminding its readers that "we conceive it to be the duty of every Southerner to repudiate every appeal to prejudice.... Persons who fan the flame of racial hatred are enemies of the people and their free institutions." Hodding Carter, editor of the *Delta Democrat-Times* in Greenville, Mississippi, ridiculed Bilbo as a disciple of the "master race theory." He also challenged his supposed "courage" in speaking his mind, since it took little bravery "to rampage against Italians and Catholics who in this State are in such a small minority, or against Jews, whose numbers here are infinitely small, or against Negroes, who don't vote or talk back."[47]

Bilbo's language and actions did not turn most of Mississippi's white voters—or the white South in general—against him. J. C. Grubbs, a farmer from central Mississippi, applauded "the fight you put up for Good old U.S.A." John Flanagan, originally from Mississippi but living in Mobile, backed Bilbo entirely. He told the senator that "*this is a White Man's Country*, World Wars or not! We didn't fight this war to give the Negros the equal rights as whites!" A Houston, Texas, man, who claimed to write on behalf of "all my many friends," praised the Mississippian for his "courage and fighting spirit." If Bilbo's language and actions had diminished his standing among a host of detractors across the country, he correctly calculated that his discriminatory language would play well among white Mississippians and other white Southerners.[48] And in the end, Bilbo only really had to appeal to the small segment of white Mississippians who had the right to cast a ballot in his upcoming 1946 re-election vote. Bilbo would win that battle, but he would not win the war to impose his larger vision of a complete and permanent separation of the white and Black races on the nation.

10
Political Crossroads, 1946: Black Voters and White Resistance

Just before noon on Friday, January 3, 1947, the US Senate assembled to organize itself for the 80th session of Congress. The first order of business was to swear in the thirty-six newly elected senators, in alphabetical order, to a body that had a Republican majority for the first time in more than a decade. After Connecticut's Raymond Baldwin took the oath, next up was Mississippi senator Theodore G. Bilbo, elected the previous summer to a third term. As Bilbo, with sunken cheeks and a food-stained jacket, reached the front of the chamber, Glen Taylor, Democrat from Idaho, objected to seating the Mississippi senator. Political observers had expected such a move, though most believed Republicans would lead the effort against Bilbo.[1]

Speculation about whether senators would seat the Mississippi senator had circulated for weeks, ever since he faced investigation by not one, but two, Senate committees in December 1946. A Special Committee to Investigate Senatorial Campaign Expenditures had examined charges that Bilbo intimidated Black voters during his campaign, and a Special Committee to Investigate the National Defense Program probed allegations that he had benefited financially from cozy arrangements with war contractors. Although Bilbo's attempt to block Black voters in Mississippi drew the most media attention, including a dramatic public hearing in Jackson, the committee report released on the morning of January 3 generally dismissed those misdeeds. Instead, senators took more seriously the less-publicized charges that Bilbo had profited unfairly because of wartime mobilization. The national defense committee concluded, in findings released a day earlier, that "the evidence presented to this committee clearly indicates that Senator Bilbo improperly used his high office as United States Senator for his personal gain in his dealings with war contractors."[2]

Southern Democrats objected to the effort to prevent Bilbo's readmission to the US Senate. They wanted him seated, after which the Senate could investigate further. Removing Bilbo later, however, would be a tougher task than blocking him from ever joining the 80th Congress. Although the US Senate could refuse to admit an elected member by a majority vote, once a senator was seated, expulsion required a two-thirds vote. Southern senators began a filibuster, which halted the typically routine process of welcoming newly elected members to the Senate club. The debate over Bilbo's fate continued for more than twenty-four hours. Finally, late Saturday afternoon, the majority leader for the previous decade, Democrat Alben Barkley of Kentucky, offered a compromise. Barkley told the lawmakers that Bilbo was "an ill man." He had cancer of the mouth and had to return to New Orleans for treatment and recovery that might take months. Barkley proposed that "the certificate of the Senator-elect from Mississippi lie on the table without prejudice and without action," until Bilbo could return. The Senate agreed unanimously with this motion, and the swearing in of new senators resumed. Bilbo left the chamber, and the next morning, he got in his gray Cadillac for the long drive south. Separately, the Senate agreed to let him continue to receive his Senate salary, despite the delay in officially seating him.[3]

A week later, another southern political drama unfolded in Atlanta. In the summer of 1946, James V. Carmichael, a protégé of Ellis Arnall (who could not succeed himself), won the popular vote for governor in the Democratic primary. Eugene Talmadge, however, became the Democratic nominee, since he won the county-unit tally—a Georgia version of the national Electoral College. After winning the typically uncontested general election in November, Talmadge died in late December, before he assumed office. The state legislature, controlled by Talmadge forces and scheduled to meet on January 13, pointed to a long-forgotten law that allowed the legislature, in such situations, to select the governor from the top two "living" vote-getters. Talmadge and his supporters had known the end was near, and in the November election, several hundred people had written in the name of his son, Herman Talmadge. Several hundred voters had also named Carmichael in the November balloting.[4]

At the same time, Arnall claimed he had to serve until his successor was chosen. Some of his supporters interpreted that statement to mean he wanted to serve until the next scheduled election in 1950. Arnall, however, vowed to stay on the job only until the incoming lieutenant governor, M. E. Thompson, assumed office. After midnight on the morning on January 15, with Talmadge supporters packing the galleries, the legislature counted the write-in votes. Carmichael had 669 and Herman Talmadge 617. But a "misplaced" box suddenly appeared from the Talmadges' home county of Telfair, which upped Talmadge's total to 675. The legislature moved quickly to certify Talmadge as the candidate with the most write-in votes, and he immediately took the oath of office as Georgia's new governor.[5]

Talmadge went to the governor's office in the state capitol, but Arnall refused to relinquish the space. He had locked himself in the chief executive's office, so Talmadge and his supporters battered the door down. As the two principals waged a war of words, supporters of the two camps squared off more violently. Talmadge supporters smashed office furniture. Fistfights broke out between the partisans. Finally, with the dispute unresolved, everyone went home, but the next morning, Talmadge returned and set up a second governor's office in a reception area of the state capitol. Both men started naming their respective slates of government appointees. At some point during the day, Talmadge gained control of Arnall's office, changed the locks, and moved his operation to the official governor's office. Two days later, after Thompson took his oath of office, Arnall officially resigned, and Thompson became the third person that week to lay claim to the Georgia governor's office. Arnall had already filed a lawsuit seeking an injunction

Governor Ellis Arnall (waving) exiting a Georgia government building during the three-governors controversy, January 1947. After the governor-elect, Eugene Talmadge, died before taking office, Arnall spearheaded a successful effort to bar Talmadge's son, Herman, from assuming the office, despite an attempt by the Georgia legislature to install the younger Talmadge. *Courtesy Georgia Archives, Vanishing Georgia Collection, geo037*

against Talmadge's inauguration, and the Fulton National Bank of Atlanta later filed another suit to determine the rightful governor, and thus, the person who controlled state funds. It took a few months for the courts to resolve the so-called three governor's controversy; in March 1947, the Georgia Supreme Court ruled Thompson was the rightful governor and would serve until a special new election in 1948.[6]

In the spring of 1946, Max Lerner, editor of the New York newspaper *PM*, described the South as the region "still most fluid politically." The US Senate race in Mississippi and the governor's contest in Georgia in 1946 bore out that analysis, despite the utter chaos that followed the conclusion of both political battles. As Black citizens in the Deep South pressed for their political rights in the summer of 1946, the Deep South stood at a political crossroads. Bilbo's Senate re-election campaign demonstrated one strand of white political thought in the aftermath of World War II: a desire to roll back wartime measures that threatened to liberalize the region's race relations and enfranchise Black voters and an effort to reimpose a system that enshrined white supremacy absolutely. Although the war often forced white Southerners to mute their racial views, many wanted life, especially in terms of race relations, to return to prewar norms at the end of the hostilities. As one southern governor told a national reporter in 1943: "We can't enforce our Jim Crow laws now—we got to kinda wink at them. But when this is all over, we'll fix that."[7]

The 1946 governor's race in Georgia, with James Carmichael running as a surrogate for the liberal Ellis Arnall, represented a different component of postwar white political thought: an attempt to accommodate Black voting in some form while still maintaining racial segregation. Envisioning limited, yet significant, changes in the region's race relations, this strategy sought to downplay racial issues as much as possible in favor of promoting economic development for the region. In the end, neither of these white political agendas would survive 1946 fully intact—though Bilbo's proved the more resilient of the two. At the same time, despite a valiant effort, Black Southerners did not secure the right to vote in either state, due to white violence and intimidation and because the federal government refused to go beyond its wartime call for nondiscrimination in supporting Black civil rights.

The outpouring of opposition to Bilbo that occurred in the second half of 1945 continued into the new year. Bilbo remained convinced of the righteousness of his cause, and in early January, he officially announced his candidacy for a third term in the US Senate. He pledged "to wage the most strenuous fight of my life in an effort to defeat the Fair Employment Practices Commission, the anti–poll tax bill, the anti-lynching bill." In May 1946, Bilbo took a two-month leave of the Senate to return to Mississippi and campaign in earnest for his seat. Before leaving Washington, however, Bilbo joined other southern senators in halting a renewed effort to breathe life into the Fair Employment Practices Committee (FEPC). On January 17, New Mexico Democrat Dennis Chavez revived legislation to make the FEPC a permanent agency. The next day, southern senators began a twenty-four-day filibuster against the legislation, the longest delaying move in the US Senate since the 1938 southern campaign against an anti-lynching bill. Bilbo joined the speechmaking late in the fight but injected his typical bombastic touch. Speaking to an almost empty chamber, he claimed he could talk for sixty days. He complained that adoption of a permanent FEPC would damage American freedom and asked, "Are we going to let some little peckerwood come around without any right and go into your office and examine your books?" After the Senate failed to pass a cloture measure to end the filibuster, Chavez withdrew his bill. At the end of June, days before the Mississippi Democratic primary that would decide Bilbo's political future, the FEPC closed its operations for good.[8]

Once back home in Mississippi, Bilbo cast himself as a martyr. Playing on Mississippi's long history of distrusting outsiders, Bilbo recounted in his stump speeches all the attacks on him by the northern press and northern organizations and held himself up as the defender of Mississippi values against "Communists, nigger-lovers, and Yankee crackpots." He told an audience in Pontotoc in May that he knew, "beyond every reasonable doubt, that our race is in jeopardy." He also promoted his preferred solution to the "race problem." Speaking at an event in Tupelo on May 17, Bilbo described himself as "the man with the guts and intelligence" to send Black Americans back to Africa. Although other issues arose during the 1946 contest—including debates over the meaning of renewed organizing efforts in the South by the American Federation of Labor (AFL) and the Congress of Industrial Organizations (CIO)—race dominated the proceedings. For Bilbo, the possibility of Black people voting in the July 2 Democratic primary represented an immediate danger to white supremacy. He told a campaign rally in Greenwood on June 5 that he sought to prevent Black voting "in the interest of all mankind, and in the interest of white supremacy for our dear Southland." After hearing that Black citizens had recently voted in a city election in Pass Christian on the Mississippi Gulf Coast, Bilbo called the exercise of Black suffrage there "one of the most damnable demonstrations of demagoguery in our Southland."[9]

US Senator Theodore Bilbo (right) campaigns for re-election in 1946 in Collins, Mississippi. During the campaign, the senator urged white Mississippians to prevent Black voting to preserve white supremacy. *Theodore G. Bilbo Papers, Historical Manuscripts, University of Southern Mississippi*

In early 1946, Black men and women in Mississippi, including many veterans, organized to encourage voting in the July primary. The Forrest County Colored Committee of 100 urged Black citizens in Hattiesburg to pay their poll tax by February 1. The group hoped to register 5,000 Black voters. In February, a statewide meeting of Black leaders from around the state (with representatives from forty-four of the state's eighty-two counties) met in Jackson and drew up a list of demands to Governor Thomas Bailey and the state legislature for "full equality and an end to discrimination against their race." Organized by A. W. Wells, a railroad clerk, the petition to state leaders included a call for abolishing the poll tax. Reportedly "shocked" and "alarmed" by the Black proposal, state lawmakers responded by appointing a special committee charged with bolstering the state's "white" primary. In March, Black veterans in Jackson formed a chapter of the American Veterans Committee (AVC), a national group formed in 1943 as a politically liberal alternative to existing veterans' groups, such as the American Legion. Louis Miles, originally from Louisiana and a student at Jackson College (now Jackson State University), led the Jackson AVC chapter. Black veterans in other locales around the state organized themselves into more informal collectives, such as the group that formed in Jefferson Davis County in mid-May. That group had two stated purposes: providing better recreation opportunities for the youth of the county and the "Promoting of Better Citizenship."[10]

The Mississippi Progressive Voters League (MPVL), originally organized in late 1944, also made a renewed push to mobilize Black voters in the state. In mid-May 1946, the group held a two-day meeting in Jackson, attended by about fifty Black leaders from around the state, including many veterans. At the opening session, President T. B. Wilson—a retired schoolteacher and real estate broker—said his group wanted to challenge the notion that outside groups stirred up Black Mississippians to ask for the ballot. Wilson emphasized that the MPVL consisted of Black Southerners "striving to bring about a spirit of better cooperation and good-will" between the races by "gaining for Mississippi Negroes the right to vote in all primaries." The *Jackson Daily News* later misquoted Wilson as saying, "We challenge the right of anyone to prevent us from voting." The paper added that Black people should stay away from the polls on July 2, as "the best way to prevent unhealthy and unhappy results." Although Wilson wrote a letter to the paper seeking to correct his quoted statement, the editor, Fred Sullens, doubted the retraction and advised Wilson that "'challenge' is a good word for him to leave alone." In addition to urging all Black citizens to vote, especially veterans who did not have to pay the poll tax, per a bill recently passed by the state legislature, the MPVL also launched a $20,000 fundraising campaign to support its voting rights effort.[11]

Despite the efforts of Black activists in Mississippi, only a tiny percentage of eligible Black voters came out during the first half of 1946 to try to register to vote. For example, by late May, although the capital city had tens of thousands of eligible Black voters, only 400 Black citizens in Jackson had signed on to the voting rolls since the beginning of the year. At the time of the July 2 election, about 5,000 Black residents had registered to vote statewide, though Mississippi had a voting-eligible Black population of 350,000. The reason for the tepid response to the Black voter mobilization campaign in Mississippi was simple: fear of reprisal. County circuit clerks handled voter registration, and Black citizens in the state had long observed that those who had tried to register faced intimidation or violence of various sorts. If election officials did allow them to register, those same officials then turned them away on election day for any number of reasons. Bilbo's campaign revived these long-standing concerns.[12]

By June 1946, fears about registering to vote seemed increasingly sensible, given the treatment potential registrants faced and the increasingly incendiary rhetoric coming from white leaders. As Bilbo pointed out during the campaign, circuit clerks needed "to devise difficult questions for negroes attempting to register by interpreting the Constitution." He also told the clerks that if they could not "think up enough questions to disqualify undesirables, then write Bilbo or any good lawyer." Some Black people who tried to register faced more than just difficult questions. On June 12, Etoy Fletcher, discharged from the military less than two months earlier, attempted to register in Brandon, east of Jackson. After the circuit clerk at the Rankin County courthouse turned him away, a white gang kidnapped him, took him to some nearby woods, and beat him.[13]

Although Bilbo had railed against Black voting from the beginning of his campaign, by late May his speeches included threats of racial violence for any Black citizens trying to participate in the political process. Following reports of the MPVL convention, Bilbo said that members of the group "should be atomically bombed and exterminated from the face of the earth." That ridiculous comment perhaps evinced little fear, but Bilbo's new stump speech more ominously included a call for Mississippians to keep the Democratic primary "clean and white." It also urged "every red-blooded Anglo-Saxon man in Mississippi to resort to any means" to prevent Black voting and noted that "if you don't know what that means, you are just not up on your persuasive measures." Black Mississippians recalled Bilbo statements that were even more explicitly threatening. For example, L. J. Sibbe of Crystal Springs relayed to the Senate investigating committee in December 1946 what he heard Bilbo say in a campaign speech on the radio: "Don't allow any niggers to vote. Keep them down. If you let them vote—if they go to the polls to vote, pour gasoline on them, and everybody knows what to do next." John James remembered an equally disturbing excerpt from a speech he heard Bilbo give at the courthouse in Bay St. Louis in June 1946: "The best way to keep a nigger from voting is to see him the night before, and if any nigger was caught trying to organize the voters, to tar and feather him and don't forget the match."[14]

Even if Bilbo's language was not as explicit as that remembered by Black citizens, everyone in Mississippi would have understood the meaning of the more subtle threats the media attributed to Bilbo.[15] In Mississippi during World War II, racial lynchings continued to decline, although two incidents involving extralegal killings of Black Mississippians occurred in October 1942. A white mob hanged two Black teenage boys in east-central Mississippi, after they allegedly assaulted a teenage white girl, and less than a week later, another group of white vigilantes took a Black man from a prison in southern Mississippi and killed him. Racial violence spiked anew throughout the South once the war ended. Civil rights leader Amzie Moore said that white residents in the Mississippi Delta at the end of the war formed a Home Guard to protect white women. He believed that in the first few months after the war "black men were being killed at the rate of one per week."[16]

Bilbo's "any means" remarks focused national attention on the Mississippi campaign. In late June, representatives of the New York Civil Rights Congress came to Mississippi and determined that Bilbo had pulled a "blanket of terror" over the state. Indeed, in the days prior to the election, even the MPVL had largely suspended its Black voting rights efforts. Black labor leader A. Philip Randolph asked President Harry Truman to send the army into Mississippi "to safeguard the sacred civil rights of the Negroes to cast their vote." The day before the July 2 election, the National Association for the Advancement of Colored People (NAACP) requested that the Justice Department deploy FBI agents as poll watchers to "prevent bloodshed and violation of constitutional rights in Mississippi." US Attorney General Tom Clark said he would use the "full force" of the Justice Department to protect Black voters in Mississippi but did not deploy federal agents. The executive secretary of Louisiana's NAACP noted that if the Justice Department could not protect "this basis [sic] right of Democracy then it is time that the Federal Government close its doors and let the fascist Bilbo and his 'ilk' run the show." The US Senate's Special Committee to Investigate Senatorial Campaign Expenditures, however, refused to scrutinize Bilbo's campaign, since all the official complaints came from outside Mississippi.[17]

White Mississippians offered few criticisms of Bilbo's campaign, and even some white Northerners applauded his efforts. The day before the election, Emily and Kenneth Drisler of New York City wrote the Mississippi senator "as two unfortunate New Yorkers who have suffered from the very aggressive campaign and extreme madness of the colored in New York" and congratulated Bilbo "on the splendid work you are doing." Arthur C. Wilson of Hyannis, Massachusetts, offered Bilbo his support for "your uphill battles against the negroes and communists, whose efforts to destroy our way of life, as enjoyed in the pre-Eleanor days, can be seen everywhere." Wilson noted that "the Jews get me down too, but it's the negroes who get me mad."[18] Both white supremacy and antisemitism had adherents nationwide.

Bilbo had four opponents in the Democratic primary race, a group he collectively dubbed "the four peckerwoods." His most formidable opponent was Tom Ellis, a former train dispatcher and clerk of the state supreme court. Ellis presented himself as a middle-of-the-road candidate and did not attack Bilbo directly. For the anti-Bilbo forces, Ellis represented the best alternative. Future governor William Winter, then serving with the US Army in the Philippines, told his parents that Mississippi could "never hope to cope with the negro question with any degree of satisfaction with the like of Bilbo in the driver's seat," although "a man like Tom Ellis, who stands as clearly and uncompromisingly for white supremacy as Theodore claims to stand, could be a real asset to the state in Washington." As the racial moderate Winter recognized, Ellis shared Bilbo's concerns about Black voting, though without the over-the-top rhetoric. Ellis did not support Black voting, since he believed Black people had "not advanced far enough for an intelligent participation in the government of this country."[19]

On Election Day, Bilbo secured an outright victory with 51 percent of the votes, and thus avoided a runoff election. Thirty percent of voters chose Ellis. Perhaps as many as 3,000 of the 5,000 registered Black voters cast a ballot. Other Black people tried to participate in the July 2 election, but various efforts to suppress the Black vote marred Election Day. Armed white mobs blocked some Black citizens from the polls, as in Decatur, where the Evers brothers, Medgar and Charles, and their World War II veteran colleagues tried to cast ballots. In McComb, town officials arrested an elderly Black man as he approached his polling place; other Black residents of town decided not to participate in the election. A similar situation occurred in Grenada. Seventy-two-year-old minister R. S. Bostick, the son of slaves, tried to vote on election day, but the sheriff turned him away. The preacher later recounted that other potential Black voters "got afraid to go, so they told me; so, nobody else didn't try." On the Gulf Coast, signs around Biloxi announced, "Negroes vote at your own risk." In Gulfport, white men at the polling station beat a local NAACP leader and his wife, Varnado and Earnestine Collier; a city policeman directed the Colliers to the location of their thrashing. And in nearby Pass Christian, where Black citizens had recently voted in a city contest, the election board told potential Black voters that they could cast a ballot in the white primary if they painted their faces white. In both Jackson and Greenville, election officials at some precincts let Black men and women vote but immediately set their ballots aside in separate envelopes, informing them that their votes had been challenged (an action allowed under Mississippi's election laws). Many more instances of Black voter intimidation occurred, some surfacing in reports in the weeks and months following the election. Bilbo remained brazenly reactionary in victory. Days after his election, he urged the governor to call a special session of the Mississippi legislature to find a way "to keep our Democratic primaries all white."[20]

As 1946 dawned in Georgia, the upcoming election season seemed to offer hope for a more progressive politics than in Mississippi. After all, Ellis Arnall's administration had overseen an extension of the suffrage to eighteen-year-olds and many Black citizens. Though Arnall had done little to alleviate the state's racial problems, he hoped that racial concerns would not consume state politics in favor of further economic development initiatives that would help all the state's residents. However, the reality of increasing numbers of Black Georgians casting a ballot led to a sustained white backlash to Black empowerment, and violence and intimidation accompanied Talmadge's victory. The suppression of the Black vote during Georgia's 1946 gubernatorial race exceeded that in Bilbo's Mississippi campaign, although the Georgia contest attracted far less national attention.

Events in early 1946 suggested that biracial politics might indeed succeed in Georgia. Black citizens voted in several elections without incident, including the balloting for mayors in Athens, home to the University of Georgia, and Valdosta, a small city in south Georgia. White residents of Valdosta even praised Black citizens for their conduct during the election. In Atlanta, a coalition of Black leaders, including chapters of the National Urban League and the NAACP, formed the All-Citizens' Registration Committee, which enrolled 7,000 new Black voters in Georgia's Fifth Congressional District. A special election in the district held in February to fill a vacated seat attracted twenty candidates, including one woman, Helen Mankin. A World War I veteran and state legislator, Mankin won the contest, largely by winning the Black vote. The only candidate to secretly attend a meeting of Black citizens, Mankin also supported Arnall, while most of the other candidates backed Talmadge.[21]

Federal court decisions added to the optimism. In March 1946, the Fifth Circuit Court of Appeals ratified the Georgia District Court decision in *King v. Chapman*, the case that had outlawed the Georgia white primary in 1945. In early April, the US Supreme Court, which had ruled the Texas white primary unconstitutional in 1944, refused to hear an appeal of this decision. This victory over the white primary, one of the major disfranchising mechanisms used by southern states, further spurred Black voter registration efforts across Georgia, especially in urban areas. Then, in early June, the US Supreme Court decided, in *Morgan v. Virginia*, that segregation in interstate transportation was illegal. Although it was not a direct assault on segregation, the court decision asserted that Jim Crow transportation laws in some states interfered with interstate commerce.[22]

Less hopeful developments, however, accompanied these signs of progress. White supremacist groups in Georgia, especially in the Atlanta area, re-emerged by the end of the war. The Ku Klux Klan (KKK), always strong in Georgia, had largely gone quiet for most of the war years, especially after the conviction of eight KKK members in 1940 for flogging scores of Black people in the Atlanta area (although the Georgia governor at the time, Eugene Talmadge, pardoned the criminals). In 1945, the KKK re-emerged in the city. That fall, the KKK held a cross burning at nearby Stone Mountain, site of the second Klan's founding during World War I. Reports circulated that the Atlanta police force had numerous KKK members. In February 1946, Roy Harris, Speaker of the Georgia House of Representatives, told a Klan leader in Atlanta that he was "100 percent for what the Klan believed in." Those beliefs included instructions issued by one Atlanta Klavern two days after Mankin's election, which suggested that floggings and lynchings represented the best solution to the "n____r problem" and encouraged all KKK members to arm themselves. James Shipp, a Klansman, had also organized a separate white supremacist group, the Commoner Party, in late 1944. Headquartered in Conyers, a town east of Atlanta, the Commoners promoted the repeal of the Fifteenth Amendment to the US Constitution—which had guaranteed the right to vote to Black men in 1870—and urged "the reduction of the Negro race to citizenship without the right of franchise."[23]

The Georgia gubernatorial contest in 1946 had three candidates: James Carmichael and two former governors, Eugene Talmadge and Ed Rivers. Talmadge, seeking a fourth stint in the governor's mansion, promised in his platform to support a "progressive" program that would give "better jobs, opportunities and a better livelihood to the people of our State." Yet Talmadge, a slightly better-looking but equally venomous version of Bilbo, saw no need for any major changes in southern life. In fact, World War II had only bolstered Talmadge's belief, like Bilbo's, that the South needed to hold on to the old ways more tightly. The Talmadge campaign focused almost exclusively on maintaining white supremacy, the tried-and-true approach that had defined his previous political races. For this election, Talmadge could point to the recent upsurge in Black activism, as well as the court decisions sanctioning Black voting and outlawing racial segregation on interstate buses and trains. Talmadge promised to repeal Black voting and stop what he described as a "nigra takeover." He told voters that if Georgia did not preserve the white primary, all segregation laws would end, "even those which prohibit intermarriage."[24]

Talmadge's message appealed to many white Georgians worried about perceived threats to traditional race relations, but some of the state's most powerful economic interests also supported Talmadge, including the railroads, the Georgia Power Company, textile owners, and some leaders of the Coca-Cola Company. The power company, perhaps the most influential political force in the state, reportedly supported Talmadge because it felt slighted by the Arnall administration. As labor leader Lucy Randolph Mason observed, the Arnall administration was "disliked by the majority of the powerfully wealthy men in Georgia." Mason and others also believed that key economic leaders in the state paid Ed Rivers to enter the race, to split the anti-Talmadge vote.[25]

The revitalized KKK supported Talmadge, and the former governor welcomed the endorsement. Klan leaders in Atlanta met with Talmadge in April as the campaign got underway. "Exalted Cyclops" Sam Roper said that when he asked Talmadge how to keep Black Georgians from voting, the candidate handed him a piece of paper with the word "Pistols" written on it. "Grand Dragon" Dr. Samuel Green said Talmadge told him that if elected he would remove from office every person who did not support "white supremacy and 100 percent Americanism." In May 1946, 2,000 Klan members held another cross burning at Stone Mountain, and the group's leaders claimed to have as many as 50,000 members statewide, including 20,000 in the Atlanta metropolitan area. By May 1946, Fulton County alone had 20,000 registered Black voters. Atlanta Klan leaders had also apparently plotted to assassinate NAACP leader A. T. Walden, although they never followed through with those plans. Beyond actual members, the KKK had support among white Georgians unaffiliated with the organization. A retired Methodist minister in Fort Valley noted that he was not a KKK member but thought "the Klan is needed." The preacher believed that "a fiery cross from every hilltop in Dixie will do more to stay the gale that is blowing toward social equality than the preaching from ten thousand Christless pulpits."[26]

Talmadge's main opponent in 1946 was James Carmichael, a man Arnall supporters had identified, as early as 1944, as a logical successor to the Georgia governor. Partly disabled as a teenager after being hit by a streetcar in his native Cobb County, Carmichael had a successful career as a state legislator and attorney. In 1943, Arnall appointed Carmichael to serve both as head of the Georgia Department of Revenue and as a member of the commission charged with revising the state's constitution. In July 1944, soon after Larry Bell named Carmichael general manager of the Bell Bomber Plant, the *Atlanta Constitution* suggested he should run for governor in 1946. People who supported Arnall liked Carmichael and saw him as a fellow New South progressive and an "Arnall-type candidate." During the 1946 campaign, Carmichael ran a "good government" campaign, one that emphasized fiscal conservatism, economic development, and educational progress. Carmichael's campaign attracted significant support. Ninety percent of Georgia newspapers endorsed the thirty-five-year-old Carmichael, and liberals, veterans, and young people signed on to his campaign. A straw poll of students at the University of Georgia in June 1946 produced 1,601 votes for Carmichael and only 195 for Eugene Talmadge.[27]

On the issue of Black voting, Talmadge accused Carmichael and one of his major press supporters, *Atlanta Constitution* editor Ralph McGill, of "plotting to integrate the races." While Carmichael did pronounce the court ruling outlawing the white primary in Georgia as the final word on the matter, he rejected the Talmadge approach while also reassuring white voters that he fully supported white supremacy. Carmichael lambasted Talmadge for playing the race card merely to get elected, pointing out that Talmadge had always threatened that if he lost an election, racial segregation would end and "Negroes would rule Georgia," but neither of those things ever happened. Carmichael also berated Talmadge for embracing the KKK, a group he equated with "Hitler's Storm Troopers." Carmichael vowed to follow the law, including recent court rulings, but he also assured white voters that he had a background "as steeped in Southern tradition as Talmadge" and promised "that as long as I am Governor, Negroes will not attend white schools, there will be no interracial marriages, and there will be no mixing of the races in our institutions."[28]

Governor Arnall took the same approach. He told a statewide radio audience in June that both Talmadge and Ed Rivers invoked race as a "false issue" and a "smoke screen." Arnall said he believed the state's white citizens "will not be misled into believing that there is a gigantic conspiracy of yard men, farm hands, cooks, wash women and children's nurses to overthrow the government of Georgia." A month earlier, speaking at the First National Conference on Citizenship in Philadelphia, Arnall had promoted the right of all Americans to a free ballot, declaring that "the right to vote was the foundation stone in a democracy of all civil liberties."[29]

Arnall also tried to blunt the role of the KKK in the campaign. On May 30, he directed his attorney general to take action to revoke the group's non-profit corporation charter (reissued two months earlier) and to work with the US attorney general to examine the KKK's activities in the state. The assistant attorney general assigned to the case, Dan Duke, revealed in mid-June that thirty-eight Atlanta police officers were Klan members. In a civil lawsuit filed by the state of Georgia a week later seeking a revocation of the state KKK's charter, the Arnall administration claimed the organization had tried to gain control of the police and other government agencies to render the state "incapable of carrying out that part of the state Constitution that guarantees protection of persons and property." At the same time, Arnall announced that the FBI had uncovered a plot by a KKK group in south Atlanta to assassinate him, a charge that Klan leader Sam Green denied. Despite the threats against him by the KKK, Arnall addressed a large audience at an "All Faiths and Races Celebration" on July 4 at Stone Mountain, organized by the Fifth District of the Georgia Department of the American Legion.[30]

On election day, July 17, Carmichael won the popular vote, garnering 313,389 votes to Talmadge's 297,245 and River's 69,489. Black men and women cast more than 12 percent of the ballots (85,000), and perhaps 98 percent of those chose Carmichael. Talmadge, however, won the county unit vote—the tally that actually counted—with 242 unit votes to Carmichael's 146 (Rivers won the other 22 unit votes). Somewhat like the process used with the Electoral College to decide presidential races at the national level, the county-unit system awarded votes based on counties won. Each of Georgia's 159 counties had a value of either 2-, 4-, or 6-unit votes, although these designations did not equitably reflect the state's population. Instead, rural areas in the state received disproportionate representation (again, much like the national Electoral College). Fulton County, which encompassed much of the Atlanta metro area and had a population of 392,688, cast 6-unit votes, while Echols County in rural south Georgia, which had a population of 2,964, cast 2-unit votes. Overall, Georgia's eight largest counties had 30 percent of the state's population but only received 12 percent of the unit votes.

Among other inequities, this system diluted the emerging Black vote in the state, concentrated in the state's urban areas. During the campaign, neither Carmichael nor Arnall questioned the county-unit system.[31]

Despite the significant Black vote in Georgia's gubernatorial contest, thousands of Black citizens who had registered to vote never got a chance to cast a ballot. Talmadge and his supporters played a major role in turning away Black voters. Much like Bilbo in Mississippi, Talmadge issued threatening warnings to would-be Black voters during the gubernatorial campaign. In a statewide radio address one week before the election, Talmadge proclaimed that "wise Negroes will stay away from the white folk's ballot boxes on July 17. We are the true friends of the Negroes, always have been, and always will be as long as they stay in the definite place we have provided for them." In addition to fearmongering, the Talmadge campaign, utilizing provisions of state law, organized a sophisticated and well-coordinated movement to challenge registered Black voters. A "mass challenge" plan originated in Talmadge's

Black men and women line up to vote in the July 17, 1946, Democratic primary in Marietta, Georgia, home to the Bell Bomber plant. Although white leaders across the state warned Black voters to stay away from the polls, more than 80,000 showed up to cast a ballot. *Bettmann/Contributor; Getty Images*

Atlanta headquarters in the month before the election; Talmadge's son and campaign manager, Herman, played a key role in enacting the scheme. The Talmadge campaign sent thousands of challenge forms to its county leaders throughout the state. Local citizens then obtained lists of Black registered voters and methodically filled out the challenge forms, which triggered a hearing before the local Board of Registrars for the disputed cases.[32]

In late June and early July, Boards of Registrars conducted voter qualification examinations in more than 20 percent of the state's 159 counties. In most counties, local officials saw no reason to follow the Talmadge directive and challenge small numbers of registered Black voters, since his victory seemed assured in their locales. In places where the challenge scheme was implemented, most Black citizens failed to appear when summoned by the Board of Registrars and were summarily disqualified as voters. A few came to the proceedings with legal counsel, although most faced the sham proceedings without such aid. In some cases, as in Wilkes County, members of the Board of Registrars allegedly "financed" the purge operations. Challenges targeted only Black voters, but many of the hearings carried at least a hint of impartiality, by approving some of those called before the boards. In other cases, all those challenged were purged. The US Justice Department officially had a "hands-off" policy toward the Black voter challenge in Georgia, similar to the stance it had adopted during the Bilbo campaign, but in a few cases, US attorneys threatened to intervene in the proceedings. Talmadge, however, objected to even this tepid federal response. During a state radio address a week before the election, he criticized US attorneys for "intimidating" Georgia residents and said it would "not be inappropriate to warn some of these fellows to be careful." He also repeated his admonition that Black Georgians stay away from polling places, since "neither the U.S. Attorneys nor Jimmy Carmichael will have a corporal guard to back them up."[33]

In addition to the purge of Black voters in the runup to the July 17 balloting, white Georgians employed other methods to limit Black voting. In several counties, white individuals took the advice Bilbo had offered them weeks earlier and sought to intimidate Black voters before the election. White vigilantes burned crosses in several Black neighborhoods. In at least two locales, including Taylor County, signs went up stating that any Black people who voted would die or "will never vote again." In Grady County, in southwest Georgia, white farmers and merchants visited the homes of Black citizens. Heavily armed, the white callers told the Black residents not to vote and threatened to kill them if they did. In addition, on the day of the election, groups of white people physically prevented Black citizens from voting at some precincts. In Meriwether County, home to Warm Springs, where polio-stricken FDR had visited often during his presidency and had died a year earlier, white citizens used a variety of voter suppression techniques: a Board of Registrars hearing, a cross burning in a Black neighborhood on the night before the election, and an assault of fifty-two Black voters by a white mob armed with sticks and rocks at a polling place on election day. The FBI at the time, and later investigations by scholars, concluded the Black voter suppression effort by the Talmadge camp proved decisive in securing the southern demagogue's victory.[34]

In addition to Carmichael, Helen Mankin, running for a full term in the US House of Representatives in July 1946, fell victim to Georgia's racial politics and the inequities of the state's county-unit system. She lost her race after election officials altered voting procedures for her district in a blatant effort to dilute the Black vote in Fulton County, one of the centers of Black political mobilization in the state. When Mankin triumphed earlier in the February 1946 special election, her victory resulted from winning the popular vote, as the Fifth Congressional District had decided in 1930 to switch from the county-unit system of determining its congressional elections to relying on popular vote totals. A few weeks before the July 17 vote, however, a district committee favorable to her main opponent, Judge James C. Davis, voted to return to the county-unit system. The district had three counties; Fulton and DeKalb both had approximately 80,000 voters, and Rockdale had only about 8,000 voters. Davis knew he would poll poorly in Fulton, which would likely cost him the election. District committee members at their meeting openly stated that they changed election procedures to defeat Mankin and "control the Negro vote." On July 17, Mankin won in Fulton (with 6 county-unit votes), and like Carmichael, she won the popular vote in the Fifth District race. Judge Davis, however, won the election by securing the county unit votes of DeKalb (6) and Rockdale County (2).[35]

The national media saw some progress in the Georgia election results, but a wave of racial violence accompanied both the Bilbo and Talmadge victories. In late July, *Life* magazine reported that 150,000 Black citizens voted in the Georgia election (an overestimation of almost 100 percent) and editorialized that the contest gave "some hope to the hopeless" concerning the South. Adopting the mantra of the Arnall administration, the national publication believed that "economic improvement has seemed to soften, if only minutely, the sharp, ferocious distinction of color." By the time these statements appeared in print, however, a white mob in Walton County had violently murdered four Georgians. One of the Black men, Roger Malcolm, had stabbed his white employer during a confrontation and was arrested. After being freed on bond, an armed group of more than twenty white men stopped his car outside of Monroe and executed him, his wife, and another Black couple, the Dorseys. The violence in Georgia, however, had begun the day after the election. In Butler, a Black veteran, Macio Snipes, cast the only Black ballot in Taylor County. True to the warning posted prior to the vote, a group of white men came to Snipes's home the next day and shot him dead. In August, the Columbians, a new white supremacy group, organized in Atlanta. The leaders described the group as a "patriotic society," devised to "create voting solidarity among all white American citizens" and "build a progressive white community." In fact, the Columbians were an openly fascist organization that had as many as 500 official adherents, and members of the group assaulted Black residents of Atlanta throughout the late summer and into the fall of 1946.[36]

In Mississippi in the weeks after Bilbo's election, racial violence also flared. In late July, five white men beat and killed a Black laborer, Leon McTatie, in Holmes County for allegedly stealing a saddle. After McTatie's body was found in a bayou in another county, his assailants, including McTatie's employer, admitted to beating but not killing him. McTatie's wife testified at a preliminary hearing that the five white men brought her husband to their house, badly beaten with his hands tied, and asked her about the saddle. When she could offer no information, the men drove off with McTatie. A later examination of McTatie's corpse suggested it had been thrown from an automobile. Two boys who worked on the same plantation as McTatie later admitted to taking the saddle. There was sufficient evidence against the five men to hold a trial, but an all-white jury "deliberated" for just ten minutes before freeing McTatie's attackers.[37]

A week later, a deputy sheriff, John Lewis, killed a Black man, Buddy Wolf, at a Black restaurant in south Mississippi because the deputy did not like Wolf's demeanor. Though a grand jury indicted Lewis for the murder, the case never went to trial. Overall, in a four-week period following the 1946 elections, white murderers killed at least ten Black people in the Deep South. Far from seeing the election contests that summer as promoting any kind of racial progress, the *Pittsburgh Courier* equated Bilbo and Talmadge with Adolf Hitler, noting that all three used "racial hate" to secure political power.[38]

Following the 1946 elections in Mississippi and Georgia, Black Americans and their allies called for federal action to end lynching and to rid the South of officials like Bilbo. Black actor and singer Paul Robeson chaired a group called the American Crusade Against Lynching (ACAL), and in September the organization staged protests in several northern cities. In Chicago, 1,000 people attended a rally supporting both Bilbo's ouster from the Senate and asking for an end to the recent spate of racial killings in the South. A rabbi told the crowd that "negro people must be proud of the fact they are colored and stamp out Fascism here." Later that month, delegates from around the country attended an ACAL convention in Washington, DC, which included a meeting with President Truman and an evening mass meeting at the Lincoln Memorial, where Robeson, among others, performed. In Mississippi, both the NAACP and the Civil Rights Congress, working separately, renewed their efforts to have Bilbo removed from the US Senate. The Civil Rights Congress secured affidavits from forty-eight Black Mississippians claiming that during Bilbo's campaign, he had "advocated, counseled, inspired, encouraged, incited, aided and abetted" white Mississippians "to commit acts of violence and intimidation" against Black voters.[39]

All this activity spurred the federal government to take some action in Mississippi. The complaints collected by the Civil Rights Congress led the Senate's Special Committee to Investigate Senatorial Campaign Expenditures to take another look at Bilbo's campaign. After receiving the complaints from Black Mississippians on September 16, the committee dispatched three investigators to the state to conduct a preliminary investigation. The agents received no help from state officials, and after securing offices in Jackson's Federal Building, Bilbo rented space just down the hall, which seemed a calculated move to intimidate potential witnesses. Despite the difficulties, the investigators obtained testimony from 500 individuals and recommended a full committee inquiry. When the special committee met in mid-November, the chairman, Allen J. Ellender, proclaimed his devotion to white supremacy and said Mississippi officials had acted "within their legal rights" in preventing Black Mississippians from voting in a white primary that was prescribed by state law. He thought pursuing the matter further represented "a useless expense of public funds." Nevertheless, Ellender agreed to go along with the wishes of the full committee, which decided to hold public hearings in early December in Mississippi.[40]

The four days of hearings began on December 2 in downtown Jackson. A mural of a stereotypically idyllic Southern plantation dominated the hearing room: enslaved Black people picking cotton, one playing the banjo, and a steamboat in the background. About 150 Black witnesses, many of them veterans or members of the MPVL, showed up to recount their struggles in registering to vote or casting a ballot on July 2. The NAACP had offered to provide counsel for those testifying, but the Senate committee rejected that request. The willingness of so many Black Mississippians to openly testify against a sitting US senator from the state became one of the most noteworthy aspects of the hearings. The *Pittsburgh Courier* rightly described their action as "courageous." Accompanied by five lawyers, Bilbo also joined the proceedings, looking "old and ill," according to a *Newsweek* correspondent, and missing several teeth because of recent oral surgery.[41]

Senator Ellender tightly controlled the proceedings of the five-member committee and consulted with the Mississippi senator frequently. As *The Nation* noted, Chairman Ellender "was determined from the start to excuse Bilbo." The two other Democratic members, Burnet Maybank of South Carolina and Elmer Thomas of Oklahoma, also proved sympathetic to their Democratic colleague. Ellender offered two contradictory arguments to discredit the case being made against Bilbo by Black Mississippians. At times, he slighted the notion of Black voter intimidation and claimed that Black apathy led to the small number of Black voters. He essentially ignored the fear factor that had long worked to limit Black suffrage in the state (and in his own Louisiana). At other times, Ellender observed that white people had always kept Black people from voting in Mississippi's Democratic primary, so Bilbo had done nothing that many others had not done. Some members of the committee even tried to justify Bilbo's campaign remarks by suggesting that his media statements during the campaign may have spurred Black voting.[42]

Committee members, including the two Republicans on the panel (Bourke Hickenlooper of Iowa and Styles Bridges of New Hampshire), also believed that many of the Black witnesses came forward only at the prodding of outside meddlers. Such assumptions gave credence to the claims of white Southerners that if left to their own devices, Black folks would not bother with things like voting and elections. Yet the Black witnesses who testified made clear that developments during the war had spurred Black political activism in Mississippi. Varnado Collier, beaten along with his wife at the Gulfport voting precinct, recounted how he had long wanted to vote, an idea bolstered in his mind by the *Smith v. Allwright* decision. Collier said he thought the ruling would have convinced everyone that Black people could vote in Democratic primaries. When Senator Ellender questioned

J. B. Raiford of Tylertown about whether it was "common knowledge" that the Democratic primary existed only for white people, Raiford admitted he knew that but also added that "we citizens of that community were real citizens, and we decided we was entitled to vote." C. N. Eiland of Louisville said he voted because he had seen a newspaper story that said the US Department of Justice "had advised all Southern States to let the colored people vote, and I thought by that, that they could vote." Lusta Prichard, also from Gulfport, noted he "was drafted into the Army just like all the other white boys were. I felt that if I was good enough to go into the Army and serve the country, I was good enough to have ... my portion of the say in my representative."[43]

The county circuit clerks also testified at the hearings and largely confirmed that they fulfilled Bilbo's charge to suppress the Black vote. The clerks verified that they asked potential Black voters—and only Black voters—impossible questions about the Mississippi Constitution during the registration process. Wendell Holmes, circuit clerk in Pike County, said Bilbo had just reminded the clerks to keep doing what they had always done. Clifford Field, Adams County clerk, admitted, with total equanimity, that he treated Black registrants differently than he did white ones. Even those circuit clerks who registered Black voters testified to discouraging them from returning to cast a ballot. Emmett Reynolds, the circuit clerk in Winston County, enrolled Black voters, but he told them to stay away on Election Day. Reynolds told Black citizens, his "friends," they were "just a little early trying" to vote in Mississippi.[44]

On day four of the hearings, Bilbo got his chance to speak. The senator claimed he had done nothing wrong, and in any event, according to Mississippi law Black citizens could not vote in the state's Democratic primary, only the general elections held in November. Bilbo also asserted that if any violence or intimidation had occurred during the July 2 election, well, he had nothing to do with any of that. As to the "any means" necessary comment, Bilbo said the newspapers misquoted him and pointed to a radio address the night before the election in which he had used the phrase "lawful means." In addition, Bilbo noted that if he was guilty of damaging the "foundations of orderly and democratic government"—as charged in the complaint against him—then "every white man in Mississippi for 56 years" shared that guilt. Bilbo had a string of other excuses: Black Mississippians should not vote in the Democratic primary because they were all Republicans (apparently he was unaware of the shifting political allegiances of Black Americans in the FDR era), he had only tried to help Black Mississippians by telling them not to vote, outside agitators had "coached" all the Black witnesses against him, and the real purpose behind the attack on Bilbo was to destroy white supremacy.[45]

Less than a week after the Jackson hearings, the Senate Special Committee to Investigate the National Defense Program had Bilbo back on the hot seat again, this time for hearings in Washington. This committee, chaired by Democrat Harley Kilgore of West Virginia, was composed of six Democrats and four Republicans and proved less inclined than the Ellender-led group to give Bilbo a pass. The testimony partly showed that Bilbo had done nothing improper in helping his constituents secure war contracts, although he became so involved in mobilization negotiations that military officials found him annoying. The most damaging charges against Bilbo arose from a series of gifts and favors Bilbo received from those war contractors he had helped. For example, F. T. Newton of Hattiesburg said he gave Bilbo $25,000 for Wall Doxey's 1942 US Senate race, although Doxey said he knew nothing about such a contribution. Bilbo got to testify on the seventh and final day of the hearings. As in Jackson two weeks earlier, he partly blamed outside agitators—"all-out Negro groups and Communist groups of America"— for pressing the charges against him. Bilbo suggested that his re-election to the US Senate represented a complete "exoneration from these charges." The committee disagreed. In a six-to-one vote (two senators abstained), it concluded that Bilbo did gain economically from his self-serving relationship with war contractors grateful to Bilbo for his help in gaining a share of the nation's economic mobilization funds. Only Tom Connally of Texas objected to the final committee report.[46]

While the Senate's war contractor investigation of Bilbo led to a hard-hitting report against the senator, far from the exoneration he thought he deserved, the three Democrats on the Senate's voter intimidation investigation panel largely cleared Bilbo of wrongdoing. As Elmer Thomas of Oklahoma explained before the release of the final report, Mississippi's election system, not Senator Bilbo, prevented Black people from voting in the July 2 election. According to Thomas, "Bilbo did nothing that almost every other politician in Mississippi hasn't done." The two Republicans on the committee filed a minority report, which concluded that "the primary campaign in Mississippi was illegally and unconstitutionally inflamed by [the] advocacy of Senator Bilbo."[47]

The split decision on Bilbo's actions largely reflected public opinion on the senator's suitability to continue to sit in the upper chamber of the nation's legislature. Even some white Southerners found the war-profiteering charges against Bilbo disturbing. An Atlanta man told Georgia senator Richard Russell that Bilbo's dealings with war contractors left no doubt that the Mississippian "has used his position as a Senator in a most disgraceful manner." At the same time, Bilbo's effort to defend white supremacy by limiting the Black vote had substantial support among white Americans, even beyond the South. For example, a policeman from Oregon told Bilbo in December 1946 that he "and millions of white Americans everwhere [sic] are for you.... In my opinion, the negro is the greatest threat in America today and we must find ways and means of stopping them before it is to [sic] late." An Illinois Republican, a telegraph operator, blamed "jewish communists" for the attacks on Bilbo, people "who would like to mix up the races in intermarriage, and mongrelize the whole population."[48] Such sentiments helped cement the compromise in the US Senate, between Democrats and Republicans and between Northerners and Southerners, that delayed action in January 1947 on whether to allow Bilbo to take his seat.

Bilbo's return to the Senate remained uncertain throughout the first half of 1947. Even though he had several more operations, one of which removed part of his jawbone, Bilbo kept insisting he would return to Washington to reclaim his seat in Congress. But he never made it back. He died in August of peripheral neuritis, a complication of his cancer surgeries. Five thousand mourners, including the entire Mississippi political establishment, attended his funeral in south Mississippi, a ceremony paid for by the US Senate. The minister who preached at the service said Bilbo "died a martyr to the ... real, true principles of American Democracy." Bilbo could have written this claim himself, but it hardly rang true for the thousands of Americans who had fought a terrible war for a more expansive form of democracy than Bilbo's narrow, whites-only vision. And in the end, it turned out Bilbo exaggerated his impoverishment; his estate was worth $100,000 (more than $1.2 million in 2022). Three months after Bilbo's death, his Mississippi colleague, Senator Jim Eastland, offered a resolution in the Senate conveying "profound sorrow and deep regret" over Bilbo's passing. The declaration passed unanimously.[49]

In Georgia, the brutal slaying of the two Monroe couples a week after Talmadge's election attracted the most federal attention in that state. President Truman, reportedly "horrified" when he heard about the killings, ordered his attorney general, Tom Clark, to mobilize the US Justice Department to investigate the murders, as well as "any other crimes of oppression." Clark called the murders "an affront to decent Americanism. Only due process of law sustains our claim to orderly self-government." Both the FBI and the Georgia Bureau of Investigation launched a full-press probe to uncover the killers of the four Black citizens. The FBI interviewed 2,500 people as part of its investigation. In December, the case went to a federal grand jury of twenty-one white men and two Black men, but after three weeks of testimony, the jury still could not positively identify any of the killers, so it issued no indictments. On other matters, such as the obstacles faced by Black voters during the 1946 Georgia Democratic primary campaign and election, the response of the Truman administration remained more muted. Despite the coordinated and sustained effort by white leaders in Georgia to suppress the Black vote, the federal government claimed it could do little to hold Talmadge or his supporters accountable. Although the FBI collected significant evidence of a statewide conspiracy managed by the Talmadge campaign to purge voter registration lists of Black voters, the Justice Department concluded that existing federal statutes remained too weak to sustain a prosecution.[50]

Federal officials believed they could mount a case in Georgia only if they secured incriminating evidence from Eugene Talmadge or his son Herman. Two of the three US attorneys in Georgia thought that the federal government could only successfully prosecute the Talmadges if one or both of them would admit in an interview "that they had formed a conspiracy to keep the negroes from voting in Georgia." That outcome seemed unlikely, but federal officials struggled to decide whether they should even interview the men. FBI agents in Georgia warned director J. Edgar Hoover to tread lightly in dealing with Talmadge. The Georgia feds pointed out that the US government would have to deal with the Georgia demagogue soon as the leader of Georgia's government, and if the feds tried to interview Talmadge or his son, they would simply cry "states' rights" to delegitimize the federal investigation. Once Eugene Talmadge got wind of the federal inquiry, he did indeed attack the effort—by claiming he did not need to engage in a conspiracy to suppress the Black vote. Talmadge suggested that white Democrats "are by precept opposed to Negro participation in white Democratic primaries and none of them had to be told or led to take the necessary steps to remove those who were not qualified, and who were forced into the party." The investigation of Black voter suppression in Georgia, generally unnoted by the national press, soon ended.[51]

Beyond the unsuccessful federal investigation of the 1946 Democratic primary race in Georgia, local groups in the state attacked the county-unit system, which had defeated both James Carmichael and Helen Mankin as well as diluted the state's Black vote. In the weeks after the election, an interracial group, Georgia Veterans for Majority Rule (GVMR), organized to challenge the county-unit arrangement. Assisted by Margaret Fisher of the Southern Conference for Human Welfare and Lucy Randolph Mason of the CIO, the GVMR quickly engineered the filing of two federal lawsuits, one seeking an injunction against Talmadge's election and the other seeking an order invalidating the election of James C. Davis, Mankin's opponent. Both legal actions maintained that the county-unit system violated the equal protection clause of the Fourteenth Amendment. Mankin, though a longtime opponent of the county-unit system, tried to get her attorney to dismiss the lawsuit filed on her behalf. Because of the election dispute, she had recently convinced the Fifth Congressional District Democratic Committee to place her name on the November ballot, along with Davis's, and she thought the lawsuit might lead to a reversal of that decision. In an August 26 decision, the three-judge panel agreed that the county-unit system created "glaring inequality" among Georgia's voters, but it upheld the voting method, noting that "our system of government, state and federal, has never sought nor demanded that each voter should have equal voting influence, though that might seem an ideal of democracy." In October, a divided US Supreme Court declined to hear an appeal of the cases, clearing the way for victories by Talmadge and Davis in November.[52]

As the courts pondered how to resolve the three-governors controversy in Georgia that followed Talmadge's untimely death, Ellis Arnall disengaged from the battle and resumed his quest for national prominence. His book about the newest of New Souths, *The Shore Dimly Seen*, published the day after the November 1946 election, quickly garnered national attention. The *New York Times*, *The New Yorker*, and other prominent publications favorably reviewed the book, and Arnall wrote articles for national outlets such as the *Atlantic* highlighting the book's themes. National pundits embraced the Georgian as a "spokesman for the New South." His message of economic uplift and diversification for the South—rather than the racial retrenchment preached by Bilbo and Talmadge—resonated with audiences beyond the South. A book reviewer for *Newsweek* approved of Arnall's analysis of the region: "He [Arnall] thinks there really is no 'Negro problem,' but a national minorities problem. Eventually, when its economy is straightened out, the South will have little to worry about." Others, however, saw little to applaud in Arnall's analysis of life in the South. Ruth Wilson, a white author writing in the NAACP's *Crisis* in May 1947, called Arnall a "phony liberal" and asked,

"How dimly does Ellis Arnall see? . . . Is his sight so dim that he has not seen the civil rights of Negroes customarily disregarded?" Following the gubernatorial controversy in Georgia in January 1947, sales of Arnall's book rose 75 percent. In late February, it sold 1,000 copies a week, and *Publisher's Weekly* touted it as future best-seller. During late 1946 and early 1947, Arnall also undertook a lecture tour of more than forty cities that earned him tens of thousands of dollars.[53]

In 1946, Ellis Arnall and Theodore Bilbo each envisioned a future path for the South shaped in response to the transformations of World War II. Arnall sought to build on the economic changes wrought by the war. He wanted to move Georgia toward more reliance on industry, operating within a national environment without regional handicaps such as the freight-rate differential. He favored some limited reforms of the state's racial arrangements, most notably extending the vote to Black citizens. He refused to consider an end to racial segregation, although he did support an improvement in segregated services and facilities. Arnall hoped that any real consideration of racial matters could be laid aside in favor of his economic project. A rising economic tide would lift all boats, making any direct confrontation with racial segregation unnecessary. These plans fit nicely with those of national liberals, who also hoped that a steadily improving economy would obviate the need to address lingering social problems. Although national Democrats viewed Arnall as perhaps the best hope for a new kind of southern politics, few other politicians in the region embraced the Arnall approach of incremental racial reform and southern economic development.

Bilbo drew different lessons from the four years of economic and social turmoil that accompanied World War II. To Bilbo, the war represented a full-frontal assault on the South's institutions, and he vowed to organize the manning of the barricades to repel the attack. Much of his concern centered on the challenges to the existing system of race relations the war encouraged, developments that threatened to undermine not only segregation and disfranchisement but what he deemed the very survival of white civilization. Bilbo had a defensive and backward-looking vision for the future, which generated national animosity directed pointedly at him. He became the symbol for the South's devotion to its long-held embrace of the values of the past, and many people outside the South in 1946, after all the upheaval of the war years, found that kind of unbendable traditionalism decidedly unreasonable. Bilbo, however, saw himself as a martyr to preserving the righteous cause of white supremacy. As he told a New York woman in

1946, he submitted to all the criticisms he faced because he felt he had to "let the white people of this country know what they are facing."[54]

Neither Bilbo nor Arnall saw his vision for the South completely fulfilled. In Bilbo's 1946 Senate re-election campaign, he pressed for his fellow white Mississippians to limit Black voting. Bilbo won his election, but his inflammatory rhetoric led to an investigation by the US Senate (as well as another Senate investigation into his self-serving entanglements with war contractors). His victory in Mississippi suggested the continuing strength of white supremacy in the Deep South, but the congressional voting investigation indicated a new level of federal concern to protect the efforts by Black Mississippians—heightened during the war—to secure the right to vote. Although it would take Black activists almost two decades of struggle to totally banish the Bilbo dream of maintaining American apartheid, Black Mississippians breached the walls guarding white supremacy's front lines in the state in 1946. Much to the chagrin of Bilbo and other white Southerners, after World War II, there would be no return to a world where white supremacy was so secure it needed no defense.

Arnall's dreams for the future also came crashing down in the 1946 Georgia gubernatorial election. He hoped that the election of his progressive protégé, James Carmichael, would continue the Arnall plan: deemphasizing racial matters in favor of improving the economy of Georgia and the South. Carmichael, however, not only lost the election because of Georgia's undemocratic county-unit voting system, but Eugene Talmadge mounted a campaign that led to a revival in Georgia of both racial violence and white supremacy groups. Arnall continued to intrigue national observers as the political incarnation of a South that looked more like the rest of the country—a perception that continued for a brief time to give Georgia a progressive sheen Mississippi never had. After 1946, however, Arnall had no political base in Georgia, which hampered his efforts to secure any kind of national political office. Herman Talmadge won the 1948 gubernatorial election and mounted a strong defense of white supremacy, one that Bilbo would have viewed as a hopeful sign for the survival of the white race. Arnall lived until 1992, but he never held public office again.[55]

Epilogue

The home front battles of World War II in the Deep South produced both winners and losers, some clear outcomes as well as some inconclusive results. Wartime mobilization brought significant change to the region's economy, while further embedding the elite, white control of economic life that had characterized the South since the antebellum period. The coming of war plants and military camps to the Deep South completed the agricultural revolution begun in the region during the 1930s. Southern agriculture, which had defined the region's economy for more than a century, looked much different by the end of World War II than it had at the beginning of the Great Depression. Large growers, who had long relied on a ready supply of cheap labor—especially Black farm laborers, tenants, and sharecroppers—accelerated their move toward diversifying and mechanizing farming operations.

Federal war policy helped the Deep South's major agricultural interests weather this transition, by shielding the rural labor market from the worst impacts of out-migration caused by economic and military mobilization and by propping up commodity prices, especially for cotton. Federal agricultural policy during World War II did much less to support the more numerous small farming operations in the Deep South, further abetting the postwar movement toward capital-intensive and large agricultural concerns, a trend that continued to accelerate over the next three decades and that largely benefited a relatively small number of agriculturalists. As a result, the rural out-migration that began during World War II continued in the decades that followed. Millions left the region's rural districts between 1940 and 1980 and never returned.[1]

World War II also provided a new wave of industrial growth in the Deep South. While much of the federal investment in economic mobilization during World War II created industrial concerns that did not outlast the war, some continued to thrive in the postwar years and even continue as important economic concerns today. Ingalls Shipbuilding in Pascagoula diversified its production and became Mississippi's largest postwar employer. Other war plants were repurposed; after a few years of inactivity, the Bell Bomber Plant in Marietta, Georgia, re-emerged by the early 1950s as a major part of the Lockheed Corporation's aircraft manufacturing business.

After the war, the federal government continued to pump money into the region's economy, primarily to support the military-industrial complex associated with the Cold War; this spending further helped fuel industrial expansion in the Deep South. During the 1950s, 20 percent of the income growth in Mississippi came from federal spending. In the 1960s, the National Aeronautics and Space Agency located its major facilities in the South, including operations in Mississippi and Alabama. At the same time, after World War II, communities in the Deep South accelerated their efforts to attract industry to the region—an increasing imperative as agricultural employment declined. Business leaders touted the region as a low-wage, anti-union haven for established industrial concerns elsewhere in the nation. In a sense, Ingalls Shipbuilding, which kept wages as low as possible and labor unions at arm's length during the war, represented a model for postwar employers in the Deep South to emulate.[2]

As war towns developed during World War II in the Deep South in places like Pascagoula, the federal government provided help with the problems associated with rapid industrialization and urbanization—in areas such as housing, health care, and public education. In the postwar era, Deep South states continued to rely on federal aid to help alleviate economic and social challenges, even as politicians in the region increasingly railed against "big government" and federal interference. The South, however, needed continued federal help in the postwar era. Despite the increased prosperity that Sunbelt industrialization and urbanization brought to the Deep South, the economic benefits remained unevenly distributed (as they did nationally). In 1986, the Southern Growth Policies Board noted the growing divide that defined the South's postwar economy: "The sunshine on the Sunbelt has proved to be a narrow beam of light, brightening futures along the Atlantic Seaboard, and in large cities, but skipping over many small towns and rural areas." Racial inequity remained a major economic impediment for the Deep South in the postwar decades, much as it had during World War II. As long as the region continued to focus energy on keeping Black people down, it could never fully prosper. In its devotion to white supremacy, the Deep South created a self-inflicted economic wound of profound proportions, one that could not be healed by simply adjusting regionally discriminatory railroad rates or attracting more low-wage industry to the region.[3]

During World War II, the federal government played a major role in the racial battles fought on the Deep South home front. At the outset of the conflict, the federal government proclaimed its support for nondiscrimination in the huge projects of economic and military mobilization. Rather than a direct challenge to legal racial segregation in the South and the de facto version of racial separation elsewhere, the nondiscrimination provisions of the Selective Service and Training Act of 1940 and the Fair Employment Practices Committee (FEPC) of 1941 supported the separate but equal mandate of the US Supreme Court's 1896 decision in *Plessy v. Ferguson*. That racial standard had rarely been upheld, yet the federal government called for its implementation as part of the mobilization for World War II. In one sense, federal action in this area seemed quite bold, worthy of a country that proclaimed it fought against totalitarianism to preserve freedom and democracy. The nondiscrimination efforts of the US government during the war, however, had only limited success.

By the end of the war, the US military had made some small, but significant, advances in ending discrimination within its own units and its own facilities. But the military fell far short of ending unequal treatment for Black soldiers, especially in locations like the Deep South, where surrounding white communities rejected the idea of nondiscrimination entirely. The federal effort to end employment discrimination during the war had even less success in the Deep South than in other parts of the country. While the military answered directly to the national government and faced more pressure to implement nondiscrimination measures, when it came to economic discrimination, the federal government had to convince private employers to abandon long-standing prejudices against non-white workers and end a system of unequal economic opportunity.

Employers across the nation, particularly in the South, fiercely resisted the nondiscrimination recommendations of the FEPC, a government agency that had no enforcement powers. Only when the massive economic and military mobilization project created a severe labor shortage (sometime in 1943) did Black men and women start to secure a significant share of war jobs. And once the conflict ended, even those delayed gains quickly evaporated. White Southerners—and their northern allies—blocked efforts at the end of the war to establish a permanent FEPC, which could have helped Black Americans secure a more equitable share of postwar employment opportunities. In October 1946, the Mississippi office of the US Employment Service helped fill more than 6,500 nonagricultural jobs. It recommended white people for 86 percent of the professional and skilled jobs and Black citizens for 92 percent of the unskilled positions. African Americans could not even obtain a fair portion of the educational, housing, and health benefits provided by the GI Bill—passed by Congress in 1944 to reward and support all who had served in the World War II military—especially in the South, where white administrators ran the programs. In 1947, of more than 3,000 Veterans Administration home loans approved in Mississippi cities, only two went to Black veterans.[4]

Despite the general failure of the federal government's nondiscrimination efforts during World War II, the existence of the policies and their ineffectiveness helped tarnish the long-term viability of racial segregation. Black Americans, including those in the South, received additional affirmation that racial discrimination could not end without eliminating the system of racial apartheid. By the late 1940s, the National Association for the Advancement of Colored People (NAACP) had shifted its legal assault on racial segregation from trying to enforce separate but equal to attacking the existence of racial segregation head-on. The federal government continued its commitment to the principle of nondiscrimination in the postwar period—in part because of the ideological Cold War that developed with the Soviet Union—but also increasingly rejected racial segregation as incompatible with those ideals. In 1948, President Harry S. Truman issued an executive order that eventually led to the desegregation of the armed forces. Although complete integration of the army did not come until the early 1950s, during the Korean War and only after President Truman replaced General Douglas MacArthur with General Matthew B. Ridgway in April 1951, the military became the first major American institution to abolish racial segregation.[5] By the early 1950s, the US Supreme Court signaled its acceptance of the NAACP's new legal strategy, culminating with the decision in *Brown v. Board of Education*, which declared school segregation inherently unconstitutional, a violation of the equal protection clause of the Fourteenth Amendment.

During World War II, a small minority of southern leaders in the Deep South seemed willing to embrace the nondiscrimination approach promoted by the federal government. Georgia governor Ellis Arnall and other southern moderates and liberals agreed that changes in racial relations needed to occur to improve the lives of the Deep South's Black citizens, although the governor did not want to abolish the system of racial segregation. Some of these white leaders, including Arnall, favored expanding voting rights for Black citizens. They wanted the South to spend less time focusing on racial matters to take advantage of the new economic possibilities created by the war, such as increased industrialization. Non-Southerners viewed the Arnall approach as a viable path forward for the South. His views promised to end the worst racial abuses of southern life without directly challenging white supremacy, a stance that resonated with much of the white public nationally, which really had little interest in securing full freedom for Black Americans. Ironically, the Arnall approach would have likely preserved a form of "practical segregation" much longer than the Bilbo-style insistence on total racial separation and openly discriminatory treatment of Black Americans.[6]

As the elections of 1946 in Georgia and Mississippi demonstrated, however, most white Southerners in the Deep South at the end of World War II did not favor putting economic development ahead of preserving racial privilege. They would continue to defend white democracy in the decades that followed. As the federal government increasingly moved from supporting nondiscrimination to opposing racial segregation, Arnall-style white moderation evaporated in the face of calls by southern white political leaders to protect white supremacy. After the national Democratic Party adopted a pro–civil rights plank at its 1948 national convention, white Democrats in the Deep South launched the States' Rights Party (Dixiecrats), which carried the states of Louisiana, Mississippi, Alabama, and South Carolina in the 1948 presidential election. After the *Brown* decision in 1954, white Southerners avidly supported a massive resistance movement to halt school desegregation, which delayed the end of dual schools until the early 1970s. But Black communities, often led by military veterans, also continued to mobilize and fight for the next two decades to end the undemocratic practices of racial segregation and Black disfranchisement.

The racial battle line drawn across America's home front in World War II—to ensure a greater measure of democracy for all citizens or to preserve white democracy—saw sustained skirmishes in the two decades after the overseas fighting ended. The federal government continued to aid the Black freedom struggle, often reluctantly and generally when faced with criticism about its commitment to promote democracy in its fight against the totalitarianism of its communist enemy, the Soviet Union. White southern moderates and liberals—as well as most white Northerners—offered only lackluster and generally silent support for racial change. Although Black activists eventually succeeded in ridding the country of legal segregation and the most overt forms of Black disfranchisement, they did not completely vanquish the white supremacy that Theodore Bilbo had worked tirelessly to preserve.

Acknowledgments

This project would not have been possible without the help of many others. As usual, the patient assistance and deep knowledge of librarians and archivists—from the Jackson Library at the University of North Carolina Greensboro (UNCG) to the National Archives and many other locales—proved indispensable in locating and accessing the evidence that undergirds this narrative. I would especially like to thank Jennifer Brannock and Andrew Rhodes of the Special Collections department at the University of Southern Mississippi for their unfailing helpfulness as I worked through scores of boxes in the Bilbo and Colmer Papers.

Numerous friends, colleagues, and family members read various drafts of the manuscript and/or provided lodgings and fellowship during research trips, including Curtis Austin, Chip and Jennifer Bolton, Lynn Bolton, Brad Bond, Kevin Farrell, Mary Beth and Sean Farrell, Watson Jennison, Jeff Jones, Scott Thompson, and Tom Ward. The two anonymous readers for Oxford University Press offered essential suggestions for improvement, Meghan Drury provided critical recommendations about how to downsize a lengthy manuscript, and Jeffrey Patton crafted the excellent maps. John Z. Kiss, dean of UNCG's College of Arts and Sciences, supplied both financial and moral support for my work. Nancy Toff of Oxford University Press encouraged this project when I first mentioned it to her many years ago at a conference, and she has given indispensable and timely aid ever since at every stage of the publication process.

A special thanks to my wife, Leslie, who has offered not only consistent support for this project but also more than thirty years of encouragement and faith. Finally, I dedicate this book to my teachers. I have had many wonderful ones over the course of my life, but my Hall of Fame includes Clyde Dease, Shirley Stough, Terry Harper, Neil McMillen, Ted Schmidt, Bill Chafe, Ray Gavins, and Larry Goodwyn.

Notes

Abbreviations

ADAH	Alabama Department of Archives and History, Montgomery
Army-AG	Army-AG Decimal File 1940–45, Records of the Adjutant General's Office, 1917–, Record Group 407, National Archives, College Park, Maryland.
AU: FDR	Archives Unbound: Franklin D. Roosevelt and Race Relations, 1933–1945
AU: NNC	Archives Unbound: African America, Communists, and the National Negro Congress, 1933–1947
BAA	*Baltimore Afro-American*
BAE	Records of the Division of Program Surveys, Project Files, 1940–45, Records of the Bureau of Agricultural Economics, Record Group 83, National Archives, College Park, Maryland
BPUSM	Theodore G. Bilbo Papers, McCain Library and Archives, University of Southern Mississippi, Hattiesburg
CD	*Chicago Defender*
CPUSM	William M. Colmer Papers, McCain Library and Archives, University of Southern Mississippi, Hattiesburg
DDT	*Greenville (Miss.) Delta Democrat-Times*
DPLC	Delta and Pine Land Company Records, Special Collections, Mitchell Memorial Library, Mississippi State University, Starkville
DSU	Charles W. Capps Jr. Archives, Delta State University, Cleveland, Mississippi
DUKE	David M. Rubenstein Rare Book & Manuscript Library, Duke University, Durham, North Carolina
Emory	Stuart A. Rose Manuscript, Archives, and Rare Book Library, Emory University, Atlanta, Georgia
FBI-46 Election	Federal Bureau of Investigation Records on the 1946 Georgia Election, Georgia Historical Society, Savannah
FEP-NA	Selected documents from Records of the Committee on Fair Employment Practice: Record Group 228, National Archives (microfilm)
Hearings, 1943	*Hearings before a Subcommittee of the Committee on Education and Labor, United States Senate, December 16–18, 1943*, 78th Cong.
Hearings, 1946	*Hearings before the Special Committee to Investigate Senatorial Campaign Expenditures, December 2–5, 1946*, 79th Cong.

IAMAW	International Association of Machinists and Aerospace Workers Records, 1901–1974, International President's Office Records (microfilm)
LC	Library of Congress, Washington, DC
MDAH	Mississippi Department of Archives and History, Jackson
NA-ATL	National Archives, Atlanta, Georgia
NA-CP	National Archives, College Park, Maryland
NA-DC	National Archives, Washington, DC
NYAN	*New York Amsterdam News*
NYT	*New York Times*
PQHV-BFS: FGR	ProQuest History Vault, Black Freedom Struggle in the 20th Century: Federal Government Records
PQHV-BFS: ORP1	ProQuest History Vault, Black Freedom Struggle in the 20th Century: Organizational Records and Personal Papers, Part 1
PQHV-NAACP: BDAC	ProQuest History Vault, NAACP Papers: Board of Directors, Annual Conferences, Major Speeches, and National Staff Files
PQHV-NAACP: BDBF	NAACP Papers: Branch Department, Branch Files, and Youth Department Files
PQHV-NAACP: EVH	ProQuest History Vault, NAACP Papers: The NAACP's Major Campaigns—Education, Voting, Housing, Employment, Armed Forces
PQHV-NAACP: SAL	ProQuest History Vault, NAACP Papers: The NAACP's Major Campaigns—Scottsboro, Anti-Lynching, Criminal Justice, Peonage, Labor, and Segregation and Discrimination Complaints and Responses
PQHV-NAACP: SS	ProQuest History Vault, NAACP Papers: Special Subjects
Russell	Richard B. Russell Library for Political Research and Studies, University of Georgia, Athens
SHC	Southern Historical Collection, The Louis Round Wilson Special Collections Library, University of North Carolina at Chapel Hill
SOAL	Doy Leale McCall Rare Book and Manuscript Library, University of South Alabama, Mobile
USMC	Shipbuilding Records of Commissioner Howard L. Vickery, 1941–1945, Records of the United States Maritime Commission, Record Group 178, National Archives, College Park, Maryland
UM	Special Collections, University of Mississippi Libraries, Oxford
WHE	Senate Subcommittee on Wartime Health and Education, Records of the United States Senate, Record Group 46, National Archives, Washington, DC
WMC	Records of the War Manpower Commission, Record Group 211, National Archives, Atlanta, Georgia

Introduction

1. Lawrence J. Nelson, *King Cotton's Advocate: Oscar G. Johnston and the New Deal* (Knoxville: University of Tennessee Press, 1999), ch. 7; Oscar Johnston to John J. Corson, July 6, 1942, and Oscar Johnston to Orrin H. Swayze, February 23, 1942, both in Box 44, DPLC. For an example of how welfare capitalism operated in a northern industrial setting, see Lizabeth Cohen, *Making a New Deal: Industrial Workers in Chicago, 1919–1939*, 2nd ed. (Cambridge: Cambridge University Press, 2008), ch. 4.
2. Oscar Johnston to Harry D. Wilson, January 16, 1942, Oscar Johnston to John E. Mitchell Jr., January 23, 1942, Oscar Johnston to C. E. Bellion, March 25, 1942, D. R. Gavin to G. W. Meek, May 16, 1942, Oscar Johnston to John J. Corson, July 6, 1942, John J. Corson to Oscar Johnston, July 17, 1942, and Oscar Johnston to John J. Corson, July 21, 1942, all in Box 44, DPLC; Nelson, *King Cotton's Advocate*, 229; James E. Pate, "Mobilizing Manpower," *Social Forces* 22 (December 1943): 154–162.
3. Documents in the case of David Reed, Box 15, Series 23, WMC.
4. As used in this study, "Deep South" refers to the states of Louisiana, Mississippi, Alabama, and Georgia.
5. US Department of Agriculture, Census of Agriculture Historical Archive, 1940 Census Publications, http://agcensus.mannlib.cornell.edu/AgCensus/censusParts.do?year=1940; Farm Population in the South, 1940, excerpt from the *Southern Agriculturalist*, Box 46, Ralph E. McGill Papers, Emory; A. D. Stewart, "Some Background Facts on Mississippi Agriculture and Farm Living Conditions," n.d., 1943, Box 1027, BPUSM; Walter W. Wilcox, *The Farmer in the Second World War* (Ames: Iowa State College Press, 1947), 13.
6. Edward L. Ayers, *The Promise of the New South: Life after Reconstruction* (New York: Oxford University Press, 1992), ch. 5; US Census Bureau, 1940 Census of Population: Vol. 1, https://www.census.gov/library/publications/1942/dec/population-vol-1.html.
7. Douglas A. Blackmon, *Slavery by Another Name: The Re-Enslavement of Black Americans from the Civil War to World War II* (New York: Doubleday, 2008); J. Morgan Kousser, *The Shaping of Southern Politics: Suffrage Restriction and the Establishment of the One-Party South, 1880–1910* (New Haven, CT: Yale University Press, 1974); Neil R. McMillen, *Dark Journey: Black Mississippians in the Age of Jim Crow* (Urbana: University of Illinois Press, 1990), part IV.
8. Pete Daniel, *Breaking the Land: The Transformation of Cotton, Tobacco, and Rice Cultures since 1880* (Urbana: University of Illinois Press, 1986), esp. ch. 5 and 8; Roger Biles, *The South and the New Deal* (Lexington: University of Kentucky Press, 1994), ch. 3; Nelson, *King Cotton's Advocate*, ch. 7.
9. Biles, *The South and the New Deal*, ch. 4, 6, and 8; Ira Katznelson, *Fear Itself: The New Deal and the Origins of Our Time* (New York: W. W. Norton, 2013), part II. Harvard Sitkoff, in *A New Deal for Blacks: The Emergence of Civil Rights as a National Issue: The Depression Decade* (New York: Oxford University Press, 1978), ix, notes that "For civil rights, the depression decade proved to be a time of planting, not harvesting."
10. "The Good War," *NYT*, August 31, 1989; Tracy Campbell, *The Year of Peril: America in 1942* (New Haven, CT: Yale University Press, 2020); Studs Terkel, *"The Good War": An Oral History of World War II* (New York: New Press, 1984); John Bodnar,

The "Good War" in American Memory (Baltimore: Johns Hopkins University Press, 2010); Michael C. C. Adams, *The Best War Ever: America and World War II*, 2nd ed. (Baltimore: Johns Hopkins University Press, 2015).

11. Gilbert C. Fite, *Cotton Fields No More: Southern Agriculture, 1865–1980* (Lexington: University Press of Kentucky, 1984), ch. 6–7; Bruce J. Schulman, *From Cotton Belt to Sunbelt: Federal Policy, Economic Development, and the Transformation of the South, 1938–1980* (New York: Oxford University Press, 1991); James C. Cobb, *The Most Southern Place on Earth: The Mississippi Delta and the Roots of Regional Identity* (New York: Oxford University Press, 1992).

12. Alfred J. Wright, "Recent Changes in the Concentration of Manufacturing," *Annals of the Association of American Geographers* 35 (December 1945): 159–162; Dillard B. Lasseter, "The Impact of the War on the South and Implications for Postwar Developments," *Social Forces* 23 (October 1944): 21; Pete Daniel, "Going among Strangers: Southern Reactions to World War II," *Journal of American History* 77 (December 1990): 886–911.

13. Merl E. Reed, *Seedtime for the Modern Civil Rights Movement: The President's Committee on Fair Employment Practice, 1941–1946* (Baton Rouge: Louisiana State University Press, 1991); Richard M. Dalfiume, *Desegregation of the U.S. Armed Forces: Fighting on Two Fronts, 1939–1953* (Columbia: University of Missouri Press, 1969); Sherie Mershon and Steven Schlossman, *Foxholes & Color Lines: Desegregating the U.S. Armed Forces* (Baltimore: Johns Hopkins University Press, 1998).

14. Reed, *Seedtime for the Modern Civil Rights Movement*, introduction; Patricia Sullivan, *Lift Every Voice: The NAACP and the Making of the Civil Rights Movement* (New York: New Press, 2009), 253–255; Executive Order 8802, https://www.eeoc.gov/history/executive-order-8802. The name of the committee created by Executive Order 8802 was officially the President's Committee on Fair Employment Practice. In May 1943, President Roosevelt reorganized the committee with Executive Order 9346, and the committee was renamed the Fair Employment Practices Committee. See Reed, *Seedtime for the Modern Civil Rights Movement*, 10. For the sake of simplicity, the latter name is used throughout this work.

15. Frederick Douglass, *The Life and Times of Frederick Douglass* (Radford, VA: Wilder Publications, 2008), 222; Manning Marable, *W. E. B. Du Bois: Black Radical Democrat*, updated ed. (New York: Routledge, 2005), 97; Bernard C. Nalty, *Strength for the Fight: A History of Black Americans in the Military* (New York: Free Press, 1986); Robert B. Edgerton, *Hidden Heroism: Black Soldiers in America's Wars* (Boulder, CO: Westview Press, 2001); Kara Dixon Vuic, "Gender, the Military, and War," in *At War: The Military and American Culture in the Twentieth Century and Beyond*, ed. David Kieran and Edwin A Martini (New Brunswick, NJ: Rutgers University Press, 2018), 201.

16. Patrick S. Washburn, "The *Pittsburgh Courier*'s Double V Campaign in 1942," *American Journalism* 3 (1986): 73–86; Sullivan, *Lift Every Voice*, ch. 7; World War II Rumor Project Collection, 1942–1943, Library of Congress, https://www.loc.gov/resource/afc1945001.afc1945001_ms07107/?sp=35; Kevin M. Kruse and Stephen Tuck, eds., *Fog of War: The Second World War and the Civil Rights Movement*

(New York: Oxford University Press, 2012), 6–7; Jacquelyn Dowd Hall, "The Long Civil Rights Movement and the Political Uses of the Past," *Journal of American History* 91 (March 2005): 1233–1263. Also see Stephen G. N. Tuck, *Beyond Atlanta: The Struggle for Racial Equality in Georgia, 1940–1980* (Athens: University of Georgia Press, 2001), ch. 1.

17. Charles L. Zelden, *The Battle for the Black Ballot: Smith v. Allwright and the Defeat of the Texas All White Primary* (Lawrence: University Press of Kansas, 2004); Jennifer E. Brooks, *Defining the Peace: World War II Veterans, Race, and the Remaking of Southern Political Tradition* (Chapel Hill: University of North Carolina Press, 2004); Steven F. Lawson, *Black Ballots: Voting Rights in the South, 1944–1969* (New York: Columbia University Press, 1976), ch. 4.

18. Patricia Sullivan, *Days of Hope: Race and Democracy in the New Deal Era* (Chapel Hill: University of North Carolina Press, 1996); William A. Link, "Frank Porter Graham, Racial Gradualism, and the Dilemmas of Southern Liberalism," *Journal of Southern History* 86 (February 2020): 10–18.

19. Jason Morgan Ward, *Defending Democracy: The Making of a Segregationist Movement and the Remaking of Racial Politics, 1936–1965* (Chapel Hill: University of North Carolina Press, 2011).

Chapter 1

1. Elmo Scott Watson, "Keeping Up the Fourth Estate," *The Rotarian*, November 1943, 40; Sara Elizabeth Morris, "Working to Save the Farm: Indiana and Mississippi Rural Women, 1940–1990" (PhD diss., Purdue University, 2011), 85; "Wickard Accepts Invitation to Open Nation-wide Thanks for Harvest," *Victory*, September 22, 1942; "Farm Crop Limit Hinted by Wickard," *NYT*, October 4, 1942; *Food for Freedom: Informational Handbook, 1943* (Washington, DC: US Department of Agriculture, 1942), 3.

2. Daniel Kryder, *Divided Arsenal: Race and the American State during World War II* (Cambridge: Cambridge University Press, 2000), 212–213; John C. Culver, *American Dreamer: A Life of Henry A. Wallace* (New York: W. W. Norton, 2001), 227; Charles Kenneth Roberts, *The Farm Security Administration and Rural Rehabilitation in the South* (Knoxville: University of Tennessee Press, 2015), ch. 9.

3. Pete Daniel, "Going among Strangers: Southern Reactions to World War II," *Journal of American History* 77 (December 1990): 886; Morton Sosna, "Introduction," in *Remaking Dixie: The Impact of World War II on the American South*, ed. Neil R. McMillen (Jackson: University Press of Mississippi, 1997), xv; Bruce J. Schulman, *From Cotton Belt to Sunbelt: Federal Policy, Economic Development, and the Transformation of the South, 1938–1980* (New York: Oxford University Press, 1991), 101; Harry Schwartz, "Hired Farm Labor in World War II," *Journal of Farm Economics* 24 (November 1942): 828; James N. Gregory, *The Southern Diaspora: How the Great Migrations of Black and White Southerners Transformed America* (Chapel

Hill: University of North Carolina Press, 2005), ch. 1; James C. Cobb, *Industrialization and Southern Society, 1877–1984* (Lexington: University of Kentucky Press, 1984), 51–52; John W. Jeffries, *Wartime America: The World War II Home Front* (Chicago: Ivan R. Dee, 1996), 79; Roger W. Lotchin and David R. Long, "World War II and the Transformation of Southern Urban Society: A Reconsideration," *Georgia Historical Quarterly* 83 (Spring 1999): 29–57; Office of War Information, Report on Wartime Migration, April 1944, Box 254, Records of Clyde M. Vandeburg, Records of the Office of War Information, Record Group 208, DC-CP. Also see Isabel Wilkerson, *The Warmth of Other Suns: The Epic Story of America's Great Migration* (New York: Vintage Books, 2010), which offers a detailed examination of Black migration in twentieth-century America, including during the World War II era.
4. Wilkerson, *The Warmth of Other Suns*, 177–179.
5. This portrait of the impact of economic mobilization during World War II on the population of northeast Mississippi is drawn from nineteen interviews conducted with a cross-section of residents from Tishomingo, Alcorn, and Lafayette Counties in 1944 by the BAE. The interviewer reports on these conversations are in Box 3, BAE (hereinafter referred to as Northeast Mississippi Migration Stories). The interviewees included four Black tenants/laborers, four white farmers (small holdings), four white tenants, three white farmers (large holdings), and three white agricultural officials (an FSA supervisor, a county extension agent, and an agricultural field man for the Tennessee Valley Authority).
6. This portrait of the impact of economic mobilization during World War II on the population of the Mississippi Delta is drawn from ten interviews conducted with a cross-section of residents from Coahoma County in 1944 by the BAE. The interviewer reports on these conversations are in Box 3, BAE (hereinafter referred to as Coahoma County Migration Stories). The interviewees included three Black sharecroppers, one Black teacher, one white planter, one white plantation manager, two people from white sharecropper families, and two white agricultural officials (a female FSA office assistant and an administrative officer for the AAA).
7. Northeast Mississippi Migration Stories.
8. "Negro Farmers Learn to Be Self-Sufficient," n.d., 1943, reel 81, Tuskegee Institute News Clippings File; "Sir William Gives Advice," *Southern Frontier*, July 1943; Claude A. Barnett and F. D. Patterson to Claude R. Wickard, June 26, 1942, and "Study Conditions among Negro Farmers" (press release), May 14, 1942, both in PQHV-BFS: ORP1; Coahoma County Migration Stories; Annual Report of Delta Council, 1943–1944, 41, Box 1, Delta Council Collection, DSU.
9. Roscoe Arant, "The Southeastern States in a War Economy," Box 1, Governor's Subject Files, Office of the Governor, Georgia Archives, Atlanta. Arant was a Regional Business Consultant for the US Department of Commerce, and his territory included Alabama, Georgia, Florida, southern Mississippi, southern Louisiana, and eastern Tennessee.
10. W. G. Hood (County Agent), "Farm Talk," *Anniston (Ala.) Star*, September 14, 1941; Letter from D. E. Whittington to Theodore Bilbo, February 4, 1942, Box 1025,

BPUSM; Lawrence J. Nelson, *King Cotton's Advocate: Oscar G. Johnston and the New Deal* (Knoxville: University of Tennessee Press, 1999), 229.
11. W. R. Brumfield to Theodore Bilbo, January 26, 1942, Box 1025, Joe C. Watson to Theodore Bilbo, February 26, 1942, Box 1025, and Theodore Bilbo to Joe C. Watson, March 2, 1942, Box 1125, all in BPUSM. The WPA was originally called the Works Progress Administration when it was created in 1935, but the name of the agency was changed to Work Projects Administration in 1939.
12. Joe L. Teaver to Theodore Bilbo, April 5, 1943, Box 768, BPUSM; Annual Report of Delta Council, 1943-1944, 11; Coahoma County Migration Stories.
13. Northeast Mississippi Migration Stories; Coahoma County Migration Stories.
14. Hood, "Farm Talk"; "Survey Shows City Attracting Many Migrants," *Atlanta Constitution*, February 1942, reel 78, Tuskegee Institute News Clippings File; "Fall Harvest Gets Underway," *Yank: The Army Newspaper*, October 7, 1942, Service Newspapers of World War II, Adam Matthew Digital; "150 Soldiers to Harvest Crops in Sandersville," *Atlanta Daily World*, August 19, 1943; "Thomas County Farmers Seek City Folks' Aid," *Atlanta Constitution*, August 27, 1943; Otey M. Scruggs, "The Bracero Program under the Farm Security Administration, 1942-1943," *Labor History* 3 (Spring 1962): 149-168; Nan Elizabeth Woodruff, *American Congo: The African American Freedom Struggle in the Delta* (Cambridge, MA: Harvard University Press, 2003), 203.
15. Press release, September 3, 1943, Box 583, Records of Clyde M. Vandeburg; Judy Barrett Litoff and David C. Smith, "'To the Rescue of the Crops': The Women's Land Army during World War II," *Prologue* 25 (Winter 1993): 347-358; Stephanie A. Carpenter, *On the Farm Front: The Women's Land Army in World War II* (DeKalb: Northern Illinois University Press, 2003), ch. 8.
16. Uncle Percy Ray to T. G. Abernathy [sic], June 30, 1943, and J. H. Friend to Thomas G. Abernathy [sic] (telegram), June 12, 1943, both in Box 414, Thomas G. Abernathy Collection, UM; J. H. Faison to James O. Eastland, July 2, 1943, and James O. Eastland to W. T. Wynn, June 22, 1943, both in Box 124, Series 3, Subseries 1, James Oliver Eastland Collection, UM; Annual Report of Delta Council, 1943-1944, 11; Jason Morgan Ward, "'Nazis Hoe Cotton': Planters, POWs, and the Future of Farm Labor in the Deep South," *Agricultural History* 81 (Fall 2007): 471-492; Dennis J. Mitchell, *A New History of Mississippi* (Jackson: University Press of Mississippi, 2014), 372.
17. David E. Bernstein, *Only One Place of Redress: African Americans, Labor Regulations, and the Courts from Reconstruction to the New Deal* (Durham, NC: Duke University Press, 2001), ch. 1; "How Not to Get Workers," *Time*, October 19, 1942; "Georgia Jails Personnel Agent, Fine Company $1,000," *Southern Patriot*, February/March 1943; Herbert Roback, "Legal Barriers to Interstate Migration," *Cornell Law Quarterly* 28 (1942-1943): 286-312; Annual Report of Delta Council, 1943-1944, 11.
18. Douglas A. Blackmon, *Slavery by Another Name: The Re-Enslavement of Black Americans from the Civil War to World War II* (New York: Doubleday, 2008), part 2; Woodruff, *American Congo*, 195-197; Coahama County Migration Stories; Michael J. Klarman, *From Jim Crow to Civil Rights: The Supreme Court and the Struggle for Racial Equality* (New York: Oxford University Press, 2006), 86-88; Charles S. Johnson, *To*

Stem This Tide: A Survey of Racial Tension Areas in the United States (Boston: Pilgrim Press, 1943), 27.

19. Lonnie Frank Kimbrough affidavit, January 2, 1945, reel 22, Peonage Files, US Department of Justice.
20. Lonnie Frank Kimbrough affidavit, January 2, 1945; Lonnie Kimbrough affidavit, n.d., fall 1944, reel 11, Peonage Files; "Chicago Judge Frees Plantation Fugitive, Denounces System," *Atlanta Daily World*, December 12, 1944.
21. George Q. Flynn, *The Mess in Washington: Manpower Mobilization in World War II* (Westport, CT: Greenwood Press, 1979), ch. 6; Committee Representing Lowndes County Farmers to Theodore G. Bilbo, January 13, 1942, Box 1049, BPUSM.
22. Louis J. Ducoff et al., "Effect of the War on the Agricultural Working Force and on the Rural-Farm Population," *Social Forces* 21 (May 1943): 408; Albert A. Blum, "The Farmer, the Army and the Draft," *Agricultural History* 38 (January 1964): 35–39; "Senators Rebuff Military Leaders," *Baltimore Sun*, March 12, 1943; Lloyd G. Reynolds, "Labor Problems of a Defense Economy," *American Economic Review* 40 (May 1950): 228.
23. Cobb, *The Most Southern Place on Earth*, 199; Flynn, *The Mess in Washington*, ch. 6; Northeast Mississippi Migration Stories.
24. Woodruff, *American Congo*, 203; Coahoma County Migration Stories.
25. Blum, "The Farmer, the Army and the Draft," 36–39; "Senators Rebuff Military Leaders"; Clip Sheet, "Federal Legislation on Farm Labor," March 31, 1943, Folder 42, Jesse Daniel Ames Papers, 1866–1972, SHC, https://finding-aids.lib.unc.edu/03686/#folder_42#1; "Sees Slavery Threat in Newest Labor Bills," *Cleveland Call and Post*, April 3, 1943; "National War Service," *NYT*, February 9, 1943; "U.S. Scraps Measuring System for Deferring Farm Workers," *Atlanta Constitution*, March 30, 1944.
26. "War Manpower Developments: Regulation of Enlistment of Men in Federal Posts and War Industry," *Journal* (American Water Works Association) 34 (November 1942): 1735; Charles D. Chamberlain, *Victory at Home: Manpower and Race in the American South during World War II* (Athens: University of Georgia Press, 2003), ch. 3; Annual Report of Delta Council, 1943–1944, 11.
27. David M. Kennedy, *The American People in World War II: Freedom from Fear, Part Two* (New York: Oxford University Press, 1999), 215–216; Andrew H. Bartels, "The Office of Price Administration and the Legacy of the New Deal, 1939–1946," *Public Historian* 5 (Summer 1983): 12–19; David Ginsburg, "The Emergency Price Control Act of 1942: Basic Authority and Sanctions," *Law and Contemporary Problems* 9 (Winter 1942): 39–43; Walter L. Randolph to John H. Bankhead, January 30, 1942, Box 6, John Hollis Bankhead Papers, ADAH; Meg Jacobs, *Pocketbook Politics: Economic Citizenship in Twentieth-Century America* (Princeton, NJ: Princeton University Press, 2005), ch. 5.
28. Kryder, *Divided Arsenal*, 213; Morris H. Hansen, *Statistical Abstract of the United States, 1943* (Washington, DC: Department of Commerce, 1944), 401; Mitchell, *A New History of Mississippi*, 372; "South Leads the Nation: Increased Value Farm Real Estate," 1943, excerpt from the *Southern Agriculturalist*, Box 46, Ralph E. McGill Papers.

29. Cobb, *The Most Southern Place on Earth*, 200; Walter Sillers to Dorothy Lee Black, March 5, 1945, Box 26, Walter Sillers Jr. Papers, DSU; Interviewer report on conversation with County Agent in Floyd County, Georgia, September 21, 1944, Box 4, BAE.
30. Woodruff, *American Congo*, 207–213; Mitchell, *A New History of Mississippi*, 372; H. L. Mitchell, "A Ceiling on Cotton Pickers' Wages," September 10, 1945, and Leslie Perry to Messrs. Dudley, Hastie and White, October 11, 1945, both in part 13C, reel 2, Papers of the NAACP; Minutes of the Meeting of the Board of Directors, October 8, 1945, PQHV-NAACP: BDAC.
31. A. D. Stewart, "The Farm Security Program in Mississippi," n.d., 1943, Box 1027, BPUSM; "The Nation: Farm Bloc Split," *NYT*, April 18, 1943; "Attitudes toward FSA Tenant Purchase Program," January 1946, Box 11, BAE; John Curl, *For All the People: Uncovering the Hidden History of Cooperation, Cooperative Movements, and Communalism in America*, 2nd ed. (Oakland, CA: PM Press, 2012), 174.
32. John Echeverri-Gent, *The State and the Poor: Public Policy and Political Development in India and the United States* (Berkeley: University of California Press, 1993), 71; *Agricultural Appropriation Bill for 1944: Hearings before the Subcommittee of the Committee on Appropriations, House of Representatives*, 78th Cong. (1943), 1616–1619 (Oscar Johnston testimony); Annual Report of Delta Council, 1943–1944, 38.
33. Nelson, *King Cotton's Advocate*, 216–217; Annual Report of Delta Council, 1943–1944, 38.
34. Bruce J. Reynolds, *Black Farmers in America, 1865–2000: The Pursuit of Independent Farming and the Role of Cooperatives* (Washington, DC: US Department of Agriculture, 2002), Appendix Table 2; "Spread of Tenancy Has Been Checked, Farm Security Official Predicts," *Southern Frontier*, November 1945.
35. Patricia Sullivan, *Days of Hope: Race and Democracy in the New Deal Era* (Chapel Hill: University of North Carolina Press, 1996), 128; "Attack FSA Stand on Poll Tax Loans," *NYT*, February 7, 1942; "Farm Security Office Accused of Aiding Dixie Poll Tax Discrimination," *Philadelphia Tribune*, January 24, 1942; R. K. Greene to E. S. Morgan, January 3, 1942, Box 1027, BPUSM.
36. Arthur Evans, "Anti–New Deal Trend Sighted in Mississippi," *Chicago Daily Tribune*, January 21, 1943; Annual Report of Delta Council, 1943–1944, 38; "Abolition of FSA Credit Funds for Farmers Held Blow to War," *NYT*, April 22, 1943; "Little Farmers Dig In for Victory," *Southern Frontier*, April 1943.
37. Woodruff, *American Congo*, ch. 6; Nelson, *King Cotton's Advocate*, 212–217; "Long-Time Tenure Objectives," May 1941, and Will Whittington to Oscar Johnston, November 28, 1942, both in Box 44, DPLC.
38. "FSA Farmers Led All Others in Increase of Vital War Crops," *Southern Patriot*, May 1943; Stewart, "The Farm Security Program in Mississippi."
39. Roberts, *The Farm Security Administration and Rural Rehabilitation in the South*, ch. 9; "Trouble in Food," *Time*, January 25, 1943; "FSA Borrowers Increase Food Production in '43," *Philadelphia Tribune*, August 5, 1944.
40. Sullivan, *Days of Hope*, 127–129; "The Nation: Farm Bloc Split"; Nelson, *King Cotton's Advocate*, 225; C. P. Trussell, "Farm Security Agency Restored by Senate, 66–12, With Funds," *NYT*, June 11, 1943; *Congressional Record*, June 10, 1943, 5641.

41. *Congressional Record*, June 10, 1943, 5634; W. A. Dallas to Theodore G. Bilbo, April 9, 1943, Box 768; James F. Fail to Theodore G. Bilbo, June 2, 1943, Box 779; and W. E. Tucker to Theodore Bilbo, May 25, 1943, and Theodore Bilbo to W. E. Tucker, both in Box 1027, all in BPUSM.
42. Theodore Bilbo to F. Jeff Eubanks, November 26, 1943, Box 1027, BPUSM; Sullivan, *Days of Hope*, 128; Jonathan Daniels to The President, June 14, 1943, Box 13, Series 1.3, Jonathan Daniels Papers, SHC; Roberts, *The Farm Security Administration and Rural Rehabilitation in the South*, 191–200; Paul Warwick, "87 Farmers, Ex-Tenants, Gather to Receive Deeds," *Atlanta Constitution*, December 1, 1944; Cecile Davis, "FSA Farmer, with $1,700 in '41, Now Worth $11,038," *Atlanta Constitution*, December 1, 1944.
43. Royall Brandis, "Cotton Competition. U.S. and Egypt, 1929–1948," *Southern Economic Journal* 19 (January 1953): 340; "Wickard Urges Crop Diversion in Cotton Belt," *New York Herald Tribune*, December 5, 1944; Henry B. Kline, "Cotton Facing Crisis as Result of Subsidies, New Competition and Imminent Mass Production," *St. Louis Post-Dispatch*, March 11, 1945.
44. *Hearings before the Subcommittee of the Committee on Appropriations, House of Representatives*, 1639–1640; Virginius Dabney, "The Dynamic New South," *NYT*, October 17, 1943; Schulman, *From Cotton Belt to Sunbelt*, 103; Annual Report of Delta Council, 1943–1944, 5.
45. D. Clayton Brown, *King Cotton in Modern America: A Cultural, Political, and Economic History since 1945* (Jackson: University Press of Mississippi, 2011), preface and ch. 7; "Commodity Developments: Cotton Growers Get Plan to Concentrate Production and Cut Costs," *Barron's National Business and Financial Weekly*, December 11, 1944; Nelson, *King Cotton's Advocate*, 230.
46. "The Deep South Looks Up," *Fortune* 28 (July 1943): 218; R. N. Hopson to J. O. Eastland, April 20, 1944, Box 47, Series 3, Subseries 4, James Oliver Eastland Collection; Coahoma County Migration Stories; Gregory, *The Southern Diaspora*, 32.

Chapter 2

1. "Pocomoke III (AV-9)," Dictionary of American Navy Fighting Ships, https://www.history.navy.mil/research/histories/ship-histories/danfs/p/pocomoke-iii.html; John Bunker, *Heroes in Dungarees: The Story of the American Merchant Marine in World War II* (Annapolis, MD: Naval Institute Press, 1995), ch. 2; "First All-Welded Steel Ship," n.d., Pascagoula Harbor and Shipyard, Subject File, MDAH; "New Cargo Liner Launched in South," *NYT*, June 9, 1940.
2. Tracy Campbell, *The Year of Peril: America in 1942* (New Haven, CT: Yale University Press, 2020), 252; William Sturkey, *Hattiesburg: An American City in Black and White* (Cambridge, MA: Harvard University Press, 2019), 207.
3. Pete Daniel, "Going Among Strangers: Southern Reactions to World War II," *Journal of American History* 77 (December 1990): 909; U.S. Bureau of the Budget, *The United*

States at War: Development and Administration of the War Program by the Federal Government (Washington, DC: GPO, 1946), ch. 6; Frederic C. Lane, *Ships for Victory: A History of Shipbuilding under the U.S. Maritime Commission in World War II* (Baltimore: Johns Hopkins University Press, 1951), ch. 1; "The Deep South Looks Up," *Fortune* 28 (July 1943): 97–100, 218. Deadweight tonnage is a measure of how much weight a ship can carry.

4. Robert Bogdan, *Freak Show: Presenting Human Oddities for Amusement and Profit* (Chicago: University of Chicago Press, 1988), 2, 112–113, 206–207; William L. Slout, *Olympians of the Sawdust Circle: A Biographical Dictionary of the 19th Century American Circus* (San Bernardino, CA: Borgo Press, 1988), 143. Biographical information on Horace Ingalls from various documents in Ancestry.com.

5. Hodding Carter and Anthony Ragusin, *Gulf Coast Country* (New York: Duell, Sloan & Pearce, 1951), 191; George M. Cruikshank, *A History of Birmingham and Its Environs: A Narrative Account of Their Historical Progress, Their People, and Their Principal Interests*, vol. 1 (Chicago: Lewis Publishing Co., 1920), 208; Richard Austin Smith, "The Haunted House of Ingalls," *Fortune* 57 (May 1958): 119, 121; "Steel Magnate Ingalls Dies at Odds with Son," *St. Louis Post-Dispatch*, July 12, 1951; "Birmingham for Tax Cut," *NYT*, November 19, 1923. Biographical information on Robert Ingalls from various documents in Ancestry.com.

6. Robert I. Ingalls, *Shipbuilding* (New York: Newcomen Society of England, 1947), 10; Jerry St. Pe, *A Salute to American Spirit: The Story of Ingalls Shipbuilding Division of Litton* (New York: The Newcomen Society of the United States, 1988), 7–8; Robert F. Couch, "The Ingalls Story in Mississippi, 1938–1958," *Journal of Mississippi History* 26 (August 1964): 193–196; A. J. Grassick, "New Ingalls Shipyard," *Marine Engineering and Shipping Review*, February 1, 1940, 44; Thomas A. Kelly, "The Impact of World War II on the Pascagoula Area: A Study of Economic Change," *Social Science Bulletin* 3 (Summer 1950): 2.

7. Smith, "The Haunted House of Ingalls," 233–234; Hearings, 1943, 647; Couch, "The Ingalls Story in Mississippi, 1938–1958," 198; Thomas M. McClellan to William M. Colmer, January 10, 1941, and Thomas M. McClellan to Commander Philip Lemler and Asa Groves, January 14, 1941, both in Box 301, CPUSM; Lane, *Ships for Victory*, 27–28; Kelly, "The Impact of World War II on the Pascagoula Area," 3–5; Ingalls, *Shipbuilding*, 13–14.

8. "The Deep South Looks Up," 218; St. Pe, *A Salute to American Spirit*, 10; "A Shipyard Designed for Building Welded Ships," *Marine Engineering and Shipping Review*, February 1, 1940, 35; "The Deep South Turns to Shipbuilding," *Machinery*, November 1942, Box 6, Mississippi Industries Collection, UM; R. H. Macy, "Production Notes on C-3 Ships," *Marine Engineering and Shipping Review*, June 1, 1943, 193; Carter and Ragusin, *Gulf Coast Country*, 187, 192; Bem Price, "South's Shipbuilding Mushrooms from Doldrums to Big Industry," *DDT*, July 24, 1941; Ingalls, *Shipbuilding*, 12–15.

9. Smith, "The Haunted House of Ingalls," 119, 121, 228; "Report of Conference in Office of Mr. Harry G. Thornton, Regional Director, WPB, Thursday, November 18, 1943," and Randolph Feltus to Claude Pepper, January 4, 1944, both in Box 26, WHE.

10. Lane, *Ships for Victory*, 1–10, 124–126, 679; Robert Ingalls to John H. Bankhead, November 20, 1940, Box 301, CPSUM; War Production Board, "Report on the Pascagoula, Mississippi, Area," December 8, 1943, Box 26, WHE.
11. Lane, *Ships for Victory*, 1; "The Boss," *Fortune* (July 1943): 216; Major Enacted Tax Legislation, 1940–1949, https://www.taxpolicycenter.org/laws-proposals/major-enacted-tax-legislation-1940-1949; Ingalls, *Shipbuilding*, 21.
12. Macy, "Production Notes on C-3 Ships," 193; US Employment Service of Mississippi, "Resurvey of the Employment Situation in the Pascagoula, Mississippi Area," June 1, 1942, Series 12, Box 19, and War Manpower Commission, "Estimate of In-Migration into the Pascagoula, Mississippi Labor Market Area," February 22, 1943, Series 12, Box 2, both in WMC; Kelly, "The Impact of World War II on the Pascagoula Area," 4. Carter and Ragusin, *Gulf Coast Country*, 194, claim that even at peak employment in 1944, 60 percent of the Ingalls workforce came from Mississippi.
13. "Germ of 'Agricultural Revolution' Seen in South's Drift to Industry," *Anniston (Ala.) Star*, December 17, 1942; Joel Williamson, *Elvis Presley: A Southern Life* (New York: Oxford University Press, 2014), 96–97; US Employment Service of Mississippi, "Resurvey of the Employment Situation in the Pascagoula, Mississippi Area"; War Manpower Commission, "Labor Market Developments Report," December 15, 1943, Series 12, Box 9, WMC; War Manpower Commission, "Estimate of In-Migration into the Pascagoula, Mississippi Labor Market Area," February 22, 1943; C. F. Floyd to E. J. Kelly, October 30, 1943, Box 1, ADDSCO Records, SOAL; Hearings, 1943, 672.
14. "Germ of 'Agricultural Revolution' Seen in South's Drift to Industry"; Kelly, "The Impact of World War II on the Pascagoula Area," 4; "150 Enrolled in Six Classes at Vocation School," *Gulfport/Biloxi (Miss.) Daily Herald*, November 9, 1940; "1,400 War Workers Trained at Pascagoula School," *Ingalls News*, October 29, 1942; War Manpower Commission, "Labor Market Developments Report," December 15, 1943.
15. U.S. Department of Labor, *A Statistical Summary of the Pascagoula Shipbuilding Area: Jackson County, Mississippi* (Washington, DC: U.S. Department of Labor, 1943); Nelson Lichtenstein, *Labor's War at Home: The CIO in World War II* (Cambridge: Cambridge University Press, 1982), 111; Information from an interview with Nollie Nichols, December 1, 1943, Box 29, WHE; H. B. Harrison to Theodore G. Bilbo, May 18, 1943, Box 1049, BPUSM; Ingalls, *Shipbuilding*, 22; Hearings, 1943, 1046.
16. R. I. Ingalls to William M. Colmer, February 16, 1942, and February 23, 1942, both in Box 301, CPUSM; Hearings, 1943, 651; Agnes E. Meyer, *Journey through Chaos* (New York: Harcourt, Brace & Co., 1944), 196–199.
17. "Report on the Pascagoula, Mississippi, Area," December 8, 1943; Hearings, 1943, 623, 651, 658; Brief of Facts for Regional Management Labor Committee, *John W. Wilson v. Ingalls Shipbuilding Corporation*, Series 15, Box 14, WMC; W. R. Guest to W. M. Colmer, March 27, 1942, R. I. Ingalls to James Forrestal, February 11, 1942, and R. I. Ingalls to William M. Colmer, February 16, 1942, and February 23, 1942, all in Box 301, CPUSM.

18. Herbert G. Gutman, *Work, Culture, and Society in Industrializing America: Essays in American Working-Class and Social History* (New York: Vintage, 1977); Hearings, 1943, 651, 665; "10,000 Workers Form Rickenbacker Corps," *NYT*, January 2, 1943; "'Racketeers' Howling Now, 'Rick' Declares," *Atlanta Constitution*, March 27, 1943; W. David Lewis, *Eddie Rickenbacker: An American Hero in the Twentieth Century* (Baltimore: Johns Hopkins University Press, 2005), 458–460; "Rickenbacker 'Re-Captured,'" *Southern Patriot*, February–March 1943. A closed shop is a workplace where membership in a union is a requirement of employment.
19. "Are You a 'Quit-Early?'" *Ingalls News*, August 27, 1942; Sandra K. Behel, "The Mississippi Home Front during World War II: Tradition and Change" (PhD diss., Mississippi State University, 1989), 32.
20. U.S. Department of Labor, *A Statistical Summary of the Pascagoula Shipbuilding Area*; Andrew E. Kersten, *Labor's Home Front: The American Federation of Labor during World War II* (New York: New York University Press, 2006), 73; William J. Breen, "The State and Workplace Reform in the South: War Manpower Commission Initiatives and Employer Resistance on the Gulf Coast in World War II," *Gulf South Historical Review* 18 (2003): 12; Clarence Mitchell to George M. Johnson, April 13, 1943, in Denton L. Watson, ed., *Papers of Clarence Mitchell*, 2 vols. (Athens: Ohio University Press, 2005), 1:61–62; Lane, *Ships for Victory*, 654; War Manpower Commission, "Labor Market Developments Report," December 15, 1943; U.S. Department of Labor, *A Statistical Summary of the Pascagoula Shipbuilding Area*, 9.
21. Hearings, 1943, 653; Monro B. Lanier to Emory S. Land, September 23, 1943, and Commissioner Carmody to Chairman Land, September 29, 1943, both in Box 582, USMC; R. I. Ingalls to William M. Colmer, February 16, 1942.
22. War Manpower Commission, "Report on Pascagoula, Mississippi," December 10, 1942; U.S. Department of Labor, *A Statistical Summary of the Pascagoula Shipbuilding Area*, 4–5; Moss Point Historic District, Application for National Register of Historic Places, 48, https://www.apps.mdah.ms.gov/nom/dist/226.pdf; "1,400 War Workers Trained at Pascagoula School"; "Women Welders on Job!" *Ingalls News*, September 24, 1942.
23. War Manpower Commission, "Report on Pascagoula, Mississippi," December 10, 1942; "Women Welders on the Job!"; 1930 and 1940 U.S. Census Schedules for Harrison County, Mississippi, Ancestry.com; Carter and Ragusin, *Gulf Coast Country*, 187; "Vera Anderson, Pascagoula Welding Champ to be Honored Guest in N.Y.," *Greenville (Miss.) Delta-Democrat Times*, December 6, 1943.
24. "Women Welders on Job!" *Ingalls News*, September 24, 1942; "Feminine Notes," *Ingalls News*, October 22, 1942; "Feminine Notes," *Ingalls News*, October 29, 1942; "Estimate of In-Migration into the Pascagoula, Mississippi Labor Market Area," February 22, 1943; War Manpower Commission, "Labor Market Developments Report," December 15, 1943; "The Victor," *Ingalls News*, June 4, 1943; Lane, *Ships for Victory*, 257; Hearings, 1943, 652; "Pipe Dept. News," *Ingalls News*, October 22, 1942; "Yard Notes," *Ingalls News*, March 11, 1943; "Ingalls Yard Uses First Women Keel-Layers in Gulf Coast History," *Ingalls News*, November 5, 1942.

25. Behel, "The Mississippi Home Front during World War II," 71–72; Hearings, 1943, 700–704.
26. Breen, "The State and Workplace Reform in the South," 24; "Ingalls Yard Can Use 3,000 More Men, Women," *Ingalls News*, October 22, 1942; "Badly Needed . . . Welders," *Ingalls News*, October 29, 1943; War Manpower Commission, "Employment Service Operations," *Social Security Bulletin* 6 (May 1, 1943): 37; Hearings, 1943, 672–673, 929.
27. "Two Little Sisters," *Ingalls News*, November 5, 1942; "Welfare of Women Workers Important Item at Ingalls," *Ingalls News*, October 8, 1943; Behel, "The Mississippi Home Front during World War II," 71–72. Biographical information on Maude Ladner from Ancestry.com.
28. Numerous advertisements dated between June 8, 1944, and August 31, 1944, all in Box 1, ADDSCO Records. See also Melissa A. McEuen, *Making War, Making Women: Femininity and Duty on the American Home Front, 1941–1945* (Athens: University of Georgia Press, 2011), 191–193.
29. Hearings, 1943, 736–742; Meyer, *Journey through Chaos*, 211.
30. "Two Beauties Are First Female Sheet Metal Trade Delegates," *Atlanta Constitution*, January 16, 1943; "A Hundred Dollar Smile!" *Ingalls News*, February 25, 1943; "First National Women's Welding Contest Was Close, Hard Battle, Ingalls' Vera Anderson Wins Out over Oregon's Hermina Strmiska," *Ingalls News*, June 4, 1943; "Vera Anderson, Pascagoula Welding Champ to be Honored Guest in N.Y."; "Welding Champ Shares Spotlight at Jackson Fair," *Ingalls News*, October 22, 1943; "Woman Welder Retains 'Crown,'" *NYT*, January 30, 1944.
31. Bruce Nelson, "Organized Labor and the Struggle for Black Equality in Mobile during World War II," *Journal of American History* 80 (December 1993): 962; Mary Perez, "Welder Symbolized Women During World War II," *Charleston (S.C.) Post and Carrier*, October 3, 2013, https://www.postandcourier.com/features/welder-symbolized-women-during-wwii/article_658d8d2b-8dea-51b0-a2ff-6e110508b7c9.html; "Georgia's 'Miss Swing Shift' . . . Emma Harwell," *The Bellringer*, August 1944; "Meet the Champion Welder," *Ingalls News*, October 8, 1943.
32. J. G. Magrath, "Welded Ships from Singing River—III," Marine Engineering and Shipping Review, January 1, 1944, 194; George Q. Flynn, *The Mess in Washington: Manpower Mobilization in World War II* (Westport, CT: Greenwood Press, 1979), 178–179; "A Reporter Reports on a Woman Welder," *Ingalls News*, November 5, 1942; McEuen, *Making War, Making Women*, 207–209.
33. War Manpower Commission, "Labor Market Developments Report," December 15, 1943; War Manpower Commission, "Report on Pascagoula, Mississippi," December 10, 1942, Series 12, Box 19, WMC; Hearings, 1943, 652; W. R. Guest to C. F. Palmer, August 2, 1941, Box 581, USMC.
34. War Manpower Commission, "Report on Pascagoula, Mississippi," December 10, 1942; War Manpower Charts and Statistical Information Relating to the Alabama Dry Dock and Shipbuilding Company, February 1943, DocsTeach, National Archives, https://www.docsteach.org/documents/document/war-manpower-charts-and-stat

istical-information-relating-to-the-alabama-dry-dock-and-shipbuilding-corporation; John LeFlore, "Taps Sound for Skilled Negro Workers in Dixie Shipyards," *CD*, August 25, 1945; Judy Barrett Litoff, "Southern Women in a World at War," in *Remaking Dixie: The Impact of World War II on the American South*, ed. Neil R. McMillen (Jackson: University Press of Mississippi, 1997), 61–62; Enoc P. Waters, "Color Lines Blurred in Strange New Orleans, City of Contrasts," *CD*, March 20, 1943; "Jobs Denied Women in New Orleans," *CD*, March 13, 1943; "First Woman Welder at Higgins Industries," *Pittsburgh Courier*, May 6, 1944.

35. William M. Colmer, "An Appeal for Ship Production," *Congressional Record*, March 26, 1942, Appendix, 1220; R. I. Ingalls to William M. Colmer, March 27, 1942, Box 301, CPUSM; "Speed Output or Face Angry Public, Nelson Warns Labor, Management," *Atlanta Constitution*, March 24, 1942.

36. Julian E. Zelizer, "Confronting the Roadblock: Congress, Civil Rights, and World War II," in *Fog of War: The Second Word War and the Civil Rights Movement*, ed. Kevin M. Kruse and Stephen Tuck (New York: Oxford University Press, 2012), 38.

37. Lichtenstein, *Labor's War at Home*, 96–97; James B. Atleson, *Labor and the Wartime State: Labor Relations and Law during World War II* (Urbana: University of Illinois Press, 1998), 49–50 and ch. 9; "Roosevelt Bars Double-Time Pay for Sunday and Holiday Work," *NYT*, September 10, 1942; Michael Goldfield, *The Southern Key: Class, Race, and Radicalism in the 1930s and 1940s* (New York: Oxford University Press, 2020), 72–73; Ira Katznelson, *Fear Itself: The New Deal and the Origins of Our Time* (New York: W. W. Norton, 2013), 389–390.

38. Mrs. J. E. Ellis to Senator Bilbo, May 24, 1943, and Emmette Beaube to Theodore G. Bilbo, October 27, 1943, both in Box 1109, Grady E. Griffin to Theodore G. Bilbo, May 15, 1943, Box 1049, all in BPUSM; O. B. Cutrer Sr. to Bill Colmer, January 16, 1943, and R. E. Anderson to W.M. Colmer, August 24, 1943, both in Box 507, CPUSM.

39. Donald Crumpton Mosley, "A History of Labor Unions in Mississippi" (PhD diss., University of Alabama, 1965), 134–136; Decision and Direction of Election in the Matter of The Ingalls Shipbuilding Corporation and Metal Trades Department, affiliated with A.F. of L., March 20, 1940, and "Shipbuilding Employees to Ballot" (press release), National Labor Relations Board, March 21, 1940, both in Series 6.3, Box 5, Industrial Union of Marine and Shipbuilding Workers of America Records, Special Collections and University Archives, University of Maryland, College Park.

40. "White AFL Union in Birmingham Goes to Bat for Negroes; Secures Equal Pay for Equal Work Hours," *Houston (Tex.) Negro Labor News*, April 19, 1944; Herbert R. Northrup, "The Negro and Unionism in the Birmingham, Ala., Iron and Steel Industry," *Southern Economic Journal* 10 (July 1943): 39; Robert C. Weaver, "Racial Employment Trends in National Defense," *Phylon* 2 (1941): 358; telegram from Walter White to Sidney Hillman, March 11, 1941, and "Protest Gets Protection for Negro Labor in New Iron Works Contract" (press release), March 28, 1941, both in PQHV-NAACP: EVH.

41. Kersten, *Labor's Home Front*, ch. 3; Ingalls, *Shipbuilding*, 294; Louis Stark, "Metal Unions Vote 'No Strike' Policy," *NYT*, January 6, 1941; Lane, *Ships for Victory*, ch. 9;

"AFL Ratifies Pact for Shipyards along Gulf Coast," *Hartford (Conn.) Courant*, August 4, 1941.

42. "In re Ingalls Shipbuilding Corporation and Pascagoula Metal Trades Council (AFL)," November 15, 1941, *Labor Relations Reference Manual* 9 (1940–1941): 815–816; W. H. Lawrence, "2 NDMB Rulings Bar Union Shop; A.F.L. Ship Workers Lose Demand," *NYT*, November 15, 1941; H. B. Harrison to Theodore Bilbo, January 4, 1942, Box 1041, and W. H. Barker to Theodore G. Bilbo, June 26, 1945, Box 1049, both in BPUSM; "Ingalls Shipyards Closed Down as Workers Strike," *DDT*, October 13, 1941; "Gulf Ship Plant Is Shut by Strike," *NYT*, October 14, 1941.

43. Atleson, *Labor and the Wartime State*, 30; "In re Ingalls Shipbuilding Corporation and Pascagoula Metal Trades Council (AFL)," 815–816; Bruce J. Schulman, *From Cotton Belt to Sunbelt: Federal Policy, Economic Development, and the Transformation of the South, 1938–1980* (New York: Oxford University Press, 1991), 78–79; E. B. McNatt, "Toward a National Wartime Labor Policy: The Union-Security Issue," *Journal of Business of the University of Chicago* 16 (January 1943): 64–65; H. B. Harrison to Theodore Bilbo, January 4, 1942, Box 1041, BPUSM.

44. Lichtenstein, *Labor's War at Home*, 96; Hearings, 1943, 607, 609, 619, 653; *Ingalls News*, issues from 1942 to 1944.

45. H. A. Barlett to Eric Peterson, October 26, 1942, H. A. Barlett to F. D. Laudemann, May 13, 1943, and May 22, 1943, all on reel 46, IAMAW; Hearings, 1943, 609.

46. H. A. Barlett to Eric Peterson, November 27, 1942, reel 46, IAMAW; "Two Beauties Are First Female Sheet Metal Trades Delegates"; "Dixie AFL Meet Scores Discrimination," *BAA*, January 30, 1943; "Southern War Labor Conference Convenes in Atlanta," *Southern Patriot*, February/March 1943; Kersten, *Labor's Home Front*, ch. 3; War Manpower Commission, "Report on Pascagoula, Mississippi," December 10, 1942.

47. H. A. Barlett to F. D. Laudemann, January 16, 1945, and April 12, 1945, reel 46, IAMAW; Lichtenstein, *Labor's War at Home*, 133–135; Information from an interview with Nollie Nichols, December 1, 1943.

48. Burton R. Morley to Frank A. Constangy, November 26, 1943, and Frank A. Constangy to Burton R. Morley, November 29, 1943, Series 8, Box 1, WMC.

49. "Ingalls Shipyard Strike Grows; 900 More Leave Jobs," *Jackson Daily News*, April 9, 1944; "Assails Shipyard Halt," *NYT*, April 11, 1944; E. L. Mancil to Theodore G. Bilbo, February 21, 1945, Box 1041, BPUSM; "WLB Sets Hearing at Pascagoula on Order Compliance," *DDT*, February 23, 1945.

50. "Strike of 10,000 Cripples Shipyard," *NYT*, February 25, 1945; "Near 6,000 Pascagoula Shipyard Workers out on Strike," *DDT*, February 25, 1945; "Ingalls Strikers Are Warned They Face Induction," *DDT*, February 27, 1945; "Shipyard Strike in Mississippi in Fifth Day," *Benton Harbor (Mich.) News-Palladium*, February 28, 1945; Hearings, 1943, 619; H. A. Barlett to Eric Peterson, November 30, 1942, reel 46, IAMAW; "Shipyard Men Are Due Back," *Baltimore Sun*, March 1, 1945.

51. "Contract Committeeman," *Alabama*, March 17, 1944, 11; Russell Porter, "Ship Plant Turns to Diesel Engines," *NYT*, October 3, 1945; Max Forester, "Jobs Outlook Called Bright in Ingalls Yard," *New York Herald Tribune*, October 3, 1945; Ninth

Annual Report, Department of Labor, State of Georgia, to the Governor and General Assembly, 1945, Georgia Archives, Atlanta; Lichtenstein, *Labor's War at Home*, 221; John LeFlore, "Alabama Unemployment Called Future Race Relations Gauge," *CD*, March 2, 1946; Unemployment Rate for the United States, 1940–1946, Federal Reserve Economic Data, https://fred.stlouisfed.org/series/M0892BUSM156SNBR.

52. Porter, "Ship Plant Turns to Diesel Engines"; Forester, "Jobs Outlook Called Bright in Ingalls Yard"; Donald Grant, "Outlook Bright for Shipbuilding at Ingalls Yards in Mississippi. 18 Vessels Under Construction Now," *St. Louis Post-Dispatch*, October 3, 1945; "Strikes Shut Off Supplies, Cause Ingalls Lay-Offs," *DDT*, February 22, 1946; George Horne, "Shipbuilding Jobs Show Steady Drop," *NYT*, December 8, 1946; "Ingalls Shipyard May Close in Dispute," *Jackson Daily News*, March 23, 1946; "R. I. Ingalls Sr., 69, An Industrialist," *NYT*, July 13, 1951; Ingo Heidbrink, "The Business of Shipping: An Historical Perspective," in *The Blackwell Companion to Maritime Economics*, ed. Wayne K. Talley (Malden, MA: Wiley-Blackwell, 2012), 46; Couch, "The Ingalls Story in Mississippi, 1938–1958," 201–205.

53. Behel, "The Mississippi Home Front during World War II," 88; Edward K. to Theodore Bilbo, July 15, 1945, Box 1071, BPUSM.

54. "Ingalls Shipyard May Close in Dispute"; John LeFlore, "3,000 Join Hate Strike," *CD*, March 30, 1946; James C. Cobb, *The Selling of the South: The Southern Crusade for Industrial Development, 1936–90* 2nd ed. (Urbana: University of Illinois Press, 1993), 101–102.

Chapter 3

1. Birmingham Hearing transcript, June 1942, John Beecher to Lawrence Cramer, April 30, 1942, and Donald M. Nelson to Malcolm S. MacLean, May 14, 1942, all in reel 17, FEP-NA.
2. "President's Committee on Fair Employment Practice" (WPB press release), April 5, 1942, and John Beecher to George Johnson, April 15, 1942, both in PQHV-BFS: ORP1; "Five Are Preparing Material," *Kansas City Call*, May 29, 1942; Merl E. Reed, *Seedtime for the Modern Civil Rights Movement: The President's Committee on Fair Employment Practice, 1941–1946* (Baton Rouge: Louisiana State University Press, 1991), 68.
3. Lawrence W. Cramer to John Beecher, May 2, 1942, reel 78, FEP-NA; B. M. Phillips, "Coca Cola, Bell Aircraft, Vultee, Ala. Drydock Agree to Obey FDR," *BAA*, June 27, 1942; Cliff Mackay, "'Buck-Passing' in Job Training Charged," *Atlanta Daily World*, June 20, 1942; James Carmichael testimony, Birmingham Hearing transcript, June 1942.
4. Phillips, "Coca Cola, Bell Aircraft, Vultee, Ala. Drydock Agree to Obey FDR"; Mackay, "'Buck-Passing' in Job Training Charged."
5. "Labor Practice Hearings Set," *Gadsden (Ala.) Times*, June 14, 1942; "Birmingham Journal Raps FEP Hearings," *CD*, June 27, 1942; *Alabama* quoted in Doris Kearns Goodwin, *No Ordinary Time: Franklin & Eleanor Roosevelt: The Home Front in World War II* (New York: Simon & Schuster, 1994), 330–331; Virginius Dabney, "Nearer and

Nearer the Precipice," *The Atlantic*, January 1943, 100; Reed, *Seedtime for the Modern Civil Rights Movement*, 70–71; George S. Schuyler, "Views and Reviews," *Pittsburgh Courier*, August 15, 1942.

6. John Morton Blum, *V Was for Victory: Politics and American Culture during World War II* (New York: Harcourt Brace Jovanovich, 1976), 183; Earl Brown and George R. Leighton, "The Negro and the War," Public Affairs Pamphlets, No. 71, 1944, 9–11, 14, Box 57, Walter Sillers Jr. Papers, DSU; Dewey W. Grantham, "The South and Congressional Politics," in *Remaking Dixie: The Impact of World War II on the American South*, ed. Neil R. McMillen (Jackson: University Press of Mississippi, 1997), 28.

7. Patrick S. Washburn, "The *Pittsburgh Courier* and Black Workers in 1942," *Western Journal of Black Studies* 10 (Fall 1986): 110; George Q. Flynn, *The Mess in Washington: Manpower Mobilization in World War II* (Westport, CT: Greenwood Press, 1979), 166–167.

8. Charles S. Johnson and Clifton R. Jones, "Memorandum on Negro Internal Migration, 1940–1943," August 16, 1943, AU: FDR; Bureau of Agricultural Economics, Preliminary Report on Mobile Survey, April 22, 1942, Box 12, BAE.

9. "National Defense Labor Problems: The Weaver Appointment," *The Crisis*, October 1940, 319; E. R. Plowden to J. L. LeFlore, April 4, 1941, J. L. LeFlore to E. R. Plowden, May 1941, and J. L. LeFlore to Robert C. Weaver, April 23, 1942, all in reel 4, John L. LeFlore Papers, SOAL; J. L. LeFlore to Walter White, July 28, 1941, PQHV-NAACP: EVH.

10. J. L. LeFlore to W. J. Trent Jr., June 8, 1941, July 14, 1941, August 7, 1941, and August 16, 1941, and J. L. LeFlore to John M. Carmody, July 1941, all in reel 4, John L. LeFlore Papers; J. L. LeFlore to Walter White, August 11, 1941, PQHV-NAACP: EVH; "Housing Labor Dispute Denied," *Mobile Press*, July 23, 1941; Walter White to Francis Biddle, October 10, 1941, PQHV-NAACP: EVH.

11. Negro Schools and Colleges in Mississippi Having Vocational Training Facilities, and the Types of Courses Each Is Equipped to Give, December 1, 1941, PQHV-BFS: FGR; John Beecher Field Report, Trip to Jackson and Flora, Mississippi, May 14–16, 1942, reel 77, FEP-NA; Reed, *Seedtime for the Modern Civil Rights Movement*, 68; Merl E. Reed, "The FEPC, the Black Worker, and the Southern Shipyards," *South Atlantic Quarterly* 74 (1975): 449.

12. "Some of the Highlights of the Public Career of Mobile NAACP Executive Secretary John L. LeFlore, 1925–1950," n.d., 1950, PQHV-NAACP: BDBF; Birmingham Hearing transcript, June 1942; Herbert R. Northrup, "Organized Labor and Negro Workers," *Journal of Political Economy* 51 (June 1943): 219–221; Herbert R. Northrup, "Negroes in a War Industry: The Case of Shipbuilding," *Journal of Business of the University of Chicago* 16 (July 1943): 168.

13. Glenn Feldman, *The Great Melding: War, the Dixiecrat Rebellion, and the Southern Model for America's New Conservatism* (Tuscaloosa: University of Alabama Press, 2015), 47; "Threats to National Unity in the South," Statement of the Southern Delegation of the National Negro Congress, August 6, 1942, AU: NCC; "Dixon

Charges Agency with Disrupting South's White-Negro Segregation," *Gadsden (Ala.) Times*, August 4, 1942.
14. J. Mills Thornton III, "Segregation and the City: White Supremacy in Alabama in the Mid-Twentieth Century," in *Fog of War: The Second Word War and the Civil Rights Movement*, ed. Kevin M. Kruse and Stephen Tuck (New York: Oxford University Press, 2012), 56; Frank M. Dixon to Ralph D. Williams, July 22, 1942, *Congressional Record*, July 24, 1942, Appendix, 2949.
15. "Our One Cause for Fear," *Montgomery (Ala.) Advertiser*, July 26, 1942; "People Rally Behind Gov. Dixon in the Fight for South's Principles," *Greenville (Ala.) Advocate*, August 6, 1942; "Dixon Supported," *Albany-Decatur (Ala.) Daily*, July 27, 1942; "Cheers for Governor Dixon, for Congressman Manasco," *Cullman (Ala.) Democrat*, July 30, 1942. For more on Dixon and the FEPC, see Feldman, *The Great Melding*, ch. 8.
16. Ira Katznelson, *Fear Itself: The New Deal and the Origins of Our Time* (New York: W. W. Norton, 2013), part II; Walter White to Franklin D. Roosevelt, August 19, 1942, AU: FDR; "Say Dixie Bloc Can Refuse FEPC Funds," *Cleveland Call and Post*, August 15, 1942; Tracy Campbell, *The Year of Peril: America in 1942* (New Haven, CT: Yale University Press, 2020), 211–212; Daniel Kryder, *Divided Arsenal: Race and the American State during World War II* (Cambridge: Cambridge University Press, 2000), 94–101; Marjorie McKenzie, "Pursuit of Democracy," *Pittsburgh Courier*, August 15, 1942; "Colored Americans Are Suspicious," *Pittsburgh Courier*, September 26, 1942; Reed, *Seedtime for the Modern Civil Rights Movement*, 74–76; Charles D. Chamberlain, *Victory at Home: Manpower and Race in the American South during World War II* (Athens: University of Georgia Press, 2003), 59–60, 133.
17. Lawrence D. Cramer to Alabama Shipbuilding and Drydock Corporation, November 19, 1942, reel 17, FEP-NA; "Labor Market Development Report Entailing the Ratio of Non-whites and Women in the Workforce . . . ," June 12, 1943, Reports, Tabulations, and Compilations, 1936–1951, WMC (online).
18. Summary of a Report to the Industrial Relations Department of the National Urban League for Social Service among Negroes on the Race Riots in the Alabama Dry Dock and Shipbuilding Company Yards in Mobile, Alabama, n.d., 1943, PQHV-NAACP: EVH; Rev. H. E. Carter, "Say Skilled Workers in Mobile Rated Unskilled Despite FEPC," *BAA*, January 2, 1943.
19. FEPC, Field Investigation Report, June 8, 1943, PQHV-BFS: FGR; Burton R. Morley to John Griser, May 3, 1943, Burton R. Morley to John M. Griser, May 20, 1943, and B. C. Knerr to Burton Morley, May 22, 1943, all in Central Files and Monthly MOPAC Area Reports, 1936–1951, WMC (online); Hervey Allen (WMC Regional Information Representative), Report, n.d. June 1943, Speeches by Members of Regional Office Staff and Other Material, 1936–1951, WMC (online); Northrup, "Negroes in a War Industry," 169.
20. Northrup, "Negroes in a War Industry," 169; Bruce Nelson, "Organized Labor and the Struggle for Black Equality in Mobile during World War II," *Journal of American History* 80 (December 1993): 978; Victor H. Bernstein, "The Story of a Race Riot: Women Joined Men in Clubbing and Stoning Negro Ship Workers," *PM*, May

31, 1943; FEPC, Field Investigation Report, June 8, 1943; "8 Hurt in Mobile in Inter-Race Fray," *NYT*, May 26, 1943; "Race Riot Flares between White, Negro Workers in Mobile, Alabama Shipyard," *Cleveland Call and Post*, June 5, 1943.

21. Bernstein, "The Story of a Race Riot." Press reports at the time, as well as those of the War Department, estimated the number of injured workers as fewer than twenty. The FEPC investigation offered fifty as a "conservative estimate" of the number of Black casualties. See FEPC, Field Investigation Report, June 8, 1943. The National Urban League Field Secretary, Franklin O. Nichols, believed the number of injuries might have been as high as 100. See Franklin O. Nichols to Lester Granger, May 29, 1943, Part VI, Box A69, Records of the National Urban League, LC. Information on Clifford L. Williams from various documents in Ancestry.com.

22. Jane Dailey, "The Sexual Politics of Race in World War II," in Kruse and Tuck, eds., *Fog of War*, 157; Marilynn S. Johnson, "Gender, Race, and Rumours: Re-examining the 1943 Race Riots," *Gender & History* 10 (August 1998): 259–263.

23. Hervey Allen (WMC Regional Information Representative), Report, n.d. June 1943; FEPC, Field Investigation Report, June 8, 1943.

24. Hervey Allen (WMC Regional Information Representative), Report, n.d. June 1943; FEPC, Field Investigation Report, June 8, 1943.

25. FEPC, Field Investigation Report, June 8, 1943; "Statement of Proposed Solution for Settlement of Difficulties at Shipyard of the Alabama Dry Dock and Shipbuilding Company . . .," May 28, 1943, PQHV-BFS: FGR.

26. FEPC, Field Investigation Report, June 8, 1943; "Statement of Proposed Solution for Settlement of Difficulties at Shipyard of the Alabama Dry Dock and Shipbuilding Company . . .," May 28, 1943, and Telegram, Francis J. Haas to J. M. Griser, June 2, 1943, both in PQHV-BFS: FGR; "Mobile Race Riot Laid to Company," *NYT*, June 13, 1943; Nelson, "Organized Labor and the Struggle for Black Equality in Mobile during World War II," 982.

27. Hervey Allen (WMC Regional Information Representative), Report, n.d. June 1943; "Mobile Race Riot Laid to Company."

28. John P. Davis, "Segregated Pattern in Industry Looms as Result of FEPC Decision in Mobile Case," *Pittsburgh Courier*, June 12, 1943; Reed, *Seedtime for the Modern Civil Rights Movement*, 117–122; "Surrender in Mobile," *Pittsburgh Courier*, June 19, 1943; Telegram, Walter White to Paul McNutt, June 9, 1943, and Telegram, J. L. LeFlore to Francis E. Haas, June 6, 1945, all in PQHV-NAACP: EVH.

29. "Negro Workers Urged to Return to Shipyard Jobs," *Dothan (Ala.) Eagle*, May 27, 1943; Bernstein, "The Story of a Race Riot"; Nelson, "Organized Labor and the Struggle for Black Equality in Mobile during World War II," 981; Robert A. Hill, ed., *The FBI's RACON: Racial Conditions in the United States during World War II* (Boston: Northeastern University Press, 1995), 275; FEPC, Field Investigation Report, June 8, 1943; "'Back-To-ADDSCO' Move Grows: Normal Force Seen by Monday, WMC Declines Job Transfers," *Mobile Press*, May 30, 1943; Clarence Mitchell to Lawrence Cramer and George M. Johnson, June 1, 1943, PQHV-BFS: FGR.

30. Clarence M. Mitchell to Truman Gibson Jr., August 10, 1943, PQHV-BFS: FGR; Reed, "The FEPC, the Black Worker, and the Southern Shipyards," 457–459; John LeFlore, "Taps Sound for Skilled Negro Workers in Dixie Shipyards," *CD*, August 25, 1945.
31. John LeFlore, "Inefficiency Is Charged to Welders," *CD*, September 25, 1943; LeFlore, "Taps Sound for Skilled Negro Workers in Dixie Shipyards"; Pete Daniel, *Standing at the Crossroads: Southern Life in the Twentieth Century* (Baltimore: Johns Hopkins University Press, 1996), 146.
32. Joseph F. Battley to Chief of Staff, Army Service Forces, May 31, 1944, and Telephone conversation between Colonel Boyer and Miss Hardy, Fourth Service Command, May 31, 1944, both in PQHV-BFS: FGR; John LeFlore, "Workers Defy Threat of Riot; Break Record," *CD*, June 10, 1944.
33. Thomas A. Scott, "Winning World War II in an Atlanta Suburb: Local Boosters and the Recruitment of Bell Bomber," in *The Second Wave: Southern Industrialization from the 1940s to the 1970s*, ed. Philip Scranton (Athens: University of Georgia Press, 2001), 4–8, 12; Jacob Vander Meulen, *Building the B-29* (Washington, DC: Smithsonian Institution Press, 1995), 75; Leston Faneuf, *Lawrence D. Bell: A Man and His Company, "Bell Aircraft"* (New York: Newcomen Society in North America, 1958), 16; Pete Inglis, *Restored to Honor: Georgia's B-29, Sweet Eloise* (Marietta, GA: GRAFCO Productions, 2001), 80.
34. Faneuf, *Lawrence D. Bell*, 8–17.
35. Karen Ferguson, "The Politics of Exclusion: Wartime Industrialization, Civil Rights Mobilization, and Black Politics in Atlanta, 1942-1946," in *The Second Wave*, 62; William Y. Bell testimony, Birmingham Hearing transcript, June 1942; Chamberlain, *Victory at Home*, 50–52; "Ga. Teachers Adopt Double 'V' Program," *Pittsburgh Courier*, May 2, 1942; "'No Equal Pay for Negro Workers'—Talmadge," *Pittsburgh Courier*, March 21, 1942.
36. Robert C. Weaver, "Negro Employment in the Aircraft Industry," *Quarterly Journal of Economics* 59 (August 1945): 598–614.
37. Folder, "Labor: Bell Aircraft Co., N.Y., 1940–1941," PQHV-NAACP: EVH; Merl E. Reed, "Bell Aircraft Comes South: The Struggle by Atlanta Blacks for Jobs during World War II," in *Labor in the Modern South*, ed. Glenn T. Eskew (Athens: University of Georgia Press, 2001), 103.
38. Weaver, "Employment in the Aircraft Industry," 617; Minutes of the Seventh Regional Labor Supply Committee, March 18, 1942, reel 78, FEP-NA; A. F. Smith to B. F. Ashe, December 23, 1942, Series 12, Box 1, WMC; Lamar Q. Ball, "All Idle Atlantans Must Be Put to Work, Conference Reveals," *Atlanta Constitution*, February 9, 1943.
39. Clarence W. Mitchell to Cy W. Record, February 28, 1942, and Lawrence D. Bell to Sidney Hillman, March 10, 1942, both in Reel 78, FEP-NA.
40. Reed, "Bell Aircraft Comes South," 104; William Y. Bell testimony, Birmingham Hearing transcript, June 1942.
41. William Y. Bell testimony and M.D. Mobley testimony, Birmingham Hearing transcript, June 1942; Richard W. Croop, interview by Thomas A. Scott, December 15, 1998, transcript, Kennesaw State University Archives, Kennesaw, Georgia; "Bell's 1st Year Points Way to South's Future," *Atlanta Constitution*, April 13, 1944.

42. Rufus Jarman, "Mechanical Courses to Train 3,300 Here for Work in Bell Aircraft Plant to Start Middle of April," newspaper clipping, Box 1, Blair Family Papers, Kennesaw State University Archives; John Beecher to Will W. Alexander, February 27, 1942, reel 77, FEP-NA; "Local Situation Due to Come Up for Airing at Birmingham F.E.P. Hearing," *Atlanta Daily World*, June 17, 1942.
43. Reed, *Seedtime for the Modern Civil Rights Movement*, 190; M. D. Mobley testimony, Birmingham Hearing transcript, June 1942; Gerald David Jaynes and Robin M. Williams Jr., *A Common Destiny: Blacks and American Society* (Washington, DC: National Academy Press, 1989), 59.
44. Reed, "Bell Aircraft Comes South," 112–126; Moss Myles Kendrix, "Fail to Provide Defense Training for Ga. Workers," *CD*, May 2, 1942; "Atlanta, Ga., Urban League Wins Fight; Aided by FEPC, NMS," *Pittsburgh Courier*, December 5, 1942.
45. Ferguson, "The Politics of Exclusion," 64–66; Madrid Boyd Turner, "A Study of One Hundred Skilled Negro Workers at Bell Aircraft Corporation and the Problems Encountered in Adapting to a Peacetime Economy" (MA thesis, Social Work, Atlanta University, 1946), 32; Reed, "Bell Aircraft Comes South," 120–125.
46. Meulen, *Building the B-29*, 81–84; A. Bruce Hunt to Frank Constangy, February 19, 1944, Series 20, Box 1, WMC; Denton L. Watson, ed., *The Papers of Clarence Mitchell Jr.*, 2 vols. (Athens: Ohio University Press, 2005), 2:355. Also see Michelle Brattain, *The Politics of Whiteness: Race, Workers, and Culture in the Modern South* (Princeton, NJ: Princeton University Press, 2001), ch. 3.
47. Bryant H. Prentice Jr. to Dillard Lasseter, July 6, 1944, and William H. Shell to Dillard B. Lasseter, February 13, 1945, both in Series 20, Box 1, WMC; James V. Carmichael to J. R. Henderson, August 11, 1944, Box 4, James Vinson Carmichael Papers, Emory.
48. William H. Shell to Dillard B. Lasseter, February 13, 1945, and June 30, 1945, both in Series 20, Box 1, WMC; Turner, "A Study of One Hundred Skilled Negro Workers at Bell Aircraft Corporation and the Problems Encountered in Adapting to a Peacetime Economy," 3–9, 31; "Memorandum on Negro Employment at Bell Aircraft Company," November 3, 1944, Part VI, Box A70, Records of the National Urban League.
49. Clarence M. Mitchell to W. Don Ellinger, February 28, 1945, Box 5, Thomas Scott Papers, Kennesaw State University Archives; Chamberlain, *Victory at Home*, 47–48; Reed, "Bell Aircraft Comes South," 122–126; Joe B. Gabriel, interview by Thomas A. Scott, October 23, 2000, transcript, Kennesaw State University Archives.
50. Chamberlain, *Victory at Home*, 141–142; Turner, "A Study of One Hundred Skilled Negro Workers at Bell Aircraft Corporation and the Problems Encountered in Adapting to a Peacetime Economy," 34; "Memorandum on Negro Employment at Bell Aircraft Company," November 3, 1944.
51. Witherspoon Dodge to Clarence M. Mitchell, March 12, 1945, Box 5, Thomas Scott Papers; William H. Shell to Dillard B. Lasseter, June 30, 1945, Series 20, Box 1, WMC.
52. Northrup, "Organized Labor and Negro Workers," 218; "UAW Controls 90 Pct. at Bell," *Atlanta Constitution*, March 3, 1944; Reed, "Bell Aircraft Comes South," 123–127; Chamberlain, *Victory at Home*, 138–139; George W. Crockett Jr. to Witherspoon Dodge, February 5, 1945, Box 5, Thomas Scott Papers.

53. US Office of War Information, News Bureau, Information Digest, August 4 and 9, 1941; Cy W. Record Field Report, February 25, 1942, reel 77, FEP-NA.
54. Clarence Mitchell to Robert C. Weaver, April 23, 1942, C. F. Burke to Sidney Hillman, March 17, 1942, Robert C. Weaver to Mary Anderson, March 25, 1942, Resolution, Jackson Citizens to President Franklin D. Roosevelt, Both Houses of Congress, et al., April 18, 1942, and John Beecher Field Report, Trip to Jackson and Flora, Mississippi, May 14–16, 1942, all in reel 77, FEP-NA.
55. Clarence Mitchell to Robert C. Weaver, April 23, 1942, Resolution, Jackson Citizens to President Franklin D. Roosevelt, Both Houses of Congress, et al., April 18, 1942, and John Beecher Field Report, Trip to Jackson and Flora, Mississippi, May 14–16, 1942, all in reel 77, FEP-NA.
56. John Beecher Field Report, Trip to Jackson and Flora, Mississippi, May 14–16, 1942; Constance McLaughlin Green et al., *United States Army in World War II: The Technical Services, The Ordnance Department: Planning Munitions for War* (Washington, DC: Center of Military History, 1990), 144; "Mississippi Ordnance Plant (Flora, MS)," Record Group 156, Records of the Office of the Chief of Ordnance, 1940–1966 (Morrow, GA: National Archives of Atlanta, n.d.), 67; John H. Young III, "Race Prejudice Left Doors of 18 Million Dollar Plant Closed," *Pittsburgh Courier*, February 24, 1945.
57. Perry W. Howard to Captain Eugene Davidson, September 12, 1941, Robert C. Weaver to Lawrence W. Cramer, September 24, 1941, and Monro B. Lanier to Lawrence W. Cramer, November 4, 1941, all in Reel 78, FEP-NA.
58. LeFlore, "No Upgradings, Firings Facing Labor in South"; A. Bruce Hunt to Dillard B. Lasseter, August 4, 1944, and Charles A. Ballard to J. M. Bryant, October 3, 1944, both in Series 20, Box 3, WMC; "Number in Training by Course Title and Location as of January 31, 1944, State of Mississippi," Series 11, Box 19, WMC.
59. Chamberlain, *Victory at Home*, 159; Thomas A. Scott, "Bell Bomber," *New Georgia Encyclopedia*, https://www.georgiaencyclopedia.org/articles/government-politics/bell-bomber.
60. "14,401 Workers Needed in Dixie 'Must' Plants," *Atlanta Constitution*, January 25, 1945; Luther Francis Yancey Jr., "Unloose the Hate Chains" (editorial cartoon), *BAA*, February 20, 1943; Reed, *Seedtime for the Modern Civil Rights Movement*, ch. 10.

Chapter 4

1. William M. Tuttle Jr., *Daddy's Gone to War: The Second World War in the Lives of America's Children* (New York: Oxford University Press, 1995), 64–65; Randolph Feltus to Fred Cumbus, December 13, 1943, Box 26, WHE; Jean Byers, *A Study of the Negro in Military Service* (Washington, DC: US Department of Defense, 1950), 19; "Senate Seeks Cure for Juvenile Crime," *Christian Science Monitor*, November 29, 1943; Alexander Rudolph Stoesen, "The Senatorial Career of Claude D. Pepper" (PhD diss., University of North Carolina, 1965), 170–175.

2. Hearings, 1943, iii–v, 804–809; Ella J. Baker to Lucille Black, March 20, 1943, PQHV-NAACP: BDBF; Membership Report, Jackson County, Mississippi, June 5, 1943, part 26A, reel 14, Papers of the NAACP. The Pascagoula Civic Improvement Association and the Jackson County NAACP chapter had an overlapping membership. Edward B. Wright Jr., a member of both groups, worked as a chauffeur for the US Maritime Commission in 1943, though he had previously worked at Ingalls.
3. James Thrasher, "Boomtown, U.S.A.," *Coshocton (Ohio) Tribune*, December 20, 1943; Hearings, 1943, 602, 969. In early 1943, Pascagoula experienced a temporary shortage of both meat and milk, but those problems lasted only a couple of months. See Report of Conference in Office of Mr. Harry G. Thornton, November 18, 1943, Box 26, and Minutes of Hearing Regarding Food Shortage Held at Pascagoula, March 22, 1943, Box 27, both in WHE; and "Milk Shortage in County Ends with Opening of Fresh Milk Depot Today," *Pascagoula Chronicle-Star combined with the Moss Point (Miss.) Advertiser*, April 30, 1943.
4. Hearings, 1943, 969–970; Drew Pearson, "Washington Merry-Go-Round," *Anniston (Ala.) Star*, January 9, 1944; Randolph Feltus to Claude Pepper, January 4, 1944, Box 26, WHE.
5. By August 1943, the federal government had spent $6.7 billion on the construction of war plants and military facilities and on contracts for war-related industries in the southern states of Alabama, Florida, Georgia, Mississippi, North Carolina, South Carolina, and Tennessee. See "War Contracts in the South," *Atlanta Constitution*, August 9, 1943.
6. John W. Jeffries, *Wartime America: The World War II Home Front* (Chicago: Ivan R. Dee, 1996), 85–86; US Department of Labor, *A Statistical Summary of the Pascagoula Shipbuilding Area: Jackson County, Mississippi* (Washington, DC: U.S. Department of Labor, 1943), 2; Adam Rome, *The Bulldozer in the Countryside: Suburban Sprawl and the Rise of American Environmentalism* (New York: Cambridge University Press, 2001); Lizabeth Cohen, *A Consumers' Republic: The Politics of Mass Consumption in Postwar America* (New York: Alfred A. Knopf, 2003), ch. 5.
7. Report on Pascagoula, Mississippi, December 10, 1942, Box 19, Series 12, WMC; US Department of Labor, *A Statistical Summary of the Pascagoula Shipbuilding Area*, 12; Thomas A. Kelly, "The Impact of World War II on the Pascagoula Area: A Study of Economic Change," *Social Science Bulletin* 3 (Summer 1950): 7; Hearings, 1943, 671, 785, 1008; Robert Ingalls to William M. Colmer, Box 301, CPUSM; US Bureau of Yards and Docks, *Building the Navy's Bases in World War II: History of the Bureau of Yards and Docks and the Civil Engineer Corps, 1940–1946*, 2 vols. (Washington, DC: Government Printing Office, 1947), 2:380.
8. Robert Ingalls to Admiral E. S. Land, June 18, 1941, and Robert Ingalls to Thomas M. Woodward, Box 581, E. S. Land to R. I. Ingalls, August 11, 1941, and A. F. Coon to R. I. Ingalls, Box 582, all in USMC.
9. "Foresee Integration in Defense Program," *CD*, June 28, 1941; A. F. Coon to C. F. Palmer, June 30, 1941, and W. R. Guest to C. F. Palmer, August 2, 1941, both in Box 581, USMC.

10. Edward B. Wright Jr. to Mr. Coons, September 14, 1941, and Edward B. Wright Jr. to A. F. Coon, September 19, 1941, both in Box 582, USMC; Charles Van Devander, "U.S. Defense Housing Built for Negroes Goes to Whites," *Washington Post*, January 28, 1942; Gerald Van Dusen, *Detroit's Sojourner Truth Housing Riot of 1942: Prelude to the Race Riot of 1943* (Cheltenham: The History Press, 2020).
11. W. R. Guest to A. F. Coon, March 25, 1942, Box 582, USMC; Hearings, 1943, 1008.
12. Hearings, 1943, 653–656; 756, 764, 785–786, 803, 1028–1029; Jeffries, *Wartime America*, 86; John B. Blandford Jr. to Rear Admiral H. L. Vickery, January 10, 1944, Box 582, USMC. Part of the Eastlawn development, the section with houses was also often called the Maritime Housing Project. To avoid confusion, Maritime Housing Project is used here to identify the first federal housing project built by the Navy.
13. W. R. Guest to A. F. Coon, March 25, 1942, Box 582, USMC; Harrison Otis and J. Warren McCleskey, interview by Leroy and Peterson, November 24, 1943, interview notes, Box 27, City Officials of Pascagoula, interview by Carl Malmberg and Leroy, December 1, 1943, interview notes, Box 28, and Resolution, Pascagoula PTA, May 17, 1944, Box 26, all in WHE; Hearings, 1943, 763–769, 796–797, 803, 823; Kelly, "The Impact of World War II on the Pascagoula Area," 7–8; Richardson Wood, "The Shambles around the War Plant," *Harper's Magazine*, August 1, 1951, 49.
14. Hearings, 1943, 765, 784, 803–804; "Tenants Appeal to Congressmen for Relief Action," *Pascagoula Chronicle-Star combined with Moss Point Advertiser*, November 19, 1943; Committee for Congested Production Areas, Pascagoula Area, Mississippi, reports, February 15, 1944, and July 31, 1944, both in PQHV-BFS: FGR.
15. D. E. Lawrence to P. J. Duff, July 9, 1943, Box 582, USMC; Report of Conference in Office of Mr. Harry G. Thornton, November 18, 1943; Agnes E. Meyer, *Journey through Chaos* (New York: Harcourt, Brace, 1944), 197–198; Hearings, 1943, 786; S. Burton Heath, "Mississippi Boom—Town Has Housing Surplus; Its Ship-Builders Prefer to Live on Farm," *Indiana (Pa.) Gazette*, August 7, 1943; Harrison G. Otis to Tenants, March 20, 1944, Box 1039, BPUSM.
16. Neil R. McMillen, *Dark Journey: Black Mississippians in the Age of Jim Crow* (Urbana: University of Illinois Press, 1989), 14; Hearings, 1943, 805, 994; "Open Homes Unit to Men at Ship-Yards," *CD*, March 28, 1942.
17. "Open Homes Unit to Men at Ship-Yards"; Hearings, 1943, 785–786, 1029; W. L. McMillan, interview by Mr. Leroy, December 4, 1943, interview notes, Box 26, and Mr. Peterson, Report on Tour of Pascagoula's Federal Housing Projects, November 30, 1943, Box 27, both in WHE.
18. Mr. Peterson, Report on Tour of Pascagoula's Federal Housing Projects, November 30, 1943; Hearings, 1943, 843, 991; W. L. McMillan interview; M. L. Brown and E. B. Wright Jr., interview by Mr. Leroy, December 8, 1943, interview notes, Box 27, WHE.
19. Some Problems of the Negro in Mobile, October 9, 1942, Box 4, BAE; Labor Market Developments Report Entailing the Ratio of Non-whites and Women in the Workforce, Labor Demands, Labor Turnover, Training, Absenteeism, Overstaffing, and Related Community Problems such as Day Care, Laundries, and Transportation, June 12, 1943, WMC; Bruce Nelson, "Organized Labor and the Struggle for Black

Equality in Mobile during World War II," *Journal of American History* 80 (December 1993): 958; "Marietta Makes Application for 1000 More Housing Units," *Cobb County (Ga.) Times*, January 4, 1945, and "Growing Gracefully" (editorial), *Marietta (Ga.) Daily Journal*, January 2, 1945, newspaper clippings, both in Box 2, Blair Family Papers, Kennesaw State University Archives, Kennesaw, Georgia; "Marietta Didn't Go Boom!" *The Bellringer*, September 1944; Joe B. Gabriel, interview by Thomas A. Scott, October 23, 2000, transcript, Kennesaw State University Archives.

20. Karen Kruse Thomas, *Deluxe Jim Crow: Civil Rights and American Health Policy, 1935–1954* (Athens: University of Georgia Press, 2011), ch. 2–4.

21. Hearings 1943, 641, 674; Lincoln Allen, "Medical Needs of the War Industry Areas," *Science & Society* 8 (Winter 1944): 30–31; Thomas J. Ward Jr., *Black Physicians in the Jim Crow South* (Fayetteville: University of Arkansas Press, 2003), 39–40.

22. Hearings, 1943, 851; US Department of Labor, *A Statistical Summary of the Pascagoula Shipbuilding Area*, 12; McMillen, *Dark Journey*, 172.

23. Hearings, 1943, 666, 684, 687, 696, 734–735, 742, 850; Thomas, *Deluxe Jim Crow*, ch. 2–4; D'Ann Campbell, *Women at War with America* (Cambridge, MA: Harvard University Press, 1984), 179; War Production Board, Report on the Pascagoula, Mississippi, Area, 15, December 8, 1943, Box 26, and C. M. McGill to C. L. Williams, November 19, 1942, Box 28, both in WHE.

24. Elizabeth Temkin, "Driving Through: Postpartum Care during World War II," *American Journal of Public Health* 89 (April 1999): 587–589; Hearings, 1943, 642, 846–849; Thomas, *Deluxe Jim Crow*, 98–99.

25. Thomas, *Deluxe Jim Crow*, 127–129; Daniel S. Hirshfield, *The Lost Reform: The Campaign for Compulsory Health Insurance in the United States from 1932 to 1943* (Cambridge, MA: Harvard University Press, 1970), 163–165.

26. Hearings, 1943, 961–962.

27. William A. Link, *The Paradox of Southern Progressivism, 1880–1930* (Chapel Hill: University of North Carolina Press, 1992), 142–159; County Board of Supervisors, interview by Carl Malmberg and Truslow, December 7, 1943, interview notes; and Report of R. T. Westman to the Jackson County Board of Supervisors, December 1, 1943, all in Box 28, WHE; Hearings, 1943, 860–862.

28. L. C. Spencer, interview by Peterson and Truslow, December 11, 1943, interview notes, Box 28, WHE; Hearings, 1943, 684, 865–867.

29. David M. Kennedy, *The American People in World War II: Freedom from Fear, Part Two* (New York: Oxford University Press, 1999), 225–228; Tracy Campbell, *The Year of Peril: America in 1942* (New Haven, CT: Yale University Press, 2020), 201–202; L. C. Spencer interview; Hearings, 1943, 638, 669.

30. M. L. Brown and E. B. Wright Jr. interview; Hearings, 1943, 806–808.

31. Thomas, *Deluxe Jim Crow*, 62–68, 129–134; James H. Jones, *Bad Blood: The Tuskegee Syphilis Experiment* (New York: Free Press, 1981); Hearings, 1943, 843–845; Report from Arthur E. Fink to Eliot Ness (Social Protection Division of the FSA), May 25, 1943, Box 29, WHE.

32. Hearings, 1943, 675, 692, 844, 856; Statement of Dr. Hoff, December 8, 1943, Box 29, WHE.

33. Thomas, *Deluxe Jim Crow*, 135–136; Hearings, 1943, 855–859.
34. W. R. Gulley and others to Pat Harrison and Theodore Bilbo, January 23, 1941, Box 1071, BPUSM; Hearings, 1943, 914–915; Minutes of Hearing Regarding Food Shortage Held at Pascagoula, March 22, 1943, Box 27, WHE.
35. Hearings, 1943, 744–746, 748, 781, 916, 919; Tuttle, *Daddy's Gone to War*, 73; Michael C. C. Adams, *The Best War Ever: America and World War II*, 2nd ed. (Baltimore: Johns Hopkins University Press, 2015), 97–102; Steven Mintz and Susan Kellogg, *Domestic Revolutions: A Social History of American Family Life* (New York: Free Press, 1988), 165–167.
36. "National Go-To-School Drive," n.d., 1944, Box 255, Records of Clyde M. Vandeburg, Records of the Office of War Information, Record Group 208, NA-CP; Hearings, 1943, 730, 733; Thomas R. Wells, interview by Carl Malmberg, Peterson, and Leroy, November 30, 1943, interview notes, Box 27, and Mr. and Mrs. Easton King, interview by Carl Malmberg and Truslow, November 22, 1943, interview notes, Box 26, both in WHE; Report from Arthur E. Fink to Eliot Ness (Social Protection Division of the FSA), May 25, 1943; Report of Conference in Office of Mr. Harry G. Thornton, November 18, 1943.
37. Thomas R. Wells interview; Draft of Report on Pascagoula, n.d., 1944, Box 26, WHE; Hearings, 1943, 916.
38. Meyer, *Journey through Chaos*, 200–201.
39. Hearings, 1943, 912, 914–916, 921; M. L. Brown and E. B. Wright Jr. interview.
40. W. R. Gulley and others to Pat Harrison and Theodore Bilbo, January 23, 1941; Hearings, 1943, 912, 920, 928.
41. Charles C. Bolton, *The Hardest Deal of All: The Battle over School Integration in Mississippi, 1870–1980* (Jackson: University Press of Mississippi, 2005), 20, 40–41; S. 1313, 77th Congress, 1st Session (1941); "Mississippi's Interest in Federal Aid for Elementary and Secondary Schools S. 1313," n.d., 1942, Box 1020, BPUSM; Hearings, 1943, 942; "S-1313 Reported Out: South Could Use Money," *Southern Frontier*, July 1942.
42. "School Aid," *Washington Post*, November 28, 1942; "Dispute Given Governor on U.S. School Aid," *Atlanta Constitution*, April 10, 1942; H. M. Ivy to Theodore G. Bilbo, June 19, 1943, Box 1020, BPUSM; *Hearings before a Subcommittee of the Committee on Education and Labor, United States Senate, Seventy-Eighth Congress, April 6–8, 1943*, 78th Cong.; "To Equalize Opportunity," *Atlanta Constitution*, August 9, 1943; C. P. Trussell, "Southerners Kill School Aid Bill as Discrimination Bar Is Adopted," *NYT*, October 21, 1943.
43. *Congressional Record*, October 20, 1943, 8558–8570; Trussell, "Southerners Kill School Aid Bill as Discrimination Bar Is Adopted"; Theodore Bilbo to Mrs. J. M. Kirkpatrick, October 26, 1943, Box 1020, BPUSM; Harry McAlpin, "GOP Trickery Beats U.S. Education Bill," *CD*, October 30, 1943.
44. Interviewer Reports on Conversations with Residents in Northeast Mississippi, Box 3, BAE.
45. Interviewer Reports on Conversations with Residents in Northeast Mississippi, Box 3, BAE.

46. US War Department, *Is a Crime Wave Coming?* (Washington, DC: Government Printing Office, 1946), 13–18; Sandra Moncrief, *The Phantom Barber* (North Charleston, SC: CreateSpace Independent Publishing Platform, 2015), ch. 1–3; Johnnie Richardson Rape Case from Pascagoula, Mississippi, January 1, 1944–December 31, 1944, PQHV-NAACP: SAL; *Wiley v. State*, 197 Miss. 21. Headline in Pascagoula Chronicle Star, June 16, 1942.
47. Moncrief, *The Phantom Barber*, 7–31; J. L. LeFlore to Thurgood Marshall, June 23, 1944, reel 2, John L. LeFlore Papers, SOAL; "Young Pascagoula Negro Held for Murder and Rape of Nellie Ricks," *DDT*, February 27, 1944; *Wiley v. State*, 197 Miss. 21.
48. Johnnie Richardson Rape Case from Pascagoula, Mississippi, January 1, 1944–December 31, 1944.
49. McMillen, *Dark Journey*, part IV; Johnnie Richardson Rape Case from Pascagoula, Mississippi, January 1, 1944–December 31, 1944; "Gets New Trial in Rape Case," *CD*, May 20, 1944.
50. Advance Press Release for Report on Juvenile Delinquency, October 1943; Advance Press Release from the US Department of Labor, April 1944; and Fact Sheet: Wartime Problems of American Children, all in Box 2, Records of Natalie Davisen, Program Manager for Homefront Campaigns, 1943–1945, Records of the Office of War Information, Record Group 208, NA-CP.
51. Malvina Lindsay, "The Gentler Sex: In Defense of Parents," *Washington Post*, December 6, 1943; Adams, *Best War Ever*, 97–101; Mintz and Kellogg, *Domestic Revolutions*, 165–167.
52. Hearings, 1943, 934; Moncrief, *The Phantom Barber*, 4; W. F. Bond and Sara Ricks, interview by Carl Malmberg, interview notes, November 25, 1943, Misdemeanors in Police Court, Pascagoula, Mississippi, July 1 to November 23, 1943, Inclusive; Misdemeanors in Justice of the Peace Court, District III, July 1 to November 29, 1943, Inclusive; Report of Robert G. Caldwell, Social Protection Representative for Mississippi, Federal Security Agency, November 30, 1943; and Report of a Tour of Taverns Near Pascagoula by investigative staff and Mr. and Mrs. Easton King, reported by Peterson, December 4, 1943, all in Box 26, WHE.
53. Hearings, 1943, 657; Kenneth Underwood, "The Church Meets Boomtown Problems," *Religious Education* 39 (January 1, 1944): 36; Draft of Report on Pascagoula, n.d., 1944; Report of a Tour of Taverns Near Pascagoula by investigative staff and Mr. and Mrs. Easton King, reported by Peterson, December 4, 1943, Box 26, WHE.
54. Hearings, 1943, 621, 705, 738, 753–758; Report of Inter-Church Committee to the Sub-committee on Wartime Heath and Education, December 8, 1943, Box 26, WHE; Mr. and Mrs. Easton King interview; Harrison Otis and J. Warren McCleskey interview.
55. Hearings, 1943, 621, 658–659, 883, 988; War Production Board, Report on the Pascagoula, Mississippi, Area, December 8, 1943, Box 26, WHE.
56. Committee for Congested Production Areas, Pascagoula, Mississippi, Report, February 15, 1944, and Report, July 31, 1944.
57. Eleanor Ferguson Straub, "Government Policy toward Civilian Women During World War II" (PhD diss., Emory University, 1973), 285–296; Tuttle, *Daddy's Gone*

to War, 75–83; Howard Dratch, "The Politics of Child Care in the 1940s," *Science & Society* 38 (Summer 1974): 167–204.
58. Tuttle, *Daddy's Gone to War*, 75–83; Dratch, "The Politics of Child Care in the 1940s," 167–204; Emilie Stoltzfus, *Citizen, Mother, Worker: Debating Public Responsibility for Child Care after the Second World War* (Chapel Hill: University of North Carolina Press, 2003), 37–38.
59. Hearings, 1943, 753, 759–761, 918, 929–930.
60. Hearings, 1943, 971; Hodding Carter and Anthony Ragusin, *Gulf Coast Country* (New York: Duell, Sloan & Pearce, 1951), 194–195; Harry Hewes, "War-Boom Town Refuses to Become a Ghost Town," *The American City* 60 (July 1945): 88.

Chapter 5

1. S. D. Redmond to President, Southern Railroad Co., August 11, 1942, Box 1075, Army-AG.
2. J. Clay Smith Jr., *Emancipation: The Making of the Black Lawyer, 1844–1944* (Philadelphia: University of Pennsylvania Press, 1993), 298–320; Charles H. Wilson Sr., *God! Make Me a Man: A Biographical Sketch of Dr. Sidney Dillion Redmond* (Boston: Meador Publishing Co., 1950); "Dr. S. D. Redmond," *NYT*, February 13, 1948.
3. S. D. Redmond to President, Southern Railroad Co., August 11, 1942, and E. E. Norris to C. H. Buford, September 15, 1942, both in Box 1075, Army-AG.
4. Bernard C. Nalty, *Strength for the Fight: A History of Black Americans in the Military* (New York: Free Press, 1986), ch. 5, 7, and 8; Robert B. Edgerton, *Hidden Heroism: Black Soldiers in America's Wars* (Boulder, CO: Westview Press, 2001), 47–82.
5. Jean Byers, *A Study of the Negro in Military Service* (Washington, DC: US Department of Defense, 1950), 62; James C. Cobb, *Industrialization and Southern Society, 1877–1984* (Lexington: University of Kentucky Press, 1984), 51–52; "The Impact of Camp Shelby upon Hattiesburg, Mississippi," unreleased report of the Office of War Information, November 23, 1942, AU: FDR; David M. Kennedy, *The American People in World War II: Freedom from Fear, Part Two* (New York: Oxford University Press, 1999), 286; Ernest Herndon, "Camp Van Dorn Major Impact Here during War," *McComb (Miss.) Enterprise-Journal*, August 4, 1989; L. M. Caulfield, *Camp Van Dorn, Centreville, Mississippi, 1942–1947* (n.p., 1986).
6. Mississippi House of Representatives delegation to General George C. Marshall, April 30, 1942, Box 1076, Army-AG; W. V. Pruit to Army Chief of Staff, August 14, 1942, Box 1074, Army-AG; "Asks North Posts for Negro Troops," *NYT*, August 3, 1942; "Bankhead Request Is Rejected by Army," *NYT*, August 14, 1942.
7. John Morton Blum, *V Was for Victory: Politics and American Culture during World War II* (New York: Harcourt Brace Jovanovich, 1976), 184–185; Sherie Mershon and Steven Schlossman, *Foxholes & Color Lines: Desegregating the U.S. Armed Forces* (Baltimore: Johns Hopkins University Press, 1998), ch. 2; Richard M.

Dalfiume, *Desegregation of the U.S. Armed Forces: Fighting on Two Fronts, 1939–1953* (Columbia: University of Missouri Press, 1969), ch. 2; Andrew E. Kersten, *A. Philip Randolph: A Life in the Vanguard* (Lanham, MD: Rowman & Littlefield, 2007), 53–55; Gilbert Ware, *William Hastie: Grace under Pressure* (New York: Oxford University Press, 1985), ch. 8.

8. "Selective Service and Training Act of 1940," https://www.loc.gov/item/uscode1940-005050a003/; Digest of War Department Policy Pertaining to Negro Military Personnel, January 1, 1944 (War Department Policy in Regard to Negroes, October 16, 1940), Online Documents: Desegregation of the Armed Forces, Harry S. Truman Presidential Museum and Library, www.trumanlibrary.org. Approximately 350,000 women volunteered for military service during the war, though "there was an underrepresentation of women from the South" in the World War II military. See D'Ann Cambell, *Women at War with America: Private Lives in a Patriotic Era* (Cambridge, MA: Harvard University Press, 1984), 20–23.

9. Byers, *A Study of the Negro in Military Service*, 7–27; Nalty, *Strength for the Fight*, 136; Kennedy, *The American People in World War II*, 209; G. C. Marshall to Secretary of War, December 1, 1941, in *Blacks in the United States Armed Forces: Basic Documents*, ed. Morris J. MacGregor and Bernard C. Nalty, 13 vols. (Wilmington, DE: Scholarly Resources, 1977), 5:114–115.

10. A. L. Ford to Henry L. Stimson, July 31, 1942, and John W. Martyn to A. L. Ford, August 10, 1942, both in Box 1075, Army-AG; A. Leonard Allen to Robert P. Patterson, September 21, 1945; Robert P. Patterson to A. Leonard Allen, October 26, 1942; and Mrs. Fred Haynes to President Roosevelt, September 24, 1942, all in Box 1073, Army-AG; Report of Sara Kennedy, November 1942, PQHV-NAACP: BDAC; Ulysses Lee, *The Employment of Negro Troops* (Washington, DC: Center of Military History, US Army, 1994), 408–412; H. S. Milton, ed., *Utilization of Negro Manpower in the Army: A 1951 Study* (Chevy Chase, MD: Operations Research Office, Johns Hopkins University, 1955), 560; Tracy Campbell, *The Year of Peril: America in 1942* (New Haven, CT: Yale University Press, 2020), 233–234.

11. Capt. H. Ficklen, "You're in the Army Now," *Chicago Daily News*, October 6, 1942; Louise Thompson to Henry Stimson, October 9, 1942; and Stanley J. Grogan to Editor, *Chicago Daily News*, January 6, 1943, all in Box 1073, Army-AG; Robert F. Darden III, "Dallas Morning News Editorial Cartoonists: Influences of John Knott on Jack "Herc" Ficklen and William McClanahan" (MA thesis, Journalism, North Texas State, 1978), ch. 3; Byers, *A Study of the Negro in Military Service*, 27–28. Ficklen's comic appeared in papers around the country.

12. Robert P. Patterson to Walter White, August 17, 1942, PQHV-NAACP: EVH; "Air Base Buses to Comply with Segregation Law," *DDT*, July 22, 1942.

13. Robin D. G. Kelley, *Race Rebels: Culture, Politics, and the Black Working Class* (New York: Free Press, 1994), 62; Julia E. Baxter to Walter White, September 24, 1943, part 9A, reel 9, Papers of the NAACP; Boyte Austin Presnell, "The Impact of World War II on Race Relations in Mobile, Alabama, 1940–1948" (MA thesis, Atlanta University, 1972), 37–38; "Hearing Due Today in Negro's Death," *Mobile Register*, August 18, 1942; "Some Problems of the Negro in Mobile," October 9, 1942, Box 4,

BAE; Margaret A. Burnham, *By Hands Now Known: Jim Crow's Legal Executioners* (New York: W. W. Norton, 2022), 78–83.

14. Office of War Information, "Community Tensions in Three Army Camp Impact Areas," December 9, 1942, 9–27, Special Services Division, Report No. 100, AU: FDR; "The Impact of Camp Shelby upon Hattiesburg, Mississippi," 21–22, 33; Donald Young to Francis Keppel, June 9, 1943, Box 37, General Correspondence of John J. McCloy, 1941–1945, Records of the Office of the Secretary of War, Record Group 107, NA-CP.

15. MacGregor and Nalty, *Blacks in the United States Armed Forces*, 5: 168; Lee, *Employment of Negro Troops*, 97–98; W. A. Brower, "Soldier Slain, 1 Hurt at Army Camp in Miss.," *BAA*, June 12, 1943; "The Impact of Camp Shelby upon Hattiesburg, Mississippi," 34; C. C. Park (Inspector General) to Commanding General, Third Army, June 16, 1943, in US Dept. of the Army, *A Historical Analysis of the 364th Infantry in World War II* (Washington, DC: US Dept. of the Army, 1999); Black soldier from the 369th Coast Artillery Regiment to Billy Rowe, April 29, 1943, Box 1070, Army-AG; Motley, *The Invisible Soldier*, 162; Bryan D. Booker, *African Americans in the United States Army in World War II* (Jefferson, NC: McFarland & Co., 2008), 288; Order of Colonel Schmid, "Off Limits Area," March 19, 1943, and Map of Camp Gordon, Georgia, both in PQHV-NAACP: EVH.

16. Claude Montgomery Jr., interview by Neil McMillen, December 2, 1994, Vol. 597, Mississippi Oral History Program, University of Southern Mississippi.

17. Morris J. MacGregor, *Integration of the Armed Forces, 1940–1965* (Washington, DC: Government Printing Office, 1989), ch. 2; Lee, *Employment of Negro Troops*, 134; Will V. Neely, "Jim Crow Absent at Ft. Benning," *Kansas City Call*, October 9, 1942; Pete Jarman to Henry L. Stimson, June 8, 1943, Box 1068, Army-AG.

18. "Soldiers Segregated at Hospital," *CD*, October 2, 1943; Abner Spiers to Senator Bilbo, February 10, 1942, Box 1084, BPUSM; Pete Jarman to Henry L. Stimson, June 8, 1943, and Henry L. Stimson to Pete Jarman, June 16, 1943, both in Box 1068, Army-AG; J. M. Housworth to Senator Russell, August 22, 1942, and John W. Martyn to Richard B. Russell, June 4, 1942, both in Box 1075, Army-AG.

19. Thomas A. Guglielmo, "A Martial Freedom Movement: Black G.I.s' Political Struggles during World War II," *Journal of American History* 104 (March 2018): 879–903, explores various expression of activism by Black soldiers during the war. Neil R. McMillen, "Fighting for What We Didn't Have: How Mississippi's Black Veterans Remember World War II," in *Remaking Dixie: The Impact of World War II on the American South*, ed. Neil R. McMillen (Jackson: University Press of Mississippi, 1997), 93–110, shows that service in the conflict affected Black Mississippians in different, and often contradictory, ways.

20. Ware, *William Hastie*, 113–114; Douglas Walter Bristol Jr., "Terror, Anger, and Patriotism: Understanding the Resistance of Black Soldiers during World War II," in *Integrating the U.S. Military: Race, Gender, and Sexual Orientation since World War II*, ed. Douglas W. Bristol Jr. and Heather Marie Stur (Baltimore: Johns Hopkins University Press, 2017), 15–17; Jack D. Walker to his mother, March 26, 1941, and Edward J. Cox to Walter White, April 7, 1941, both in part 7A, reel 24, Papers of the NAACP; Thomas H. Brewer to Judge William Hastie, July 16, 1941, William H. Hastie

to the Secretary of War, October 15, 1941, and William H. Hastie to the Adjutant General, January 23, 1942, all in PQHV-BFS: FGR.
21. Information on Lummus from Ancestry.com. According to the 1940 census, of the 139 soldiers who lived in the barracks with Lummus in April 1940, all but six were born in the South.
22. Alexa Mills, "A Lynching Kept Out of Sight," *Washington Post*, September 2, 2016; "Soldier's Body Found Hanging from Trees near Ft. Benning," *Chicago Bee*, April 17, 1941, and "Negro Soldier Killed by Lynchers," flyer, April 14, 1941, both in PQHV-BFS: FGR; Jack D. Walker to his mother, March 29, 1941, and Roy Wilkins to President Roosevelt, April 18, 1941, both in part 7A, reel 24, Papers of the NAACP; James Albert Burran, "Racial Violence in the South During World War II" (PhD diss., University of Tennessee, 1977), 32, 44–45; Lee, *Employment of Negro Troops*, 348.
23. Mills, "A Lynching Kept Out of Sight"; Roy Wilkins to President Roosevelt, April 18, 1941, part 7A, reel 24, Papers of the NAACP.
24. "Tuskegee Reports 4 1941 Lynchings," *Robesonian* (Lumberton, NC), January 2, 1942; Jesse Daniel Ames, *The Changing Character of Lynching: Review of Lynching, 1931–1941, with a Discussion of Recent Developments in This Field* (Atlanta: Commission on Interracial Cooperation, 1942), 39.
25. Lee, *Employment of Negro Troops*, 323–325; George Grant to the War Department, May 4, 1943, PQHV-NAACP: EVH.
26. Byers, *A Study of the Negro in Military Service*, 28, 52–54; Privates of the 364th Engineers to the NAACP, March 6, 1943, PQHV-NAACP: EVH.
27. Byers, *A Study of the Negro in Military Service*, 63.
28. Office of War Information, "Community Tensions in Three Army Camp Impact Areas," 9–27.
29. Motley, *The Invisible Soldier*, 162. For an examination of the Colfax Massacre, see Charles Lane, *The Day Freedom Died: The Colfax Massacre, the Supreme Court, and the Betrayal of Reconstruction* (New York: Henry Holt & Co., 2008).
30. Georgia M. Johnson to William H. Hastie, January 24, 1942, PQHV-BFS: FGR; "Army Justifies Force in Alexandria Riot, Puts Blame on Civilian Police," *CD*, January 31, 1942; "Blames War Department's Jim Crow Policy for Soldier Riot in South," *CD*, February 7, 1942.
31. "White and Negro Troops Clash at Alexandria; 30 Wounded," *Montgomery (Ala.) Advertiser*, January 12, 1942; Ralph Matthews, "La. Rioting Planned by Whites," *BAA*, January 22, 1942; Statement of Sgt. John Hines, January 18, 1942, PQHV-NAACP: SS; Penn Kimball, "PM's Investigation of the Alexandria, La., Race Riots," *PM*, January 21, 1942; Penn Kimball, "Army Censors Facts on Riot," *PM*, January 22, 1942; "Negroes Kept in Camp after Louisiana Riot," *NYT*, January 12, 1942; Ralph Matthews, "La. Rioting Planned by Whites," *BAA*, January 22, 1942.
32. Truman K. Gibson Jr. to George Roudebush (citing confidential War Department report), May 21, 1943, PQHV-BFS: FGR; "White and Negro Troops Clash at Alexandria"; Matthews, "La. Rioting Planned by Whites."
33. "President Asked to Investigate Race Riots in Louisiana" (Union for Democratic Action press release), January 22, 1942, Member of the 91st Engineers to Walter

White, January 13, 1942, Ralph Robinson to Mr. and Mrs. Clem Jones, January 11, 1942, Statement of Sgt. John Hines, January 18, 1942, James B. LaFourche to Walter White, January 31, 1942, and "Louisiana Disorder Investigated" (War Department press release), January 23, 1942, all in PQHV-NAACP: SS; Matthews, "La. Rioting Planned by Whites"; Kimball, "PM's Investigation of the Alexandria, La., Race Riots"; William M. Simpson, "A Tale Untold? The Alexandria, Louisiana, Lee Street Riot," *Louisiana History* 35 (Spring 1994): 133–149.

34. Statement of Mary Frances Scales, n.d., and clipping from the *Louisiana Weekly*, n.d., both in PQHV-NAACP: SS; "Army Justifies Force in Alexandria Riot, Puts Blame on Civilian Police"; Kimball, "PM's Investigation of the Alexandria, La., Race Riots"; "President Asked to Investigate Race Riots in Louisiana"; Matthews, "La. Rioting Planned by Whites"; Rachel L. Emanuel and Alexander P. Tureaud, *More Noble Cause: A. P. Tureaud and the Struggle for Civil Rights in Louisiana* (Baton Rouge: Louisiana State University Press, 2011), 87.

35. "White and Negro Troops Clash at Alexandria"; Burran, "Racial Violence in the South during World War II," 63–68; "La. Whites Alarmed by Courage Shown by Negroes during Riot," *Philadelphia Tribune*, January 31, 1942; "Night of Horror Vividly Recalled by Brutalized Victims of White MP's, State and Civilian Police in Riot," *Louisiana Weekly*, January 24, 1942; James B. LaFourche to Walter White, January 19, 1942, Thomas R. Greene memo to the Officer in Charge, March 12, 1942, and James B. LaFourche to Walter White, January 31, 1942, all in PQHV-NAACP: SS; William H. Hastie to P. L. Prattis, November 12, 1942, PQHV-BFS: FGR.

36. L. J. Frank Sr. to Theodore Bilbo, April 7, 1942, Box 1066, BPUSM.

37. For an explanation of the operation of "White law" in the Deep South during the segregation era, see Neil R. McMillen, *Dark Journey: Black Mississippians in the Age of Jim Crow* (Urbana: University of Illinois Press, 1989), part IV.

38. William H. Chafe et al., eds., *Remembering Jim Crow: African Americans Tell about Life in the Segregated South* (New York: New Press, 2001); "Community Tensions in Three Army Camp Impact Areas," 10; "All Not Well at Camp Shelby, Miss.," *BAA*, July 5, 1941; Charles C. Walker to Secretary Stimpson [sic], April 8, 1942, Box 1076, and two letters from anonymous soldiers to Secretary of War, July 1942, Box 1075, all in Army-AG; Ernest L. Spivey to Roscoe Dungee, June 2, 1942, PQHV-NAACP: EVH. Black soldiers outside of the South were also denied access to local communities because of conflicts with local law enforcement. See James C. Kayne to Secretary of War, September 14, 1942, Box 1073, Army-AG.

39. George Grant to the War Department, May 4, 1943; Burran, "Racial Violence in the South During World War II," 153; "The Impact of Camp Shelby upon Hattiesburg, Mississippi," 26; "Blames War Department's Jim Crow Policy for Soldier Riot in South"; Georgia M. Johnson to William Hastie, January 1, 1942, PQHV-BFS: FGR; "Negro Soldiers and White M.P.'s Shoot It Out in Alabama," *New York Age*, June 3, 1944; Penn Kimball, "Why Army Had Race Rioting," *PM*, January 23, 1942.

40. Ernest L. Spivey to Roscoe Dungee, June 2, 1942.

41. Burran, "Racial Violence in the South during World War II," 76–77; Statement of Pvt. John Spears, November 1, 1942, and Report of Investigation of Staff Judge Advocate,

Lieutenant Colonel Julien C. Hyer, JACD on Private Raymond Carr Case, Alexandria, Louisiana, November 13, 1942, both in PQHV-BFS: FGR. Biographical details for Raymond Carr from Ancestry.com

42. Truman K. Gibson Jr. with Steve Huntley, *Knocking Down Barriers: My Fight for Black America* (Evanston, IL: Northwestern University Press, 2005), 103; Report of Investigation of Staff Judge Advocate, Lieutenant Colonel Julien C. Hyer, JACD on Private Raymond Carr Case, Alexandria, Louisiana, November 13, 1942, Richard Donovan to Governor Sam Jones, November 13, 1942, and John J. McCloy to Francis Biddle, April 23, 1943, all in PQHV-BFS: FGR; "Jury Won't Indict Cop in Slaying," *CD*, April 24, 1943; "Hit Refusal to Try Killer of Soldier," *CD*, May 8, 1943.

43. United Service Organizations, *Operation USO: Report of the President, February 4, 1941–January 9, 1948* (New York: n.p., 1948), 1, 7, 16; "Negro Soldiers Have Trouble with MPs at Alexandria, La.," *The Southern Frontier*, February 1942; "Camp Shelby Soldiers Get a USO Center," *CD*, March 21, 1942.

44. "The Impact of Camp Shelby upon Hattiesburg, Mississippi," 26–27; Reports of the Activities of the USO Club, East 6th Street, Hattiesburg, Mississippi, June–August 1942, Box 584, Tatum Family Business Records, McCain Library and Archives, University of Southern Mississippi, Hattiesburg; "Camp Shelby, Miss.," *CD*, August 8, 1942.

45. "The Impact of Camp Shelby upon Hattiesburg, Mississippi," 27; F. M. Tatum and S. H. Blair to Blanche Best, August 18, 1942, Helen Crawley to F. M. Tatum and S. H. Blair, September 1, 1942, F. M. Tatum to Helen Crawley, September 10, 1942, Helen Crawley to F. M. Tatum, September 22, 1942, Petition from Advisory and Leadership Committee of the USO (Colored), October 12, 1942, Shelby Pickett to T. A. Rymer, February 5, 1943, and Agreement for the Operation of the Negro USO Club in the City of Hattiesburg, Miss., April 1943, all in Box 584, Tatum Family Business Records.

46. "The Impact of Camp Shelby upon Hattiesburg, Mississippi," 24; Clarence Jones affidavit, June 15, 1943, and Wilbur T. Jackson affidavit, June 11, 1943, both in PQHV-NAACP: EVH.

47. Truman K. Gibson Jr. to J. A. Ulio, May 9, 1942, and J. A. Ulio to Truman K. Gibson Jr., May 21, 1942, both in Box 1076, Army-AG.

48. Roy Wilkins to Henry L. Stimson, January 23, 1942, PQHV-BFS: FGR.

49. Roy Wilkins to Henry L. Stimson, January 23, 1942.

Chapter 6

1. Patricia Sullivan, *Lift Every Voice: The NAACP and the Making of the Civil Rights Movement* (New York: New Press, 2009), 277–281; Dominic J. Capeci Jr. and Martha Wilkerson, *Layered Violence: The Detroit Rioters of 1943* (Jackson: University Press of Mississippi, 1991); Thomas J. Sugrue, *The Origins of the Urban Crisis: Race and Inequality in Postwar Detroit* (Princeton, NJ: Princeton University Press, 1996), ch. 1; Eduardo Obregón Pagán, *Murder at the Sleepy Lagoon: Zoot Suits, Race, and Riot*

in Wartime L.A. (Chapel Hill: University of North Carolina Press, 2003); Edward J. Escobar, "Zoot-Suiters and Cops: Chicano Youth and the Los Angeles Police Department during World War II," in *The War in American Culture*, ed. Lewis A. Erenberg and Susan E. Hirsch (Chicago: University of Chicago Press, 1996), 284–309; Robert A. Hill, ed., *The FBI's RACON: Racial Conditions in the United States during World War II* (Boston: Northeastern University Press, 1995), 717; "Riot Rumors Reported in Three Big Cities," *CD*, July 10, 1943; Kenneth D. Rose, *Myth and the Greatest Generation: A Social History of Americans in World War II* (New York: Routledge, 2008), 133.

2. "History of the 364th Infantry," in U.S. Department of the Army, *A Historical Analysis of the 364th Infantry in World War II* (Washington, DC: US Department of the Army, 1999); Truman K. Gibson Jr. with Steve Huntley, *Knocking Down Barriers: My Fight for Black America* (Evanston, IL: Northwestern University Press, 2005), 14; Mark V. Tushnet, *Making Civil Rights Law: Thurgood Marshall and the Supreme Court, 1936–1961* (New York: Oxford University Press, 1994), 64–66. The army's *Historical Analysis* contains a narrative history of the 364th, an analysis of the regiment's personnel over time, and summaries of several interviews with members of the 364th who served during World War II.

3. Thomas J. Ward Jr., "Competent Counsel: Thurgood Marshall, the Black Press, and the Alexandria Soldiers' Rape Trials," *Louisiana History* 61 (Summer 2020): 229–266. After World War II ended, the War Department created a Clemency Board, which reviewed more than 27,000 cases in which a convicted offender was still imprisoned; the Board reduced or ended the sentence in 85 percent of these cases. See Arthur E. Farmer and Richard H. Wels, "Command Control—Or Military Justice," *New York University Law Quarterly Review* 24 (April 1949): 265.

4. "History of the 364th Infantry"; Elmer P. Gibson to Truman K. Gibson Jr., July 14, 1943, PQHV-BFS: FGR; "Feel Commanding Officer's Inhumanity Provoked Riot," *Pittsburgh Courier*, January 2, 1943.

5. Judge Advocate General's Department, *Board of Review: Holdings, Opinions, and Reviews* 16 (1942–1943): 341–348.

6. "History of the 364th Infantry"; Interview with Robert Thomson, in US Department of the Army, *A Historical Analysis of the 364th Infantry in World War II*; Judge Advocate General's Department, *Board of Review: Holdings, Opinions, and Reviews* 20 (1942–1943): 169–188.

7. "History of the 364th Infantry"; Judge Advocate General's Department, *Board of Review: Holdings, Opinions, and Reviews* 20 (1942–1943): 169–188; Ollie North Courts-Martial Transcript, January 1, 1943–December 31, 1943, PQHV-NAACP: EVH; "News from Home: Arizona," *Yank: The Army Newspaper*, March 12, 1943, Service Newspapers of World War II, Adam Matthew Digital; "2 Killed, 12 Shot in Negro-Troop Riot at Phoenix," *New York Herald Tribune*, November 28, 1942.

8. "History of the 364th Infantry"; "Armored Cars Patroled [sic] City," *BAA*, December 12, 1942; Judge Advocate General's Department, *Board of Review: Holdings, Opinions, and Reviews* 20 (1942–1943): 169–188; Louis R. Lautier to Thurgood Marshall,

November 29, 1943, PQHV-BFS: FGR; Ollie North Courts-Martial Transcript, January 1, 1943–December 31, 1943.
9. "History of the 364th Infantry"; Interview with Robert Thomson; C. C. Park (Inspector General) to Commanding General, Third Army, June 16, 1943, in US Department of the Army, *A Historical Analysis of the 364th Infantry in World War II*; Irvin C. Wiley to Whom It May Concern, June 1, 1943, PQHV-BFS: FGR; Carroll Case, *The Slaughter: An American Atrocity* (Asheville, NC?: FBC, Inc., 1998), 26–30 (Inspector General's report of June 8, 1943).
10. Interview with Robert Thomson; Ulysses Lee, *The Employment of Negro Troops* (Washington, DC: Center of Military History, US Army, 1994), 367.
11. C. C. Park (Inspector General) to Commanding General, Third Army, June 16, 1943; Interview with Robert Thomson; W. A. Brower, "Soldier Slain, 1 Hurt at Army Camp in Miss.," *BAA*, June 12, 1943; Lathe B. Row to Inspector General, September 21, 1943, Box 472, Security-Classified General Correspondence 1942–1945, Records of the War Department General and Special Staffs, Record Group 165, NA-CP; Interview with Samuel D. Smith, in US Department of the Army, *A Historical Analysis of the 364th Infantry in World War II*; Prentice Thomas to Truman K. Gibson, June 9, 1943, PQHV-NAACP: EVH; William E. Hughes and Samuel W. Rosso, interview with author, February 12, 2018, interview notes in author's possession. Hughes and Rosso were both boys living in Centreville at the time of the 1943 events, aged ten and thirteen respectively.
12. Lee, *The Employment of Negro Troops*, 366–368; Motley, *The Invisible Soldier*, 126–127.
13. Clarence Jones affidavit, June 15, 1943, Riots and Disorders, Assault, Suicide, and Homicide, Violence against African American Military Personnel, June 1943–April 1945, BFS-PQHV; Interview with Robert Thomson; "Two Others Die in Dixie Race Outbreak," undated *CD* news clipping, June 1943, Box 1067, Army-AG. I found no corroboration for either of these killings. The army's investigation in the 1990s of the personnel records of the 364th did not uncover the deaths of any members of the 364th Regiment in late May 1943 other than William Walker. See "Personnel Investigation."
14. Motley, *The Invisible Soldier*, 124; C. C. Park (Inspector General) to Commanding General, Third Army, June 16, 1943; John Edgar Hoover to the Attorney General, June 5, 1943, Box 1068, Army-AG; Case, *The Slaughter*, 26–30.
15. Prentice Thomas to Truman K. Gibson, June 9, 1943; Lathe B. Row to Inspector General, September 21, 1943; Case, *The Slaughter*, 26–30; C. C. Park (Inspector General) to Commanding General, Third Army, June 16, 1943; Hughes and Rosso interview.
16. Case, *The Slaughter*, 26–30; C. C. Park (Inspector General) to Commanding General, Third Army, June 16, 1943. The account of the confrontation between Hix and Watkins has been reconstructed from numerous documents in Box 1068, Army-AG. Background information on Hix from Ancestry.com.
17. James A. Burran, "Racial Violence in the South during World War II" (PhD diss., University of Tennessee, 1977), 136; James B. McIntyre, Report of Investigation,

June 2, 1943, Homicide, Assault, and Lynching, Violence against African American Military Personnel, March–November 1942, BFS-PQHV.
18. McIntyre, Report of Investigation, June 2, 1943; Certificate of Death, Pvt. William Walker, May 30, 1943, The Civil Rights and Restorative Justice Project, Northeastern University. The War Department sent Walker's sister, Flora Walker, a telegram, which said, "Pvt. William Walker died suddenly at 4:45 pm, May 30 in the Station hospital." See "Two Others Die in Dixie Race Outbreak."
19. Case, *The Slaughter*, 26–30; C. C. Park (Inspector General) to Commanding General, Third Army, June 16, 1943; John Edgar Hoover to the Attorney General, June 5, 1943; Certificate of Death, Pvt. William Walker, May 30, 1943.
20. McIntyre, Report of Investigation, June 2, 1943. None of the army or other federal investigators made or mentioned the connection between the two incidents involving Hix and Black soldiers, though his reported comment at the hospital suggests his anti-Black reputation may have been well known.
21. Brief and Argument in Support of Petition for Clemency, In the Matter of Milan G. Brown, n.d., 1944?, Courts-Martial, Including Rape, Murder, and Mutiny, January 1, 1945–December 31, 1949, NAACP-PQHV; Judge Advocate General's Department, *Board of Review: Holdings, Opinions, and Reviews* 44 (1945): 359–361; C. C. Park (Inspector General) to Commanding General, Third Army, June 16, 1943.
22. C. C. Park (Inspector General) to Commanding General, Third Army, June 16, 1943; Report of Homer B. Scretchings, November 10, 1943, in US Department of the Army, *A Historical Analysis of the 364th Infantry*; Case, *The Slaughter*, 26–30, 48; Motley, *The Invisible Soldier*, 127; Burran, "Racial Violence in the South during World War II," 137; Irvin C. Wiley to Whom It May Concern, June 1, 1943.
23. C. C. Park (Inspector General) to Commanding General, Third Army, June 16, 1943; Corporal Anthony J. Smirely Jr. to E. Washington Rhodes, May 30, 1943, Riots and Disorders, Assault, Suicide, and Homicide, Violence against African American Military Personnel, June 1943–April 1945, BFS-PQHV; Irvin C. Wiley to Whom It May Concern, June 1, 1943; "Governor Asks for Investigation of Camp Van Dorn," *DDT*, June 1, 1943.
24. Wilbur T. Jackson statement, June 11, 1943, and Corporal Anthony J. Smirely Jr. to E. Washington Rhodes, May 31, 1943, both in PQHV-BFS
25. Wilbur T. Jackson statement, June 11, 1943, and Corporal Anthony J. Smirely Jr. to E. Washington Rhodes, May 31, 1943, both in PQHV-BFS: FGR; Case, *The Slaughter*, 26–30; John Edgar Hoover to the Attorney General, June 5, 1943.
26. Paul B. Johnson to Theodore Bilbo, May 31, 1943, Box 1066, BPUSM; Memo from George F. Kennedy to Officer in Charge, June 12, 1943, in US Department of the Army, *A Historical Analysis of the 364th Infantry*. For examples of press coverage that promoted the "clean out Mississippi" statement, see "Governor Asks for Investigation of Camp Van Dorn," and "Colored Troops at Centreville Accused 'Fomenting' Race Riots; Governor Requests U.S. Probe," *Jackson Clarion Ledger*, May 31, 1943.
27. "Death Reports at Camp Van Dorn Are Greatly Exaggerated by Rumor," no date, early June 1943, *McComb (Miss.) Enterprise-Journal*, Subject File: Camp Van Dorn,

MDAH; Telegram, Mrs. W. Warren to Adjutant General, May 31, 1943, Box 1068, Army-AG; Clarence Jones affidavit, June 15, 1943.

28. Neil A. Wynn, *The African American Experience during World War II* (Lanham, MD: Rowman & Littlefield, 2010), 48; Vito Marcantonio to President Franklin D. Roosevelt, June 16, 1943, in Appendix to the *Congressional Record*, June 24, 1943, 3205; Lee, *The Employment of Negro Troops*, 366–375; "District Attorney Reveals Rape of White Woman by Negro Soldiers; State Offers Reward," *Jackson Clarion-Ledger*, June 5, 1943; J. P. Coleman to Thomas G. Abernethy, August 10, 1943, BPUSM.

29. Burran, "Racial Violence in the South during World War II," 148–149; Colored Americans to Inspector General's Dept., June 1943, PQHV-BFS: FGR; "The Attack on Duck Hill," *Time*, September 13, 1943; "6 Soldiers Get 10–15 Yrs. in Shooting," *BAA*, September 11, 1943; "Two More Sentenced in Duck Hill Shooting, Five Others Acquitted; Civil Officials Praise 'Army's Action'" (Associated Negro Press Release), September 13, 1943, PQHV-BFS: ORP1.

30. G. M. Halloran to Commanding General, Fourth Service Command, June 26, 1943, PQHV-BFS: FGR; "Negro Soldier Shot, Wounded by Patrolman," *Jackson Clarion-Ledger*, June 7, 1943; "15 Jailed, 2 Shot in Another Army Riot," *BAA*, June 19, 1943.

31. "Camp Stewart Soldiers Riot; One Is Killed," *Atlanta Constitution*, June 11, 1943; "Camp Stewart Riot Lasted for 3 Hours," *BAA*," July 3, 1943; "Fear Serious Racial Clashes at Camp Stewart, Ga., between Men of 369th and Georgia 'Crackers,'" *New York Age*, May 8, 1943; James R. O'Hanlon, "Army Investigates Negro-White Battle in South's 'Powder Keg,'" *PM*, June 11, 1943; J. A. Ulio to Assistant Chief of Staff, May 15, 1943, and William D. Alford to Franklin D. Roosevelt, May 11, 1943, both in Box 1070, Army-AG. Also see Daniel Kryder, *Divided Arsenal: Race and the American State during World War II* (New York: Cambridge University Press, 2000), ch. 6.

32. Marvin E. Fletcher, *America's First Black General: Benjamin O. Davis, Sr., 1880–1970* (Lawrence: University Press of Kansas, 1989).

33. Virgil L. Peterson to Chief of Staff, June 4, 1943, and Roy Wilkins to Truman K. Gibson Jr., May 14, 1943, both in PQHV-BFS: FGR; Prentice Thomas to Walter White, May 14, 1943, PQHV-NAACP: EVH.

34. "Camp Stewart Riot Lasted for 3 Hours"; Lee, *The Employment of Negro Troops*, 371–372; Bell Irvin Wiley, *The Training of Negro Troops* (Washington, DC: Historical Section, Army Ground Forces, 1946), 50–51.

35. Case, *The Slaughter*, 26–30; C. C. Park (Inspector General) to Commanding General, Third Army, June 16, 1943; Courtney H. Hodges, Decision on Recommendations of Inspector General, June 21, 1943, in US Department of the Army, *History of the 364th Infantry*; Michael Newton, *Unsolved Civil Rights Murder Cases, 1934–1970* (Jefferson, NC: McFarland, 2016), 127; Lee, *The Employment of Negro Troops*, 368.

36. C. C. Park (Inspector General) to Commanding General, Third Army, June 16, 1943.

37. Corporal Anthony J. Smirely Jr. to E. Washington Rhodes, May 30, 1943; Thomas Joyce, "The 'Double V' Was for Victory: Black Soldiers, the Black Protest, and World War II" (PhD diss., Ohio State University, 1993), 298–299.

38. C. C. Park (Inspector General) to Commanding General, Third Army, June 16, 1943; Judge Advocate General's Department, *Board of Review: Holdings, Opinions, and Reviews* 44 (1945): 359–363.
39. Case, *The Slaughter*, 26–30; John Andrew Kirk, "Black Activism in Arkansas, 1940–1970" (PhD diss., University of Newcastle upon Tyne, 1997), 71–78; Virgil L. Peterson, The Hall of Valor Project, https://valor.militarytimes.com/hero/18034; "History of the 364th Infantry"; "Negro Soldiers to Remain at Camp Van Dorn as Conditions Become Normal," *Atlanta Daily World*, July 7, 1943; "Cop Lets 'Em Fight in Vicksburg, Miss.," *BAA*, July 24, 1943; "Negro Troops to Keep Guns in Mississippi," *NYAN*, July 10, 1943.
40. Memo from George F. Kennedy to Officer in Charge, June 12, 1943; Report of Homer B. Scretchings, November 10, 1943.
41. Memo from George F. Kennedy to Officer in Charge, June 12, 1943; "History of the 364th Infantry."
42. Corp. Marold Blythe (Letter to the Editor), *NYAN*, July 24, 1943; Lee, *The Employment of Negro Troops*, 368–369; Statement of J. B. Meriwether, July 5, 1943, in US Department of the Army, *A Historical Analysis of the 364th Infantry*; Louis B. Lautier to Carl Murphy, July 19, 1943, PQHV-BFS: FGR.
43. Courtney H. Hodges, Decision on Recommendations of Inspector General, June 21, 1943; Memo of Homer E. Shields, June 4, 1943, and Charles Hudson to Costella Hudson, June 16, 1943, both in Box 1067, Army-AG; "History of the 364th Infantry"; Lathe B. Row to Inspector General, September 21, 1943, and R. A. Meredith to Chief of Staff, US Army, October 14, 1943, both in Box 472, Security-Classified General Correspondence 1942–1945, Records of the War Department General and Special Staffs, Record Group 165, NA-CP.
44. Lathe B. Row to Inspector General, September 21, 1943; Robert P. Patterson to Thomas G. Abernethy, February 22, 1944, Box 382, Thomas G. Abernethy Collection, UM.
45. Case, *The Slaughter*; Roberto Suro and Michael A. Fletcher, "Mississippi Massacre, or Myth? Army Tries to Put to Rest Allegations of 1943 Slaughter of Black Troops," *Washington Post*, December 23, 1999. Case designed his book largely as a work of fiction, but a long opening chapter offers a historical account about the massacre of Black soldiers at Camp Van Dorn.
46. "Personnel Investigation," in US Department of the Army, *A Historical Analysis of the 364th Infantry in World War II*; Suro and Fletcher, "Mississippi Massacre, or Myth?"; Scott Tynes, "Army Officially Refutes Claim of Massacre," *Brookhaven (Miss.) Daily Leader*, November 16, 1998.
47. Case, *The Slaughter*, 6; Statement of J. B. Meriwether, July 5, 1943; Donald Adderton, "Old Rumor Makes for Dramatic Reading, But Does Disservice to Truth of the 364th," *Biloxi Sun Herald*, November 14, 1998; Geoffrey F. X. O'Connell, "Missing in Action," June 11 2001, Inthesetimes.com, https://inthesetimes.com/issue/25/14/oconnell2514.html. Martzall's military records show that he entered service in September 1943, months after the racial turmoil at Camp Van Dorn took place (though before the massacre he claimed occurred later that fall). See Application for World War II Compensation of William Penn Martzall, April 6, 1950, Ancestry.com.

48. Case, *The Slaughter*.
49. William F. Holmes, in "Whitecapping: Agrarian Violence in Mississippi, 1902–1906," *Journal of Southern History* 35 (May 1969): 165–185, explains the practice of whitecapping in southwest Mississippi in the late nineteenth and early twentieth centuries, when small white farmers, fearful of economic marginalization, directed their anxieties into attacks on their Black neighbors.
50. "History of the 364th Infantry."
51. Carroll Case, interview by Neil McMillen, April 12, 1996, Vol. 672, Mississippi Oral History Program, University of Southern Mississippi, Hattiesburg.
52. Motley, *The Invisible Soldier*, 61, 128; Memorandum for Record, October 19, 1943, Box 472, Security-Classified General Correspondence 1942–1945, Records of the War Department General and Special Staffs Record Group 165, NA-CP; "History of the 364th Infantry." Goodman received a promotion to full colonel in March 1945 and to brigadier general before he retired from service in November 1946. He died on March 6, 1947, at the age of fifty-five, and is buried in Arlington National Cemetery. See Ancestry.com.
53. Gibson with Huntley, *Knocking Down Barriers*, 19.

Chapter 7

1. J. L. Horace, "Report of Visits to Nine Southern Army Camps and Camp Communities Where Negro Soldiers Are Stationed . . .," Box 242, General Correspondence, 1939–1947, Records of the Office of the Inspector General, Record Group 159, NA-CP; Arthur W. Womack, "Dorie Miller to Be Memorialized at Annual Meet of Church Council" (Associated Negro Press Release), May 24, 1944, PQHV-BFS: ORP1; "Asks Roosevelt End Camp Discrimination," *NYT*, June 21, 1943; War Department to Edgar J. Brown, n.d., June 1943, Box 1067, Army-AG.
2. Horace, "Report of Visits to Nine Southern Army Camps and Camp Communities"; Truman K. Gibson to Jonathan Daniels, February 24, 1944, PQHV-BFS: FGR; "John J. McCloy," *Economist*, March 18, 1989, 28.
3. Richard M. Dalfiume, "The "Forgotten Years" of the Negro Revolution," *Journal of American History* 55 (June 1968): 106; Kai Bird, *The Chairman: John J. McCloy, The Making of the American Establishment* (New York: Simon & Schuster, 1992), 186–189; Truman K. Gibson Jr. with Steve Huntley, *Knocking Down Barriers: My Fight for Black America* (Evanston, IL: Northwestern University Press, 2005), 109–110; J. Todd Moye, *Freedom Flyers: The Tuskegee Airmen of World War II* (New York: Oxford University Press, 2010), 170.
4. Charles W. Wade to Theodore G. Bilbo, June 5, 1943, Box 1084, and J. P. Coleman to Thomas G. Abernethy, August 10, 1943, Box 788, BPUSM.
5. Patrick S. Washburn, "The Pittsburgh Courier's Double V Campaign in 1942," *American Journalism* 3 (1986): 73–86; Patrick S. Washburn, *A Question of Sedition: The Federal Government's Investigation of the Black Press during World*

War II (New York: Oxford University Press, 1986); Paul Alkebulan, *The African American Press in World War II: Toward Victory at Home and Abroad* (Lanham, MD: Lexington Books, 2014), ch. 5; Richard M. Dalfiume, *Desegregation of the U.S. Armed Forces: Fighting on Two Fronts, 1939–1953* (Columbia: University of Missouri Press, 1969), 87.
6. Westbrook Pegler, "Fair Enough," *Atlanta Constitution*, June 30, 1943; "Confiscate *Defender* in Dixie Camp," *CD*, July 24, 1943; "Negro Press 'Hot-Foot' of Dixie Causes Ban from Mississippi Camp," *People's Voice (New York, N.Y.)*, July 31, 1943.
7. Judge William H. Hastie, "Only Federal Action Can Protect Negroes in the Army" (syndicated column), *York (Pa.) Gazette & Daily*, June 16, 1943; Roy Wilkins to Truman Gibson, June 24, 1943, PQHV-BFS: FGR.
8. Horace, "Report of Visits to Nine Southern Army Camps and Camp Communities"; J. A. Ulio to Joseph Gray Wylie, June 28, 1943, Box 1067, Army-AG.
9. Dalfiume, *Desegregation of the U.S. Armed Forces*, 82; G. C. Marshall to Commanding Generals, July 3, 1943, *Blacks in the United States Armed Forces: Basic Documents*, edited by Morris J. MacGregor and Bernard C. Nalty, 13 vols. (Wilmington, DE: Scholarly Resources, 1977), 5:270–271; John J. McCloy to Chief of Staff, July 3, 1943, AU: FDR; Digest of War Department Policy Pertaining to Negro Military Personnel, January 1, 1944 (Protection of Arms and Ammunition, July 10, 1943), Online Documents: Desegregation of the Armed Forces, Harry S. Truman Presidential Museum and Library, www.trumanlibrary.org.
10. "Educational Program for Colored Troops, July 29, 1943," PQHV-NAACP: EVH.
11. "Educational Program for Colored Troops, July 29, 1943"; "Words of Wisdom," *Atlanta Constitution*, September 10, 1943; "Comments on General Stockton's Order to Soldiers at Camp Stewart, Ga.," *BAA*, August 21, 1943; Daniel Kryder, *Divided Arsenal: Race and the American State during World War II* (New York: Cambridge University Press, 2000), 201–205; Luther Francis Yancey Jr., "The Golden Rule" (editorial cartoon), *BAA*, August 14, 1943.
12. L. R. Forney to General Bissell (Assistant Chief of Staff for Intelligence), January 13, 1944, and M. G. White to the Chief of Staff, January 13, 1944, both in Box 472, Security-Classified General Correspondence 1942–1945, Records of the War Department General and Special Staffs, Record Group 165, NA-CP; J. S. Leonard to Assistant Secretary of War, December 17, 1943, in MacGregor and Nalty, eds., *Blacks in the United States Armed Forces*, 5:281–287.
13. J. A. Ulio to Commanding Generals, January 7, 1944, in MacGregor and Nalty, eds., *Blacks in the United States Armed Forces*, 5:303–305; Ulysses Lee, *The Employment of Negro Troops* (Washington, DC: Center of Military History, US Army, 1994), 211; Jean Byers, *A Study of the Negro in Military Service* (Washington, DC: US Department of Defense, 1950), 41.
14. Joel and Jimmy to Truman K. Gibson, May 17, 1944; Conversation between Mr. T. K. Gibson Jr. and James P. Phinnie of Camp Shelby, Mississippi, May 18, 1944; and Edward Stern to Director of Military Training, A. S. F., n.d., June 1944, all in PQHV-BFS: FGR.

15. Dalfiume, *Desegregation of the U.S. Armed Forces*, 93; J. S. Leonard to Assistant Secretary of War, December 17, 1943, in MacGregor and Nalty, eds., *Blacks in the United States Armed Forces*, 5:281–287; "Are the Cards Stacked? Many Negro Combat Units Being Broken Up," *Pittsburgh Courier*, October 30, 1943.
16. War Department, "Command of Negro Troops," February 29, 1944, in MacGregor and Nalty, eds., *Blacks in the United States Armed Forces*, 5:307–325; Byers, *A Study of the Negro in Military Service*, 42–44; "Mixed Units Studied by War Department," *Pittsburgh Courier*, May 13, 1944; Kryder, *Divided Arsenal*, 156–157.
17. Memo to the Chief of Staff, March 12, 1943, Online Documents: Desegregation of the Armed Forces.
18. Gibson and Huntley, *Knocking Down Barriers*, 112–113; War Department, "Command of Negro Troops," February 29, 1944, 5:311.
19. Ruth Benedict and Gene Weltfish, *The Races of Mankind*, Box 57, Walter Sillers Jr. Papers, DSU; "Army Blocked on Distribution of Racial Booklet, May Says," *Washington Post*, March 6, 1944; Charles King, *Gods of the Upper Air: How a Circle of Renegade Anthropologists Reinvented Race, Sex, and Gender in the Twentieth Century* (New York: Doubleday, 2019), 317–318; James Marlow and George Zielke, "Storm over a Pamphlet," *Hattiesburg American*, March 10, 1944; Theodore G. Bilbo to Earnest Sevier Cox, April 17, 1944, Box 6, Earnest Sevier Cox Papers, DUKE.
20. Minutes of Meeting of Advisory Committee on Negro Troop Policy, February 29, 1944, and John J. McCloy to Secretary of War, March 2, 1944, both in MacGregor and Nalty, eds., *Blacks in the United States Armed Forces*, 5:326–331, 334; H. S. Milton, ed., *Utilization of Negro Manpower in the Army: A 1951 Study* (Chevy Chase, MD: Operations Research Office, Johns Hopkins University, 1955), 564.
21. "War Dep't. Maps Probe of Jim Crow in Army Camps," *NYAN*, July 10, 1943; Digest of War Department Policy Pertaining to Negro Military Personnel, January 1, 1944 (Recreation Facilities, March 10, 1943), and J. B. Leonard to Assistant Secretary of War, May 25, 1943, both in Online Documents: Desegregation of the Armed Forces; Francis Yancey Jr., "A Sign of Real Progress" (editorial cartoon), *BAA*, May 15, 1943; Dalfiume, *Desegregation of the U.S. Armed Forces*, 88. Ironically, when the men of the 364th tried to integrate a post exchange and a theater at Camp Van Dorn in late May 1943, they probably knew nothing of the recent army directive, which had legitimized their protests.
22. J. S. Leonard to Assistant Secretary of War, December 17, 1943; Minutes of Meeting of Advisory Committee on Negro Troop Policies, February 29, 1944; and J. A. Ulio to Commanding Generals, July 8, 1944, all in MacGregor and Nalty, eds., *Blacks in the United States Armed Forces*, 5:284–285, 330–331, and 340–341.
23. J. A. Ulio to Commanding Generals, July 8, 1944; "Army Denies Louis and Ray Were Jailed on Jim Crow Protest" (Associated Negro Press Release), April 3, 1944, PQHV-BFS: ORP1; Michael Lee Lanning, *The Court-Martial of Jackie Robinson: The Baseball Legend's Battle for Civil Rights during World War II* (Guilford, CT: Stackpole Books, 2020).
24. "Governor Protests Army's Negro Policy," *NYT*, August 25, 1944; Jeanne Theoharis, *The Rebellious Life of Mrs. Rosa Parks* (Boston: Beacon Press, 2013), 50.

25. *Congressional Record*, August 24, 1944, 7295; Report on Editorial in the *Jackson Daily News*, September 1, 1944, AU: FDR; David E. Dunn, "Sparks' Wire on Segregation Gets Response," *Montgomery (Ala.) Advertiser*, September 6, 1944.
26. Lee, *The Employment of Negro Troops*, 397–399; Byers, *A Study of the Negro in Military Service*, 84–85.
27. Leslie S. Perry to Truman Gibson, November 10, 1944, PQHV-BFS: ORP1; Byers, *A Study of the Negro in Military Service*, 85; B. O. Davis to the Inspector General, June 16, 1944, Box 1065, Army-AG; Weekly Intelligence Summary, August 19, 1944, through August 25, 1944, and Weekly Intelligence Summary, September 9, 1944, through September 15, 1944, both in Box 262, Office Assistant Secretary of War Civilian Aide to the Secretary, Racial Situation in the Army 1944–January 1946, Records of the Office of the Secretary of War, Record Group 107, NA-CP; Audie S. Ellis and others to Franklin D. Roosevelt, August 31, 1944, and Report on telephone call from Lt. W. F. Sibley, September 1, 1944, both in AU: FDR.
28. Walter White to Robert P. Patterson, September 21, 1944; "Action against Col. Edgerly if Charge Is Proved" (NAACP Press Release), October 5, 1944; John J. McCloy to Walter White, November 13, 1944; and Anonymous report to Walter White, November 5, 1945, all in PQHV-NAACP: EVH; "Colonel Says Anti-Segregation Order Observed at Ft. Benning," *Atlanta Daily World*, September 12, 1944; Racial Incident Report, January 17, 1945, Box 261, Office Assistant Secretary of War Civilian Aide to the Secretary, Racial Situation in the Army 1944–January 1946.
29. Racial Situation in the United States, December 23, 1944 to January 6, 1945, AU: FDR.
30. J. L. LeFlore to Truman K. Gibson, June 15, 1944, and J. L. LeFlore to Brig. Gen. James A. Mollison, June 28, 1944, both in PQHV-BFS: FGR; John LeFlore, "In Court Martial," *CD*, July 8, 1944.
31. Race Incident, Brookley Field, Ala., report, May 25, 1944, Box 17, Office of the Commanding General, Chief of Staff for Service Commands Correspondence Files, 1943–1945, Records of the Army Air Forces [AAF], Record Group 18, NA-CP; John LeFlore, "Whites Ignore Commands of Negro Sentry," *CD*, June 3, 1944; James Albert Burran, "Racial Violence in the South During World War II" (PhD diss., University of Tennessee, 1977), 203–204.
32. Burran, "Racial Violence in the South during World War II," 204–205; LeFlore, "In Court Martial"; LeFlore, "Whites Ignore Commands of Negro Sentry"; "Negroes and Whites Stage Gun Battle," *Dothan (Ala.) Eagle*, May 25, 1944; "General Quells Outbreak of Negro Troops," *Rome (Ga.) News-Tribune*, May 25, 1944; "Good American Soldiers," *Birmingham News*, May 31, 1944. Biographical information for Mollison from Ancestry.com.
33. LeFlore, "Whites Ignore Commands of Negro Sentry"; Burran, "Racial Violence in the South during World War II," 205–206; LeFlore, "In Court Martial"; "Nine Negro Soldiers Convicted in Shooting at Brookley Field," *Anniston (Ala.) Star*, June 30, 1944. Among the nine convicted: Willie Fleetwood, Rome, Georgia; Edward C. Reece, Bibb County, Georgia; Willie E. Wright, Bibb County, Georgia; Willie B. Lane, Florida; and Enos Bailey, Kentucky. See Ancestry.com.

34. A disgusted Negro Trooper to *Cleveland Call & Post*, August 16, 1944, in Phillip McGuire, *Taps for a Jim Crow Army: Letters from Black Soldiers in World War II* (Lexington: University of Kentucky Press, 2015), 196–197; Neil R. McMillen, *Dark Journey: Black Mississippians in the Age of Jim Crow* (Urbana: University of Illinois Press, 1989), 233–237; Danielle L. McGuire, *At the Dark End of the Street: Black Women, Rape, and Resistance—A New History of the Civil Rights Movement from Rosa Parks to the Rise of Black Power* (New York: Vintage Books, 2010), 24–31; "27 Negro Soldiers Arrested," newspaper clipping, August 26, 1944; "Riot Is Narrowly Averted," September 2, 1944; Walter White to Tabitha Petran, October 4, 1944; and Thurgood Marshall to Henry L. Stimson, November 3, 1944, all in PQHV-NAACP: EVH; "Army Probes Rioting in Louisiana Town," *NYAN*, August 26, 1944.
35. Alexandria, Louisiana Racial Tensions, n.d., 1944?, Series 1.3, Box 13, Jonathan Daniels Papers, SHC; Burran, "Racial Violence in the South during World War II," 213–214; "27 Negro Soldiers Arrested."
36. Thurgood Marshall and Edward R. Dudley, Memorandum on Behalf of Sergeant Conway F. Price, n.d., 1944, and Army Press Release, n.d., 1944, both in PQHV-NAACP: EVH; "Army Probes Rioting in Louisiana Town."
37. Burran, "Racial Violence in the South during World War II," 214–215; "More Negro Soldiers Convicted," *NYT*, September 28, 1944; John E. Rousseau Jr., untitled report on Camp Claiborne courts-martial, n.d., 1944; Charles B. Coleman to Leslie S. Perry, May 26, 1945; "2 More Negro Soldiers Guilty in Mutiny Trials," newspaper clipping, n.d., 1944; and Walter White to Tabitha Petran, October 4, 1944, all in PQHV-NAACP: EVH. Among the Camp Claiborne soldiers convicted by court-martial were George S. Washington of Houston, Texas; Ernest B. Collier of Orlando, Florida; and Philip Davis of Montgomery, Alabama.
38. *History of the 31st Infantry Division in Training and Combat, 1940–1945* (Nashville: Battery Press, 1993), 10; CG, Southern Defense Command to War Department, August 25, 1944, and John S. Myers, File Memo, September 4, 1944, both in Box 1789, Internal Security Division, Emergency Protection Branch, Race Riots and Strikes, 1942–1945, Records of the Office of the Provost Marshall General, 1941–, Record Group 389, NA-CP; Burran, "Racial Violence in the South during World War II," 211–212; Joseph Wright to NAACP, May 23, 1945, and Joseph Wright to Edward R. Dudley, August 2, 1945, both in PQHV-NAACP: EVH; "Probe Camp Killing of Private by Lieutenant," *Long Beach (Calif.) Independent*, September 5, 1944.
39. Lou Layne to Truman Gibson, June 17, 1944, Box 205, Civilian Aide to the Secretary—Subject File, Records of the Office of the Secretary of War, Record Group 107, NA-CP; E. W. Gruhn to Chief of Staff, Army Service Forces, October 17, 1944, Box 13, Office of the Commanding General, Lt. General Somervell's Desk File, 1942–1943, Records of Headquarters Army Service Forces, Record Group 160, NA-CP. Layne had his transfer request accepted; the Army moved him to Staten Island, New York. See Truman Gibson Jr. to Lou Layne, August 14, 1944, PQHV-BFS: FGR.
40. E. J. Kahn Jr. and Henry McLemore, *Fighting Divisions* (Washington, DC: Infantry Journal Press, 1946), 124–125; Daniel K. Gibran, *The 92nd Infantry Division and*

the Italian Campaign in World War II (Jefferson, NC: McFarland Publishing, 2001); Moye, *Freedom Flyers*; Charles W. Sasser, *Patton's Panthers* (New York: Simon & Schuster, 2004); David P. Colley, *Blood for Dignity: The Story of the First Integrated Combat Unit in the U.S. Army* (New York: St. Martin's Press, 2003).

41. "The Luckless 92nd," *Newsweek*, February 26, 1945; Milton Bracker, "Negroes' Courage Upheld in Inquiry," *NYT*, March 15, 1945; John Chabot Smith, "Army Studying More Effective Negro Training," *New York Herald Tribune*, March 15, 1945.

42. Roi Ottley, "The Troops' Own Story on 92d Division's Record Reflects Failures of American Democracy," *PM*, June 11, 1945; *The Crisis*, April 1945, 97.

43. Paul Sann, "Gibson: The Negro Proves He Can Fight," *New York Post*, April 9, 1945; Statement of Truman K. Gibson Jr., Civilian Aide to the Secretary of War, at Press Conference, Monday, April 9, 1945, Washington, DC, and "NAACP Votes against Leadership of Gibson" (NAACP Press Release), May 24, 1945, both in PQHV-NAACP: EVH.

44. Fred Atwater, "Dixie Echoes 92nd Slurs," *CD*, April 7, 1945; *Congressional Record*, June 29, 1945, 6994–6995; "Says French Negroes Raped 5,000," *New York Daily News*, June 30, 1945; "Solon Claims Negro Troops Are Failure," *Shreveport (La.) Times*, June 30, 1945.

45. "The Negro Soldier," Appendix to the *Congressional Record*, February 1, 1946, 430; Walter White, *A Man Called White: The Autobiography of Walter White* (Athens: University of Georgia Press, 1995), 251; John Edgerton, *Speak Now against the Day: The Generation before the Civil Rights Movement in the South* (New York: Knopf, 1994), 326–327; "Senator Eastland's Eruption," *Macon (Ga.) News*, July 9, 1945, part 18B, reel 3, Papers of the NAACP; "Rule by Demagogues," *Time*, July 9, 1945; A Negro Member of the United States Navy to Theodore Bilbo, n.d., summer 1945, Box 1084, BPUSM.

46. Telegram, P. H. Sanders to Senator T. G. Bilbo, July 10, 1945; Robert H. Lavender to Senator Bilbo, August 6, 1945; and Theodore G. Bilbo to Robert H. Lavender, August 15, 1945, all in Box 1067, BPUSM; Rawn James Jr., *The Double V: How Wars, Protest, and Harry Truman Desegregated America's Military* (New York: Bloomsbury Press, 2013), 180–182. By the last months of the war, about 200 Navy vessels had racially mixed crews. See Gerald Astor, *The Right to Fight: A History of African Americans in the Military* (Novato, CA: Presidio Press, 1998), 314.

47. "A New Outlook," *Life* magazine, October 29, 1945, 6, 8; Nan Elizabeth Woodruff, *American Congo: The African American Freedom Struggle in the Delta* (Cambridge, MA: Harvard University Press, 2003), 224–225.

48. Dalfiume, *Desegregation of the U.S. Armed Forces*, 149.

49. Dalfiume, *Desegregation of the U.S. Armed Forces*, 149–155; James, *The Double V*, 210–212; Alan L. Gropman, *The Air Force Integrates, 1945–1964* (Washington, DC: Office of Air Force History, US Air Force, 1985), 46–59, 281–285; US Board of Officers on Utilization of Negro Manpower in the Post-War Army, *Policy for Utilization of Negro Manpower in the Post-War Army: Supplemental Report of War Department Special Board on Negro Manpower* (Washington, DC: War Department, 1946).

Chapter 8

1. "The Freight-Rate Battle," *Fortune* 30 (October 1944): 149–154, 193–200; *Minutes of the Meeting of the Southern Governors' Conference, 1943* (Atlanta: The Conference, 1943); Cliff Mackay, "The Globe Trotter: Let's Adopt a Slogan," *Atlanta Daily World*, August 8, 1943.
2. *Minutes of the Meeting of the Southern Governors' Conference, 1943*; Sam H. Jones, as told to James Aswell, "Will Dixie Bolt the New Deal," *Saturday Evening Post*, March 6, 1943, 20–22, 45.
3. "The President Tours a Rebellious South," "Southern Governors Head the 'Revolt' against the New Deal," and "The Not-So-Solid South," *Life*, May 3, 1943, 17–21; "Arnall Confers with Roosevelt for Five Hours," *Atlanta Constitution*, April 21, 1943; H. C. Nixon, "The Southern Governors' Conference as a Pressure Group," *Journal of Politics* 6 (August 1944): 344.
4. Gladstone Williams, "Arnall, George Hold Parley with Roosevelt," *Atlanta Constitution*, February 12, 1942; Bruce J. Schulman, *From Cotton Belt to Sunbelt: Federal Policy, Economic Development, and the Transformation of the South, 1938–1980* (New York: Oxford University Press, 1991), 129; John Chamberlain, "Arnall of Georgia," *Life*, August 6, 1945, 69–76; Harold Paulk Henderson, *The Politics of Change in Georgia: A Political Biography of Ellis Arnall* (Athens: University of Georgia Press, 1991), ch. 1 and 2. In 1942, Talmadge was completing his third two-year term as Georgia's governor, after winning election in 1932, 1934, and 1940. Beginning with the 1942 election, Georgia governors began serving four-year terms.
5. Edwin Camp, "Talmadge Stirs Up a Storm," *NYT*, July 27, 1941; Walter Davenport, "The Fuehrer of Sugar Creek," *Collier's*, December 6, 1941, 71–72; Sue Bailes, "Eugene Talmadge and the Board of Regents Controversy," *Georgia Historical Quarterly* 53 (December 1969): 410–412.
6. Bailes, "Eugene Talmadge and the Board of Regents Controversy," 412–417; Henderson, *The Politics of Change in Georgia*, ch. 3; "New Regents Oust Georgia Educators," *NYT*, July 15, 1941. Pittman represented a lesser target than Cocking, perhaps because Talmadge found it harder to tag Pittman, a Mississippi native, with the "foreigner" label.
7. Walter White to Editor of the *Atlanta Constitution*, July 16, 1941, part 18C, reel 22, Papers of the NAACP; "Georgia Students Burn Their Governor in Protest of His Academic Meddling," *Life*, October 27, 1941, 43–45; "Conference Drops Georgia University," *NYT*, October 14, 1941; "College Body Bars 10 in Georgia Group," *NYT*, December 5, 1941.
8. Henderson, *The Politics of Change in Georgia*, ch. 3; "Salaries in Fulton County, Ga.," *The Southern Frontier* 1 (February 1940): 1; "Equal Pay Suit Draws Fire of Supt. Collins," *Atlanta Daily World*, February 19, 1942; Atlanta Urban League, "A Report of Public School Facilities for Negroes in Atlanta, Georgia," 1944, Part VI: Box A69, Records of the National Urban League, LC; "Governor Hits Equal Salaries for Negroes," *Atlanta Constitution*, February 27, 1942; John McCray, "The Need for Changing," *Atlanta Daily World*, April 25, 1942; Cliff MacKay, "Reeves' Stand in Pay

Issue Draws Praise," *Atlanta Daily World*, April 18, 1942. Also see Tomiko Brown-Nagin, *Courage to Dissent: Atlanta and the Long History of the Civil Rights Movement* (New York: Oxford University Press, 2011), 87–93.

9. "Mr. Arnall, Would You Call the Activities of This Racial Equality Board 'Spurious,'" 1942, Eugene Talmadge Pamphlets, McCain Library and Archives, University of Southern Mississippi, Hattiesburg; Julian Harris, "Georgia Will Vote in Bitter Primary," *NYT*, September 6, 1942; John T. Kneebone, *Southern Liberal Journalists and the Issue of Race, 1920–1944* (Chapel Hill: University of North Carolina Press, 1985), 193–194.

10. Christopher A. Brooks and Robert Sims, *Roland Hayes: The Legacy of an American Tenor* (Bloomington: Indiana University Press, 2015), ch. 11; Commission on Interracial Cooperation, "The Roland Hayes Incident," July 29, 1942, Folder 41, Jessie Daniel Ames Papers, SHC; "Segregation on Trial: 'White Supremacy! In South to Stay,'" *Pittsburgh Courier*, August 1, 1942; "Gov. Talmadge Warns Negroes," *NYT*, July 24, 1942.

11. Commission on Interracial Cooperation, "The Racial Issue in Political Campaigns—1942," August 17, 1942, PQHV-NAACP: BDAC; "Georgia Warns Militia to Expect Race Conflict," *PM*, August 13, 1942; "Camp Publishes 'Alert' Letter to State Guard," undated newspaper clipping, August 1942, Box 4, BAE; "Georgia Guard on Alert," *NYT*, August 12, 1942; C. E. Gregory, "Arnall Says Talmadge Seeks Racial Troubles," *Atlanta Journal*, August 10, 1942; William Anderson, *The Wild Man from Sugar Creek: The Political Career of Eugene Talmadge* (Baton Rouge: Louisiana State University Press, 1975), 210.

12. Form letter from Dorothy Tilly, August 11, 1942, Box 3, Glenn W. Rainey Papers, Emory; Andrew W. Manis, "'City Mothers': Dorothy Tilly, Georgia Methodist Women, and Black Civil Rights," in *Before Brown: Civil Rights and White Backlash in the Modern South*, ed. Glenn Feldman (Tuscaloosa: University of Alabama Press, 2004), 132–133; E. M. Martin to Walter White, August 27, 1942, PQHV-NAACP: BDAC.

13. "Voting for Victory," *New Republic*, September 21, 1942, 348; J. C. Chunn, "Talmadge's Defeat Proves Race Issue Is Dead in Dixie," *Pittsburgh Courier*, September 19, 1942; "Lessons of Talmadge Defeat," *CD*, September 26, 1942; "The Shape of Things," *The Nation*, September 19, 1942, 223.

14. Walter Davenport, "Unanimous Arnall," *Collier's*, July 24, 1943, 16, 57; "Georgia's New Peach," *Saturday Evening Post*, August 28, 1943, 6; Henderson, *The Politics of Change in Georgia*, ch. 4 and 5; Gerald W. Johnson, "Arnall of Georgia—and '48," *American Mercury*, August 1946, 177.

15. "Georgia's New Peach"; Ellis Arnall to All State Department Heads, Officials and Employees, February 25, 1943, Box 3, H. W. Caldwell Papers, Hargrett Rare Book and Manuscript Library, University of Georgia Libraries, Athens; Henderson, *The Politics of Change in Georgia*, ch. 7; John Temple Graves, "This Afternoon," *Birmingham Post*, April 29, 1946.

16. Brown-Nagin, *Courage to Dissent*, 33–38, details the "culture of lawlessness" and white violence that Black residents in Georgia had to endure during this era.

17. Merl E. Reed, *Seedtime for the Modern Civil Rights Movement: The President's Committee on Fair Employment Practice, 1941–1946* (Baton Rouge: Louisiana State University Press, 1991), 222–225; Harry McAlpin, "Atlanta City Council Asks Ouster of FEPC Office and White Director," *CD*, December 18, 1943; "Atlanta FEPC Grows—Ignores City Councilmen," *CD*, January 29, 1944.
18. Kevin J. McMahon, *Reconsidering Roosevelt on Race: How the Presidency Paved the Road to Brown* (Chicago: University of Chicago Press, 2004), 168–175; "Arnall Asked to Arrest Cop, Sheriff in Georgia Lynching," *BAA*, February 27, 1943.
19. Henderson, *The Politics of Change in Georgia*, 137; Ronald H. Bayor, *Race and the Shaping of Twentieth-Century Atlanta* (Chapel Hill: University of North Carolina Press, 1996), 27; "Governor Arnall's Speech," *Atlanta Daily World*, November 11, 1944; Malcolm W. Bayley, "They're Comin' Up in Georgia," *Christian Science Monitor*, June 24, 1944, 2.
20. "Suspend Teacher Who Sued for Same Pay Given Whites," *Pittsburgh Courier*, December 5, 1942; Brown-Nagin, *Courage to Dissent*, 90; V. W. Hodges, "First Round of Equal Pay Suit Ends; Judge Orders Briefs Filed," *Atlanta Daily World*, January 25, 1944; V. W. Hodges, "Board Contends Pay Now Equal," *Atlanta Daily World*, July 13, 1944; Henderson, *The Politics of Change in Georgia*, ch. 7.
21. Glenda Gilmore, *Defying Dixie: The Radical Roots of Civil Rights, 1919–1950* (New York: W. W. Norton, 2008), 394–397; "A Survey of Opinions Held by Mississippi and Alabama White People Regarding Negroes," n.d., 1942, PQHV-NAACP: BDAC; Harvard Sitkoff, "African American Militancy in the World War II South: Another Perspective," in *Remaking Dixie: The Impact of World War II on the American South*, ed. Neil R. McMillen (Jackson: University Press of Mississippi, 1997), 79–80; Stephen G. N. Tuck, *Beyond Atlanta: The Struggle for Racial Equality in Georgia, 1940–1980* (Athens: University of Georgia Press, 2001), 43. The Southern Conference for Human Welfard came out against racial segregation in 1946. See Numan V. Bartley, *The Creation of Modern Georgia*, 2nd ed. (Athens: University of Georgia Press, 1990), 198.
22. Mackay, "The Globe Trotter: Let's Adopt a Slogan"; Herman Hancock, "Teen-Agers Will Ballot in '44 without Having to Pay Tax," *Atlanta Constitution*, August 4, 1943.
23. Robert A. Garson, *The Democratic Party and the Politics of Sectionalism, 1941–1948* (Baton Rouge: Louisiana State University Press, 1974), 44–48; "Three States Act on Soldier Vote," *NYT*, January 4, 1944; *Congressional Record*, January 14, 1944, Appendix, 209; Spike Washington, "Primary Rules Not Affected by Soldier Vote Bill in Assembly," *Atlanta Daily World*, January 5, 1944.
24. Robert Mickey, *Paths out of Dixie: The Democratization of Authoritarian Enclaves in America's Deep South, 1944–1972* (Princeton, NJ: Princeton University Press, 2015), 120; Southern Conference for Human Welfare, "A Memorandum on the Suffrage in Georgia," 1940, Part VI: Box A73, Records of the National Urban League, LC; "Vote for G. I. Negroes Asked," *Atlanta Constitution*, January 7, 1944; Southern Regional Council, "The White Primary, 1944: With Special Reference to Georgia," n.d., 1945?, reel 218, Southern Regional Council Papers; Tuck, *Beyond Atlanta*, 44–66.
25. Nancy Beck Young, *Why We Fight: Congress and the Politics of World War II* (Lawrence: University of Kansas Press, 2013), 173–174; Gilmore, *Defying Dixie*,

337–341; Charles L. Zelden, *The Battle for the Black Ballot: Smith v. Allwright and the Defeat of the Texas All White Primary* (Lawrence: University Press of Kansas, 2004); John Morton Blum, *V Was for Victory: Politics and American Culture during World War II* (New York: Harcourt Brace Jovanovich, 1976), 211–212; Bayley, "They're Comin' Up in Georgia," 2.

26. Robert A. Lively, "The South and Freight Rates: Political Settlement of an Economic Argument," *Journal of Southern History* 14 (August 1948): 361; Kenneth Stewart, "Ellis Arnall: A Liberal Grows in Georgia," *PM*, August 18, 1946.
27. Lively, "The South and Freight Rates," 357–384; Henry Wallace, "Transportation Monopoly and Discriminatory Rates Keep South and West in a Colonial Status," *Southern Patriot*, November 1943; E. R. Oliver, "The South and Its Freight Rates," speech to the Chattanooga Kiwanis Club, July 27, 1943, Box 1, Governor's Subject Files, Office of the Governor, Georgia Archives, Atlanta.
28. Lively, "The South and Freight Rates," 379–382; Henderson, *The Politics of Change in Georgia*, ch. 8; Gladstone Williams, "Full U.S. Moral Force Thrown behind Arnall," *Atlanta Constitution*, December 29, 1944; Ellis Arnall, interview by Mel Steely and Ted Fitz-Simons, April 2, 1986, transcript, Digital Library of Georgia, https://dlg.usg.edu/record/uwg_phc_arnall19860402; "Arnall Accuses Railroads of Plot," *NYT*, January 3, 1945; "Georgia Rebels Again," *Time*, April 9, 1945; "ICC Delays Freight Rate Cut; Arnall Charges 'Favor' to Rails," *Atlanta Constitution*, October 27, 1945.
29. Schulman, *From Cotton Belt to Sunbelt*, 129; "Arnall Asks Negro's Friends to Join Freight Rate Fight" (Associated Negro Press Release), June 7, 1944, PQHV-BFS: ORP1; "The Freight-Rate Battle," 198.
30. David M. Jordan, *FDR, Dewey, and the Election of 1944* (Bloomington: Indiana University Press, 2011), 139; Stewart, "Ellis Arnall"; Ellis Arnall, interview by Harold Paulk Henderson Sr., July 19, 1985, transcript, Russell; "Reporter Arnall Gets the News," *Atlanta Constitution*, June 23, 1944; "Arnall Sees Roosevelt Willing," *Washington Post*, June 23, 1944.
31. George H. Gallup, *The Gallup Poll: Public Opinion, 1935–1971*, 3 vols. (New York: Random House, 1972), 1:456–457; Glenn Feldman, *The Great Melding: War, the Dixiecrat Rebellion, and the Southern Model for America's New Conservatism* (Tuscaloosa: University of Alabama Press, 2015), 92; Stewart, "Ellis Arnall"; Ralph McGill, "Arnall Ends Two Busy Days with Roosevelt Talk," *Atlanta Constitution*, August 30, 1944; Ellis Arnall, interview by Harold Paulk Henderson Sr., July 19, 1985; clipping from *Pathfinder* magazine, September 11, 1944, Box 1, Alvan S. Arnall Collection of Ellis G. Arnall Materials, Russell; M. L. St. John, "Arnall Wins Favor on Speaking Tour," *Atlanta Constitution*, November 5, 1944.
32. Henderson, *The Politics of Change in Georgia*, 85–92; M .L. St. John, "Poll Tax to Die, Arnall Declares," *Atlanta Constitution*, January 24, 1945; Selden Menefee, "America at War: Southern Statesman," *Washington Post*, March 1, 1945; "Poll Tax Repeal Sent to Georgia Governor," *NYT*, February 6, 1945; Ellis Arnall, interview by Harold Paulk Henderson Sr., July 19, 1985; Ellis Arnall, "Arnall Describes Provisions to Eliminate 'Dictatorships,'" *Atlanta Constitution*, April 1, 1945.

33. Jennings Perry, "Georgia's Decision Will Echo in South," *PM*, February 13, 1945; Henderson, *The Politics of Change in Georgia*, 92; "A Tribute to Governor Arnall of Georgia," 1945, reel 1, Southern Regional Council Papers; Cliff MacKay, "Georgia Moves to Poll Tax-Free Column" (Associated Negro Press Release), February 7, 1945, PQHV-BFS: ORP1; McMahon, *Reconsidering Roosevelt on Race*, 157. Feldman, *The Great Melding*, 84, notes that liberals during the World War II era believed that a hidden southern liberalism would be revealed if the region's voting restrictions were removed.

34. Southern Regional Council, "The White Primary, 1944"; "Things We Can Do to Help," *Atlanta Daily World*, May 26, 1944; Brown-Nagin, *Courage to Dissent*, 49; Herman "Skip" Mason Jr., *Politics, Civil Rights, and Law in Black Atlanta* (Charleston, SC: Arcadia Publishing, 2000), 34, 36; Southern Regional Council, "The White Primary: Stop Worrying," pamphlet, May 1944, reel 218, Southern Regional Council Papers. The exact number of Black Georgia voters who registered in the aftermath of the *Smith v. Allwright* decision is uncertain, but their numbers had probably more than doubled by June 1944 over the 1940 numbers (from 11,500 to 25,000). See Southern Conference for Human Welfare, "A Memorandum on the Suffrage in Georgia," and Southern Regional Council, "The White Primary, 1944."

35. Southern Regional Council, "The White Primary, 1944"; "Georgians 'Reaffirm' 'White Supremacy,'" *NYT*, June 8, 1944; "Ga. Negro Demos to Fight Vote Ban" (Associated Negro Press Release), June 12, 1944, and "Southern White Woman Hits Ban on Negro Voting" (Associated Negro Press Release), June 21, 1944, both in PQHV-BFS: ORP1; Citizens Democratic Club of Fulton County to J. Lon Duckworth, June 21, 1944, and Mrs. Dorothy Q. Rainey to J. Lon Duckworth, June 20, 1944, both in part 4, reel 7, Papers of the NAACP.

36. Eugene Martin to Walter White, July 26, 1944, PQHV-NAACP: BDAC; "Ask Ga. Legislature to Repeal Primary Laws" (Associated Negro Press Release), June 14, 1944, and "Georgia Governor Gets Committee Approval on Negro Vote Ban" (Associated Negro Press Release), June 26, 1944, both in PQHV-BFS: ORP1; "Biddle Sent Affidavits on Georgia Primary Ban," July 6, 1944, and Telegram from C. A. Scott to Roy Wilkins, July 5, 1944, both in part 4, reel 7, Papers of the NAACP.

37. Tuck, *Beyond Atlanta*, 65; Brown-Nagin, *Courage to Dissent*, 49; C. A. Scott to Thurgood Marshall, November 24, 1944, part 4, reel 7, Papers of the NAACP; Southern Regional Council, "The White Primary, 1944"; J. Edgar Hoover to Jonathan Daniels, July 4, 1944, AU: FDR; Victor H. Bernstein, "Negro 'Token Vote' to Test Georgia Jim Crow Primary," *PM*, July 3, 1944.

38. Thurgood Marshall to A. T. Walden, July 26, 1944; Francis Biddle to C. A. Scott, December 1, 1944; A. T. Walden to Francis Biddle, March 12, 1945; Thurgood Marshall to C. A. Scott, April 18, 1945; and Testimony of J. Lon Duckworth, n.d., 1944 or 1945, all in part 4, reel 7, and W. M. Thomas to Thurgood Marshall, part 4, reel 8, all in Papers of the NAACP; "File Ga. Suit to Smash Primary," *Atlanta Daily World*, August 25, 1944; John LeFlore, "Georgia Upholds Negroes' Vote," *CD*, October 20, 1945; Calvin Kytle and James A. Mackay, *Who Runs Georgia?* (Athens: University of

Georgia Press, 1998), 254; Southern Regional Council, "The White Primary, 1944"; "Studying to Irritate the South," *Macon Telegraph*, June 16, 1945.

39. "Georgia Poll Tax Out; Negroes Still Barred," *CD*, February 10, 1945; "Arnall Replies to Colored Leaders," *BAA*, March 3, 1945; LeFlore, "Georgia Upholds Negroes' Vote"; "Negroes Get Vote in Georgia Primary," *NYT*, October 13, 1945; Ora W. Eads letter to the editor, *Atlanta Constitution*, October 23, 1945; "Gov. Arnall Asks Appeal," *Atlanta Daily World*, October 14, 1945. Information on Eads from Atlanta City Directory, 1945, Ancestry.com.

40. "People in the Limelight: Ellis Arnall," *New Republic*, February 12, 1945, 214; Drew Pearson, "In Praise of Georgia's Governor," *Louisville Courier-Journal*, March 31, 1945; Ellis Arnall to Evalyn Walsh, April 5, 1945, Box 5, Evalyn Walsh McLean Papers, LC; Stewart, "Ellis Arnall"; Eustace Gay, "Facts and Fancies: Southern 'Liberals,'" *Philadelphia Tribune*, July 7, 1945.

41. Stewart, "Ellis Arnall"; "Dixie Liberals Pussyfoot: Social Equality Scares Arnall," *CD*, July 7, 1945; Fritz Lord, "Arnall Urges Rights: Racial Problems Are Only Economic, Georgia's Governor Asserts in Interview," *Louisville Times*, June 26, 1945; "Arnall Bars Negroes on Social Equality," *NYT*, June 28, 1945. The Lord title appeared in the paper's second edition. The first edition had the title, "Arnall Asks Equality, What Difference Does It Make if You Eat with Negroes?" The Associated Press and the Associated Negro Press picked up the story when it had its original title. See "Georgia Governor Denies Racial Equality Statement" (Associated Negro Press Release), July 4, 1945, PQHV-BFS: ORP1.

42. Ellis Arnall, as told to Walter Davenport, "Revolution Down South," *Collier's*, July 28, 1945, 17, 71–72; "Georgia Governor Shows Moral Courage," *Philadelphia Tribune*, July 28, 1945; Chamberlain, "Arnall of Georgia"; Stewart, "Ellis Arnall"; Josh Skinner, "Arnall Faces Tough Decision on U.S. Solictorship Offer," *Atlanta Constitution*, September 6, 1945.

Chapter 9

1. "His Honor Speaks," *Time*, April 3, 1944, 23; "Bilbo Urges Re-Election of Self, Roosevelt; Says Race Equality Is Taught," *McComb (Miss.) Daily Journal*, March 23, 1944; Charles Pope Smith, "Theodore G. Bilbo's Senatorial Career, The Final Years: 1941–1947" (PhD diss., University of Southern Mississippi, 1983), 132.

2. Theodore G. Bilbo, "The War; Constitutional Government; and the Race Issue—America's Greatest Unsolved Domestic Problem," March 22, 1944, *Congressional Record*, April 17, 1944, Appendix, 1795–1802.

3. Bilbo, "The War"; "'Mayor' Bilbo Wants Slum Dweller Sent to Farms," *Atlanta Daily World*, March 19, 1944; Smith, "Theodore G. Bilbo's Senatorial Career, The Final Years: 1941–1947," 106.

4. Bilbo, "The War"; "Delta State Asks Full Probe of 'Social Equality' Charges," *Memphis Commercial Appeal*, March 24, 1944; "Mrs. Louise Perry Denies Charges Made by Bilbo," *Bolivar (Cleveland, Miss.) Commercial*, March 24, 1944; "Committee Report

Backs Teacher Accused by Bilbo," n.d., March 1944, Box 1011, BPUSM; "Teacher's Act Is Condemned," *Memphis Press-Scimitar*, March 30, 1944.

5. Jason Morgan Ward, *Defending White Democracy: The Making of a Segregationist Movement and the Remaking of Racial Politics, 1936-1965* (Chapel Hill: University of North Carolina Press, 2011).

6. Chester M. Morgan, *Redneck Liberal: Theodore G. Bilbo and the New Deal* (Baton Rouge: Louisiana State University Press, 1985), 226-228; Neil R. McMillen, *Dark Journey: Black Mississippians in the Age of Jim Crow* (Urbana: University of Illinois Press, 1989), 36; Nancy Beck Young, *Why We Fight: Congress and the Politics of World War II* (Lawrence: University Press of Kansas, 2013), 173-174; "House by 252 to 84 Votes to Outlaw Southern Poll Tax," *NYT*, October 14, 1942; Charles S. Johnson, *To Stem This Tide: A Survey of Racial Tension Areas in the United States* (Boston: The Pilgrim Press, 1943), 68.

7. Ira Katznelson, *Fear Itself: The New Deal and the Origins of Our Time* (New York: W. W. Norton, 2013), part II; "Absentee Senators Ordered Arrested for Poll-Tax Fight," *Los Angeles Times*, November 15, 1942; Frederick R. Barkley, "Senate Filibuster Near End," *NYT*, November 22, 1942; Theodore Bilbo to Brinkley Morton, November 25, 1942, Box 1076, and Theodore Bilbo to Reverend Sam Franklin, November 17, 1942, Box 1077, both in BPUSM; C. W. Fowler, "Labor Forces Plan New Poll Tax Drive in '43, as Senate Buries Bill," *CIO News*, November 30, 1942.

8. George H. Gallup, *The Gallup Poll: Public Opinion, 1935-1971*, 3 vols. (New York: Random House, 1972), 1:271, 403; Steven White, *World War II and American Racial Politics: Public Opinion, The Presidency, and Civil Rights Advocacy* (New York: Cambridge University Press, 2019), 54-57; W. M. Burt to Theodore G. Bilbo, November 19, 1942, Box 1076, and Sam H. Franklin Jr. to Theodore Bilbo, November 17, 1942, and Charles S. Fox to Theodore Bilbo, November 23, 1942, both in Box 1077, all in BPUSM; Ward, *Defending White Democracy*, 56-57.

9. James Marlow, "The Home Front," *Jackson (Miss.) Daily News*, June 13, 1945; David Brinkley, *Washington Goes to War* (New York: Alfred A. Knopf, 1988), 203.

10. Sam Lacey, "Big Wind Bilbo on Loose, Set for Poll Tax Filibuster," *CD*, June 5, 1943; "Washington Notes," *New Republic*, December 13, 1943; "Washington Notes," *New Republic*, April 3, 1944; "Of All Things," *The New Yorker*, January 27, 1945, 51; "Bilbo Blames Mrs. Roosevelt and Others for Threat to Filibuster," *Washington Tribune*, December 18, 1943; Theodore Bilbo to C. G. Smith, May 31, 1943, Box 1076, BPUSM.

11. Smith, "Theodore G. Bilbo's Senatorial Career, The Final Years: 1941-1947," 139-145; Merle E. Reed, *Seedtime for the Modern Civil Rights Movement: The President's Committee on Fair Employment Practice, 1941-1946* (Baton Rouge: Louisiana State University Press, 1991), 156-172; Report of the Secretary for the July 1945 meeting of the Board, PQHV-NAACP: BDAC; "Bilbo Opens Fire on FEPC," *Baltimore Sun*, June 28, 1945. Also see Ward, *Defending White Democracy*, 78-83.

12. Glenn Feldman, *The Great Melding: War, the Dixiecrat Rebellion, and the Southern Model for America's New Conservatism* (Tuscaloosa: University of Alabama Press, 2015), 43-44; Katznelson, *Fear Itself*, part II; Audio recording of the May 24, 1946, episode of *Meet the Press*, LC; "Agency Bill Voted with FEPC Funds," *NYT*, June 21,

1944; *Hearings before the Committee on Labor, House of Representatives, on H. R. 3986, H. R. 4004 and H. R. 4005*, 78th Cong., (1944).
13. Mrs. J. C. Boyer to Theodore Bilbo, June 23, 1945, Box 1022, BPUSM. Boxes 1022, 1023, and 1024 of the Bilbo Papers are full of letters from correspondents from Mississippi and around the country writing in support of Bilbo's position opposing the FEPC.
14. Southern Conference for Human Welfare press release, June 27, 1945, Box 41, Thomas G. Abernethy Collection, UM; A Petition from Citizens of the State of Georgia, June 1945, Box 512, Glenn W. Rainey Papers, Emory.
15. Margaret Fisher to Glenn and Dot, June 28, 1945, and A Petition from Citizens of the State of Georgia, June 1945, both in Box 512, Glenn W. Rainey Papers, Emory; Theodore Bilbo to William Holmes Borders, June 19, 1945, Box 1024, BPUSM; "Atlantans Score Bilbo's Attack on FEPC Petitions," *Jackson Daily News*, June 24, 1945.
16. Thomas G. Abernethy to Charles L. Horn, May 27, 1944, Box 41, Thomas G. Abernethy Collection; *Congressional Record*, June 16, 1944, 6014.
17. "Election Officials Deny Mississippi Negroes Vote in Democratic Primary," *Atlanta Daily World*, September 4, 1942; Carsie A. Hall to Thurgood Marshall, August 26, 1942, PQHV-NAACP: EVH; Commission on Interracial Cooperation, "The White Primaries Disturb the South," August 31, 1942, PQHV-NAACP: SS.
18. Charles C. Bolton, "Race and Wartime Politics during the Administration of Governor Thomas L. Bailey (1944–1946)," *Journal of Mississippi History* 81 (Spring/Summer 2019): 48–51; Rob F. Hall, "Negro-Baiter Runs Last in Mississippi [sic] Race," *Daily Worker (New York, N.Y.)*, August 10, 1942; "Southern Leaders Prepare to Resist," *NYT*, April 4, 1944; J. Wesley Dixon to Attorney Marshall, August 28, 1944, PQHV-NAACP: EVH; John P. Davis, "Miss. Whites Use Force and Other Restrictions against Majority Negro Population," *Pittsburgh Courier*, June 10, 1944; "Attempt of Negroes to Vote in Jackson Election Halted," *Jackson Clarion-Ledger*, July 8, 1944; "Plan Miss. Battle on White Primary," *CD*, November 11, 1944; Steven F. Lawson, *Black Ballots: Voting Rights in the South, 1944–1969* (New York: Columbia University Press, 1976), 101; Mississippi NAACP chapter documents, 1942–1946, reel 14, Part 26A, Papers of the NAACP; Patricia Sullivan, *Lift Every Voice: The NAACP and the Making of the Civil Rights Movement* (New York: New Press, 2009), ch. 7.
19. Charles C. Bolton, "Mississippi's School Equalization Program, 1945–1954: 'A Last Gasp to Try to Maintain a Segregated Educational System,'" *Journal of Southern History* 66 (November 2000): 781–814; "Miss. Teachers Ask Equal Salaries, Better Buildings," *Atlanta Daily World*, March 25, 1943; "Miss. Teachers Warned on Equal Salary by State," *CD*, October 23, 1943; Petition to His Excellency Governor Tom Bailey and the Members of the Mississippi Legislature, February 8, 1944, and Walter Sillers to Bishop Theodore D. Bratton, January 31, 1944, both in Box 65, Walter Sillers Jr. Papers, DSU; Bolton, "Race and Wartime Politics during the Administration of Governor Thomas L. Bailey (1944–1946)."
20. "Bilbo Threatens New Civil War over FEP Bill," *CD*, February 24, 1945; Bilbo, "The War"; Theodore Bilbo to D. H. McCoy, James Chrestman, and Baxter D. Ward, July

29, 1943; Mrs. R. G. Burt to Theodore G. Bilbo, June 16, 1944; and Theodore G. Bilbo to Mrs. R. G. Burt, June 20, 1944, all in Box 1084, BPUSM.

21. "Mississippi Mob Slays Man over Rich Farm," *Pittsburgh Courier*, August 26, 1944; Eldridge Simmons affidavit, August 1, 1944, reel 25, Part 7A, Papers of the NAACP; Dudley J. Hughes, *Oil in the Deep South: A History of the Oil Business in Mississippi, Alabama, and Florida, 1859–1945* (Jackson: University Press of Mississippi, 1993); "Current Topics of Interest in Wall Street," *NYT*, May 17, 1944; Elizabeth Wilson, "4 White Men Freed in Slaying of Negro Preacher," *PM*, October 8, 1944.

22. Steven Hahn, *A Nation under Our Feet: Black Political Struggles in the Rural South from Slavery to the Great Migration* (Cambridge, MA: Harvard University Press, 2003), ch. 7, 453–454, 468–471; "Sen. Bilbo Plans 'Back to Africa' Bill," *CD*, April 22, 1939; *Congressional Record*, April 24, 1939, 4650–4671; Michael W. Fitzgerald, "'We Have Found a Moses': Theodore Bilbo, Black Nationalism, and the Greater Liberia Bill of 1939," *Journal of Southern History* 63 (May 1997): 303.

23. Fitzgerald, "'We Have Found a Moses'" 293–320; C. L. R. James et al., *Fighting Racism in World War II* (New York: Pathfinder, 1980), 88.

24. Harry McAlpin, "Silver Lining," *CD*, January 23, 1943; Theodore Bilbo to I. C. Caldwell, October 21, 1942, Box 1066, and Edward D. Clarkson to Theodore G. Bilbo, April 6, 1944, Box 817, both in BPUSM; "Senator Stages Show in U.S. Senate, 'He Comes On,'" *Kansas City Plaindealer*, November 27, 1942; *Congressional Record*, June 20, 1944, 6253. Stenographers for the *Congressional Record* doctored Bilbo's speech to remove the racially offensive slurs he made during his remarks. See Young, *Why We Fight*, 125.

25. Flyer for Grand Mass Meeting Given in Honor of Marcus Garvey's Birthday, August 1941, and Eardlie John to Theodore G. Bilbo, August 11, 1941, both in 18B, reel 13, Papers of the NAACP; "Harlem Turns Thumbs Down on Bilbo—Make Costumes for Elks," *New York Amsterdam Star-News*, August 23, 1941.

26. James N. Hatchett to Theodore Bilbo, March 28, 1944, PQHV-NAACP: SS.

27. Bolton, "Race and Wartime Politics during the Administration of Governor Thomas L. Bailey (1944–1946)," 9–13; Ed S. Lewis Jr., "Suggestions for County Chairmen," April 17, 1944, Box 57, Walter Sillers Jr. Papers; Joseph E. Lowndes, *From the New Deal to the New Right: Race and the Southern Origins of Modern Conservatism* (New Haven, CT: Yale University Press, 2008), 14–15; Turner Catledge, "New Deal Faces Mississippi 'Bolt'; Uninstructed Slate Is Possible," *NYT*, May 30, 1944.

28. Gallup, *The Gallup Poll*, 1: 456–457; Theodore G. Bilbo to R. M. Kelly, June 12, 1944, and Theodore G. Bilbo to John M. Kuykendall, May 20, 1944, both in Box 1108, BPUSM; Roger Daniels, *Franklin D. Roosevelt: The War Years, 1939–1945* (Urbana: University of Illinois Press, 2016), 415–416; John LeFlore, "Bilbo Threatens to Bolt if Demos Blast Poll Tax," *CD*, July 8, 1944.

29. Theodore G. Bilbo to Earnest Sevier Cox, November 4, 1945, and November 17, 1945, both in Box 6, Earnest Sevier Cox Papers, DUKE.

30. Theodore Bilbo to Evelyn Gandy, June 13, 1945; Theodore Bilbo to Evelyn Gandy, April 30, 1945; and Evelyn Gandy to Theodore Bilbo, fall 1945, all in Box 1035,

BPUSM; Smith, "Theodore G. Bilbo's Senatorial Career, The Final Years: 1941–1947," 169–170; Theodore G. Bilbo, *Take Your Choice: Separation or Mongrelization* (Poplarville, MS: Dream House Publishing Co., 1947). The correspondence between Bilbo and Gandy in 1945 and 1946, in which Bilbo regularly used the phrase "our book," makes it clear that Gandy played the major role in writing Bilbo's book. See letters in Box 1035, BPUSM.

31. Theodore Bilbo to Evelyn Gandy, April 30, 1945, Box 1035, BPUSM; Smith, "Theodore G. Bilbo's Senatorial Career, The Final Years: 1941–1947," 169–170; Bilbo, *Take Your Choice: Separation or Mongrelization*.

32. Glenda Gilmore, *Defying Dixie: The Radical Roots of Civil Rights, 1919–1950* (New York: W. W. Norton, 2008), 394–397; Robert L. Fleegler, "Theodore G. Bilbo and the Decline of Public Racism, 1938–1947," *Journal of Mississippi History* 68 (Spring 2006): 15–18; "Mass Meeting Asks Removal of Bilbo as Capital Mayor," *Jackson Clarion-Ledger*, April 14, 1944; "Sen. Bilbo Replies to Capital Critics," *Greenwood (Miss.) Commonwealth*, April 13, 1944; Racial Situation in the United States, April 24, 1944, Box 104, Central Decimal Files, October 1942–May 1944, Records of the Army Air Forces, Record Group 18, NA-CP; "Foes of Poll Tax Hit Bilbo Speech," *Jackson Clarion-Ledger*, March 24, 1944; Pvt. A. Burns to Theodore G. Bilbo, May 27, 1944, Box 1067, BPUSM; Young Men's Guild Bible Class to President Franklin Delano Roosevelt, April 13, 1944, AU: FDR.

33. W. H. Rucker to Senator Bilbo, April 6, 1944, and Phil Davis to Theodore G. Bilbo, April 7, 1944, both in Box 817, BPUSM.

34. Congressional Record, July 24, 1945, 7994–7998.

35. "Arnold Hartley Lets Bilbo Have It—First in Italian, Then in English," *Variety*, August 1, 1945; "Italian, Negro, Jew Say to Oust Bilbo," *NYAN*, October 27, 1945; Theodore Bilbo to Lesley Lucas, October 25, 1945, Box 1127, BPUSM; "Bilbo Threatens Minority Groups with Deportation," *Jewish Advocate*, August 2, 1945; "Bilbo's 'Fascist Sentiments' Surprise White Woman; Jews and Negroes Threatened" (Associated Negro Press Release), July 30, 1945, PQHV-BFS: ORP1.

36. "Arnold Hartley Lets Bilbo Have It—First in Italian, then in English"; Roy Wilkins to All NAACP units, July 26, 1945, 18B, reel 3, Papers of the NAACP; Thelma M. Dale to Friends, August 2, 1945, AU: NNC; "Drive to Send Bilbo Back to Dixie," *CD*, August 11, 1945.

37. See, e.g., "Aroused Jews Ask That Bilbo 'Go,'" *NYAN*, August 11, 1945; "Magazine Publishers Assn. Assails Bilbo," *NYAN*, August 18, 1945; "Sen. Bilbo Condemned in Annual Sons of Italy Conference Here," *Boston Daily Globe*, August 19, 1945.

38. "Wagner-Mead Statement Hits Bilbo 'Insults,'" *New York Herald Tribune*, August 11, 1945; "Both N.Y. Parties War on Bilbo," *CD*, September 1, 1945; Adam Lapin, "Labor, Negroes Are Aroused by Fascist Attacks on Minorities," *Sunday Worker (New York, N.Y.)*, August 5, 1945; "'Disgrace to Senate,' Taft Says in Branding Mississippi's Bilbo," *Pittsburgh Courier*, August 18, 1945; "Taft Discloses Senate Move to Impeach Bilbo," *Jewish Advocate*, August 16, 1945; "Bilbo Will Run Again," *NYT*, August 24, 1945.

39. A Veteran to Runt, n.d., 1945, and An ex-Negro sailor to Nazi Scum, n.d., 1945, both in Box 1085, Crew of the SS *Marne* to Senator Bilbo, October 31, 1945, Box 1127, all in BPUSM.
40. Mrs. Charles Bell to Theodore Bilbo, n.d., September 1945, and Theodore Bilbo to Mrs. Bell, September 25, 1945, both in Box 1024, BPUSM. Details on Paul Bell and his family from Ancestry.com. In a January 1941 speech to Congress, FDR enumerated the "four freedoms" Americans needed to defend as war approached: freedom of speech, freedom of worship, freedom from want, and freedom from fear.
41. Max Johnson, "Soldiers Clash in Race Riots in Italy," *Cleveland Call and Post*, August 25, 1945.
42. "Reward for Hitler," *New York Herald Tribune*, August 14, 1945; Michael R. Beschloss, *The Conquerors: Roosevelt, Truman and the Destruction of Hitler's Germany, 1941–1945* (New York: Simon & Schuster, 2002), 256; Edward A. Harris, "Bilbo 'Explains' Racial Position to Congressmen," *St. Louis Post-Dispatch*, September 23, 1945; Theodore Bilbo to Adelaide Simon, October 12, 1945, Box 1024, BPUSM.
43. "The Big Idea of Edward Bykowski," *PM*, September 23, 1945; "Bilbo's Home Picketed by Disabled Veteran," *Washington Star*, August 29, 1945; "White War Hero Pulls Picket on Bilbo in Capital," *Cleveland Call and Post*, September 8, 1945; Venice T. Spraggs, "Bilbo Defends Self in Congress," *CD*, September 15, 1945; Ira Wolfert, "Five Ways to Cheat Death," *Reader's Digest*, April 1944, 35–36; Jeff Spevak, *22 Minutes: The USS Vincennes and the Tragedy of Savo Island: A Lifetime Survival Story* (Guilford, CT: Lyons Press, 2019), 6; "Veteran Tells What He Wanted to Say to Bilbo," *PM*, September 9, 1945.
44. "The Big Idea of Edward Bykowski"; "Bilbo's Home Picketed by Disabled Veteran"; "White War Hero Pulls Picket on Bilbo in Capital"; "Veteran Tells What He Wanted to Say to Bilbo"; John DeFerrari, *Lost Washington, D.C.* (Charleston, SC: The History Press, 2011), 36.
45. "Sends Iron Cross to Bilbo . . .," *Daily Worker*, October 8, 1945; "Giant Protest Rally to Oust Bilbo," ad, *Daily Worker*, October 15, 1945; "1,200 at Rally Urge Bilbo Go," *Daily Worker*, October 20, 1945; "Bykowski and Allies Resume Picketing of Bilbo's Home," *CD*, October 20, 1945; Art Shields, "Negro, White Officers Join GI Picket Line; Bilbo Looks, Flees," *Daily Worker*, October 22, 1945.
46. Dorothy K. Funn to Max [Yergan] and Thelma, October 17, 1945, AU: NNC; "Permanent Picket Lines Ask Bilbo Ouster," *CD*, December 22, 1945; "Stage Mass Meeting," *Philadelphia Tribune*, December 1, 1945.
47. "Dixie, Methodist Women Blast Bilbo, Eastland," *CD*, August 25, 1945; "Southern Papers Repudiate Bilbo," *The Jewish Exponent*, August 3, 1945; "Mississippi Editor Talks Back to Bilbo in Defense of Downtrodden Minorities," *Memphis World*, August 10, 1945.
48. J. C. Grubbs to Theodore G. Bilbo, September 18, 1945; John E. Flanagan to Theodore G. Bilbo, October 13, 1945; and J. M. Smith to Theodore Bilbo, October 15, 1945, all in Box 1023, BPUSM; "Mississippi Mud," *Newsweek*, August 6, 1945.

Chapter 10

1. "Bilbo Is Given the Brush-Off," *Life*, January 13, 1947, 20–21; "That Man," *Time*, January 13, 1947, 21.
2. Anne M. Butler and Wendy Wolff, *United States Senate Election, Expulsion, and Censure Cases, 1793–1990* (Washington, DC: Government Printing Office, 1995), 376–379; "Practically Guilty," *Time*, January 6, 1947, 20; *Investigation of the National Defense Program, Transactions between Senator Theodore G. Bilbo and Various War Contractors, Additional Report*, January 2, 1947.
3. A. Wigfall Green, *The Man Bilbo* (Baton Rouge: Louisiana State University Press, 1963), 115–117; Paul Wooten, "Ellender Blasts 'Gestapo' Tactics," *New Orleans Times-Picayune*, January 5, 1947; *Congressional Record*, January 4, 1947, 71–109; "That Man"; "Bilbo Forces Give In to GOP as Filibuster Dies; Solon on Sick Leave; Others Take Oath," *Jackson Clarion-Ledger*, January 5, 1947; "Congress: Pepper and Bilbo," *Newsweek*, January 20, 1947, 27.
4. Charles S. Bullock III et al., *The Three Governors Controversy: Skullduggery, Machinations, and the Decline of Georgia's Progressive Politics* (Athens: University of Georgia Press, 2015), 1–7, ch. 5; "Talmadge Is Dead at 62 in Georgia," *NYT*, December 22, 1946; "Georgia: Wool Hat Rebellion," *Newsweek*, January 27, 1947, 21–24.
5. Bullock et al., *The Three Governors Controversy*, 1–7, ch. 5; "Georgia: Wool Hat Rebellion," *Newsweek*, January 27, 1947, 21–24. The "missing" Telfair box had several irregularities, including a list of supposed write-in votes oddly cast in alphabetical order and the names of some dead citizens. See Stephen G. N. Tuck, *Beyond Atlanta: The Struggle for Racial Equality in Georgia, 1940–1980* (Athens: University of Georgia Press, 2001), 70.
6. "Georgia: Wool Hat Rebellion," *Newsweek*, January 27, 1947; "Battle in Georgia on Governorship Is Taken to Court," *NYT*, January 16, 1947; "Two Governors: A Legal Tangle and Fisticuffs," *Manchester Guardian*, January 16, 1947; "Georgia: Votes Dimly Seen," *Newsweek*, February 3, 1947; "Talmadge Ousted in Georgia; Court Gives Thompson Reins," *NYT*, March 20, 1947.
7. Patricia Sullivan, *Days of Hope: Race and Democracy in the New Deal Era* (Chapel Hill: University of North Carolina Press, 1996), 193–194; "The Deep South Looks Up," *Fortune* 28 (July 1943): 223–224.
8. Robert L. Fleegler, "Theodore G. Bilbo and the Decline of Public Racism, 1938–1947," *Journal of Mississippi History* 68 (Spring 2006): 18; "Just Two More Times," *Time*, January 7, 1946; Frederick C. Othman, "Bilbo Puts Mississippi Resolution at Start of His Filibuster Speech," *Jackson Daily News*, January 30, 1946; "Threatened 60-Day Filibuster on FEPC Launched by Bilbo," *Memphis Commercial Appeal*, January 31, 1946; James E. Roper, "Filibuster Ends Chance of FEPC Bill's Passage," *Jackson Daily News*, February 10, 1946; "FEPC Dies as Bilbo Wins Renomination," *Christian Century*, July 17, 1946, 885. "Peckerwood" was a demeaning term used to refer to poor whites.
9. Robert S. Bird, "Bilbo Strikes Pose as Martyr and Gets Votes," *New York Herald Tribune*, June 30, 1946; Senator Theodore Bilbo Campaign Speech (Pontotoc), May

7, 1946, transcript, MDAH; Notes on the 1946 campaign, Box 24, Ross A. Collins Papers, LC; "Bilbo Seeks to Keep Negroes from Voting," *DDT*, June 6, 1946; "Bilbo Condemns Negro Voting at Pass Christian," *Biloxi (Miss.) Daily Herald*, June 6, 1946.

10. Flyer, Forrest County Colored Committee of 100, n.d., January 1946?, Box 1067, BPUSM; "Negroes Want Full Equality," *Memphis Press-Scimitar*, February 18, 1946; John LeFlore, "Mississippi Negroes Gird for War with Jim Crow," *CD*, March 9, 1946; John LeFlore, "Mississippi Seeks Way to Keep White Primary," *CD*, March 2, 1946; "American Veterans Committee: A New Organization for the Men and Women of This War," pamphlet, n.d., 1940s, Box 11, Glenn W. Rainey Papers, Emory; Estamore A. Wolfe, Report on the Jackson Chapter of the American Veterans Committee, n.d., January or February 1947, Box 188, American Veterans Committee Records, Special Collections Research Center, Gelman Library, George Washington University, Washington, DC; Hearings, 1946, 115, 372; Louis A. Miles, World War II Enlistment Records, 1938-1946, Ancestry.com; "Negro Veterans Form Club," *Prentiss (Miss.) Headlight*, May 16, 1946.

11. Report on the Session of the Mississippi Progressive Voters League, May 16-17, 1946, Box 1067, BPUSM; Policies Adopted by Mississippi Progressive Voters League, May 16-17, 1946, Box 2, Kenneth Toler Papers, Special Collections, Mitchell Memorial Library, Mississippi State University, Starkville; "Voters League Meets; Will Raise $20,000 to Carry Out Its Program," *Atlanta Daily World*, May 28, 1946; "Don't Try It" (editorial), *Jackson Daily News*, May 19, 1946; Letter to the Editor (T. B. Wilson), *Jackson Daily News*, May 27, 1946.

12. "400 Hinds Negroes Register to Vote since January," *Jackson Daily News*, May 21, 1946; "Primaries: White Supremacy," *Newsweek*, July 15, 1946, 30-31; John Dittmer, *Local People: The Struggle for Civil Rights in Mississippi* (Urbana: University of Illinois Press, 1994), 3, 6-7; Lois Hicks statement, Report #22, October 10, 1946, Box 15, Special Committee to Investigate Campaign Expenditures, Records of the United States Senate, Record Group 46, NA-DC.

13. Hearings, 1946, 46-55, 139-140, 192; Steven F. Lawson, *Black Ballots: Voting Rights in the South, 1944-1969* (New York: Columbia University Press, 1976), 107-110; Notes on the 1946 campaign, Box 24, Ross A. Collins Papers; Various reports compiled by investigators, October and November 1946, Box 15, Special Committee to Investigate Campaign Expenditures.

14. "'The Man' Hauls Out a New One: Atomic Threats," *CD*, June 1, 1946; "Bilbo Adamant in Face of Senate Investigation," *Austin (Tex.) Statesman*, June 28, 1946; "Bilbo Urges Mississippi Men to Employ 'Any Means' to Bar Negroes from Voting," *NYT*, June 23, 1946; Hearings, 1946, 157, 216.

15. The exact substance of Bilbo's racial remarks during the 1946 campaign is probably lost to history, as the print media that covered the campaign, both North and South, self-censored the worst language. As *Collier's* noted, it did not publish Bilbo's campaign remarks "*in toto*," because of "vile, profane, and inflammatory" language. See Henry Henderson and Sam Shaw, "Bilbo," *Collier's*, July 6, 1946.

16. Jason Morgan Ward, *Hanging Bridge: Racial Violence and America's Civil Rights Century* (New York: Oxford University Press, 2016); "Mississippi Mob Lynches a

Slayer," *NYT*, October 18, 1942; Egerton, *Speak Now against the Day*, 361–365; James C. Cobb, *The Most Southern Place on Earth: The Mississippi Delta and the Roots of Regional Identity* (New York: Oxford University Press, 1992), 212–213.

17. Garry Boulard, "'The Man' versus 'The Quisling': Theodore Bilbo, Hodding Carter, and the 1946 Democratic Party," *Journal of Mississippi History* 51 (August 1989): 201–212; Hearings, 1946, 39; Telegram, A. Philip Randolph to Harry S. Truman, June 27, 1946, Box 1, Papers of A. Philip Randolph, LC; Telegram, Walter White to Tom Clark, July 1, 1946, and Daniel E. Byrd to Thurgood Marshall, July 3, 1946, both in Part 4, Reel 9, Papers of the NAACP; "Bilbo Adamant in Face of Senate Investigation"; "Bilbo Probe Is Referred to Special Group," *Jackson Daily News*, July 1, 1946; "Senators Refuse Inquiry on Bilbo," *NYT*, July 2, 1946.

18. Emily and Kenneth Drisler to Theodore Bilbo, July 1, 1946, Box 1144, and Arthur C. Wilson to Theodore Bilbo, Box 935, both in BPUSM.

19. Peter Edson, "Bilbo Takes Out after the 'Peckerwoods,'" *Austin (Tex.) Statesmen*, May 13, 1946; Hodding Carter, "'The Man' from Mississippi—Bilbo," *NYT*, June 30, 1946; "Ellis Opens Campaign" (press release), May 10, 1946, Box 1, Kenneth Toler Papers; William Winter to Daddy and Mama, July 8, 1946, copy in author's possession; Lawson, *Black Ballots*, 106.

20. Hearings, 1946, 100, 157, 198–199, 327–329; "Primaries: White Supremacy"; "Bilbo Election Violence Told in Mississippi," *CD*, July 20, 1946; Patricia Sullivan, *Lift Every Voice: The NAACP and the Making of the Civil Rights Movement* (New York: New Press, 2009), 318; Daniel E. Byrd to Thurgood Marshall, July 3, 1946, Part 4, reel 9, Papers of the NAACP; "Bilbo Pushes Vote Curb," *NYT*, July 6, 1946. Medgar and Charles Evers were leaders in the Mississippi civil rights movement during the 1950s and 1960s. A white supremacist assassinated Medgar in 1963.

21. M. L. St. John, "Discusses Negro Vote in Georgia," *Atlanta Constitution*, February 27, 1946; "It Is Time for a Change," *Atlanta Daily World*, January 13, 1946; Tuck, *Beyond Atlanta*, 60–61; "Introducing Mrs. Mankin," n.d., 1946, Box 17, Glenn W. Rainey Papers, Emory; Lorraine Nelson Spritzer, *The Belle of Ashby Street: Helen Douglas Mankin and Georgia Politics* (Athens: University of Georgia Press, 1982).

22. Craig Lloyd, "Primus E. King (1900–1986)," *New Georgia Encyclopedia*, https://www.georgiaencyclopedia.org/articles/history-archaeology/primus-e-king-1900-1986; Derek Charles Catsam, *Freedom's Main Line: The Journey of Reconciliation and the Freedom Rides* (Lexington: University of Kentucky Press, 2009), ch. 1.

23. Tomiko Brown-Nagin, *Courage to Dissent: Atlanta and the Long History of the Civil Rights Movement* (New York: Oxford University Press, 2011), 37; "Danger: Stormtroopers at Work," *Southern Patriot*, July 1946; Civil Rights Congress, *We Charge Genocide* (New York: Civil Rights Congress, 1951), 204; Commoner Party of the United States of America, *Organization Plan of the Commoner Party of the United States of America* (Conyers, GA: n.p., 1944)

24. Thomas A. Scott, ed., *Cornerstones of Georgia History: Documents That Formed the State* (Athens: University of Georgia Press, 1995), 201–203; Tuck, *Beyond Atlanta*, 66; Kevin Kruse, *White Flight: Atlanta and the Making of Modern Conservatism*

(Princeton, NJ: Princeton University Press, 2005), 24; "'Red Gallus Gene': Despite Big Negro Vote, Talmadge Is Re-elected Governor of Georgia," *Life*, July 29, 1946, 32–33.

25. Lucy Randolph Mason to Beverley, September 24, 1946, Box 4, Lucy Randolph Mason Papers, DUKE; "The Majority Loses," *The New Republic*, July 29, 1946; Robert Mickey, *Paths out of Dixie: The Democratization of Authoritarian Enclaves in America's Deep South, 1944–1972* (Princeton, NJ: Princeton University Press, 2015), 126; Calvin Kytle and James A. Mackay, *Who Runs Georgia?* (Athens: University of Georgia Press, 1998), 43, 95, 239.

26. *We Charge Genocide*, 205; "Report from the Nation," *NYT*, May 19, 1946; E. T. Baker III, "Georgia Modern Home of the Ku Klux Klan," *Baltimore Sun*, May 23, 1946; Brown-Nagin, *Courage to Dissent*, 41; Letter to the Editor (George B. Culpepper Sr.), *Macon Telegraph and News*, April 14, 1946.

27. Harold Paulk Henderson, *The Politics of Change in Georgia: A Political Biography of Ellis Arnall* (Athens: University of Georgia Press, 1991), 79–81; George Berry, interview by Bob Short, April 6, 2013, videotape, Reflections on Georgia Politics Oral History Collection, Russell; Jennifer E. Brooks, "Winning the Peace: Georgia Veterans and the Struggle to Define the Political Legacy of World War II," in *Before Brown: Civil Rights and White Backlash in the Modern South*, ed. Glenn Feldman (Tuscaloosa: University of Alabama Press, 2004), 260–267; Notes on telephone conversation between Henry A. Wallace and Ellis G. Arnall, May 10, 1946, reel 66, Henry A. Wallace Papers; "Georgia Primary: Newly Enfranchised Kids Give the Campaign the Young College Spirit," *Life*, July 1, 1946.

28. Gene Roberts and Hank Klibanoff, *The Race Beat: The Press, the Civil Rights Struggle, and the Awakening of a Nation* (New York: Alfred A. Knopf, 2006), 30; "Carmichael Paints Talmadge as Paul Revere of Race Issue," *Atlanta Constitution*, June 5, 1946; "Carmichael Ties Klan to Opponents' Necks," *Atlanta Daily World*, May 23, 1946.

29. C. E. Gregory, "Arnall Says State on Trial, Calls Racial Issue Screen," *Atlanta Journal*, June 23, 1946; Benjamin Fine, "Arnall Demands End of Poll Taxes," *NYT*, May 18, 1946.

30. "Georgia Orders Action to Revoke Charter of Klan," *NYT*, May 31, 1946; "Duke Charges Atlanta Police Klan Members," *Atlanta Daily World*, June 15, 1946; "Georgia Sues to Lift Charter of Ku Klux Klan," *Daily Worker (New York, N.Y.)*, June 21, 1946; Marvin O'Neal Jr. to J. Edgar Hoover, June 22, 1946, Subgroup CVI, Box 115, Richard B. Russell Collection, Russell; "Klan Dragon Denies Any Plot on Arnall," *NYT*, June 23, 1946; "Survey Shows Vet Organizations Stand Firm on Fighting Bigotry," *Jewish Advocate*, September 26, 1946.

31. Henderson, *The Politics of Change in Georgia*, 167–168; Joseph L. Bernd, "White Supremacy and the Disfranchisement of Blacks in Georgia, 1946," *Georgia Historical Quarterly* 66 (Winter 1982): 502; Mickey, *Paths out of Dixie*, 79; Notes on telephone conversation between Henry A. Wallace and Ellis G. Arnall, May 10, 1946.

32. *We Charge Genocide*, 206; Mickey, *Paths out of Dixie*, 126; M. Neil Andrews to FBI Special Agent in Charge, August 20, 1946, FBI-46 Election; Bernd, "White Supremacy and the Disfranchisement of Blacks in Georgia, 1946," 497–498.

33. Tuck, *Beyond Atlanta*, 66–67; Report of Special Agent Robert M. Barwick, Long County, September 3, 1946, FBI-46 Election; *We Charge Genocide*, 206–207; Bernd,

"White Supremacy and the Disfranchisement of Blacks in Georgia, 1946," 495; M. O. Smith to NAACP, September 10, 1946, Part 4, reel 7, Papers of the NAACP.
34. *We Charge Genocide*, 207; Sarah Ayako Barksdale, "Prelude to a Revolution: African-American World War II Veterans, Double Consciousness, and Civil Rights 1940–1955" (PhD diss., University of North Carolina, 2014), 245; Various reports from Grady and Meriwether Counties, FBI-46 Election; Tuck, *Beyond Atlanta*, 67; Bernd, "White Supremacy and the Disfranchisement of Blacks in Georgia, 1946."
35. "Introducing Mrs. Mankin"; Tuck, *Beyond Atlanta*, 69; *Contested Congressional Election for Georgia Fifth Congressional District Seat, Hearing before the House Subcommittee on Elections, Committee on House Administration*, 80th Cong. (March 16, 1948).
36. "The South" (editorial), *Life*, July 29, 1946; Laura Wexler, *Fire in a Canebrake* (New York: Scribner, 2003); "Racial: Men with Guns," *Newsweek*, August 5, 1946; "Georgia Mob of 20 Men Massacres 2 Negroes, Wives; One Was Ex-GI," *NYT*, July 27, 1946; Egerton, *Speak Now against the Day*, 365; Art Shields, "Bare New Georgia Lynch-Murder: Negro Shot, Pistol Whipped," *Daily Worker (New York, N.Y.)*, July 30, 1946; NAACP, Lynching Record for 1946, PQHV-NAACP: SAL; Barksdale, "Prelude to a Revolution," 245; Report on Death of Macio Snipes, June 20, 1946, reel 17, Southern Regional Council Papers; Harold B. Hinton, "Georgia Law Urged to End Subversion," *NYT*, August 20, 1946; Steven Weisenburger, "The Columbians, Inc.: A Chapter of Racial Hatred from the Post–World War II South," *Journal of Southern History* 69 (November 2003): 821–860.
37. "Mania Grips Dixie; Three New Deaths Revealed," *CD*, August 10, 1946; Edwin Campbell Vincent, "Crowds Jam Courtroom as Five White Men Are Bound Over in McAtee [sic] Death," *DDT*, August 4, 1946; "Mississippi Trial," *NYT*, October 24, 1946.
38. William Hustwit, *Integration Now: Alexander v. Holmes and the End of Jim Crow Education* (Chapel Hill: University of North Carolina Press, 2019), 29; "Mississippi Deputy Held," *NYT*, July 31, 1946; Year End Report, 2015, Civil Rights and Restorative Justice Project, Northeastern University Law School, https://repository.library.north eastern.edu/downloads/neu:m040d844t?datastream_id=content; Memorandum on Mississippi, 1946, Box 13, Special Committee to Investigate Campaign Expenditures; "Talmadge, Hitler and Bilbo," *Pittsburgh Courier*, August 3, 1946.
39. "National Leaders Endorse Crusade against Lynching," *Cleveland Call and Post*, September 14, 1946; "'Bilbo Must Go!' Anti-Lynching Rally Attendants Shout," *Jackson Daily News*, September 17, 1946; "To Open Crusade against Lynching," *NYT*, September 23, 1946; Lawson, *Black Ballots*, 104–105; Preliminary Survey and Report of Investigators Henry Patrick Kiley, Francis T. Kelly, and Roy A. Moon, 1946, Box 984, BPUSM.
40. John D. Morris, "Full Senate Inquiry Is Voted on Bilbo's Right to His Seat," *NYT*, November 17, 1946; Preliminary Survey and Report of Investigators Henry Patrick Kiley, Francis T. Kelly, and Roy A. Moon, 1946; Harold B. Hinton, "Mississippi Leans to Bilbo in Inquiry," *NYT*, December 2, 1946; Hearings, 1946, 21–22.
41. Lawson, *Black Ballots*, 106–109; "Bilbo Hearing," *Life*, December 16, 1946; "Probes: Votes and the Man," *Newsweek*, December 16, 1946; "Courageous Mississippi," *Pittsburgh Courier*, December 14, 1946; Hearings, 1946, 1.

42. Lawson, *Black Ballots*, 106–109; "The Shape of Things" (editorial), *The Nation*, December 21, 1946; Hearings, 1946, 39, 91, 108, 133, 139–140, 171.

43. Hearings, 1946, 108, 201, 243, 274, 284.

44. Lawson, *Black Ballots*, 109–110; Hearings, 1946, 178–179, 182, 185, 188–192, 204–206.

45. Hearings, 1946, 333–354.

46. *Investigation of the National Defense Program, Transactions between Senator Theodore G. Bilbo and Various War Contractors, Additional Report*, January 2, 1947; *Investigation of the National Defense Program, Transactions between Senator Theodore G. Bilbo and Various War Contractors*, December 12–19, 1946; Tris Coffin, "An Old Southern Custom," *The Nation*, December 28, 1946; John L. Cutter, "Senator Concedes He Got 'Christmas Gifts' of Car and Pieces of Furniture," *Jackson Daily News*, December 19, 1946.

47. John D. Morris, "Bilbo Condemned in Committee Poll," *NYT*, December 29, 1946; "Clearing of Bilbo on Negro Vote Seen," *NYT*, December 23, 1946; Minority Views, Special Committee to Investigate Senatorial Campaign Expenditures, 1946, Box 984, BPUSM.

48. Morris, "Bilbo Condemned in Committee Poll"; "Clearing of Bilbo on Negro Vote Seen"; E. F. Keen Jr. to Richard B. Russell, January 4, 1947, Subgroup CVI, Box 115, Richard B. Russell Collection, Russell; Bob Currie to Theodore G. Bilbo, December 15, 1946, Box 954, and Joseph F. Miller to Theodore Bilbo, January 3, 1947, Box 956, both in BPUSM.

49. "Transition," *Newsweek*, February 10, 1947; "The Periscope: Trivia," *Newsweek*, March 3, 1947; Boulard, "'The Man' versus 'The Quisling,'" 217; "He Died a Martyr," *Time*, September 1, 1947; Green, *The Man Bilbo*, 120.

50. "Truman Orders Lynchers Found; Voices Horror at Georgia Crime," *NYT*, July 31, 1946; "Clark Orders Lynching Case Be Presented to U.S. Jury," *NYT*, October 29, 1946; "Georgia Inquiry on Lynching Ends," *NYT*, December 20, 1946; M. Neil Andrews to FBI Special Agent in Charge (Atlanta), August 20, 1946, and Atlanta FBI to J. Edgar Hoover, September 10, 1946, both in FBI-46 Election.

51. M. Neil Andrews to FBI Special Agent in Charge (Atlanta), August 20, 1946; Atlanta FBI to J. Edgar Hoover, September 10, 1946; Edward A. Tamm to J. Edgar Hoover, September 20, 1946; and L. K. Mumford to D. M. Ladd, October 22, 1946, all in FBI-46 Election; "Have You Been Called On?" *Atlanta Statesman*, September 26, 1946; Bernd, "White Supremacy and the Disfranchisement of Blacks in Georgia, 1946," 510–511.

52. Jennifer E. Brooks, *Defining the Peace: World War II Veterans, Race, and the Remaking of Southern Political Tradition* (Chapel Hill: University of North Carolina Press, 2004), 50–52; Josephine Wilkins to Helen Fuller, August 17, 1946, and Lucy Randolph Mason to Mrs. Roosevelt, September 8, 1946, both in Box 4, Lucy Randolph Mason Papers; "Talmadge Election Upheld by Court," *People's Voice (New York, N.Y)*, September 7, 1946; Lewis H. Wood, "High Court Backs Georgia Unit Rule," *NYT*, October 29, 1946. The principle of one person, one vote was not established until the US Supreme Court decision in *Baker v. Carr* in 1962. See J. Douglas Smith, *On Democracy's Doorstep: The*

Inside Story of How the Supreme Court Brought "One Person, One Vote" to the United States (New York: Hill & Wang, 2014).
53. Ellis Gibbs Arnall, *The Shore Dimly Seen* (Philadelphia: J. B. Lippincott Co., 1946); *Publisher's Weekly* 150 (October 5, 1946): 1928, 2003; William B. Hamilton, "Spokesman for the New South," *NYT*, November 17, 1946; Review of *The Shore Dimly Seen*, *The New Yorker*, November 30, 1946; "New Man for a New South," *Newsweek*, November 11, 1946; Ellis G. Arnall, "The Southern Frontier," *The Atlantic*, September 1946, 30–35; Ruth Danehower Wilson, "How Dimly Does Ellis Arnall See?" *Crisis* 54 (May 1947): 138–139; "Georgia: Votes Dimly Seen"; *Publisher's Weekly* 151 (February 22, 1947): 1277; "Play 'Em as They Fall," *Time*, February 10, 1947; "Information Arnall," *Newsweek*, February 10, 1947.
54. Theodore Bilbo to Mrs. David Sanders Herstein, August 13, 1946, Box 943, BPUSM. Herstein lived in New York City.
55. Egerton, *Speak Now against the Day*, 379.

Epilogue

1. Dewey W. Grantham, *The South in Modern America: A Region at Odds* (New York: HarperCollins, 1994), 176–178, 260.
2. James C. Cobb, *The South and America since World War II* (New York: Oxford University Press, 2011), 56–63. See also Kari Frederickson, *Cold War Dixie: Militarization and Modernization in the American South* (Athens: University of Georgia Press, 2013).
3. Cobb, *The South and America since World War II*, 202–204; Charles C. Bolton, *William F. Winter and the New Mississippi: A Biography* (Jackson: University Press of Mississippi, 2013), 250.
4. Alexis Clark, "Returning from War, Returning to Racism," *NYT*, July 30, 2020; Charles D. Chamberlain, *Victory at Home: Manpower and Race in the American South during World War II* (Athens: University of Georgia Press, 2003), ch. 6.
5. Rawn James Jr., *The Double V: How Wars, Protest, and Harry Truman Desegregated America's Military* (New York: Bloomsbury Press, 2013), 237–239; Robert B. Edgerton, *Hidden Heroism: Blacks in America's Wars* (Boulder, CO: Westview Press, 2001), 169.
6. Joseph Crespino, *In Search of Another Country: Mississippi and the Conservative Counterrevolution* (Princeton, NJ: Princeton University Press, 2007).

Bibliography

Primary Sources

MANUSCRIPT SOURCES
Alabama Department of Archives and History, Montgomery
John Hollis Bankhead Papers
Charles W. Capps Jr. Archives, Delta State University, Cleveland, Mississippi
Delta Council Collection
Walter Sillers Jr. Papers
Special Collections Research Center, Gelman Library, George Washington University, Washington, DC
American Veterans Committee Records
Georgia Archives, Atlanta
Governor's Subject Files, Office of the Governor
Ninth Annual Report, Department of Labor, State of Georgia, to the Governor and General Assembly, 1945
Georgia Historical Society, Savannah
Federal Bureau of Investigation Records on the 1946 Georgia Election
Hargrett Rare Book and Manuscript Library, University of Georgia Libraries, Athens
H. W. Caldwell Papers
Kennesaw State University Archives, Kennesaw, Georgia
Blair Family Papers
KSU Oral History Project, 1973–2019
Thomas A. Scott Papers, 1975–2013
Library of Congress, Washington, DC
Audio recording of the May 24, 1946, episode of *Meet the Press*
Ross A. Collins Papers
Evalyn Walsh McLean Papers
Records of the National Urban League
Papers of A. Philip Randolph
Special Collections and University Archives, University of Maryland, College Park
Industrial Union of Marine and Shipbuilding Workers of America Records
McCain Library and Archives, University of Southern Mississippi, Hattiesburg
Theodore G. Bilbo Papers
William M. Colmer Papers
Eugene Talmadge Pamphlets
Tatum Family Business Records
Doy Leale McCall Rare Book and Manuscript Library, University of South Alabama, Mobile
ADDSCO Annual Reports
ADDSCO Records

John L. LeFlore Papers
Sherwood McBroom Brookley Field Collection
Mississippi Department of Archives and History, Jackson
Senator Theodore Bilbo Campaign Speech (Pontotoc), May 7, 1946, transcript
Subject Files
University of Mississippi Libraries, Special Collections, Oxford
Thomas G. Abernethy Collection
James Oliver Eastland Collection
Mississippi Industries Collection
Mitchell Memorial Library, Mississippi State University, Starkville
Delta and Pine Land Company Records
Kenneth Toler Papers
National Archives, Atlanta, Georgia
Records of the War Manpower Commission
National Archives, College Park, Maryland
Records of the Adjutant General's Office, 1917–
Records of the Army Air Forces [AAF]
Records of the Bureau of Agricultural Economics
Records of the Office of the Inspector General
Records of the Office of the Secretary of War
Records of the Office of War Information
Records of the United States Maritime Commission
Records of the War Department General and Special Staffs
National Archives, Washington, DC
Records of the United States Senate
Richard B. Russell Library for Political Research and Studies, University of Georgia, Athens
Alvan S. Arnall Collection of Ellis G. Arnall Materials
Reflections on Georgia Politics Oral History Collection
Richard B. Russell Collection
David M. Rubenstein Rare Book & Manuscript Library, Duke University, Durham, North Carolina
Earnest Sevier Cox Papers
Lucy Randolph Mason Papers
Southern Historical Collection, The Louis Round Wilson Special Collections Library, University of North Carolina at Chapel Hill
Jesse Daniel Ames Papers, 1866–1972
Jonathan Daniels Papers
Stuart A. Rose Manuscript, Archives, and Rare Book Library, Emory University, Atlanta, Georgia
James Vinson Carmichael Papers
Ralph E. McGill Papers
Glenn W. Rainey Papers

NEWSPAPERS AND MAGAZINES
Alabama
Albany-Decatur (AL) Daily
American Mercury
Anniston (AL) Star

Atlanta Constitution
Atlanta Daily World
Atlanta Journal
Atlanta Statesman
The Atlantic
Austin (TX) Statesman
Baltimore Afro-American
Baltimore Sun
Barron's National Business and Financial Weekly
The Bellringer
Benton Harbor (MI) News-Palladium
Biloxi (MS) Daily Herald
Biloxi Sun Herald
Biographical Register of the Officers and Graduates of the U.S. Military Academy at West Point, New York, Since Its Establishment in 1802, Supplement
Birmingham News
Birmingham Post
Board of Review: Holdings, Opinions, and Reviews
Bolivar (Cleveland, MS) Commercial
Boston Daily Globe
Brookhaven (MS) Daily Leader
Charleston (SC) Post and Carrier
The Checkerboard
Chicago Daily News
Chicago Daily Tribune
Chicago Defender
Christian Century
Christian Science Monitor
CIO News
Cleveland Call and Post
Collier's
Congressional Record
Coshocton (OH) Tribune
Cullman (AL) Democrat
The Crisis
Daily Worker (New York, NY)
Dothan (AL) Eagle
Economist
Fortune
Gadsden (AL) Times
Greenville (AL) Advocate
Greenville (MS) Delta Democrat-Times
Greenwood (MS) Commonwealth
Gulfport/Biloxi, Mississippi, Daily Herald
Harper's Magazine
Hartford (CT) Courant
Hattiesburg (MS) American
Houston (TX) Negro Labor News

Indiana (PA) Gazette
Ingalls News
Inthesetimes.com
Jackson Clarion Ledger
Jackson Daily News
Jewish Advocate
The Jewish Exponent
Kansas City Call
Kansas City Plaindealer
Life magazine
Long Beach (CA) Independent
Los Angeles Times
Louisiana Weekly
Louisville Courier-Journal
Louisville Times
Macon Telegraph
Macon Telegraph and News
Manchester Guardian
Marine Engineering and Shipping Review
McComb (MS) Daily Journal
McComb (MS) Enterprise-Journal
Memphis Commercial Appeal
Memphis Press-Scimitar
Memphis World
Meridian (MS) Star
Mobile Press
Mobile Register
Montgomery (AL) Advertiser
The Nation
New Orleans Times-Picayune
New Republic
Newsweek
New York Age
New York Amsterdam News
New York Amsterdam Star-News
New York Daily News
The New Yorker
New York Herald Tribune
New York Post
New York Times
Pascagoula Chronicle-Star combined with the Moss Point (MS) Advertiser
The People's Voice (New York, NY)
Philadelphia Tribune
Pittsburgh Courier
PM
Prentiss (MS) Headlight
Publishers Weekly
Reader's Digest

Robesonian (Lumberton, NC)
Rome (GA) News-Tribune
The Rotarian
St. Louis Post-Dispatch
Salt Lake Tribune
Saturday Evening Post
Shreveport (LA) Times
Southern Frontier
Southern Patriot
Sunday Worker (New York, NY)
Time
Variety
Victory
Washington Post
Washington Star
Washington Tribune
York (PA) Gazette & Daily

OTHER PRIMARY SOURCES

Adam Matthew Digital, Service Newspapers of World War II.
Agricultural Appropriation Bill for 1944: Hearings before the Subcommittee of the Committee on Appropriations, House of Representatives. 78th Cong. (1943).
Ancestry.com.
Archives Unbound: African America, Communists, and the National Negro Congress, 1933–1947.
Archives Unbound: Franklin D. Roosevelt and Race Relations, 1933–1945.
Dictionary of American Navy Fighting Ships. https://www.history.navy.mil/research/histories/ship-histories/danfs.html.
Commoner Party of the United States of America. *Organization Plan of the Commoner Party of the United States of America.* Conyers, GA: n.p., 1944.
Contested Congressional Election for Georgia Fifth Congressional District Seat, Hearing before the House Subcommittee on Elections, Committee on House Administration. 80th Cong. (1948).
Digital Library of Georgia. https://dlg.usg.edu.
Douglass, Frederick. *The Life and Times of Frederick Douglass.* Radford, VA: Wilder Publications, 2008.
Federal Reserve Economic Data. https://fred.stlouisfed.org/series/M0892BUSM156SNBR.
Food for Freedom: Informational Handbook, 1943. Washington, DC: US Department of Agriculture, 1942.
Gallup, George H. *The Gallup Poll: Public Opinion, 1935–1971.* 3 vols. New York: Random House, 1972.
Gibson, Truman K., Jr., with Steve Huntley. *Knocking Down Barriers: My Fight for Black America.* Evanston, IL: Northwestern University Press, 2005.
Hansen, Morris H. *Statistical Abstract of the United States, 1943.* Washington, DC: Department of Commerce, 1944.
Hearings before a Subcommittee of the Committee on Education and Labor, United States Senate, April 6–8, 1943. 78th Cong.

Hearings before a Subcommittee of the Committee on Education and Labor, United States Senate, December 16–18, 1943. 78th Cong.

Hearings before the Committee on Labor, House of Representatives, on H. R. 3986, H.R. 4004 and H. R. 4005. 78th Cong., (1944).

Hearings before the Special Committee to Investigate Senatorial Campaign Expenditures, December 2–5, 1946. 79th Cong.

"In re Ingalls Shipbuilding Corporation and Pascagoula Metal Trades Council (AFL)." November 15, 1941, *Labor Relations Reference Manual* 9 (1940–1941): 815–816.

International Association of Machinists and Aerospace Workers Records, 1901–1974, International President's Office Records (microfilm).

Investigation of the National Defense Program. Transactions between Senator Theodore G. Bilbo and Various War Contractors, December 12–19, 1946. 79th Cong.

Investigation of the National Defense Program. Transactions between Senator Theodore G. Bilbo and Various War Contractors, Additional Report, 79th Cong. (January 2, 1947).

MacGregor, Morris J., and Bernard C. Nalty, eds. *Blacks in the United States Armed Forces: Basic Documents.* 13 vols. Wilmington, DE: Scholarly Resources, 1977.

Minutes of the Meeting of the Southern Governors' Conference, 1943. Atlanta: The Conference, 1943.

Online Documents: Desegregation of the Armed Forces, Harry S. Truman Presidential Museum and Library. www.trumanlibrary.org.

Papers of the NAACP (microfilm).

Peonage Files, US Department of Justice (microfilm).

ProQuest History Vault: Black Freedom Struggle in the 20th Century.

ProQuest History Vault: NAACP Papers.

Scott, Thomas A., ed. *Cornerstones of Georgia History: Documents That Formed the State.* Athens: University of Georgia Press, 1995.

Selected documents from Records of the Committee on Fair Employment Practice: RG 228, National Archives (microfilm).

Southern Regional Council Papers (microfilm).

Tuskegee Institute News Clippings File (microfilm).

United Service Organizations. *Operation USO: Report of the President, February 4, 1941–January 9, 1948.* New York: n.p., 1948.

US Board of Officers on Utilization of Negro Manpower in the Post-War Army. *Policy for Utilization of Negro Manpower in the Post-War Army: Supplemental Report of War Department Special Board on Negro Manpower.* Washington, DC: War Department, 1946.

US Bureau of the Budget. *The United States at War: Development and Administration of the War Program by the Federal Government.* Washington, DC: Government Printing Office, 1946.

US Census Bureau. 1940 Census of Population. Vol. 1. https://www.census.gov/library/publications/1942/dec/population-vol-1.html.

US Department of Agriculture. Census of Agriculture Historical Archive, 1940 Census Publications. http://agcensus.mannlib.cornell.edu/AgCensus/censusParts.do?year=1940.

US Department of Labor. *A Statistical Summary of the Pascagoula Shipbuilding Area: Jackson County, Mississippi.* Washington, DC: US Department of Labor, 1943.

US War Department. *Is a Crime Wave Coming?* Washington, DC: Government Printing Office, 1946.

War Manpower Charts and Statistical Information Relating to the Alabama Dry Dock and Shipbuilding Company, February 1943. DocsTeach, National Archives. https://www.docsteach.org/documents/document/war-manpower-charts-and-statistical-information-relating-to-the-alabama-dry-dock-and-shipbuilding-corporation.

War Manpower Commission. "Employment Service Operations." *Social Security Bulletin* 6 (May 1, 1943): 37–41.

Watson, Denton L., ed. *Papers of Clarence Mitchell*. 2 vols. Athens: Ohio University Press, 2005.

White, Walter. *A Man Called White: The Autobiography of Walter White*. Athens: University of Georgia Press, 1995.

Wiley v. State, 197 Miss. 21.

World War II Rumor Project Collection, 1942–1943. Library of Congress. https://www.loc.gov/resource/afc1945001.afc1945001_ms07107/?sp=35.

Year End Report, 2015. Civil Rights and Restorative Justice Project. Northeastern University Law School. https://repository.library.northeastern.edu/files/neu:cj82nd46z.

Secondary Sources

ARTICLES

Allen, Lincoln. "Medical Needs of the War Industry Areas." *Science & Society* 8 (Winter 1944): 28–39.

Bailes, Sue. "Eugene Talmadge and the Board of Regents Controversy." *Georgia Historical Quarterly* 53 (December 1969): 409–423.

Bartels, Andrew H. "The Office of Price Administration and the Legacy of the New Deal, 1939–1946." *Public Historian* 5 (Summer 1983): 5–29.

Bernd, Joseph L. "White Supremacy and the Disfranchisement of Blacks in Georgia, 1946." *Georgia Historical Quarterly* 66 (Winter 1982): 492–513.

Blum, Albert A. "The Farmer, the Army and the Draft." *Agricultural History* 38 (January 1964): 34–42.

Bolton, Charles C. "Mississippi's School Equalization Program, 1945–1954: 'A Last Gasp to Try to Maintain a Segregated Educational System.'" *Journal of Southern History* 66 (November 2000): 781–814.

Bolton, Charles C. "Race and Wartime Politics during the Administration of Governor Thomas L. Bailey (1944–1946)." *Journal of Mississippi History* 81 (Spring/Summer 2019): 43–59.

Boulard, Gary. "'The Man' versus 'The Quisling': Theodore Bilbo, Hodding Carter, and the 1946 Democratic Party." *Journal of Mississippi History* 51 (August 1989): 201–217.

Brandis, Royall. "Cotton Competition. U.S. and Egypt, 1929–1948." *Southern Economic Journal* 19 (January 1953): 339–352.

Breen, William J. "The State and Workplace Reform in the South: War Manpower Commission Initiatives and Employer Resistance on the Gulf Coast in World War II." *Gulf South Historical Review* 18 (2003): 6–37.

Couch, Robert F. "The Ingalls Story in Mississippi, 1938–1958." *Journal of Mississippi History* 26 (August 1964): 192–200.

Dalfiume, Richard M. "The 'Forgotten Years' of the Negro Revolution." *Journal of American History* 55 (June 1968): 90–106.

Daniel, Pete. "Going among Strangers: Southern Reactions to World War II." *Journal of American History* 77 (December 1990): 886–911.

Dratch, Howard. "The Politics of Child Care in the 1940s." *Science & Society* 38 (Summer 1974): 167–204.

Ducoff, Louis J., et al. "Effect of the War on the Agricultural Working Force and on the Rural-Farm Population." *Social Forces* 21 (May 1943): 406–412.

Farmer, Arthur E., and Richard H. Wels. "Command Control—Or Military Justice." *New York University Law Quarterly Review* 24 (April 1949): 263–282.

Fitzgerald, Michael W. "'We Have Found a Moses': Theodore Bilbo, Black Nationalism, and the Greater Liberia Bill of 1939." *Journal of Southern History* 63 (May 1997): 293–320.

Fleegler, Robert L. "Theodore G. Bilbo and the Decline of Public Racism, 1938–1947." *Journal of Mississippi History* 68 (Spring 2006): 1–27.

Ginsburg, David. "The Emergency Price Control Act of 1942: Basic Authority and Sanctions." *Law and Contemporary Problems* 9 (Winter 1942): 22–59.

Guglielmo, Thomas A. "A Martial Freedom Movement: Black G.I.s' Political Struggles during World War II." *Journal of American History* 104 (March 2018): 879–903.

Hall, Jacquelyn Dowd. "The Long Civil Rights Movement and the Political Uses of the Past." *Journal of American History* 91 (March 2005): 1233–1263.

Hewes, Harry. "War-Boom Town Refuses to Become a Ghost Town." *The American City* 60 (July 1945): 87–88.

Holmes, William F. "Whitecapping: Agrarian Violence in Mississippi, 1902–1906." *Journal of Southern History* 35 (May 1969): 165–185.

Johnson, Marilynn S. "Gender, Race, and Rumours: Re-examining the 1943 Race Riots." *Gender & History* 10 (August 1998): 252–277.

Kelly, Thomas A. "The Impact of World War II on the Pascagoula Area: A Study of Economic Change." *Social Science Bulletin* 3 (Summer 1950): 1–8.

Lasseter, Dillard B. "The Impact of the War on the South and Implications for Postwar Developments." *Social Forces* 23 (October 1944): 20–26.

Link, William A. "Frank Porter Graham, Racial Gradualism, and the Dilemmas of Southern Liberalism." *Journal of Southern History* 86 (February 2020): 7–36.

Litoff, Judy Barrett, and David C. Smith. "'To the Rescue of the Crops': The Women's Land Army during World War II." *Prologue* 25 (Winter 1993): 347–358.

Lively, Robert A. "The South and Freight Rates: Political Settlement of an Economic Argument." *Journal of Southern History* 14 (August 1948): 357–384.

Lotchin, Roger W., and David R. Long. "World War II and the Transformation of Southern Urban Society: A Reconsideration." *Georgia Historical Quarterly* 83 (Spring 1999): 29–57.

McNatt, E. B. "Toward a National Wartime Labor Policy: The Union-Security Issue." *Journal of Business of the University of Chicago* 16 (January 1943): 64–69.

Nelson, Bruce. "Organized Labor and the Struggle for Black Equality in Mobile during World War II." *Journal of American History* 80 (December 1993): 952–988.

Nixon, H. C. "The Southern Governors' Conference as a Pressure Group." *Journal of Politics* 6 (August 1944): 338–345.

Northrup, Herbert R. "The Negro and Unionism in the Birmingham, Ala., Iron and Steel Industry." *Southern Economic Journal* 10 (July 1943): 27–40.

Northrup, Herbert R. "Negroes in a War Industry: The Case of Shipbuilding." *Journal of Business of the University of Chicago* 16 (July 1943): 160–172.

Northrup, Herbert R. "Organized Labor and Negro Workers." *Journal of Political Economy* 51 (June 1943): 206-221.

Pate, James E. "Mobilizing Manpower." *Social Forces* 22 (December 1943): 144-166.

Reed, Merl E. "The FEPC, the Black Worker, and the Southern Shipyards." *South Atlantic Quarterly* 74 (1975): 446-467.

Reynolds, Lloyd G. "Labor Problems of a Defense Economy." *American Economic Review* 40 (May 1950): 222-229.

Roback, Herbert. "Legal Barriers to Interstate Migration." *Cornell Law Quarterly* 28 (1942-1943): 286-312.

Schwartz, Harry. "Hired Farm Labor in World War II." *Journal of Farm Economics* 24 (November 1942): 826-844.

Scruggs, Otey M. "The Bracero Program under the Farm Security Administration, 1942-1943." *Labor History* 3 (Spring 1962): 149-168.

Simpson, William M. "A Tale Untold? The Alexandria, Louisiana, Lee Street Riot." *Louisiana History* 35 (Spring 1994): 133-149.

Temkin, Elizabeth. "Driving Through: Postpartum Care during World War II." *American Journal of Public Health* 89 (April 1999): 587-595.

"War Manpower Developments: Regulation of Enlistment of Men in Federal Posts and War Industry." *Journal (American Water Works Association)* 34 (November 1942): 1734-1736.

Ward, Jason Morgan. "'Nazis Hoe Cotton': Planters, POWs, and the Future of Farm Labor in the Deep South." *Agricultural History* 81 (Fall 2007): 471-492.

Ward, Thomas J., Jr. "Competent Counsel: Thurgood Marshall, the Black Press, and the Alexandria Soldiers' Rape Trials." *Louisiana History* 61 (Summer 2020): 229-266.

Washburn, Patrick S. "The *Pittsburgh Courier* and Black Workers in 1942." *Western Journal of Black Studies* 10 (Fall 1986): 109-118.

Washburn, Patrick S. "The *Pittsburgh Courier*'s Double V Campaign in 1942." *American Journalism* 3 (1986): 73-86.

Weaver, Robert C. "Negro Employment in the Aircraft Industry." *Quarterly Journal of Economics* 59 (August 1945): 597-625.

Weaver, Robert C. "Racial Employment Trends in National Defense." *Phylon* 2 (1941): 337-358.

Weisenburger, Steven. "The Columbians, Inc.: A Chapter of Racial Hatred from the Post–World War II South." *Journal of Southern History* 69 (November 2003): 821-860.

Wright, Alfred J. "Recent Changes in the Concentration of Manufacturing." *Annals of the Association of American Geographers* 35 (December 1945): 159-162.

BOOKS

Adams, Michael C. C. *The Best War Ever: America and World War II*. 2nd ed. Baltimore: Johns Hopkins University Press, 2015.

Alkebulan, Paul. *The African American Press in World War II: Toward Victory at Home and Abroad*. Lanham, MD: Lexington Books, 2014.

Ames, Jesse Daniel. *The Changing Character of Lynching: Review of Lynching, 1931-1941, with a Discussion of Recent Developments in This Field*. Atlanta: Commission on Interracial Cooperation, 1942.

Anderson, William. *The Wild Man from Sugar Creek: The Political Career of Eugene Talmadge*. Baton Rouge: Louisiana State University Press, 1975.

Arnall, Ellis Gibbs. *The Shore Dimly Seen*. Philadelphia: J. B. Lippincott Co., 1946.

Astor, Gerald. *The Right to Fight: A History of African Americans in the Military*. Novato, CA: Presidio Press, 1998.

Atleson, James B. *Labor and the Wartime State: Labor Relations and Law during World War II*. Urbana: University of Illinois Press, 1998.

Ayers, Edward L. *The Promise of the New South: Life after Reconstruction*. New York: Oxford University Press, 1992.

Bayor, Ronald H. *Race and the Shaping of Twentieth-Century Atlanta*. Chapel Hill: University of North Carolina Press, 1996.

Bernstein, David E. *Only One Place of Redress: African Americans, Labor Regulations, and the Courts from Reconstruction to the New Deal*. Durham, NC: Duke University Press, 2001.

Beschloss, Michael R. *The Conquerors: Roosevelt, Truman and the Destruction of Hitler's Germany, 1941–1945*. New York: Simon & Schuster, 2002.

Bilbo, Theodore G. *Take Your Choice: Separation or Mongrelization*. Poplarville, MS: Dream House Publishing Co., 1947.

Biles, Roger. *The South and the New Deal*. Lexington: University of Kentucky Press, 1994.

Bird, Kai. *The Chairman: John J. McCloy, The Making of the American Establishment*. New York: Simon & Schuster, 1992.

Blackmon, Douglas A. *Slavery by Another Name: The Re-Enslavement of Black Americans from the Civil War to World War II*. New York: Doubleday, 2008.

Blum, John Morton. *V Was for Victory: Politics and American Culture during World War II*. New York: Harcourt Brace Jovanovich, 1976.

Bodnar, John. *The "Good War" in American Memory*. Baltimore: Johns Hopkins University Press, 2010.

Bogdan, Robert. *Freak Show: Presenting Human Oddities for Amusement and Profit*. Chicago: University of Chicago Press, 1988.

Bolton, Charles C. *The Hardest Deal of All: The Battle over School Integration in Mississippi, 1870–1980*. Jackson: University Press of Mississippi, 2005.

Bolton, Charles C. *William F. Winter and the New Mississippi: A Biography*. Jackson: University Press of Mississippi, 2013.

Booker, Bryan D. *African Americans in the United States Army in World War II*. Jefferson, NC: McFarland & Co., 2008.

Brattain, Michelle. *The Politics of Whiteness: Race, Workers, and Culture in the Modern South*. Princeton, NJ: Princeton University Press, 2001.

Brinkley, David. *Washington Goes to War*. New York: Alfred A. Knopf, 1988.

Bristol, Douglas W., Jr., and Heather Marie Stur, eds. *Integrating the U.S. Military: Race, Gender, and Sexual Orientation Since World War II*. Baltimore: Johns Hopkins University Press, 2017.

Brooks, Christopher A., and Robert Sims. *Roland Hayes: The Legacy of an American Tenor*. Bloomington: Indiana University Press, 2015.

Brooks, Jennifer E. *Defining the Peace: World War II Veterans, Race, and the Remaking of Southern Political Tradition*. Chapel Hill: University of North Carolina Press, 2004.

Brown, D. Clayton. *King Cotton in Modern America: A Cultural, Political, and Economic History Since 1945*. Jackson: University Press of Mississippi, 2011.

Brown-Nagin, Tomiko. *Courage to Dissent: Atlanta and the Long History of the Civil Rights Movement*. New York: Oxford University Press, 2011.

Bullock, Charles S., III, et al. *The Three Governors Controversy: Skullduggery, Machinations, and the Decline of Georgia's Progressive Politics*. Athens: University of Georgia Press, 2015.

Bunker, John. *Heroes in Dungarees: The Story of the American Merchant Marine in World War II*. Annapolis, MD: Naval Institute Press, 1995.

Butler, Anne M., and Wendy Wolff. *United States Senate Election, Expulsion, and Censure Cases, 1793–1990*. Washington, DC: Government Printing Office, 1995.

Byers, Jean. *A Study of the Negro in Military Service*. Washington, DC: US Department of Defense, 1950.

Campbell, D'Ann. *Women at War with America*. Cambridge, MA: Harvard University Press, 1984.

Campbell, Tracy. *The Year of Peril: America in 1942*. New Haven, CT: Yale University Press, 2020.

Capeci, Dominic J., Jr., and Martha Wilkerson. *Layered Violence: The Detroit Rioters of 1943*. Jackson: University Press of Mississippi, 1991.

Carpenter, Stephanie A. *On the Farm Front: The Women's Land Army in World War II*. DeKalb: Northern Illinois University Press, 2003.

Carter, Hodding, and Anthony Ragusin. *Gulf Coast Country*. New York: Duell, Sloan & Pearce, 1951.

Case, Carroll. *The Slaughter: An American Atrocity*. Asheville, NC?: FBC, Inc., 1998.

Catsam, Derek Charles. *Freedom's Main Line: The Journey of Reconciliation and the Freedom Rides*. Lexington: University of Kentucky Press, 2009.

Caulfield, L. M. *Camp Van Dorn, Centreville, Mississippi, 1942–1947*. n.p., 1986.

Chafe, William H., et al., eds. *Remembering Jim Crow: African Americans Tell about Life in the Segregated South*. New York: New Press, 2001.

Chamberlain, Charles D. *Victory at Home: Manpower and Race in the American South during World War II*. Athens: University of Georgia Press, 2003.

Civil Rights Congress. *We Charge Genocide*. New York: Civil Rights Congress, 1951.

Cobb, James C. *Industrialization and Southern Society, 1877–1984*. Lexington: University of Kentucky Press, 1984.

Cobb, James C. *The Most Southern Place on Earth: The Mississippi Delta and the Roots of Regional Identity*. New York: Oxford University Press, 1992.

Cobb, James C. *The Selling of the South: The Southern Crusade for Industrial Development, 1936–90*. 2nd ed. Urbana: University of Illinois Press, 1993.

Cobb, James C. *The South and America Since World War II*. New York: Oxford University Press, 2011.

Cohen, Lizabeth. *A Consumers' Republic: The Politics of Mass Consumption in Postwar America*. New York: Alfred A. Knopf, 2003.

Cohen, Lizabeth. *Making a New Deal: Industrial Workers in Chicago, 1919–1939*. 2nd ed. Cambridge: Cambridge University Press, 2008.

Colley, David P. *Blood for Dignity: The Story of the First Integrated Combat Unit in the U.S. Army*. New York: St. Martin's Press, 2003.

Crespino, Joseph. *In Search of Another Country: Mississippi and the Conservative Counterrevolution*. Princeton, NJ: Princeton University Press, 2007.

Cruikshank, George M. *A History of Birmingham and Its Environs: A Narrative Account of Their Historical Progress, Their People, and Their Principal Interests*. 2 vols. Chicago: Lewis Publishing Co., 1920.

Culver, John C. *American Dreamer: A Life of Henry A. Wallace*. New York: W. W. Norton, 2001.

Curl, John. *For All the People: Uncovering the Hidden History of Cooperation, Cooperative Movements, and Communalism in America*. 2nd ed. Oakland, CA: PM Press, 2012.

Dalfiume, Richard M. *Desegregation of the U.S. Armed Forces: Fighting on Two Fronts, 1939–1953*. Columbia: University of Missouri Press, 1969.

Daniel, Pete. *Breaking the Land: The Transformation of Cotton, Tobacco, and Rice Cultures Since 1880*. Urbana: University of Illinois Press, 1986.

Daniel, Pete. *Standing at the Crossroads: Southern Life in the Twentieth Century*. Baltimore: Johns Hopkins University Press, 1996.

Daniels, Roger. *Franklin D. Roosevelt: The War Years, 1939–1945*. Urbana: University of Illinois Press, 2016.

DeFerrari, John. *Lost Washington, D.C.* Charleston, SC: The History Press, 2011.

Dittmer, John. *Local People: The Struggle for Civil Rights in Mississippi*. Urbana: University of Illinois Press, 1994.

Echeverri-Gent, John. *The State and the Poor: Public Policy and Political Development in India and the United States*. Berkeley: University of California Press, 1993.

Edgerton, John. *Speak Now against the Day: The Generation before the Civil Rights Movement in the South*. New York: Knopf, 1994.

Edgerton, Robert B. *Hidden Heroism: Black Soldiers in America's Wars*. Boulder, CO: Westview Press, 2001.

Emanuel, Rachel L., and Alexander P. Tureaud. *More Noble Cause: A. P. Tureaud and the Struggle for Civil Rights in Louisiana*. Baton Rouge: Louisiana State University Press, 2011.

Erenberg, Lewis A., and Susan E. Hirsch, eds. *The War in American Culture: Society and Consciousness during World War II*. Chicago: University of Chicago Press, 1996.

Eskew, Glenn T. *Labor in the Modern South*. Athens: University of Georgia Press, 2001.

Faneuf, Leston. *Lawrence D. Bell: A Man and His Company, "Bell Aircraft."* New York: Newcomen Society in North America, 1958.

Feldman, Glenn. *The Great Melding: War, the Dixiecrat Rebellion, and the Southern Model for America's New Conservatism*. Tuscaloosa: University of Alabama Press, 2015.

Feldman, Glenn, ed. *Before Brown: Civil Rights and White Backlash in the Modern South*. Tuscaloosa: University of Alabama Press, 2004.

Fite, Gilbert C. *Cotton Fields No More: Southern Agriculture, 1865–1980*. Lexington: University Press of Kentucky, 1984.

Fletcher, Marvin E. *America's First Black General: Benjamin O. Davis, Sr., 1880–1970*. Lawrence: University Press of Kansas, 1989.

Flynn, George Q. *The Mess in Washington: Manpower Mobilization in World War II*. Westport, CT: Greenwood Press, 1979.

Frederickson, Kari. *Cold War Dixie: Militarization and Modernization in the American South*. Athens: University of Georgia Press, 2013.

Gibran, Daniel. *The 92nd Infantry Division and the Italian Campaign in World War II*. Jefferson, NC: McFarland Publishing, 2001.

Gilmore, Glenda. *Defying Dixie: The Radical Roots of Civil Rights, 1919–1950*. New York: W. W. Norton, 2008.

Goldfield, Michael. *The Southern Key: Class, Race, and Radicalism in the 1930s and 1940s*. New York: Oxford University Press, 2020.

Goodwin, Doris Kearns. *No Ordinary Time: Franklin & Eleanor Roosevelt: The Home Front in World War II.* New York: Simon & Schuster, 1994.

Grantham, Dewey W. *The South in Modern America: A Region at Odds.* New York: HarperCollins, 1994.

Green, A. Wigfall. *The Man Bilbo.* Baton Rouge: Louisiana State University Press, 1963.

Green, Constance McLaughlin, et al. *United States Army in World War II: The Technical Services, The Ordnance Department: Planning Munitions for War.* Washington, DC: Center of Military History, 1990.

Gregory, James N. *The Southern Diaspora: How the Great Migrations of Black and Southerners Transformed America.* Chapel Hill: University of North Carolina Press, 2005.

Gropman, Alan L. *The Air Force Integrates, 1945–1964.* Washington, DC: Office of Air Force History, US Air Force, 1985.

Gutman, Herbert G. *Work, Culture, and Society in Industrializing America: Essays in American Working-Class and Social History.* New York: Vintage Books, 1977.

Hahn, Steven. *A Nation under Our Feet: Black Political Struggles in the Rural South from Slavery to the Great Migration.* Cambridge, MA: Harvard University Press, 2003.

Henderson, Harold Paulk. *The Politics of Change in Georgia: A Political Biography of Ellis Arnall.* Athens: University of Georgia Press, 1991.

Hill, Robert A., ed. *The FBI's RACON: Racial Conditions in the United States during World War II.* Boston: Northeastern University Press, 1995.

Hirshfield, Daniel S. *The Lost Reform: The Campaign for Compulsory Health Insurance in the United States from 1932 to 1943.* Cambridge, MA: Harvard University Press, 1970.

History of the 31st Infantry Division in Training and Combat, 1940–1945. Nashville: Battery Press, 1993.

Hughes, Dudley J. *Oil in the Deep South: A History of the Oil Business in Mississippi, Alabama, and Florida, 1859–1945.* Jackson: University Press of Mississippi, 1993.

Hustwit, William. *Integration Now: Alexander v. Holmes and the End of Jim Crow Education.* Chapel Hill: University of North Carolina Press, 2019.

Ingalls, Robert I. *Shipbuilding.* New York: Newcomen Society of England, 1947.

Inglis, Pete. *Restored to Honor: Georgia's B-29, Sweet Eloise.* Marietta, GA: GRAFCO Productions, 2001.

Jacobs, Meg. *Pocketbook Politics: Economic Citizenship in Twentieth-Century America.* Princeton, NJ: Princeton University Press, 2005.

James, C. L. R., et al. *Fighting Racism in World War II.* New York: Pathfinder, 1980.

James, Rawn, Jr. *The Double V: How Wars, Protest, and Harry Truman Desegregated America's Military.* New York: Bloomsbury Press, 2013.

Jaynes, Gerald David, and Robin M. Williams Jr. *A Common Destiny: Blacks and American Society.* Washington, DC: National Academy Press, 1989.

Jeffries, John W. *Wartime America: The World War II Home Front.* Chicago: Ivan R. Dee, 1996.

Johnson, Charles S. *To Stem This Tide: A Survey of Racial Tension Areas in the United States.* Boston: Pilgrim Press, 1943.

Jones, James H. *Bad Blood: The Tuskegee Syphilis Experiment.* New York: Free Press, 1981.

Jordan, David M. *FDR, Dewey, and the Election of 1944.* Bloomington: Indiana University Press, 2011.

Kahn, E. J., Jr., and Henry McLemore. *Fighting Divisions.* Washington, DC: Infantry Journal Press, 1946.

Katznelson, Ira. *Fear Itself: The New Deal and the Origins of Our Time*. New York: W. W. Norton, 2013.

Kelley, Robin D. G. *Race Rebels: Culture, Politics, and the Black Working Class*. New York: Free Press, 1994.

Kennedy, David M. *The American People in World War II: Freedom from Fear, Part Two*. New York: Oxford University Press, 1999.

Kersten, Andrew E. *A. Philip Randolph: A Life in the Vanguard*. Lanham, MD: Rowman & Littlefield, 2007.

Kersten, Andrew E. *Labor's Home Front: The American Federation of Labor during World War II*. New York: New York University Press, 2006.

Kieran, David, and Edwin A Martini, eds. *At War: The Military and American Culture in the Twentieth Century and Beyond*. New Brunswick, NJ: Rutgers University Press, 2018.

King, Charles. *Gods of the Upper Air: How a Circle of Renegade Anthropologists Reinvented Race, Sex, and Gender in the Twentieth Century*. New York: Doubleday, 2019.

Klarman, Michael J. *From Jim Crow to Civil Rights: The Supreme Court and the Struggle for Racial Equality*. New York: Oxford University Press, 2006.

Kneebone, John T. *Southern Liberal Journalists and the Issue of Race, 1920–1944*. Chapel Hill: University of North Carolina Press, 1985.

Kousser, J. Morgan. *The Shaping of Southern Politics: Suffrage Restriction and the Establishment of the One-Party South, 1880–1910*. New Haven, CT: Yale University Press, 1974.

Kruse, Kevin. *White Flight: Atlanta and the Making of Modern Conservatism* Princeton, NJ: Princeton University Press, 2005.

Kruse, Kevin M., and Stephen Tuck, eds. *Fog of War: The Second World War and the Civil Rights Movement*. New York: Oxford University Press, 2012.

Kryder, Daniel. *Divided Arsenal: Race and the American State during World War II*. Cambridge: Cambridge University Press, 2000.

Kytle, Calvin, and James A. Mackay. *Who Runs Georgia?* Athens: University of Georgia Press, 1998.

Lane, Charles. *The Day Freedom Died: The Colfax Massacre, the Supreme Court, and the Betrayal of Reconstruction*. New York: Henry Holt, 2008.

Lane, Frederic C. *Ships for Victory: A History of Shipbuilding under the U.S. Maritime Commission in World War II*. Baltimore: Johns Hopkins University Press, 1951.

Lanning, Michael Lee. *The Court-Martial of Jackie Robinson: The Baseball Legend's Battle for Civil Rights during World War II*. Guilford, CT: Stackpole Books, 2020.

Lawson, Steven F. *Black Ballots: Voting Rights in the South, 1944–1969*. New York: Columbia University Press, 1976.

Lee, Ulysses. *The Employment of Negro Troops*. Washington, DC: Center of Military History, US Army, 1994.

Lewis, W. David. *Eddie Rickenbacker: An American Hero in the Twentieth Century*. Baltimore: Johns Hopkins University Press, 2005.

Lichtenstein, Nelson. *Labor's War at Home: The CIO in World War II*. Cambridge: Cambridge University Press, 1982.

Link, William A. *The Paradox of Southern Progressivism, 1880–1930*. Chapel Hill: University of North Carolina Press, 1992.

Lowndes, Joseph E. *From the New Deal to the New Right: Race and the Southern Origins of Modern Conservatism*. New Haven, CT: Yale University Press, 2008.

MacGregor, Morris J. *Integration of the Armed Forces, 1940–1965.* Washington, DC: Government Printing Office, 1989.
Marable, Manning. *W. E. B. Du Bois: Black Radical Democrat.* Updated ed. New York: Routledge, 2005.
Mason, Herman "Skip," Jr. *Politics, Civil Rights, and Law in Black Atlanta.* Charleston, SC: Arcadia Publishing, 2000.
McEuen, Melissa A. *Making War, Making Women: Femininity and Duty on the American Home Front, 1941–1945.* Athens: University of Georgia Press, 2011.
McGuire, Danielle L. *At the Dark End of the Street: Black Women, Rape, and Resistance—A New History of the Civil Rights Movement from Rosa Parks to the Rise of Black Power.* New York: Vintage, 2010.
McGuire, Phillip. *Taps for a Jim Crow Army: Letters from Black Soldiers in World War II.* Lexington: University of Kentucky Press, 2015.
McMahon, Kevin J. *Reconsidering Roosevelt on Race: How the Presidency Paved the Road to Brown.* Chicago: University of Chicago Press, 2004.
McMillen, Neil R. *Dark Journey: Black Mississippians in the Age of Jim Crow.* Urbana: University of Illinois Press, 1990.
McMillen, Neil R., ed. *Remaking Dixie: The Impact of World War II on the American South.* Jackson: University Press of Mississippi, 1997.
Mershon, Sherie, and Steven Schlossman. *Foxholes & Color Lines: Desegregating the U.S. Armed Forces.* Baltimore: Johns Hopkins University Press, 1998.
Meyer, Agnes E. *Journey through Chaos.* New York: Harcourt, Brace & Co., 1944.
Mickey, Robert. *Paths out of Dixie: The Democratization of Authoritarian Enclaves in America's Deep South, 1944–1972.* Princeton, NJ: Princeton University Press, 2015.
Milton, H. S., ed. *Utilization of Negro Manpower in the Army: A 1951 Study.* Chevy Chase, MD: Operations Research Office, Johns Hopkins University, 1955.
Mintz, Steven, and Susan Kellogg. *Domestic Revolutions: A Social History of American Family Life.* New York: Free Press, 1988.
Mitchell, Dennis J. *A New History of Mississippi.* Jackson: University Press of Mississippi, 2014.
Moncrief, Sandra. *The Phantom Barber.* North Charleston, SC: CreateSpace Independent Publishing Platform, 2015.
Morgan, Chester M. *Redneck Liberal: Theodore G. Bilbo and the New Deal.* Baton Rouge: Louisiana State University Press, 1985.
Motley, Mary Penick. *The Invisible Soldier.* Detroit: Wayne State University Press, 1975.
Moye, Todd. *Freedom Flyers: The Tuskegee Airmen of World War II.* New York: Oxford University Press, 2010.
Nalty, Bernard C. *Strength for the Fight: A History of Black Americans in the Military.* New York: Free Press, 1986.
Nelson, Lawrence J. *King Cotton's Advocate: Oscar G. Johnston and the New Deal.* Knoxville: University of Tennessee Press, 1999.
New Georgia Encyclopedia. Athens, GA: Georgia Humanities Council and the University of Georgia Press, 2004–. https://www.georgiaencyclopedia.org.
Newton, Michael. *Unsolved Civil Rights Murder Cases, 1934–1970.* Jefferson, NC: McFarland, 2016.
Pagán, Eduardo Obregón. *Murder at the Sleepy Lagoon: Zoot Suits, Race, and Riot in Wartime L.A.* Chapel Hill: University of North Carolina Press, 2003.

Reed, Merl E. *Seedtime for the Modern Civil Rights Movement: The President's Committee on Fair Employment Practice, 1941–1946*. Baton Rouge: Louisiana State University Press, 1991.

Reynolds, Bruce J. *Black Farmers in America, 1865–2000: The Pursuit of Independent Farming and the Role of Cooperatives*. Washington, DC: US Department of Agriculture, 2002.

Roberts, Charles Kenneth. *The Farm Security Administration and Rural Rehabilitation in the South*. Knoxville: University of Tennessee Press, 2015.

Roberts, Gene, and Hank Klibanoff. *The Race Beat: The Press, the Civil Rights Struggle, and the Awakening of a Nation*. New York: Alfred A. Knopf, 2006.

Rome, Adam. *The Bulldozer in the Countryside: Suburban Sprawl and the Rise of American Environmentalism*. New York: Cambridge University Press, 2001.

Rose, Kenneth D. *Myth and the Greatest Generation: A Social History of Americans in World War II*. New York: Routledge, 2008.

St. Pe, Jerry. *A Salute to American Spirit: The Story of Ingalls Shipbuilding Division of Litton*. New York: Newcomen Society of the United States, 1988.

Sasser, Charles W. *Patton's Panthers*. New York: Simon & Schuster, 2004.

Schulman, Bruce J. *From Cotton Belt to Sunbelt: Federal Policy, Economic Development, and the Transformation of the South, 1938–1980*. New York: Oxford University Press, 1991.

Scranton, Philip, ed. *The Second Wave: Southern Industrialization from the 1940s to the 1970s*. Athens: University of Georgia Press, 2001.

Sitkoff, Harvard. *A New Deal for Blacks: The Emergence of Civil Rights as a National Issue: The Depression Decade*. New York: Oxford University Press, 1978.

Slout, William L. *Olympians of the Sawdust Circle: A Biographical Dictionary of the 19th Century American Circus*. San Bernardino, CA: The Borgo Press, 1988.

Smith, Douglas. *On Democracy's Doorstep: The Inside Story of How the Supreme Court Brought "One Person, One Vote" to the United States*. New York: Hill & Wang, 2014.

Smith, J. Clay., Jr. *Emancipation: The Making of the Black Lawyer, 1844–1944*. Philadelphia: University of Pennsylvania Press, 1993.

Spevak, Jeff. *22 Minutes: The USS Vincennes and the Tragedy of Savo Island: A Lifetime Survival Story*. Guilford, CT: Lyons Press, 2019.

Spritzer, Lorraine Nelson. *The Belle of Ashby Street: Helen Douglas Mankin and Georgia Politics*. Athens: University of Georgia Press, 1982.

Stoltzfus, Emilie. *Citizen, Mother, Worker: Debating Public Responsibility for Child Care after the Second World War*. Chapel Hill: University of North Carolina Press, 2003.

Sturkey, William. *Hattiesburg: An American City in Black and White*. Cambridge, MA: Harvard University Press, 2019.

Sugrue, Thomas J. *The Origins of the Urban Crisis: Race and Inequality in Postwar Detroit*. Princeton, NJ: Princeton University Press, 1996.

Sullivan, Patricia. *Days of Hope: Race and Democracy in the New Deal Era*. Chapel Hill: University of North Carolina Press, 1996.

Sullivan, Patricia. *Lift Every Voice: The NAACP and the Making of the Civil Rights Movement*. New York: New Press, 2009.

Talley, Wayne K., ed. *The Blackwell Companion to Maritime Economics*. Malden, MA: Wiley-Blackwell, 2012.

Terkel, Studs. *"The Good War": An Oral History of World War II*. New York: New Press, 1984.

Theoharis, Jeanne. *The Rebellious Life of Mrs. Rosa Parks*. Boston: Beacon Press, 2013.

Thomas, Karen Kruse. *Deluxe Jim Crow: Civil Rights and American Health Policy, 1935–1954*. Athens: University of Georgia Press, 2011.
Tuck, Stephen G. N. *Beyond Atlanta: The Struggle for Racial Equality in Georgia, 1940–1980*. Athens: University of Georgia Press, 2001.
Tushnet, Mark V. *Making Civil Rights Law: Thurgood Marshall and the Supreme Court, 1936–1961*. New York: Oxford University Press, 1994.
Tuttle, William M., Jr. *Daddy's Gone to War: The Second World War in the Lives of America's Children*. New York: Oxford University Press, 1995.
US Bureau of Yards and Docks. *Building the Navy's Bases in World War II: History of the Bureau of Yards and Docks and the Civil Engineer Corps, 1940–1946*. 2 vols. Washington, DC: Government Printing Office, 1947.
US Department of the Army, *A Historical Analysis of the 364th Infantry in World War II*. Washington DC: US Department of the Army, 1999.
Van Dusen, Gerald. *Detroit's Sojourner Truth Housing Riot of 1942: Prelude to the Race Riot of 1943*. Cheltenham: The History Press, 2020.
Vander Meulen, Jacob. *Building the B-29*. Washington, DC: Smithsonian Institution Press, 1995.
Ward, Jason Morgan. *Defending White Democracy: The Making of a Segregationist Movement and the Remaking of Racial Politics, 1936–1965*. Chapel Hill: University of North Carolina Press, 2011.
Ward, Jason Morgan. *Hanging Bridge: Racial Violence and America's Civil Rights Century*. New York: Oxford University Press, 2016.
Ward, Thomas J., Jr. *Black Physicians in the Jim Crow South*. Fayetteville: University of Arkansas Press, 2003.
Ware, Gilbert. *William Hastie: Grace under Pressure*. New York: Oxford University Press, 1985.
Washburn, Patrick S. *A Question of Sedition: The Federal Government's Investigation of the Black Press during World War II*. New York: Oxford University Press, 1986.
Wexler, Laura. *Fire in a Canebrake*. New York: Scribner, 2003.
White, Steven. *World War II and American Racial Politics: Public Opinion, The Presidency, and Civil Rights Advocacy*. New York: Cambridge University Press, 2019.
Wilcox, Walter W. *The Farmer in the Second World War*. Ames: Iowa State College Press, 1947.
Wiley, Bell Irvin. *The Training of Negro Troops*. Washington, DC: Historical Section, Army Ground Forces, 1946.
Wilkerson, Isabel. *The Warmth of Other Suns: The Epic Story of America's Great Migration*. New York: Vintage Books, 2010.
Williamson, Joel. *Elvis Presley: A Southern Life*. New York: Oxford University Press, 2014.
Wilson, Charles H., Sr. *God! Make Me a Man: A Biographical Sketch of Dr. Sidney Dillion Redmond*. Boston: Meador Publishing Co., 1950.
Woodruff, Nan Elizabeth. *American Congo: The African American Freedom Struggle in the Delta*. Cambridge, MA: Harvard University Press, 2003.
Wynn, Neil A. *The African American Experience during World War II*. Lanham, MD: Rowman & Littlefield, 2010.
Young, Nancy Beck. *Why We Fight: Congress and the Politics of World War II*. Lawrence: University Press of Kansas, 2013.
Zelden, Charles L. *The Battle for the Black Ballot*: Smith v. Allwright *and the Defeat of the Texas All White Primary*. Lawrence: University Press of Kansas, 2004.

UNPUBLISHED SOURCES

Barksdale, Sarah Ayako. "Prelude to a Revolution: African-American World War II Veterans, Double Consciousness, and Civil Rights 1940–1955." PhD diss., University of North Carolina at Chapel Hill, 2014.

Behel, Sandra K. "The Mississippi Home Front during World War II: Tradition and Change." PhD diss., Mississippi State University, 1989.

Case, Carroll. Interview by Neil McMillen. April 12, 1996. Vol. 672. Transcript. Mississippi Oral History Program, University of Southern Mississippi, Hattiesburg.

Burran, James Albert. "Racial Violence in the South During World War II." Ph.D. diss., University of Tennessee, 1977.

Darden, Robert F., III. "Dallas Morning News Editorial Cartoonists: Influences of John Knott on Jack 'Herc' Ficklen and William McClanahan." MA thesis, North Texas State, 1978.

Joyce, Thomas. "The 'Double V' Was for Victory: Black Soldiers, the Black Protest, and World War II." PhD diss., Ohio State University, 1993.

Kirk, John Andrew. "Black Activism in Arkansas, 1940–1970." PhD diss., University of Newcastle upon Tyne, 1997.

Montgomery, Claude, Jr. Interview by Neil McMillen. December 2, 1994. Vol. 597. Mississippi Oral History Program, University of Southern Mississippi.

Morris, Sara Elizabeth. "Working to Save the Farm: Indiana and Mississippi Rural Women, 1940–1990." PhD diss., Purdue University, 2011.

Mosley, Donald Crumpton. "A History of Labor Unions in Mississippi." PhD diss., University of Alabama, 1965.

Presnell, Boyte Austin. "The Impact of World War II on Race Relations in Mobile, Alabama, 1940–1948," MA thesis, Atlanta University, 1972.

Smith, Charles Pope. "Theodore G. Bilbo's Senatorial Career, The Final Years: 1941–1947." PhD diss., University of Southern Mississippi, 1983.

Stoesen, Alexander Rudolph. "The Senatorial Career of Claude D. Pepper." PhD diss., University of North Carolina, 1965.

Straub, Eleanor Ferguson. "Government Policy toward Civilian Women during World War II." PhD diss., Emory University, 1973.

Turner, Madrid Boyd. "A Study of One Hundred Skilled Negro Workers at Bell Aircraft Corporation and the Problems Encountered in Adapting to a Peacetime Economy." MA thesis, Atlanta University, 1946.

Index

For the benefit of digital users, indexed terms that span two pages (e.g., 52–53) may, on occasion, appear on only one of those pages.

Figures are indicated by *f* following the page number

Abernethy, Thomas, 167, 174, 228–29
Abrams, Wellington, 188
African Americans, 277
   and credit arrangements, 22–24
   education and, 111–12
   and education equalization, 9, 81, 204, 209–10, 230–31
   and employment at Alabama Dry Dock and Shipbuilding Company, 53, 70–71, 73–79
   and employment at Bell Aircraft (Buffalo, NY), 82
   and employment at Bell Bomber Aircraft Plant (GA), 81, 82–83, 85–88
   and employment at Higgins shipyard, 53
   and employment at Ingalls Shipbuilding Company, 52–53, 63
   and employment in Mobile, Alabama, construction industry, 69–71
   and health care, 107–9
   housing and, 98–99, 102–3
   and Jim Crow justice, 116–17
   and labor unions, 56–57, 59–60, 63, 69–70, 71, 76, 88
   and racial violence, 5, 129, 130–31, 133–36, 138–39, 143–44, 149–50, 160–61, 162, 189–91, 208, 231–32, 251–52, 260–62, 267–68, 271
   and voting rights struggle, 9–10, 215–19, 229–30, 249–50, 251, 254–56, 257–61, 259*f*, 264–65, 271
   and workforce training, 53, 66, 67, 68, 69, 70–71, 73, 74, 81, 82, 83–85, 86, 88, 90, 91

agriculture, 4, 6–7, 273
   cotton planters, 4, 6–7, 19, 20, 21–22, 25–26, 28–29, 30, 34–36
   and crop diversification, 29, 35–36
   and mechanization, 35–36
   sharecropping/tenancy, 1, 4, 5, 15–16, 17, 18, 20, 22–24, 28–30, 31–32, 34, 36, 125–26, 231–32, 273
Alabama Dry Dock and Shipbuilding Company, 42–43, 65–66, 68–69, 86, 149–50, 187–88
   Bulletin 86, 77
   the FEPC and, 65–66, 68, 70–71, 73–74, 75–79
   and the Mobile compromise, 76–79, 85–86
   the War Manpower Commission and, 74, 75–76, 78
   white riot at, 74–76, 78, 149–50
Aleutian Islands, 172
Alexandria, Louisiana, 138–45, 150, 189–90
   and racial conflict in Little Harlem district (1941), 138–41
Almond, Edward M., 193, 196
American Civil Liberties Union, 116, 216
American Crusade Against Lynching, 263
American Farm Bureau Federation, 16, 31
American Federation of Labor, 45, 54, 55, 61, 63, 90, 248
   Bridge, Structural, and Ornamental Iron Workers, 56–57
   International Association of Machinists, 88, 91–92
   International Brotherhood of Boilermakers, Iron Ship Builders, and Helpers of America, 59–60

American Federation of Labor (*cont.*)
  International Brotherhood of
    Carpenters and Joiners, 66, 69–70
  Pascagoula Metal Trades Department,
    56, 57, 58–59, 60–62, 93–94
American Medical Association, 105
American Teachers Association, 113
American Veterans Committee, 249–50
Amite County, Mississippi, 127, 232
Anderson, Minnie, 47
Anderson, R. E., 55
Anderson, Vera, 47, 50–52, 51*f*, 59–60, 61
Arnall, Ellis, 10, 223–24, 270, 271, 276–77
  and differential freight rates, 212–14
  and the Farm Security
    Administration, 34
  and Franklin D. Roosevelt, 202, 214–15, 219–20
  national profile, 214–16, 219–21, 269–70
  and the 1942 governor's election, 202–7
  and the 1944 presidential
    election, 214–15
  and the 1946 governor's election, 245–47, 256, 257–58
  opposition to the FEPC, 227
  as a progressive reformer, 207–8, 210–11, 219–20, 221, 254, 257, 271
  and the Southern Governors
    Conference, 201–2
  and voting reform, 210–12, 215–19
Association of Citizens' Democratic
  Clubs, 218
Atlanta, Georgia, 4, 20–21, 81, 82, 83–84,
  86, 87, 133–34, 149–50, 204, 208,
  217–19, 228, 254, 255, 256, 258–59, 261–62
  Atlanta Constitution, 177–78, 203–5,
    216–17, 219, 257
  Atlanta Journal, 217, 219
  Police Department, 205–6, 255–56, 258
Augusta, Georgia, 142, 143
Austin-Wadsworth Bill, 26

Babcock, Paul, 71, 74–75
Bailey, Thomas, 230–31, 249–50
Balance Agriculture with Industry
  program, 39–40, 112

Baldwin, C. B., 31, 34
Ballard, Charles, 91
Baltimore Afro-American, 26, 177–78
Bankhead, John, 27, 127–28
Barkley, Alben, 37, 244–45
Barnett, Claude, 18
Baton Rouge, Louisiana, 141, 146, 166, 167
Beecher, John, 84, 89–90
Bell Aircraft (Buffalo, NY), 80–81
Bell Bomber Aircraft Plant (GA), 51–52,
  66, 80*f*, 259*f*, 273–74
  Department 86, 85–87
  and the FEPC, 65–66, 68, 79–80, 81–82,
    83–84, 85, 86–87
  and the War Manpower Commission,
    82, 85, 86–87
Bell, Larry, 80–81, 82, 83, 257
Bell, Paul, 239
Bell, Vaughn, 83
Bell, William, 81
Belsaw, E. T., 76
Benedict, Ruth, 181
Bennette, A. N., 93–94
Bethune, Mary McLeod, 145, 216
Biddle, Francis, 174–75
Bilbo, Theodore, 10, 19–20, 63, 113,
  141–42, 159–60, 249*f*, 267, 270–71, 276–77
  anti-Bilbo movement, 236–43
  and the Farm Security
    Administration, 33–34
  and Franklin D. Roosevelt, 222–23, 234–35
  1944 speech to the Mississippi
    legislature, 222–23, 231–32,
    234, 236–37
  and the 1946 US Senate election, 247–54, 249*f*
  and nondiscrimination in the military,
    181, 195–96
  and opposition to anti-poll tax efforts,
    224–26, 238–39
  and opposition to the FEPC, 222–23,
    226–29, 237–39, 247–48
  and resettlement of African Americans
    to Africa, 222–23, 232–34, 236, 248
  and seating challenge in the 80th
    Congress, 244–45

and the Special Committee to
Investigate the National Defense
Program, 244, 266–67
and the Special Committee to
Investigate Senatorial Campaign
Expenditures, 244, 252, 263–67
*Take Your Choice: Separation or
Mongrelization*, 235–36
Birmingham, Alabama, 4, 39, 40–41,
65, 66–67
labor unions at Ingalls Iron
Works, 56–57
Black newspapers, 18, 26, 66–67, 92, 139,
141, 154, 166, 174–75, 178, 182,
185, 193–94, 201, 207, 220–21, 241
Blair, Leon, 80–81, 102–3
Blue, Clyde, 172
Booker T. Washington Aircraft School,
84–85, 86
Booker T. Washington High School, 84–
85, 209
Bostick, R. S., 253–54
bracero program, 20–21
Brookley Army Air Field, 68–69, 74–
75, 142–43
racial conflict in the area around (1944),
186–89, 191
Brooks, J. S., 49–50
Brown, Edgar J., 173
Brown, James L., 165
Brown, M. L., 93–94, 102, 107–8
Brumfield, J. R., 19–20
Brunswick, Georgia, 16, 38
Bureau of Agricultural Economics, 16, 25,
27, 102–3, 114, 130–31
Bykowski, Edward, 240–42
Byrd, Harry, 33

Calhoun County, Alabama, 19, 20–21
Camp Beauregard, 138, 143–44
Camp Claiborne, 137, 138, 139–40, 141,
142–43, 173–74
racial conflict in the area around
(1944), 189–91
364th Infantry Regiment at, 150
Camp Gordon, 131–32, 142, 143
Camp Livingston, 136–37, 138, 139–40,
141, 173–74, 189–90

Camp McCain, 17, 150, 173–74, 231
racial conflict in the area around
(1943), 160–61
Camp Shelby, 127, 131–32, 133–34, 138,
142, 146, 149–50, 161–62, 173–74,
175, 179
Camp Sibert, 183
Camp Stewart, 131–32, 149–50, 173, 174,
175, 176–77
and the Educational Program for
Colored Troops, 177–78
racial conflict in the area around
(1943), 162–64
and the 369th Coast Artillery
Regiment, 162–64
Camp Van Dorn, 127, 146, 173–74, 176–
77, 231
massacre rumors and, 168–71
and the 518th Quartermaster Regiment,
154, 158
and the 512th Quartermaster Regiment,
146, 155–56
and the 99th Infantry Regiment, 154–
55, 166–67
and the 364th Infantry Regiment, 149–
50, 153–60, 164–67, 171–72, 179
Carmichael, James V. 257
and Bell Aircraft, 65–66, 79–80, 85, 87
and the 1946 governor's election, 245–
46, 247, 257, 258–59, 271
Carmody, John M., 46, 69–70
Carroll, Omer, 159–60
Carr, Raymond, 143–44
Carter, Hodding, 242–43
Case, Carroll, 168–70
Catholic Laymen's Association of
Georgia, 208–9
Centreville, Mississippi, 127, 146, 149,
153–54, 155–56, 157, 159–60, 164–
66, 170–71
Chavez, Dennis, 247–48
Chicago, Illinois, 2, 23–24, 156, 232–33,
238, 263
Chicago Defender, 63, 138–39, 175, 207
Citizens Committee of 1,000, 173
National Negro Congress chapter in,
238, 242
Civil Rights Congress, 252, 263

Clarksdale, Mississippi, 17, 35–36
Clark, Tom, 219–20, 252, 267–68
Clay, Lucius, 79–80
Coahoma County, Mississippi, 17, 18, 20, 22–23, 25–26, 36
Coca-Cola Company, 65–66, 256
Cocking, Walter D., 203
Cold War, 274, 276, 277
Coleman, Charles B., 190–91
Coleman, J. P., 160–61, 174
Collier, Earnestine, 253–54
Collier, Varnado, 253–54, 264–65
Collins, Mississippi, 161–62, 249f
Colmer, William M., 44, 53–54, 55, 95–96
Columbians, 261–62
Columbus, Georgia, 132–33, 134–35, 142, 218–19
Commission on Interracial Cooperation, 206–7
Commoner Party, 255
Congress of Industrial Organizations, 28–29, 54, 74, 222–23, 237–38, 248, 268–69
   Industrial Union of Marine and Shipbuilding Workers of America, 56, 70–71, 74, 76–77
   Steel Workers Organizing Committee, 56
   United Automobile Workers, 88
Connally, Tom, 266
Constangy, Frank, 41
Cooper, L. M., 66
Corban, L. C., 117–18
county-unit system, 258–59, 261, 268–69, 271
Coweta County, Georgia, 202, 213–14
Cramer, Lawrence, 65–67, 77–78
Crane, J. C., 48, 118–19
Croop, Richard, 83–84
Crystal Springs, Mississippi, 20, 251

Dabney, Virginius, 66–67
Dallas, W. A., 33–34
Daniels, Jonathan, 34
Davidson, Eugene, 90
Davis, Benjamin O., 129, 162–63
Davis, James C., 261, 268–69
Davis, Lee R., 190–91
Davis, Samuel L., 209–10

Davis, T. Hoyt, 219
debt peonage, 22–23
DeKalb County, Georgia, 261
Delahoussaye, Marion, 53
Delta Council, 18, 22, 29–30, 31, 35
Delta and Pine Land Company, 1–4
Detroit, Michigan, 17, 98–99, 149–50
Dickerson, Earl, 70–71
differential freight rates, 201, 212–14
Dixon, Frank, 71–72
Dodge, Witherspoon, 87
Dolan, William, 115–16
Double V slogan, 9, 174–75
Douglas, William O., 213–14
Douglass, Frederick, 8
Doxey, Wall, 266
draft boards, 24–26
Du Bois W. E. B., 8
Duck Hill, Mississippi, 160–61, 174
Duke, Dan, 258
Dunlap, D. R., 75–76

Eastland, James, 21–22, 33, 36, 159–60, 194–95, 242–43, 267
Edgerly, John P., 185–86
Educational Program for Colored Troops, 177–78
Eiland, C. N., 264–65
Eisenhower, Dwight D., 195
Ellender, Allen J., 263, 264–65, 266
Ellis, Charles L. Jr., 157–58, 164
Ellis, Tom, 253
Emergency Maternal and Infant Care program, 104–5
Emergency Price Control Act, 27
emigrant-agent laws, 22
Etheridge, F. K., 44
Etheridge, Mark, 66–67
Evers, Charles, 253–54
Evers, Medgar, 253–54
Exchequer, 37, 40
Ezell, W. M., 168–69

Fair Employment Practices Committee, 7–8
   Birmingham hearings, 65–67, 70–71, 72–73, 74–75, 79–80, 82, 84–85, 88, 89–90

nondiscrimination mandate, 66, 68, 77–78, 88, 89, 90–91
white opposition to, 66–67, 71–73, 87, 92, 228–29
Farm Bloc, 24–25, 26
Farm Security Administration, 15–16, 18, 20, 29–35, 114–15
and the Food for Freedom program, 32–33
and Pascagoula housing, 101–2
federal aid to education, 112–14
Federal Bureau of Investigation, 79, 189–90, 252, 258–59, 260–61, 267–68
murder of Felix Hall and the, 135–36
and the 364th Infantry Regiment, 154–55, 157, 159
Federal Public Housing Authority, 95–96, 99–101, 102
Federal Works Agency, 69–70, 119–20
Ficklen, Jack "Herc" 129–30
Field, Clifford, 265
Fight for Freedom Committee, 140–41
Fletcher, Etoy, 251
Flora, Mississippi, 88, 89–90
Food for Freedom program, 15, 32–33
Fort Benning, 132–33, 133f, 134–35, 136, 142, 173–74, 185–86, 192, 202
racial conflict in the area around (1941), 134–36
Fort Hood, 183
Fort McClellan, 133–34
Fort Valley, Georgia, 204, 256
Fourteenth Amendment, 268–69, 276
Franklin, Lester, 229–30
Franklin, Morgan, 157
Fulton County, Georgia, 216–19, 256, 258–59, 261

Gandy, Evelyn, 235–36
Garvey, Marcus, 232–34
General Tire Engineering Company, 88–90
Georgia Board of Regents, 203
Georgia Veterans for Majority Rule, 268–69
GI Bill, 275–76
Gibson, Elmer, 127–28, 171f

Gibson, Truman K., 147, 150–51, 172, 175–76, 182, 193–95, 196–97
Golditch, Leonard, 237–38, 241–42
Goodman, John Forest, 152–53, 157–59, 164–65, 167, 172
Gordon, Mittie Maud Lena, 232
Graham, W. K., 76–77
Gray, George C., 140
Greater Liberia, 232–33
Green, Samuel, 256, 258
Greene, R. K., 31
Grenada, Mississippi, 17, 18, 101, 253–54
Griser, John M., 70–71, 75–77
Guerre, Louis F., 191
Guest, W. R., 39–40, 41, 52–53
Gulfport, Mississippi, 46–47, 253–54, 264–65
Gulf Shipbuilding, 66, 68–69
Gulley, Walter R., 94, 119
Guthrie, R. E., 158–59, 164–66

Haas, Francis, 77
Hall, Carsie, 229
Hall, Felix, 135–36
Halloran, George, 179
Hanson, Charles, 76–77
Hanst, K. F., 144
Harris, Ben, 84
Harris, Roy, 219, 255
Harrison, H. B., 57–58
Harrison, Pat, 112–13
Hastie, William, 128, 129, 134–35, 175–76, 196–97
Hattiesburg, Mississippi, 55, 127, 131, 138, 142, 144–46, 175, 186, 249–50
Hayes, Alzada, 205–6
Hayes, Roland, 205
Hecht, Ben, 140–41
Heidelberg, Terril, 115
Higgins, Andrew Jackson, 41–42, 53
Higgins Industries, 65, 78–79
Hillman, Sidney, 83
Hinesville, Georgia, 163
Hix, Charles, 155–57, 170–71
Hodges, Courtney, 164, 167
Holmes, Herbert, 229–30
Holmes, Wendell, 265
Holp, Marshal LeRoy, 187–89

hookworm, 106
Hoover, Lawrence, 134–35
Hopson plantation, 35–36
Horace, J. L., 173–74, 176
Houston, Charles, 196–97
Howard, Perry, 90, 163
Hudson, Donald, 188–89

Ingalls, Horace, 38–39
Ingalls News, 45, 58–59
Ingalls, Robert, 38–42, 43–44, 62–63, 93–94
   and labor unions, 53–54, 56–58, 61–62
   and Pascagoula housing, 96–98
   and women workers, 46–47, 48–49
Ingalls Shipbuilding Company, 6–7
   Athletic Club, 119
   and the FEPC, 68, 90–91
   founding of, 39–41
   health care at, 106–7, 108–9
   labor strikes at, 60–62
   labor unions at, 53–54, 56, 57–62
   and postwar operations, 63, 273–74
   and the War Manpower Commission, 91
   wartime profits, 41–42
   workers at, 42–52
International Workers Order, 129–30
Interstate Commerce Commission, 212–14
Iuka, Mississippi, 18, 114
Ivy, H. M., 113–14

Jackson County, Mississippi, 39–40, 43–44, 46–47, 93–94, 95–96, 103–4, 106, 108, 109, 111, 118
Jackson, Mississippi, 89, 116–17, 125–26, 229–30, 244, 249–50, 253–54, 263–64
Jackson Daily News, 184, 225–26, 250
Jarman, Pete, 132–33, 224
J. F. Pate Construction Company, 69–70
Johnson, Georgia, 138–39
Johnson, Paul B., 20, 159–60
Johnson, Raymond, 158
Johnston, Oscar, 1–2, 29–30, 31–32, 33, 35
Jones, Clarence, 154, 160
Jones, Sam, 201–2

Jones, Willie, 196

Kaiser, Henry, 107
Kennedy, George, 166
Kennedy, Sara, 210
Kilgore, Harley, 266
Kimbrough, Lonnie, 23–24
King, Albert, 134–36
King, Easton, 110, 117–18
King, Primus, 218–19
King v. Chapman, 218–19, 254–55
Knighton, Robert J., 155, 156–57, 159, 170
Kuger, Laverna, 59–60
Ku Klux Klan, 255, 256, 258

labor unions, 38
   popular attitudes about, 54, 55
   See also American Federation of Labor; Congress of Industrial Organizations
LaBuy, Walter, 23–24
Ladner, Maud, 48–49
Lafayette County, Mississippi, 18, 114–15
LaFourche, James B., 140
Land, E. S., 96–98
Langer, William, 113–14
Lanham Act of 1940, 95, 98, 104, 112, 119–20
Lanier, Monro B., 39–40, 41, 46, 90
Lasseter, Dillard, 87
Layne, Lou, 192
League of White Supremacy, 194–95
LeFlore, John L., 69–71, 76, 77–78, 130–31, 187
Lewis, John, 262
Life, 50, 221, 261–62
literacy test, 215–16, 224
Lockheed Corporation, 91–92, 273–74
Los Angeles, California, 81, 149–50
Louis, Joe, 171f, 183
Louisville, Kentucky, 220–21
Lummus, Robert A., 134–36
lynching, 5, 135–36, 168, 189, 251–52, 255

Mackay, Cliff, 201
Macon, Georgia, 135, 195, 211–12, 218–19, 228, 242–43
Magrath, J. G., 52

Malcolm, Roger, 261–62
Malley, Virginia, 47
Mankin, Helen, 254, 255, 261, 268–69
Marietta, Georgia, 65–66, 102–3, 259f
Marshall, George C., 127–28, 129, 176–78
Marshall, Thurgood, 218
Martin, Eugene, 206–7, 217–18
Martzall, Bill, 168–69, 170–71
Mason, Dolly, 237–38, 241–42
Mason, Lucy Randolph, 256, 268–69
Matthews, Aquilla, 145–46
Maxwell Field, 183–84, 185
May, Andrew J., 181
May, Armand, 228
McCloy, John J., 144, 173–75, 185–86, 196
   Advisory Committee on Negro Troop Policy and, 174, 176–77, 178, 179, 182–83
McCollum, Dalton, 143–44
McComb, Mississippi, 153–54, 160, 167, 229–30, 231, 253–54
McGill, Ralph, 204–5, 206–7, 257
McKnight, Ray, 139
McNair, Leslie, 164, 165–66, 167
McNutt, Paul, 77–78
McTatie, Leon, 262
Meredith, Burgess, 140–41
Meridian, Mississippi, 91, 142, 229–30
Meriwether, J. B., 168–69
Meyer, Agnes, 49–50, 111
migration, 16–19
   to Mobile, Alabama, 68–69
   rural labor markets and, 19–20, 273
Milburne, Leslie, 156, 157
Military Police, 134–35, 141–44, 160–61, 183, 189–90, 191
   in Alexandria, Louisiana, 139–41
   Black soldiers as, 139, 140–41, 142–44, 151–52, 158
   at Brookley Army Air Field, 186–89
   at Camp Shelby, 161–62
   at Camp Stewart, 162, 163–64
   at Camp Van Dorn, 153–57, 158, 159, 160, 164–65, 166–67, 168–69, 170–71
   at Fort Benning, 134–35
   in Phoenix, Arizona, 151–52
Mississippi Association of Teachers in Colored Schools, 230–31

Mississippi Ordnance Plant, 88–90, 225
Mississippi Progressive Voters League, 229–30, 250, 251, 252, 263–64
Mississippi Supreme Court, 116–17
Mitchell, Clarence, 76–77, 83, 86–87
Mobile, Alabama, 38, 42–43, 49–50, 66, 68–71, 75, 96f, 102–3
Mobley, M. D., 84
Mollison, James A., 188–89, 191
Monroe, Georgia, 261–62, 267–68
Montgomery, Alabama, 31, 135–36, 183–84
Montgomery, Claude Jr., 132
Moore, Amzie, 251–52
Morgan, E. S., 31
Morley, Burton, 60–61, 74, 75–76, 77
Municipal League of South Fulton County, 217–18
Muscle Shoals, Alabama, 17, 18

Natchez, Mississippi, 146, 166, 167, 229–30
The Nation, 207, 264
National Aeronautics and Space Agency, 274
National Association for the Advancement of Colored People, 31, 56–57, 116, 130, 276
   and anti-Bilbo efforts, 233–34, 238, 242
   and Bell Aircraft (Buffalo, NY), 82
   chapters in the Deep South, 9, 93–94, 187, 211–12, 229–30, 254
   The Crisis, 194, 269–70
   and federal aid to education, 113
   and the 1946 elections, 252, 253–54, 256, 263–64
   and military mobilization problems, 130–31, 136, 140, 144, 150, 175–76, 185–86, 187, 190–91, 193–94, 196–97
   and teacher salary equalization, 81, 204, 209
   and voting rights, 9–10, 211–12, 216–17, 218–19, 229
National Committee to Abolish the Poll Tax, 212, 225, 236–37
National Committee to Combat Anti-Semitism, 237–38

National Cotton Council, 29–30
National Defense Mediation Board, 58
National Defense Training School
   Gulfport, 46–47
   Pascagoula, 43, 46–47, 91
National Housing Agency, 95
National Labor Relations Board, 54–55
National Negro Congress, 81–82, 233–34
   and the Oust Bilbo campaign, 238, 242
National Negro Council, 173, 238
National Urban League, 81, 84–85, 86, 87, 90–91, 211–12, 254
National War Labor Board, 60–61
National Youth Administration, 74, 85–86, 110, 145
Neely, Frank, 65, 81
Nelson, Donald, 65
New Deal, 5–6, 10–11, 19–20, 22–23, 32–33, 103–4, 207
New Orleans, Louisiana, 4, 17, 38, 46, 53, 80–81, 141, 146, 231–32
New Republic, 207, 219–20
Newsweek, 193, 263–64, 269–70
Newton, F. T., 266
The New Yorker, 226, 269–70
New York Times, 222–23, 238–39, 269–70
nondiscrimination mandate of the federal government, 7–9, 204–5, 210, 223–24, 247, 275–77
Nunnally, Curtis, 188–89

O'Bryant, Charles W., 157–58, 164–65
O'Dea, Mark, 41
Office of Price Administration, 27
Office of War Information, 75–76, 77, 79, 138, 145–46
Otis, Harrison, 99–101

Pan-African Congress, 125–26
Parisius, Herbert W., 32–33
Park, C. C., 154–55, 164–65, 167
Parks, Rosa, 183–84
Pascagoula Civic Improvement Association, 93–94, 102, 107–8
Pascagoula, Mississippi, 16, 229–30, 274
   Airport Inn, 117–18
   Carver Village, 97f, 102, 119, 120
   crime in, 115–16

   Eastlawn Housing Project, 99–101, 104, 106, 119
   Gulfdale, 97f, 102, 107–8
   health care in, 104–6, 107–9
   and hearings of US Senate Subcommittee on Wartime Health and Education (1943), 93–94, 102, 103–4, 105–6, 109, 118–19, 121
   and housing, 95–102
   Inter-Church Committee, 48, 118–19
   and juvenile delinquency, 117–19
   Maritime Housing Project, 95–99
   Pelham's Point, 115–16
   public schools and, 109–12
   Recreation Commission, 119
Pass Christian, Mississippi, 248, 253–54
Patterson, F. D., 18
Patterson, Robert, 129, 130, 167, 184–85, 196
Peace Movement of Ethiopia, 232
Pearson, Drew, 94, 219–20
Pegler, Westbrook, 175
Pepper, Claude, 93, 94, 105–6, 121
Perry, Louise, 223
Peterson, Virgil, 154–55, 165–66, 196–97
Phoenix, Arizona (Camp Papago), 153–54, 158–59, 160
   and the 364th Infantry Regiment, 150–53
Picayune, Mississippi, 42–43, 133–34
Piccolo, Josephine, 237, 238, 241–42
Pittman, Marvin S., 203
Pittsburgh Courier, 9, 77–78, 89–90, 175, 207, 262, 263–64
PM, 193–94, 212–13, 247
poll tax, 31, 202, 210–11, 212, 215–16, 219–20, 222–23, 224–26, 227, 228–31, 233, 234–35, 238–39, 249–50
Porter, Ray, 171–72
post exchanges (PX), 131–32, 154–55, 158–59, 164, 183–84, 185, 187, 191
POW camps, 21–22
Presley, Elvis, 42–43
Price, William, 172
Prichard, Lusta, 264–65

"The Races of Mankind," 181
Raiford, J. B., 264–65

Rainey, Dorothy, 217
Rainey, Glenn W., 217
Randolph, A. Philip, 7–8, 128, 252
Randolph, Walter, 27
Rankin, John, 184
Reader's Digest, 221, 240–41
Redmond, S. D., 125–27, 148
Reed, David, 2
Reeves, William H., 204, 209
Revels, Hiram, 125–26
Reynolds, Emmett, 265
Richardson, Johnnie, 115, 116–17
Rickenbacker, Eddie, 45
Rickenbacker Squadron, 45
Ricks, Nellie Opal, 115–16
Rivers, E. D., 202, 255–56, 258–59
Robeson, Paul, 263
Robinson, Jackie, 183, 192–93
Robinson, (Sugar) Ray, 183
Rockdale County, Georgia, 261
Roosevelt, Eleanor, 5–6, 226–27
Roosevelt, Franklin D., 10–11, 27, 32–33, 38, 54–55, 58, 202, 207, 260–61
  the election of 1944 and, 214–15, 234–35
  race and, 72–73, 128, 212
Roper, Sam, 256
Ross, Malcom, 227, 228–29
Row, Lathe B., 167
Rucker, W. H., 237
Russell, Richard, 133–34, 266–67

Sapp, Robert, 136
Savannah, Georgia, 4, 38, 163, 211–12, 218
Scales, Mary Frances, 140–41
Scott, C. A., 216–17, 218
Scretchings, Homer, 166
Screws, M. Claude, 208
Scruggs, W. P., 23–24
Selective Service and Training Act, 8, 128, 133–34, 179, 184–85, 223–24, 275
The Shore Dimly Seen, 269–70
Sillers, Walter, 28, 230–31
Simmons, Eldridge, 231–32
Simmons, Isaac, 231–32
Sipp, John, 152
Slocum, Edna, 50
Smirely, Anthony, 159, 164–65
Smith-Connally Act, 54–55, 60–61

Smith, Dallas, 44
Smith, Howard, 54–55
Smith, Lonnie, 9–10
Smith, Samuel D., 153–54
Snipes, Macio, 261–62
Sojourner Truth Housing Project, 99
Somervell, Brehon B., 192
Southern Association of Colleges and Secondary Schools, 203–4
Southern Conference for Human Welfare, 210, 211–12, 216–17
  Committee for Georgia, 227–28
Southern Governors Conference, 201–2
Southern Growth Policies Board, 274
Southern Railway, 125, 126–27
Southern Regional Council, 206–7, 210, 216–17
Southern Tenant Farmers Union, 28–29, 31–32
Spanish Fort, Alabama, 96*f*
Sparks, Chauncey, 183–85
Spears, John, 143–44
Spencer, F. B., 79
Spencer, L. C., 103–4, 106–7
Spiers, Abner, 133–34
SS Tule Canyon, 79
States' Rights Party (Dixiecrats), 277
Stewart, A. D., 101
Stewart, Kenneth, 212–13
Stewart, Ralph, 189–90
Stimson, Henry L., 128, 147–48, 174, 182
Stockton, E. A. Jr., 177–78
Stone Mountain, Georgia, 255, 256, 258
Strmiska, Hermina, 50
Studebaker, J. W., 84
Sullens, Fred, 250
Sun Shipbuilding Company, 77–78
syphilis, 108–9
  Tuskegee study, 108

Taft, Robert A., 238–39
Talmadge, Eugene, 81, 207–8, 255
  and federal aid to education, 113
  and the 1942 governor's election, 202–7
  and the 1946 governor's election, 245, 255–61, 267–69
Talmadge, Herman, 245–47, 246*f*, 259–60, 268, 271

Tarver, Malcolm C., 33
Tatum, Frank M., 145–46
Taylor County, Georgia, 260–61, 262
Tennessee Coal, Iron, and Railroad Company, 65, 107
Thomas, Elbert, 112–13, 120
Thomas, Elmer, 264, 266
Thompson, M. E., 245–47
Thomson, Robert, 151–52, 154
Tilly, Dorothy, 206–7
Tipton, James, 91
Tishomingo County, Mississippi, 18, 25, 114
Trimble, Ernest, 76–77
Tri-State Bus Company, 131, 161–62
Truman, Harry S., 215, 219–20, 221, 252, 263, 267–68, 276
tuberculosis, 109
Turner, Henry McNeal, 232
Tuskegee Airmen, 128, 192–93
Tuskegee Institute, 70, 162–63
Tydings Amendment, 24–25, 26
Tylertown, Mississippi, 15, 264–65

Ulio, J. A., 147, 176, 182–83
Underwood, Felix J., 105–6, 109
United Service Organizations, 138
    Alexandria, Louisiana, 144–45
    Hattiesburg, Mississippi, 144–46
    Phoenix, Arizona, 151–52
US Army
    and abusive language directive, 136–37
    Army General Classification Test, 180–81
    and Black combat soldiers, 129–30, 169, 171–72, 178, 179–82, 192–94
    and Black officers, 8–9, 127–28, 129, 150, 153–54, 178–79, 185, 196–97, 239–40
    and courts-martial, 134–35, 150, 152, 161, 163–64, 165, 172, 183, 186–87, 189, 190–91
    and desegregation of recreational facilities and transportation, 182–86
    Gillem Committee, 196–97
    92nd Infantry Division, 192–95, 196–97, 239–40
    96th Infantry Division, 239
    93rd Infantry Division, 192–93
    and nondiscrimination mandate, 126–27, 132, 133–34, 136–37, 141–42, 169, 170, 172, 176–77, 179–80, 184–85, 191–92, 196, 197
    Officer Candidate School, 132–33, 133f
    761st Tank Battalion, 192–93
    Special Forces Ordnance Unit Training Center, 89–90, 225
    special training units, 179, 193
    367th Infantry Regiment, 150
    and transportation of personnel policy, 130–31
US Department of Agriculture, 15, 16, 18, 28–29, 32–33
US Employment Service, 1–2, 20–21, 22, 26–27, 42, 45–46, 67, 71, 73, 275–76
    Atlanta, Georgia, 82, 85, 86–87
    Chicago, Illinois, 2
    Greenville, Mississippi, 2
    Jackson, Mississippi, 88–90
    New Orleans, Louisiana, 53
    Pascagoula, Mississippi, 42, 52–53, 91
US Justice Department, 144, 168–69, 174–75, 218–19, 252, 260, 267–68
US Maritime Commission, 37, 38, 39–40, 41, 42–43, 76–77
    and Pascagoula housing, 95–99, 100, 119
    and women's welding contest, 50
US Office of Education, 43, 67, 70
US Public Health Service, 104, 108
USS *Pocomoke*, 37
USS *Vincennes*, 240–41
US Supreme Court, 208, 246–47, 254–55, 268–69
    Brown v. Board of Education (1954), 276
    differential freight rate case, 213–14
    Morgan v. Virginia (1945), 254–55
    Plessy v. Ferguson (1896), 7, 275
    Smith v. Allwright (1944), 9–10, 212, 216–17, 229–30, 265
University of Georgia, 203–4, 221, 254, 257

Valdosta, Georgia, 254

Vickery, Howard L., 48
Vultee Aircraft, 81–82

Wade, Charles W., 174
Wagner-Murray-Dingell Bill, 105
Wagner, Robert W. 238–39
Walden, A. T., 210, 216–17, 256
Walker, William, 149, 156–58, 159–61, 164–65, 166, 167, 170
Wallace, Henry, 16, 32–33, 213, 214–15
Walton County, Georgia, 261–62
War Food Administration, 26–27, 32–33
War Manpower Commission, 1–2, 26–27, 41, 48, 52–53, 60–61, 72–73, 92
  labor stabilization plans, 43–44, 45–46
War Production Board, 54–55, 58–59, 65, 71–72, 81, 83
Watkins, Harvey, 155–56
Watson, Joe, 19–20
Weaver, Robert C., 69
Wells, A. W., 249–50
Wells, Thomas R., 93–94, 110, 111, 120
Weltfish, Gene, 181
Whitaker, Richard, 156, 157, 159, 170
white primary, 9–10, 212, 216–20, 229–31, 254–55, 256, 257, 263
White, Walter, 7–8, 77–78, 128, 130, 185–86, 190–91, 196–97, 203–4, 206–7
Whittington, Will, 31–32
Wickard, Claude, 15–16, 32–33, 35–36
Wickham, Fred, 150–51
Wiley, Henry Lee, 115–16
Wiley, Irvin, 152–53, 158–59
Wilkins, Roy, 136, 147, 148, 175–76
Wilkinson, Horace C., 71–72, 194–95
Williams, Clifford, 75
Williams, Henry, 130–31
Williams, Luther, 168

Wilson, Ruth, 270
Wilson, T. B., 229–30, 250
Winchell, Walter, 211, 238
Winter, William, 253
Wolf, Buddy 10P39
women, 6–7, 20, 37, 63, 145, 151–52, 160, 166, 168–69, 189, 205–7, 239–40, 242–43, 251–52
  and agricultural labor, 21
  and childcare, 119–20
  and the Emergency Maternal and Infant Care program, 104–5
  and employment at the Alabama Dry Dock and Shipbuilding Company, 49, 53, 74–75
  and employment at the Bell Bomber Aircraft Plant, 51–52, 80f, 82, 84–85
  and employment at Higgins Industries, 31
  and employment at Ingalls Shipbuilding Company, 46–52, 51f, 53, 63
  and employment in Mobile, 49–50
  and labor unions, 59–60
  and the Mississippi Ordnance Plant, 88–89
  in Pascagoula, 99–100, 104–5, 111
Women's Federated Club movement, 145
Women's Land Army, 21
Works Progress Administration, 119–20
Wright, Edward B. Jr., 93–94, 98–99

Xavier University (New Orleans), 53

Yancy, Luther Francis Jr., 177–78
YMCA/YWCA, 145–46
Young, Hortense, 220–21
Young, John, 89–90